AIDS AND ADAPTATIONS

A Study of the
Administrative Processes by which
Social Services Departments help Clients
to receive Aids, and Adaptations to their Homes.

URSULA KEEBLE, M.A. (Cantab.),

*Research Assistant, London School of Economics
and Political Science, 1974–76.*

OCCASIONAL PAPERS ON SOCIAL ADMINISTRATION NO. 62

*Editorial Committee under the
Chairmanship of Professor Brian Abel-Smith
Published by The Bedford Square Press
of the National Council of Social Service*

First published 1979
© *Copyright 1979 by The Social Administration Research Trust*

ISBN 0 7199 0963 5

MADE AND PRINTED IN ENGLAND BY
WILLMER BROTHERS LIMITED
ROCK FERRY, BIRKENHEAD

CONTENTS

LIST OF TABLES

INTRODUCTION

REASONS FOR THE STUDY

In February 1972 I returned to social work in what had become part of an Inner London borough after an absence of six years, most of them spent abroad. I had read about the re-organisation of London government in 1965 and of the creation, after the Local Authority Social Services Act 1970, of integrated local authority social services departments throughout England and Wales, but I had been insulated by distance from any personal experience of the effects of either of these re-organisations. I went fresh to an area team that had itself been in existence less than a year; and to my first mixed case-load. This included three clients with severe physical handicaps.

These clients, and their families, had agreed to re-housing in what they had been led to believe would be "purpose-adapted" accommodation in a new block of flats. The flats were administered by the GLC but it was the borough which had agreed to pay for the adaptations which were to be charged against the social services vote. Unfortunately, although the flats had stood empty for some months, many of the adaptations planned had not been started at the time the clients were moved in. This meant that, in addition to the teething troubles common to any new building, people already under stress were also required to put up with the inconvenience of major structural alterations. All the disabled were dependent on wheelchairs for mobility indoors.

To add to their sense of grievance the families of the disabled clients who were not on supplementary benefit were asked to contribute towards the cost of some of the adaptations as it was the policy of the social services committee to operate a form of means-testing for all adaptations costing more than £25. Requests to disclose details of income were met with open hostility, not only because the clients felt that the adaptations ought to have been furnished before they were moved in, but also because they firmly – although wrongly – believed that since the passing of the Chronically Sick and Disabled Persons Act 1970 every local authority social services department was obliged by law to provide what was necessary free of any charge.[1]

7

Although assessment was required for adaptations costing over £25 the social services department did however provide any necessary aids to daily living free, though on loan. Because of the severity of their handicaps these three clients needed a number of aids, ranging from inexpensive items such as teapot tippers and special utensils for eating to special baths and electrically-operated track hoists. Some of the smaller aids were kept in stock[2] although the amount of paperwork needed before they were issued impeded rapid delivery. Requests for more expensive aids had to go before the social services committee, which met every six weeks. The decision to take a request to committee was made by an official of the secretariat five grades below the director and it was thought imprudent to ask committee members to consider more than two expensive requests at one sitting. To the social workers waiting for the committee to reach a verdict there appeared to be little or no feedback from the director about those requests that were turned down before reaching the committee stage. Indeed the director himself was not always informed of requests that fell by the wayside.

Nor could social workers be sure what criteria the committee applied when making its decisions. The main one appeared to be the availability of finance at the time. As the end of the financial year approached, and the inadequate budget showed signs of running out, deliberate, stringent and conscious rationing was imposed from above – again by officers well below the level of the directorate. There were also, I discovered, other times of the year when unconscious rationing took place. The clerk who ordered and issued aids saw the annual budget as divided into four equal and immutable quarters. As soon as a quarterly total came into sight, the flow of aids, never rapid, dried up completely and on one occasion stock-taking of the small aids cupboard was made to last three weeks. This clerk did not see herself as withholding a service – on the contrary, she felt herself to be dedicated to the cause of the disabled – but she saw her primary role as custodian of the rate-payers' money, a sacred trust to which she constantly referred. In this, she epitomised the attitude of the secretariat as opposed to that of the majority of the field workers.[3]

In spite of the restrictions and delays, many of them inherent in local government, the borough for which I worked was providing a better service than that of many Greater London boroughs and far beyond that of the national average. In 1972–73 it had provided, according to the annual statistics issued by the Department of Health and Social Security,[4] over 2,000 households with personal aids – 7.5 times the national average of 280 householders receiving aids. It had also provided over 370 adaptations which was 5.9 times the national average of 62 dwellings adapted in the same year.

My experience over the next year in working with the disabled taught me a good deal about their practical needs, about the daily management of their lives and about ways of reducing their handicaps. Often my disabled clients proved my best teachers and I was further helped by the one senior occupational therapist whom this borough employed in 1972 to cover all its area offices. But as the months went by I began to realise that it was not only myself who was learning on the job. Many architects, surveyors, builders and employees of the borough's technical services department came new to the idea of adaptation;[5] even the most experienced ex-welfare officers had to face new concepts of need. There was also an ever-increasing number of new and sophisticated aids from which the most appropriate had to be selected. Occupational therapists coming new from college or from hospital appointments were now constantly confronted with the challenge of disabled people living in unsuitable home accommodation.

The prevailing lack of expertise where the problems of the physically handicapped were concerned, especially at supervisory and consultancy levels, led me towards informal talks with social workers from other boroughs and with representatives of a number of voluntary bodies. These confirmed my feeling that a comparative study of the administrative processes involved in getting aids to the clients would be useful, and that the reasons for the delays over adaptations also needed to be investigated more widely. A brief feasibility study conducted towards the end of 1973 in six Greater London boroughs confirmed the impression that a great many senior administrators, as well as field-workers, shared my concern. It seemed likely that I could expect an adequate response to a constructive study in the Greater London area. The aim would be to pin-point the most frequent causes of delay and to suggest ways in which some of them might be overcome.

The study was made possible by a generous grant from the National Fund for Research into Crippling Diseases which enabled me to return to the London School of Economics and Political Science as a research worker in the Department of Social Science and Administration working to Professor Brian Abel-Smith. Indeed but for the enthusiasm for the project shown from the beginning by Professor Abel-Smith it is unlikely that anything so wide in scope could have been launched. It was over his signature that the initial letters asking for the co-operation of the directors of social services throughout the Greater London area went out and it was these letters that received a total and affirmative response from all 32 Greater London boroughs and the City of London. To all these Directors I am grateful for their co-operation and for the facilities they offered me for discussion with members of their departments at all levels.

9

A*

To those directors and assistant directors of social services departments who personally found time to spare for long and far-ranging interviews I would like to offer my special thanks. Also to those senior members of staff who drew up the full and carefully planned programmes which made it possible for me to cover so much ground in visits of one, or at most two, days. Whether closeted with individuals, poring over documents in registries, sitting in on routine weekly meetings, going round aids stores, or sharing sandwiches at specially convened working lunches, I was conscious of the care the organisers had taken to give me the fullest possible picture of the work done by staff at different levels, how the staff themselves felt about their jobs and their ideas about improving services. I cannot thank them enough for the courtesy they showed and the stimulation they gave me.

Occupational therapists of all grades contributed a great deal of provocative and constructive thought to this study and I should like to thank all those I met, whether based on social services departments, in hospitals, demonstration centres or on area health authorities. Also those at the Disabled Living Foundation who helped me when I was a social worker and, subsequently, during the course of this research.

I also benefited from the willing co-operation and advice of members of the staff of the Department of Health and Social Security, the Central Council for Education and Social Work Training, the Housing Corporations and the Housing Department of the Greater London Council.

I am grateful to many librarians and archivists and especially to the librarians of the Department of Health and Social Security, the Department of the Environment, the National Institute of Social Work and the Record-Keeper for the Director-General of the Greater London Record Office.

I would like to thank Ann Crombie, June Neill, Susan Tester, Colin Groves, William Warburton and Jonathan Bradshaw for sharing with me knowledge gained from their own researches and projects; also Mr Charles Player, recently retired from Croydon, who was able to supply a perspective of over forty years of welfare experience. For their consistent help, advice and encouragement, especially during the feasibility stage of the project, I owe a special debt of gratitude to Philip Jones and Clare Wavish, then both in Wandsworth.

Although interviews with severely disabled clients, and their relatives, formed only a small part of the project I would like to thank all those I met for their willingness to answer questions, the suggestions they offered about ways in which delays they had endured might have been avoided and their warm hospitality to a stranger.

The amount of detailed material accumulated – much of it confidential – was to present considerable problems when the time came to write the report. Here again I was able to draw on the experience, advice and constructive criticisms of Professor Abel-Smith who commented on two lengthy drafts of the original report as well as the shortened version for publication. I am deeply grateful to him for the help he gave throughout the project. My thanks are also due to Miss Sally Sainsbury, lecturer in Social Administration at the London School of Economics, for the interest she showed in the project and for reading and commenting on my manuscript.

Preparing for the study involved a good deal of secretarial work. This, together with the typing of the drafts of the report fell to Miss Bridget Atkinson of the London School of Economics who worked unflaggingly until the typescript went to the publishers. To her also I offer a very special vote of thanks. My husband helped me in innumerable ways throughout the three years which the study took to complete and which, had I not been able to rely on his patient co-operation, it would not have been possible for me to begin.

Finally I turn again to my sponsors, the National Fund for Research into Crippling Diseases, this time to thank them for the generosity that has now made possible the printing and publishing of this report.

None of the above are in any way responsible for the views expressed in this report for which I must myself take full responsibility.

NOTES

1. Many Members of Parliament made speeches reinforcing this conviction as did the coverage given to the Act by the media.

2. In 1972 the list of aids in stock showed few additions to the lists used by the Welfare Departments in 1965 although many new ones had come on to the market.

3. See the study by the Brunel Institute of Organisation and Social Studies, *Social Services Departments* (Heinemann, 1974) page 29, which sees such departments as an "agency" consisting of two groups, "the administration tend to identify with 'bureaucratic' value ... their desire is to contain costs and their instinct is to repel what they see as extravagant demands for services".

4. See DHSS, *Local Authority Social Services Departments, Aids to Households* (September 1973).

5. Although the revised and expanded edition of Selwyn Goldsmith's *Designing for the Disabled* (Royal Institute of British Architects) had been available since 1967, this handbook was not then widely known to administrators and social workers. Other guidelines, for example, *Housing People Who Are Physically Handicapped*, including notes on "mobility" housing, were not forthcoming until the Department of the Environment published Circular 74/74 in May 1974.

CHAPTER ONE

THE AIMS OF THE STUDY, METHOD AND RESPONSE

Two assumptions underlie the study that follows. The first is that many disabled people are helped to limit, reduce or overcome the problems of physical handicap by the correct use of appropriate aids to daily living. The second is that carefully designed adaptations – some of them quite small – to the homes in which disabled people are living can similarly help them to live in a more normal way than would otherwise be possible. A definition of the term "aid to daily living" and the varying definitions of adaptations used by different local authorities will be found in Chapters Six and Eleven.

The aims of the study may be summarised as follows :

(i) To investigate the administrative and financial arrangements by which the social services departments in Greater London provided aids and adaptations to disabled clients under the Chronically Sick and Disabled Persons Act 1970;
(ii) To study how priorities were established and financial control was exercised;
(iii) To identify delays and their causes;
(iv) To examine and compare different approaches to the problem and evaluate their success.

Method

The Inner and Outer boroughs of Greater London were chosen for study. This made it possible to carry out the research single-handed within the restraints of time and finance. An additional advantage was that local government reorganisation in the Greater London area had already taken place in 1965 whereas all other boroughs and county boroughs in Great Britain were in the throes of reorganisation in 1974, the year in which the study began.

Letters were sent in late 1974 and early 1975 to the directors of social services departments in the 32 Greater London boroughs and the City of London, explaining the aim of the research and asking them to grant an interview to provide an overall view of the policy adopted in each borough and of the services for the disabled provided by their departments. The letters also asked for permission to interview personnel at different levels in their organisation in order to study the chain of responsibility for the execution of policy and how it worked out in practice. This required talking to warehousemen as well as interviewing clerks, handymen and technical staff to see how aids were stored, issued and installed. Interviews were also requested with people who controlled the quality and quantity of aids supplied.

The decision to conduct personal interviews with a variety of people was welcomed by officials who felt they already had too much paper-work and it certainly contributed to their response. The assurance that all interviews would be treated as confidential and every effort made to conceal the identity of particular boroughs, although again welcomed, was nevertheless to make the writing of the report more complicated.

These personal interviews were backed up by a series of questionnaires. To begin with a comprehensive questionnaire had been worked out to cover all aspects of the study. This was then broken down into lists of questions related to the jobs of the various officials likely to be interviewed in the secretariat and also to that of occupational therapists. Where duties overlapped relevant questions appeared on more than one of the questionnaires, the main purpose of which was to ensure that interviews were conducted on similar lines and the same questions addressed to people with comparable duties in similar boroughs. To avoid formality and encourage a free flow of views the questions were not necessarily taken in the same order, but care was taken in the final minutes of the interview to see that none remained uncovered. Brief notes were made during the interviews and a full record prepared as soon as possible afterwards.

A postal survey involving so many different levels of staff would have taken some time to percolate through the system and would have been unlikely to receive either as uniform or as wide a spread of attention.

No questionnaires were devised for storemen, handymen and other manual staff as encounters with them were often unplanned and always informal.

Documentary evidence, e.g. copies of the forms on which aids were ordered and adaptations initiated, was asked for. There were no standard forms in use by all boroughs and in some boroughs formats designed for a particular purpose varied from area to area. Publications about the services available for the disabled, as required by Section 1(2) of the Chronically Sick and Disabled Persons Act 1970 were also looked at. These varied from simple leaflets to amusingly illustrated booklets. Frequently the more expensively produced included information of interest to the disabled along with a much greater volume of information about services for the elderly, whether or not some of these services were jointly used.[1]

Questions were also asked about the kinds of survey conducted and if they were considered to have been successful. This had a direct bearing on the extent of the needs identified and whether the provision of aids and adaptations was able to keep pace with the demand.

Officials of the Department of Health and Social Security were asked, before the study began, to help define what are later referred to in the report as the "grey areas", i.e. the areas of overlap between aids that are aids to home nursing and therefore a health responsibility and aids to daily living which are the responsibility of local authority social services departments. At their request a question on whether a circular of guidance from central government would be welcome was inserted. Appropriate officials also arranged visits to Demonstration Centres[2] in three teaching hospitals in the Greater London area and gave introductions to consultants advising working parties that were relevant to the provision of aids and adaptations. A visit to an area health authority Rehabilitation Centre which drew out clients from all the Greater London boroughs was also made. Two commercial exhibitions, put on by "Naidex" were also visited.[3]

A discussion about the provision of aids and adaptations by local authorities was held with senior officials of the Disabled Living Foundation and a meeting was also arranged with senior members of the British Association of Occupational Therapists. Meetings with researchers engaged in relevant work at universities, colleges of technology, colleges of engineering and colleges of further education were also arranged.

The Secretary of the Rowntree Trust was visited in the preliminary stages of the study and information was later provided by researchers for The Family Fund Project who were concerned with the provision of aids and adaptations for very severely handicapped children.

Talks were held with senior officials of the Inner London Education Authority who were concerned with rehabilitation work for multiply handicapped children and with selected teachers in schools for the multiply handicapped.

Senior architects and administrative officials of the Department of the Environment were consulted as were senior officers of the housing department of the Greater London Council.

A number of questions about the policy of local housing departments were included in the questionnaire as, although the study is limited to housing for the disabled, the amount and kind of existing housing stock available in the boroughs, the number of purpose-built dwellings and the extent of future plans to provide units of wheelchair housing and mobility housing might well influence the policy of social services committees towards finding money for costing major adaptations.

Discussions also took place with staff of the Development and Housing Section of the Housing Corporation on national policies in relation to housing people with special needs and also, in the Corporation's London office, on the work done by a team whose brief includes looking after the majority of housing associations that cater mainly for special needs housing throughout the Greater London area.

It was decided not to attempt systematic interviews with social workers as it was thought that directors of social services departments would be less willing to respond if the study were to take up the time of staff who were considered to be already over-burdened. The initial phase of the study coincided with a period of militancy on the part of social workers in some of the Inner London boroughs and this too would have made it difficult to construct a representative sample of social workers even had it been possible to conduct interviews without extending the period of research. The principal reason for not extending the study to include interviews with social workers was that as the focus was on the administrative and financial processes of providing aids and adaptations the involvement of area teams might not prove particularly fruitful.[4]

Response

In all personal contact was made with 14 directors, of whom ten granted long interviews, two held lengthy talks on the telephone and two were seen for five minutes only. Two directors extended invitations to sit in on their weekly meetings with senior staff, a third called a special meeting on aids and adaptations so that both he and the researcher could hear the views of staff at all levels. One director invited the researcher to his weekly meetings with area team managers. Because of the rhythm of the local authority financial year fewer interviews with directors took place in October and November 1974 and 1975 – the time of the budget forecasts – than in other months except for February 1975 and 1976 when frequent meetings were being called by finance committees to discuss cuts in the budget. Two directors reported that as the Association of Directors of Social Services had considered the project constructive they were making arrangements for senior members of their staff who had special knowledge of the subject to conduct interviews in their stead.

In addition to the 14 directors the following members of staff were interviewed, either formally or informally :

Assistant/Deputy Directors 21
Finance Officers 21

16

Principal Officers	18
Head Occupational Therapists	9
Administrative Officers (AP 3 – 5)	15
Occupational Therapists	36
Specialist Service Officers	6
Aids and Adaptations Officers	12
Technical Officers	6
Clerical Officers (1 – 3)	14
Assistant Technicians	6
Handymen	2
Storemen	10
Improvement Grants Officer	1
Borough Housing Research Officer	1

The number of officials in the several boroughs who answered prepared questions was :

12 in one borough
10 in two
9 in two
7 in three
6 in four
5 in four
4 in three
3 in seven
2 in one
1 in one

Contact with Clients

Because the main emphasis of the study was placed on the ways in which aids and adaptations were provided rather than on the people receiving them, contact with clients was limited to a few structured interviews with carefully selected disabled people. As a preliminary to these interviews opportunities were sought to meet numbers of disabled people informally by visits to a variety of organisations, both public and private, where physically handicapped people met at leisure. These included a session of wheel-chair dancing at a local authority centre, a discotheque evening at a mixed club for normal and physically handicapped young people (PHAB), a group of disabled scouts and rangers, a Christmas party at a school for handicapped children and a coffee evening for the mothers of handicapped children attending a pre-school group. Most of the people met were more than willing to talk about their attitudes towards the aids and adaptations provided by local authorities, and the insistence of many of them that disabled people themselves were frequently better judges of the kind of aids and adaptations they needed than social workers ensured that the questionnaire used for the structured interviews that followed were designed to contain some open-ended questions. Many of these produced constructive and valid suggestions.

It would not have been possible in the time available to take samples of clients from all the boroughs. Three boroughs were chosen, one as the result of a suggestion by its own assistant director of research and development and another through the expressed willingness on the part of the director to help in every way possible. The third borough was chosen because it was known to take an untypically generous attitude towards providing major adaptations in the private sector when the prognosis of the client's medical condition was uncertain or bad.

The selection of the clients in the first borough was determined by the time they had waited for a *major adaptation* to be completed. Letters were sent out to the eleven clients who had waited more than one year between the first request for an adaptation and the final inspection of the completed work. The letters asking if they would agree to be interviewed were posted from the London School of Economics and it was made clear that the researcher did not represent the borough and could in no way influence the progress of the adaptation. It was however hoped that the suggestions from the clients themselves would result in other disabled people being less inconvenienced in the future. All eleven were enthusiastic about being given an opportunity to air their views. In a second borough nine clients were studied, these being the only people to receive major adaptations in the years between 1971 and 1976. In the third borough just one client was seen, a man suffering from advanced multiple sclerosis.

In addition to seeing the documents kept by officers of the secretariat the confidential files of clients were also made available by the area offices concerned. This made it possible for each step in the administrative process to be accurately dated as well as to observe the interaction between different local authority departments, landlords and builders. As the recall by clients of various incidents over a lengthy period of time cannot be relied on, access to such files was considered essential if the main cause of delay were to be pin-pointed with accuracy.

Every one of the 21 clients interviewed had been subjected to unreasonable delay but none, with hindsight, said they regretted having asked for an adaptation in the first place. Two implied that to have said so would have been "ungrateful" and "impolite". Only one felt the quality of workmanship fell far below the standard that any local authority ought to have passed. All felt that the builder could have completed the job more quickly and made less mess.

One couple, however, moved to a New Town shortly after the work was completed. One man died a week after a major adaptation taking more than eighteen months had been finished. Another client, after adaptations taking two years, had begun to spend alternating months in hospital.

A sample of 21 clients is too small to offer sufficient data from which to generalise but it suggests that the questions it raises merit a larger study. Local authorities need to know more about the length of time families have continued to remain in homes that have been adapted to them; and also how much longer the disabled clients themselves remained alive.

A further sample of 46 clients in an Inner London borough who had suffered from delays over the delivery and installation of *aids* was extracted from a total of 397 clients who had received aids in the period 1 January 1976 – 1 April 1977. The 46 clients in the sample were those who had waited more than one week but less than four weeks before their aids had been delivered and were ready for use. Opposition from social workers in the five areas in which the 46 disabled persons lived was considerable and, although the assistant director responsible for aids had previously obtained permission from the area managers, it was decided not to go ahead with the interviews as planned.

Limitations of the Study

Because of the span of time between the first boroughs visited and the last some of the findings in October 1974 had already become obsolete by June 1976. On occasions the interviews themselves were to contribute to some of the changes that took place later.[5] The information presented in this report covers the position at the time of the visits.

One of the continuously changing situations during the course of this study was the result of the decision of a number of directors of social services to increase their complement of domiciliary occupational therapists. The shift away from "the more traditional methods of occupational therapy" (such as craft instruction in hospital), towards "assessment of a patient's needs and limits of ability" had already been noted by a Working Party on the Remedial Professions[6] in late 1973, which had also pointed out that "assessment for aids is not a task appropriate to a social worker".[7]

The rationale for basing domiciliary occupational therapists on local authority social services departments had come from the Seebohm Report in 1968[8] but faced with an overall shortage of the number of remedial therapists needed in both hospitals and the community, the 1973 Working Party felt it necessary to remind local

19

authorities that, after the re-organisation of the health services on 1 April 1974, "The Government had powers to transfer personnel from local authorities to health authorities . . . although it has stated that where occupational therapists were concerned their powers will be used selectively, after consultation with those most concerned".[9]

"Selective transfer" according to a health services circular in December 1974[10] was to take the form of rounding up and transferring to health authorities all those occupational therapists employed by social services departments who were "working without supervising or being supervised by occupational therapists and/or might be considered to be in danger of becoming isolated from their health service colleagues".[11]

In some of the Greater London boroughs supervision was provided by hastily establishing posts for head occupational therapists. In others services administrators resorted to new nomenclature such as "Occupational Officer" or "Advisor on Rehabilitation" as an acknowledged way of evading the government directive. In one borough after protracted consultations lasting nineteen months, an assistant director gained permission to "hang on to" three occupational therapists in three separate areas, a victory for principle, unaffected by the fact that only one of the original three was still in post. Even in those boroughs which had been employing head occupational therapists before December 1974 the situation seldom remained static and towards the end of 1975 some local authorities were beginning to freeze any vacancies that occurred as a way of cutting public expenditure. In others directors continued to beseech recalcitrant social services committees to make the employment of more domiciliary therapists a priority.

Uncertainties about the future of domiciliary occupational therapists in the employ of local authorities were intensified by the changes anticipated in the structure and professional status of the remedial professions as a whole. The 1973 Working Party had realised that, in order to encourage recruitment and avoid wastage, a greatly improved career structure would have to be provided, together with increases in salary commensurate with the wider responsibilities that remedial therapists were already assuming. This a committee, convened in May 1974 under the chairmanship of Lord Halsbury,[12] now set out to do and, because of the urgency of the situation, it managed to report jointly to the Department of Health and Social Security and the Office of Manpower Economics in December of the same year. New grades were recommended and figures for increased salaries were published in detail[13] but although interim guidance about establishing new posts in health districts was given in December 1974[14] nothing could be done about raising salaries or approval until the revisions had been scrutinised by the Whitley Council Professional and Technical Committee. An officially approved scale of salaries backdated rises in pay for all existent grades. For the new supervisory and administrative grade of district occupational therapist, still only designated, there was to be a flat rate increase of £201 a year. The fact that some – but not all – of the Greater London boroughs were paying their domiciliary occupational therapists more than their health service counterparts became for a time a bitterly divisive issue although the higher salaries they received were seldom given, by those interviewed in the course of this study as their main reason for choosing to work in local authority social services departments.[15]

Once health service pay had been brought into approximate alignment with that offered by local authorities it nevertheless became easier to make joint appointments in districts where occupational therapists were particularly thin on the ground and with hospitals where patients' services would otherwise have to be discontinued. Further impetus towards joint appointments was to come, in 1976, from Joint Finance[16] but interviews for this study had finished before it was possible to measure the repercussions of the Halsbury Report on the service as a whole.

Towards the end of this study however some senior social services administrators thought that joint appointments might well result in patients in need of aids and adaptations on discharge from hospital suffering less from hitches, duplications and delays in their provision.

Time did not permit detailed work to be done on hospital discharge procedures nor on patients obliged to wait an unnecessarily long time in hospital because aids had not been installed, or adaptations done, in their homes. Nor was it possible to make a study of patients who had been prematurely discharged from hospital without the aids and adaptations they needed to make life comfortable, convenient and safe for them at home. The problems and some possible solutions are touched on in Chapter Nine, but more research is needed in this field.

No attempt was made to investigate the provision of aids and adaptations for clients who were blind or partially-sighted, deaf or dumb. The special needs of the mentally handicapped were also excluded from the brief. Many of the aids and adaptations investigated may well have gone to clients suffering from multiple handicaps but samples of clients were deliberately restricted to those still categorised in 1974–6 by the Department of Health and Social Security as "General Classes".

The Wider Context

To help the non-specialised reader understand the background, the study is placed in a wider context in Chapters Two and Three. Chapter Two describes the general social and legislative background to the Chronically Sick and Disabled Persons Act 1970. Chapter Three discusses the problems that have arisen over financing the Chronically Sick and Disabled Persons Act. The Greater London study begins in Chapter Four with detailed references to the different ways in which the Greater London boroughs tackled the problem of finance and the varying levels of provision they achieved. Chapter Five gives the structure of a typical social services department of a Greater London borough, shows at what level aids are ordered and issued and at what points the duties of fieldwork staff involve contact with officers of the secretariat. Some new patterns of organisation, created especially to deal with the provision of aids and adaptations, are also discussed. Chapters Six and Eleven include general definitions of aids and adaptations but otherwise confine themselves, as does the rest of this report, to the findings of the study in Greater London.

NOTES

1. For suggestions by central government on the need to co-ordinate services for the elderly and the handicapped of all ages see DHSS Circular 45/71, para. 9.v.

2. The Department has given grants of extra money to six such Demonstration Centres in the Greater London area. Formerly known as Centres of Excellence, they offer, in addition to the normal services of a department of physical medicine, information and advice to social workers and domiciliary occupational therapists. Courses are also run for interested groups such as home helps and literature and video-tapes are lent to social services departments and volunary organisations. A small permanent exhibition of aids such as hoists is kept and clients and their relatives who come from the hospital catchment area may go to the centre to be shown how to use them.

3. These exhibitions are financed partially by money from the DHSS and partly by manufacturers who take stands.

4. See Smith, G., and Ames, Janet, "Area Teams in Social Work Practice: A Programme for Research", in the *British Journal of Social Work*, VI (i), 1977. Page 56. "For the most part area teams remain heavily dependent upon administrative functions performed centrally."

5. Changes that are known to have taken place because more than one visit was made are recorded. Relevant legislation since 1974 that changed procedures is also referred to as are circulars, and other documents issued since the study began.

6. *The Remedial Professions, a report of a Working Party set up by the Secretary of State for Social Service s* (The McMillan Report) London HMSO 1973.

7. *The Remedial Professions*, op. cit. Par. 29.

8. *Report of the Commission on Local Authority and Allied Personal Social Services*, Cmnd 3703 (HMSO, 1968). "The Seebohm Report", para. 253.

9. *The Remedial Professions*, par. 50. Employment by local authorities.

10. DHSS HSC (13) 102. *Occupational Therapists: Joint Review by Area Health Authorities and Loca l Authorities*. (Dec. 1974).

11. *The Remedial Professions*, Para. 23.

12. DHSS *Report of the Committee of Inquiry into the Pay and Related Conditions of Service of the Profession Supplementary to Medicine and Speech Therapists*. (The Halsbury Report). (HMSO 1975).

13. Ibid. Chapter 25 "Our Recommendations".

14. DHSS HSC (15) 101. *The Remedial Professions and Linked Therapies* (preceded by a department letter on transitional arrangements DS 36/76).

15. Advance Letter (PTA) 20/75, dated 5 November 1975.

16. See Chapter Three, p. 67 and Joint Circular HC 77/17, LAC 77/10.

CHAPTER TWO

THE LEGISLATIVE BACKGROUND TO
LOCAL AUTHORITY SOCIAL SERVICES
FOR THE DISABLED

1. *Introduction*

An early mention of "the provision of medical and surgical appliances" out of central government funds for people other than ex-members of the Armed Forces of the Crown is made in the National Insurance Act of 1911.[1] Those eligible for insurance were entitled to :

> "medical treatment and attendance, including the provision of proper and sufficient medicines, and such medical and surgical appliances as may be prescribed by regulations to be made by the Insurance Commissioners." (In this Act called "medical benefit")

The "medical and surgical" appliances referred to in the Act of 1911 were listed under two headings – "medical benefit" and "additional benefit". Among those on the first list were such things as dressings, ice-bags, splints and elastic bandages which were in common use by doctors.[2] These the insurance carriers, the "approved societies" as they came to be known, were obliged to supply. But, as Levy points out,

> "a sharp distinction is drawn between 'appliances' and things which, in ordinary parlance, would be considered appliances proper, such as artificial limbs, crutches, trusses, spectacles, dentures and so on, which are required not so much for treatment as to compensate for physical defects by mechanical means. All such appliances are available to the insured only as additional benefits ... Here then is the same old limitation that applies to all additional benefits, namely that they depend upon the financial position of the insurance carrier."[3]

The approved societies were obliged to provide all the appliances on the first list and could provide appliances from the second listed as "additional benefits". Frequently they did not have enough money to do so,[4] in which case the insured person had to apply to such charitable organisations as the Royal Surgical Aid Society which "never had enough to go round". Thus only a fraction of the need for the appliances identified by doctors was met.

When the Royal Commission on Workmen's Compensation sat in 1939–40 evidence was produced to the effect that insurance companies sometimes supplied artificial limbs but never trusses[5] and the reports of the Royal Surgical Aid Society contain ample evidence of the long periods during which workers in need of surgical appliances might have to wait.[6]

The *National Insurance (Industrial Injuries) Act of 1946* granted powers to the Minister under Section 75 to

"ensure the provision and maintenance, free of charge, or at a reduced charge, of equipment or appliances for any person who, by reason of a loss of limb or otherwise, is in need of them as the result of any injury or disease against which he was insured under this Act."[7]

Although the new powers of the Minister were only permissive, the Act brought the principle of provision for the disabled civilian worker into line with what was already available for ex-servicemen.[8]

No legislation has attempted to define "disability" except in the broadest terms – indeed it would be impracticable to try to do so. But the *Disabled Persons (Employment) Act 1944* was the first act to treat disabled people as one single category of persons, irrespective of cause.[9] As defined by this Act a disabled person was one who :

"on account of injury, disease, or congenital deformity, is substantially handicapped in obtaining or keeping employment, or in undertaking work on his own account, of a kind which apart from that injury, disease or deformity would be suited to his age, experience and qualifications . . ."[10]

It should be noted that this definition concentrates on the employability of disabled persons. The then Minister of Labour and National Service introduced compulsory registration for disabled people for the first time. These employment registers are still maintained by branches of the Department of Employment today.

The next act to provide specific benefits to disabled persons was the *National Health Service Act 1946*. Section 28 of the Act, taken in conjunction with a subsequent circular,[11] made it possible for local authority health departments to provide any medical equipment or apparatus necessary for the after care of patients in their own homes. The loan or hire of such equipment – frequently called medical loan equipment – was closely bound up with the home nursing service and has remained a responsibility of health authorities. The principle, however, of transporting such things as air cushions, bed rests and hoists to the patient at home for short periods was a precedent for supplying similar aids for longer periods when the new welfare

24

departments came into being under the *National Assistance Act 1948*. Section 29 of this Act begins by giving local authorities the power of :

"promoting the welfare of persons . . . who are deaf or dumb and other persons who are substantially and permanently handicapped by illness, injury or congenital deformity or such other disabilities as may be prescribed by the Minister."[12]

The power of "promoting welfare" went much further than the *Disabled Persons (Employment) Act 1944* had done. Under the terms of the new Act employability is now seen as a social as well as an economic concept. Local authorities are asked to make arrangements for sheltered workshops and also for hostels for workers in need of such accommodation. Nor is the need for social contact outside the framework of employment ignored although recreational facilities are mentioned in only one subsection, 29.–(f).

The latitude implicit in the term "promoting welfare", together with the hope expressed by the then Minister that local authorities will give a wider interpretation to the words "substantially and permanently", allowed the new welfare committees to provide a wide variety of new and extended services. The fact that the Minister also hoped that "in their dealings with individual handicapped persons local authorities will no doubt exercise discretion in the use of the word 'permanently' ",[13] would seem to imply that such services were intended to cater for the varying needs of as many disabled people as possible.

In statutory terms Section 29 of the National Assistance Act gives local authorities "power to make arrangements . . .

(a) for informing persons to whom arrangements under that subsection [subsection (1)] relate of the services available for them thereunder;

(b) for giving such persons instruction in their own homes or elsewhere in methods of overcoming the effects of their disabilities;

(c) for providing workshops where such persons may be engaged (whether under a contract of service or otherwise) in suitable work, and hostels where persons engaged in the workshops, and other persons to whom arrangements under subsection (1) of this section relate and for whom work or training is being provided in pursuance of the Disabled Persons (Employment) Act, 1944, may live;

(d) for providing persons to whom arrangements under subsection (1) of this section relate with suitable work (whether under a contract of service or otherwise) in their own homes or elsewhere;

(e) for helping such persons in disposing of the produce of their work;

(f) for providing such persons with recreational facilities in their own homes or elsewhere;

(g) for compiling and maintaining classified registers of the persons to whom arrangements under subsection (1) of this section relate."

More emphasis was to be put on recreational facilities after an Advisory Council on the Welfare of the Handicapped had been appointed[14] and had reported to the Minister.

The control that was to be exercised by the Minister over the implementation of Section 29 of the National Assistance Act 1948 was absolute. Section 29.–(2) made clear that arrangements could only become mandatory *"to such extent that the Minister may direct"* and Section 29.–(3) points out that they "shall [then] be carried into effect in *accordance with a scheme made thereunder*" [researcher's italics]. The "scheme" was to provide the key to all approved provision but with the apparent exception of provision for the blind, it was to prove more often than not a slow and unproductive exercise. All the provisions of Section 29 as they related to blind persons normally resident in a local authority area were, it must be noted, made mandatory on 7 June 1948,[15] just three weeks after the National Assistance Act 1948 became law. But the arrangements for the blind, unlike other categories of disabled persons, had already had years of legislative and departmental activity behind them.[16] Other categories of disabled people had to wait a good deal longer – some of them for as long as ten years – before receiving the most haphazard and sketchy of local authority welfare services.

2. *Circular 32/57: The Schemes*

The local authorities themselves had to wait more than three years before they received the next circular,[17] issued on 28 August 1951. In this the Minister announced that the Advisory Council on the Handicapped had reported and that he was issuing their recommendations in the form of two outline schemes appended to the circular. Following the success of the scheme for the Blind, it was hoped that these new schemes would help local authorities in planning provision for the Deaf or Dumb[18] or what were later to become known as the Disabled Persons (General Classes).[19] These recommendations form the bedrock of the study that follows.

From the point of view of the physically handicapped it was unfortunate that Circular 32/51 failed to convey any sense of urgency. On the contrary, having reminded local authorities that provisions for the blind under Section 29 of the Act had been mandatory since

26

June 1948, the Minister then announced in paragraph 3 that he had "no intention at present of giving any similar direction as respects the classes of handicapped persons covered by the two appended schemes." Paragraph 4 pointed out that the outline schemes had been divided into two parts, the first of which "sets out the services the council must or may provide immediately." Part II of the scheme was relegated to a remoter future when it was hoped it might be possible for local authorities to devote greater resources to bringing the recommendations in Part I "to full adequacy".

As the mandatory requirements embodied in Part I of the scheme were few in number and capable of being "brought into operation without substantial expenditure of manpower or money", the response by local authorities to implementing Section 29 of the National Assistance Act 1948 was to prove, in many instances, unduly tardy and lukewarm. From a circular issued in 1958[20] it is clear that some authorities, albeit referred to as "relatively few", had at that date not submitted any schemes at all. These the Minister courteously asked "to give renewed consideration to their adoption in the light of remarks quoted in the 1951 circular" and two years later, in 1960, the Minister decided to make the submission of schemes obligatory.[21] Researchers were, however, still to report variable and haphazard provision in many parts of England and Wales in the late Sixties.[22]

The full title of the second appended scheme is : *Scheme for the provision of Welfare Services under Section 29 and Section 30 for Handicapped Persons other than the Blind, Partially-Sighted, Deaf and Dumb"*. The inclusion of Section 30 of the Act in the title was essential as it was the section that permitted local authorities to register and employ as their agents "any voluntary organisation having for its sole or principal object the promotion of the welfare of persons to whom the last foregoing section [Section 29] applies". In many local authority areas sheltered workshops, day centres, recreation centres and luncheon clubs owed their entire existence to voluntary enterprise. Section 30 of the Act was now strengthened by the outline scheme which urged councils to use the powers they had been given to subsidise existing facilities run by voluntary associations and, by implication, extend and perhaps even improve upon them. A strong plea was entered not only to seek their co-operation but also to co-ordinate and direct their activities within an all-absorbing scheme. The use of voluntary associations as agents was never intended to preclude initiatives on the part of the local authorities in setting up projects of their own. Yet this appears to be precisely what happened. Having, as it were, paid the voluntary associations to get on with the job a great many councils sat back and coasted along as if the request for a scheme had never been made. This too may be inferred from the circular issued in 1958 in which the

27

Minister points out that over-reliance on voluntary associations is not a wholly satisfactory answer and that "adoption by an authority of powers to provide service themselves ... enables better and more uniform provision to be made."

A close examination of other clauses in the mandatory group of requirements supports the Minister's contention that they would put little strain on the existing resources of any council. The need to co-operate a bit harder with the Ministry of Labour and National Service over help with the employment (Clause 11) and training (Clause 13) of disabled people under the relevant Acts[23] goes no further than asking that the Council "shall take such steps as may be practicable" (11) or "are practicable" (13).

Employability emerges as the single thread linking all the mandatory clauses of the outline scheme – so much so that at times it seems as if Section 29 of the National Assistance Act is no more than an extension of the Disabled Persons (Employment) Act 1944 albeit in local authority terms. Other mandatory clauses, always incorporating the word "shall", are concerned with making reasonable payment to handicapped people working in sheltered workshops or social centres provided by voluntary associations, in their own homes, possibly taught by volunteers, or "elsewhere". (Clauses 6, 7 and 8). The Council is further placed under an obligation "to sell or otherwise dispose of all goods produced in the sheltered workshops" (Clause 9.– (1)) and "*shall* help handicapped persons under clauses 7 and 8, [working at home or elsewhere], to secure orders for their goods or services and to dispose of any saleable goods or other marketable articles produced by them."[24]

Even the way in which the Register of the Handicapped (General Classes) is to be kept is slanted towards capacity for work. The original injunction in Section 29.–(g) of the Act for the keeping of a classified register reappears under the outline scheme as Part I (3) "The Register".

> "(3) The Council *shall* keep a register of handicapped persons who apply for assistance and whom the Council assist under this scheme, and *shall* include therein such particulars as the Minister may from time to time direct." [italics supplied].

It is not surprising that so many clients confused this register with the one kept by the labour exchanges or considered them to be mutually exclusive.[25]

Classification had to be according to ten kinds of coded handicap, which are linked with those drawn up by the Medical Research Council and used by the Ministry of Labour and National Service since the Disabled Persons (Employment) Act 1944.[26] In addition the clerk in charge of the Register was to sub-divide the disabled persons listed into five other classes of which four were directly associated with their employability. The fifth category concerned disabled children still at school.[27]

The registration of handicapped persons was one of the mandatory services which the majority of local councils were most prepared to implement with speed. But as the registers inevitably recorded only those persons known to have asked for[28] or received a service already, including possibly those who were being helped by voluntary associations, they could serve no useful purpose for any forward planning such as that envisaged in the outline scheme. At the national level the lack of a uniform attitude towards registration made the statistics of very limited value.[29] The failure to identify anything approximating to the number of disabled persons in their areas must be postulated as one reason why so many local authorities did not feel under pressure to submit schemes.

The majority of disabled persons who wanted one of the limited services available appeared to have been willing to register, given the opportunity to do so. But the fact that it was obvious from the Act that registration under Section 29 (g) would one day become compulsory aroused sufficient opposition for the Minister to say in the outline scheme that "the handicapped person's application need be nothing more than a word to the council's welfare officer."[30] This established the principle that no service should be withheld because a disabled person refused to register. What is less clear is whether there would be sufficient welfare officers for the disabled client to have a word with. The possibility of their appointment is first mentioned in 1951 in paragraph 12 of Part I of the outline scheme which states :

"Welfare Officers
12.– (1) For the discharge of the Council's functions under this scheme there shall be employed by or on behalf of the Council such number of Welfare Officers as the council may determine,"

but until a council's scheme, which had to contain all the mandatory clauses, had been sent to and received the approval of the Minister, that council was under no obligation to employ any.

Indeed the staffing situation in welfare departments between the passing of the Act in 1948 and the approval of a scheme must have been somewhat haphazard. As far as provision under Section 29 for the handicapped was concerned it was thought that those relieving officers who had been concerned with provision of services under the poor law "could be expected to have adequate knowledge of the needs of most disabled persons".[31] A number of paid craft instructors were also appointed. Some occupational therapists who in those days still saw instruction in handicraft as part of their professional work, left hospitals and health departments and went underground to re-emerge as welfare officers. Circular 32/51 made it clear, however, that reliance on volunteer handicraft instructors – from the British Red Cross Society and the various Cripple Aid societies who are referred to as being "active in this field" – was essential. Help might also be obtained from those members of Women's Institutes who were skilled in handicraft.[32]

The mandatory duties of welfare officers, in addition to visiting the disabled themselves, were :

> "to use their best endeavours to arrange for voluntary workers to visit handicapped persons with a view to affording them comfort and encouragement and assistance in their solution of domestic and other problems confronting them, to accompany them to the places of workshops, social centres, clubs and similar centres of recreation and otherwise assist in carrying out the purposes of this scheme."[33]

Some of the problems which volunteers were expected to handle in 1951 would, in the 1970s, be more properly considered the province of professional counsellors or case-workers.

The extent to which council welfare departments developed a sense of professionalism would appear to have been intricately bound up with the submission of schemes which, on their acceptance by the Minister, automatically included the mandatory employment whenever possible of carefully selected welfare officers : "persons holding a Diploma or Certificate in Social Science or a similar qualification in social work of a comparable character." Because however of a shortage of trained personnel,[34] the Minister was also prepared to accept "persons as respects whom the Council are satisfied that they enjoy a special aptitude for the work and possess a broad knowledge of the social services and some experience in a field of welfare."[35]

The duties that "shall" be included and "shall" be distributed amongst the newly-appointed welfare officers are outlined in Part I paragraph 4 with additional permissive duties given in detail in paragraph 5. However many welfare departments must have been severely under-staffed. Part II of the outline scheme expressed the hope in paragraph 16 that :

> "the numbers of Welfare Officers, including persons engaged in teaching handicrafts, employed by or on behalf of the Council shall be sufficient to secure the efficient administration of the services,"

and that their numbers should be one of the many aspects of progressive development that local authorities were requested to keep under constant review.

Many of the volunteers recruited by welfare officers ended up as paid welfare officers themselves. A fully professional service in 1951 seemed neither to be necessary or desirable. Circular 32/51, however, concluded by saying that the Advisory Council for the Welfare of Handicapped Persons "are about to consider the question of appropriate qualifications for Welfare Officers, and the Minister ... will in due course consider ... whether it would be desirable to formulate more precisely the qualifications required."[36]

Although many of the welfare officers lacked paper qualifications, they did not lack professional expertise within the limits of the role defined for them. They were not expected to make clinical assessments of clients – there were doctors and consultants to do that – nor was it necessary for them to become involved in casework with clients although some of them, experienced in using casework methods,[37] did so if they felt it to be to the client's advantage. Essentially however they were seen as "enablers", people of experience and commonsense who could sum up what their disabled clients needed in the way of practical assistance and then see that this assistance was provided by the most appropriate person, whether home help, doctor, nurse, therapist or volunteer. Sainsbury saw the role of the welfare officers as "pivotal".[38] It was around them that a wealth of services revolved, some provided by other local authority departments, and others by appropriate agents. It was the welfare officers who were also the most likely persons to recommend such aids as then existed – and to make sure that the voluntary association or charity supplying or hiring them delivered them. If the voluntary association were acting as an agent of the council it was the welfare officers who were obliged to collect and account for the cost to the client of hiring the aid.

Aids, for so long provided exclusively by charities, do not receive a specific mention anywhere in the National Assistance Act of 1948, although council welfare departments might, presumably, provide them under the generalities of their powers to promote the welfare of disabled persons. There are also two paragraphs in the outline scheme in Circular 32/51 which might provide the necessary legal framework – paragraph 4 (1) which allows them "to assist handicapped persons in overcoming the effects of their disabilities", and paragraph 5 (1) which allows them "to provide practical assistance for handicapped persons in their homes". In the early Fifties, however, "practical assistance" was more likely to be thought of in terms of nursing or domestic help than pick-up sticks, teapot tippers – often made for clients by welfare officers – or larger equipment such as hoists.

Welfare officers were also – where opportunities to provide them existed – the most likely people to recommend one of the limited number of adaptations that the more enlightened councils were willing to provide or help with providing.

Adaptations on the other hand get their first official mention in Clause 5 (5), Part I, of the outline scheme. It is very explicit and leaves councils in no doubt whatsoever about what they are being given permissive powers to do. Part I says they may :

> "5 (5) assist handicapped persons in arrangements for the carrying out of any works of adaptation in their homes or the provision of any additional facilities designed to secure the greater comfort or convenience of such persons, and if the Council so determine defray any expenses incurred in the carrying out of any such works."[39]

This clause – particularly as it defines the permissive powers conferred on councils to defray expenses in carrying out adaptations – was to play a very important role in later years.[40]

No other kind of adaptation, as for example the installation of an inside toilet, is mentioned; not even the one that was to achieve the widest popularity – the conversion of coal-burning fires to gas or electricity. Judith Buckle in a national survey of housing for the disabled conducted in 1968, found that out of a sample of 12,738, 12 per cent of disabled people had had fires converted, but that the cost of the majority of these conversions had been paid for by relatives. A further 5 per cent of the sample had had bannister rails fitted in their homes and 4 per cent had had rails put in toilets and bathrooms; in 2 per cent of dwellings in which disabled persons lived a W.C. had either been converted or added and in 1 per cent a bathroom had been installed, often at council expense. Out of a sample of 441 clients who used wheelchairs some 20 per cent had received the ramps recommended in Part II of Appendix II of Circular 32/51, and walls had been removed or rooms converted for 1 per cent of clients in wheelchairs.[41]

These figures based on interviews in 1968 reveal how low the level of activity had remained for a full twenty years and also how low the majority of welfare departments had set their sights. Although no clear picture is available of the extent of provision throughout England and Wales in the Nineteen-Fifties, the situation as far as the Greater London area is concerned is less obfuscated thanks to the preservation of two sets of archives – those of Middlesex, which the researcher did not examine, and those of the London County Council which were made accessible. From an examination of the minutes of the health and welfare committees of the L.C.C. and from the policy files of the L.C.C. welfare department, it is possible to reconstruct a picture, albeit sketchy and incomplete, of just how far the Metropolitan boroughs were prepared to go along with the provision of aids and adaptations between 1948 and the re-organisation of London government in 1965.

As far as the provision of aids were concerned the L.C.C. followed the pattern, common to most parts of the country, of using voluntary societies as agents with the local branches of the British Red Cross and the St John's Ambulance Association providing aids both for nursing patients at home and aids for daily living or "welfare" aids. Whenever possible the aids provided were purchased from Government Training Centres but long delays in delivery frequently occurred. Wooden aids, such as bath boards and trolleys, could also be obtained in many boroughs from their own sheltered workshops but on the whole these tended to be limited in kind, heavy and cumbersome. Only a very few of them were purchased from commercial firms.

A list circulated in 1957 shows that the health department was beginning to issue an increasing number of aids made by commercial manufacturers of which only one, a kind of hoist, was also issued by the welfare department as an aid to daily living. By 1964, both departments were using various pieces of equipment made by the same five commercial manufacturers.

The picture where adaptations is concerned is even clearer. There were very few of them and those that there were were of a very limited kind, the portable wooden ramp being a top favourite.

Further correspondence with other departments shows an abortive attempt to find enough private builders with the necessary competence who were willing to work for the welfare departments.[42] There may have been a few, more substantial, adaptations but those officials interviewed who had worked for the L.C.C. as welfare officers recalled a policy at that time which was beginning to place a much heavier emphasis on clubs and recreational facilities than on adaptations.

Aids and adaptations, it should not be forgotten, although important in helping disabled clients to live at home, form only a fraction of local authority provision and of the expenditure of local authority social services departments. Even so one cannot help but ask what happened to the legislation under Section 29 on "promoting the welfare" of the disabled by extending recreational facilities and social contact. The provision of wireless sets and games, the organising of lectures and outings, the buildings of luncheon clubs and new centres, the provision of hostels for workers in sheltered conditions and the hotels and camps for holidays – all these necessary and desirable facilities remained for the most part buried amongst what the Minister called "the permissive group" of clauses in the outline scheme in Circular 32/51. The various local authorities moved at their own pace. Many of them had not even begun to make adequate provision for the physically handicapped before still more demands were being made of them. The circular issued in 1960 in which the

33

Minister finally felt able to make the adoption of schemes for the physically handicapped mandatory, also announced that, as a result the passing of the Mental Health Act 1959[43] any provision made under Section 29 of the National Assistance Act must also include making arrangements for promoting the welfare of "mentally disordered persons of any description." For local authorities who had already submitted a scheme, the circular suggests that "a simple way of enlarging it ... would be the submission of an amended scheme ..."[44] The full title of the Circular, *Welfare Services for Mentally Disordered Persons and for Handicapped Persons*, clearly indicates that there would be new demands and new drains on existing resources for which the physically handicapped would have to compete.

For a long time they had been obliged to compete with the elderly for the interest and attention of councillors who, under Section 21 of the self-same National Assistance Act 1948, had been required to attend to the building of new and alternative residential homes of various sizes and for various purposes to replace the old workhouses. Since the Children's Act younger members of the population had also made new demands on council resources, but such competition for provision is no new thing in local government. The answer to the paltry way in which the disabled were treated must lie somewhere within themselves. They had been so long accustomed to expecting so little that they failed to ask for enough.[45] And those who worked for and on their behalf, also became reconciled to being what ex-welfare officers still refer to as the "Cinderella" service.

This was not what the framers of the National Assistance Act of 1948 had intended or expected. In its preamble it boldly declares itself as "an Act to terminate the existing poor law ... and to make further provision for the welfare of the disabled, the sick, aged and other persons". And in the first circular issued after the Act the Minister spoke of the historic opportunity which this offered to local authorities who had the "will and vision to seize the opportunities ... to substitute a modern welfare service for one which had perforce to be based on outmoded legislation for the relief of destitution."[46] But allowing elderly people to pay towards their keep in local authority residential homes or disabled persons to contribute towards the cost of a service or an adaptation does not in itself confer dignity on the client. The stigma associated in the public mind with the poor law was not to be removed while so many – although not all – local authorities welfare departments continued to offer scant, haphazard services inadequately related to either known or still unidentified needs. It is not, therefore, surprising that the Seebohm Committee reporting in 1968 remarks that "the death knell of the poor law was still to be rung."

34

Yet had Section 29 of the National Assistance Act been fully implemented and schemes submitted made effective, the history of the disabled would have indeed been different. The seeds of what was later to be referred to in the House of Commons as "a charter for the disabled and chronically sick"[47] had already been sown in 1948. Had they fallen on less stony ground the legislation of the Seventies might never have been necessary.

3. *Developments in the Sixties*

Spending public money on keeping elderly people out of institutions, as well as on building new and more attractive ones, as required by Section 21 of the National Assistance Act, gathered momentum during the Sixties. The strain that this had imposed on both hospitals and local authority geriatric resources made it necessary to look more closely at the methods of caring for and coping with the increasing number of people who were surviving to a far greater age than ever before. At the same time academic studies of the effect of institutionalism[48] were beginning to show that many of the inmates of residential homes need never have been there in the first place. Some needed just a little help with washing and dressing or with negotiating a passage to the toilet. Some could not be relied upon to shop for themselves or to prepare a hot meal but were otherwise active. With a certain amount of domiciliary care, in the form of nursing auxiliaries, bathing auxiliaries, home helps and meals on wheels, an aid like a handrail in a corridor, or a minor adaptation like a half step into the back yard, they could have gone on looking after themselves for very much longer. There was little possibility of putting these people back into their own homes; but the press, who took up their cause, did much to discourage premature admissions to residential care in the future. At the other end of the spectrum, congenitally disabled infants were surviving. Some of these children could be kept out of hospitals or other institutions for at least some part of their lives if enough domiciliary support was forthcoming – and of the right kind – to alleviate the stress felt by parents and siblings.[49] A shortage of residential places for children, and the awareness of parents that institutions could not provide the care that their handicapped children needed, reinforced the expediency of what was at best always a limited choice.

Attempts by some local authorities to prove that it would be cheaper to lay on the whole gamut of domiciliary services than to create and maintain extra places in residential homes could only be hypothetical. Townsend was careful to point out how difficult it would be to arrive at the cost of changes from residential to what began to be called "community" care. The domiciliary services would not necessarily be cheaper. Such changes, he said in 1962, would

"represent a distinct shift in priorities and depend for their success on the determination of society to implement them. In particular they demand a new approach to the question of community care. We should not suppose that it is generally easier or cheaper to care for homeless and handicapped people in the community than in institutions. Effective domiciliary services are probably more difficult to organise and maintain and we have too little knowledge or experience of their short-comings ... Much will depend, in the long run, on building up a sufficient number of responsible and properly trained and paid social workers, welfare assistants, doctors and nurses."[50]

In 1957 Dr Shenfield estimated the cost of keeping an elderly person in a geriatric hospital bed as £400 a year, and in residential care as £200 a year.[51] The cost of keeping elderly people in their own homes (with some domiciliary services) was estimated at only £80–100 a year. In 1972, Jean Symons, working for the Economist Intelligence Unit with considerable data at her disposal, calculated that the average weekly cost of keeping disabled persons in their own home worked out at around £10.00 a week cheaper than in long-stay hospitals or residential homes.[52] However for families receiving constant attendance allowances and other cash benefits the margin between institutional and home care may well be much narrower. A case in 1975 of a London borough refusing to spend £6,000 on adapting a property on behalf of an eleven-year-old multiply handicapped child put the cost of residential care at £3,000 a year, or nearly £58 a week.[53]

Ideally the question at issue should be what is best for the client in the widest possible context. In some cases residential care may be the only way in which a client's needs can be met; in others it may be essential to avoid the break-up of a family. But in the Seventies it should never be the only alternative because there are too few domiciliary services,[54] because those provided are ill-organised or because there is confusion about which department should be providing them.

Departmental responsibility was firmly laid down by the Seebohm Committee which reported in 1968 that

"It is basic to our proposals that the social services department should take over responsibility for social work and occupational therapy with physically handicapped people and their families, the provision of residential and day centres for them, as well as providing home helps, meals on wheels, holidays and a sitters in service ... The health services must be concerned with medical

36

diagnosis and treatment, including medical rehabilitation, home nursing where necessary and the provision through the health visiting service of help with physically handicapped children."[55]

The Seebohm Committee also saw the provision of adaptations as the major responsibility of the new social services departments :

"But the social services department must take the major responsibility for securing early action and helping in the provision of adaptations."[56]

In this it echoes Section 29 of the National Assistance Act with the timely addition of the proviso "securing early action". The committee was well aware of the delays encountered and of people forced

"to live in unsatisfactory conditions or wait for months or years before a suitable appliance [?aid] is provided, or adaptations made or a suitable house provided."

While the Seebohm Committee was sitting another project which was to have far-reaching effects on the social services had been initiated. The Labour government then in power had asked the Office of Population Censuses and Surveys to mount a national survey to determine the numbers of adult handicapped and impaired people in Great Britain and to investigate the suitability or otherwise of the homes they lived in. The impact of this survey was anticipated in the House of Commons during the Second Reading of the *Chronically Sick and Disabled Persons Act* in December 1969 :

". . . But next year we shall have a large body of information which no previous British government, and few other governments elsewhere, have ever had. We can see for the first time just who and how many we are talking about. We shall know how many are getting a service, how many who need it are not, and what is the most effective line of advance. In other words we can get our priorities right for this group and balance these against wider priorities for the first time."[57]

This survey pointed out the deficiencies in the registers kept by local authority welfare departments and also revealed that, of those disabled people using local authority services, the majority were availing themselves of help provided, at the time of the survey, by health departments that were still part of the local authority framework.

"Not all handicapped people known to authorities appeared on the registers of (the then) welfare departments and those receiving services (i.e. 41 per cent of the handicapped) are most likely to have been benefiting from the nursing, chiropody and home help services. Only 18 per cent of the very severely handicapped were on local authority registers at the time of the survey, 11 per cent of the severely handicapped and 7 per cent of the appreciably handicapped."[58]

With such a small proportion of the substantially and permanently handicapped known to local authority welfare departments – and it was with this part of the disabled population in mind that Section 29 of the National Assistance Act 1948 had been framed – it is not surprising that dissatisfaction with welfare provision had been steadily growing throughout the Sixties. Many disabled people, no longer content to remain quiescent, had already begun to look elsewhere for support, to the self-help organisations which were proliferating.[59] Some of these had begun to organise themselves into pressure groups and, having lobbied their local councillors in vain, now turned to parliament and demanded positive action. *The Chronically Sick and Disabled Persons Act 1970*, which received the support of all parties had a triumphant passage through both Houses and went on to the statue book on 30 May 1970, the same day as the *Local Authority Social Services Act 1970*.

This latter Act translated one of the hopes expressed by the Seebohm Report that there should be new united local authority social services departments "on the rates", supported by the rates support grant and community-based. They were to be created out of the existing multiplicity of services and to absorb among others the functions of the welfare committees that had been established under Section 29 of the National Assistance Act 1948. At the same time professionalism would be encouraged as new career structures for trained professional social workers opened up. These, including the effects on the disabled of newly created posts, are discussed in detail in Chapter Five.

4. *The Chronically Sick and Disabled Persons Act 1970*

The Bill had an enthusiastic reception by all parties. Its aim was clear enough – to provide a far-reaching codification of help for disabled people. At the time the Act was passed the services envisaged were the concern of four different departments of central government – the Department of Health and Social Security, the Department of the Environment, the Department of Education and Science and the Department of Employment and Productivity. They involved traffic authorities, sanitary authorities, planning authorities, housing authorities and education authorities as well as the health and welfare departments of local authorities. Gradually most of these services were to be gathered under the umbrella of the new local authority social services departments, e.g. car badges for disabled drivers, concessionary bus fares, home helps and chiropody. The voluntary organisations which had already done so much to help the disabled, and also to safeguard their interests, were carefully included as co-opted members of various advisory and consultative bodies. Youth employment services got a special mention. Children suffering from autism and dyslexia were to have special educational treatment, as were children suffering from the dual handicap of deafness and blindness. Young patients who have to stay long periods in hospital were made a matter of special concern, as were the younger handicapped people who might be cooped up with the very old in Part III accommodation. Various kinds of research were encouraged including the founding of a long overdue Institute of Hearing Research. But the success of the Act would depend, in the first place, on identifying who the disabled were, where they were, what were their most pressing needs and how services for them could best be designed to meet those needs; and secondly on informing them of these services as they became available.

The need to inform those disabled known to the local authority of any services that could be of use to them was recognised in Section 29 (1) of the National Assistance Act 1948 but Section 1 of the Chronically Sick and Disabled Persons Act goes much further and makes such information mandatory. Those local authorities "having duties under Section 29 of the National Assistance Act" are now obliged to :

"inform themselves of the number of persons to whom that section applies within their area and of the need for making by the authority of arrangements under that section for such persons."[60]

Mr Alfred Morris, the Private Member responsible for introducing the Bill,[61] pointed out that this represented a departure from precedent :

"All previous legislation was built on self application for help. Section 1 of the Act, on the other hand, says that the onus is on the public authority to go out and find the people in need. This is a very sharp break in the law."[62]

The need to impose a duty on local authorities to seek out disabled people living in their area was partly due to the failure of disabled people to come forward of their own accord after the National Assistance Act. But it was also necessary because welfare authorities had been obliged to register and give information about their services only to people who had already asked for or received assistance, a self-limiting exercise. The new Act took the precaution of requiring local authorities to "cause to be published" information about the services they were providing. This was to result in space being taken in local newspapers, in leaflets, pamphlets and booklets being pushed through letter-boxes and posters displayed in prominent places. Not all local authorities did all these things but the majority did more than one of them.

On a national scale the media gave the Act a very favourable reception and the national press, radio and television have continued ever since to play a powerful part both in interesting the general public and keeping up the pressures necessary to make sure of its implementation. Interestingly, the provision under the Act of help with radio sets and television sets – provision of the latter has been exceptionally generous in the Greater London area as compared with the country as a whole – has meant that increasing numbers of disabled people are also at the receiving end of constant information about the problems that other disabled people are experiencing.[63]

As far as the actual provision of services for the disabled was concerned, the Act was less ambitious than was claimed. In the main, Section 2 of the *Chronically Sick and Disabled Persons Act*, the section with which this study is mainly concerned, is only Section 29 of the *National Assistance Act 1948* writ large. The occasional lecture mentioned in the clause 5 (3) outline scheme attached to Circular 32/51 is now extended to become help for adult handicapped persons to attend full-time courses of education – a facility that is often all too dependent on another facility recommended in the Act, that of access to public places of education[64] in addition to places of entertainment and sanitation.[65] There were other up-datings in keeping with the time as well as the provision of television sets as well as radios and the payment of rentals. There was also – and this was to prove most popular of all both with disabled clients and with local councillors – an obligation to help with the installation of telephones and perhaps the payment of charges for telephone rentals[66] although not of telephone bills.

The actual statutory provisions of Section 2 of the Chronically Sick and Disabled Persons Act are as follows :

> "2.–(1) Where a local authority having functions under section 29 of the National Assistance Act 1948 are satisfied in the case of any person to whom that section applies who is ordinarily resident in their area that it is necessary in order to meet the needs of that person for that authority to make arrangements for all or any of the following matters, namely :
>
> a) the provision of practical assistance for that person in his home;
>
> b) the provision for that person of, or assistance to that person in obtaining, wireless, television, library or similar recreational facilities;
>
> c) the provision for that person of lectures, games, outings or other recreational facilities outside his home or

assistance to that person in taking advantage of educational facilities available to him;

d) the provision for that person of facilities for, or assistance in, travelling to and from his home for the purpose of participating in any services provided under arrangements made by the authority under the said section 29 or, with the approval of the authority, in any services provided otherwise than as aforesaid which could be provided under such arrangements;

e) the provision of assistance for that person in arranging for the carrying out of any works of adaptation in his home or the provision of any additional facilities designed to secure his greater safety, comfort or convenience;

f) facilitating the taking of holidays by that person, whether at holiday homes or otherwise and whether provided under arrangements made by the authority or otherwise;

g) the provision of meals for that person whether in his home or elsewhere;

h) the provision for that person of, or assistance to that person in obtaining, a telephone and any special equipment necessary to enable him to use a telephone,

then, notwithstanding anything in any scheme made by the authority under the said section 29, but subject to the provisions of section 35 (2) of that Act (which requires local authorities to exercise their functions under Part III of that Act under the general guidance of the Secretary of State and in accordance with the provisions of any regulation made for the purpose), it shall be the duty of that authority to make those arrangements in exercise of their functions under the said section 29."

This appears to make a lot of highly satisfactory promises but careful analysis of the provisions of Section 2 reveals that nothing must of necessity be provided outright, let alone free. First, the local authority has to establish to its own satisfaction that need exists – for this the local authority is the sole arbiter – then it has to decide if it is the kind of need that ought to be met and only then, after such a decision has been made, is it required to do anything about it. Even then, what it does will depend on the resources available so it could be very little indeed. A council might, for example, merely "make arrangements" for the need to be met. The words to "make arrangements" form the key motif of all else that follows in Section 2 so that what at first glimpse might appear to be an end result is in practice left unresolved and inconclusive.

41

With this in mind let us take as an example Section 2.–(1)(e), which deals with adaptations. It can be seen to break down into the following steps :

    (i) the local authority has to decide, to its own satisfaction, if a need exists; (the local authority is the sole arbiter of needs)

    (ii) if a need is believed to exist then the local authority has to decide what sort of "arrangements" it must make

    (iii) to give assistance to clients

    (iv) in making other "arrangements"

    (v) for the carrying out of works of adaptation.

At which point the mandatory duties of the local authority peter out altogether.

No local authority is apparently obliged by law to see any provision through to the end, although the majority of social services departments having once taken a decision to offer some degree of help were more likely than not to do so. Even so the researcher was to find evidence of adaptations unmonitored and apparently abandoned for more than a year. The requests for simple aids, which clients had expected to result in simple acts of provision, were to become progressively more remote as waiting lists lengthened. One of the reasons for such delays was that some requests got lost in the system. Another was undoubtedly shortage of staff. But a third arose out of problems over payment.

A comparison of Section 2 of the Chronically Sick and Disabled Persons Act 1970 with Section 29 of the National Assistance Act 1948 reveals that one vital point is missing from the later Act – the need to clarify the circumstances under which clients may be expected to pay for, or contribute towards, the cost of services provided.

To insist that a local authority helps with making arrangements for a number of highly desirable services does not automatically mean that the local authority is obliged to foot either the whole or indeed any part of the bill. Yet that was the prevailing impression left on many disabled clients by the Chronically Sick and Disabled Persons Act 1970. The National Assistance Act of 1948 on the other hand had left local authority committees in no such doubt about their rights to choose the extent of the financial obligations they were prepared to incur and Section 29.–(5) states firmly :

> "A local authority may recover from persons availing themselves of any service provided under this section such charges (if any) as, having regard to the cost of the service the authority may determine, whether generally or in the circumstances of any particular case."

This section which has dealt so clearly with this issue was not repealed by the 1970 Act. Nor was it repeated or reworded so that policy in 1970 concerning the possibility of contributions by clients – whether changed or unchanged – should have been equally clear. The unrepealed subsection has not even been quoted or referred to in any of the official literature published after the Act. The first circular to be issued by the Department of Health and Social Security after the Act[67] does however safeguard the rights of local authorities to decide for themselves how much they are prepared to pay. That some local authorities will operate a form of means-testing is taken for granted in paragraph 40 which, although urging liberality, says

"This is not to imply any diminution of the statutory powers of discretion of authorities to determine charges or to waive them."

While in paragraph 7 the Circular had already stated that

"criteria of need are matters for local authorities to determine in the light of resources."

This is a far cry from the statement made by Mr Alfred Morris in the House of Commons at the Committee Stage of the Bill in which he said

"gives the individual clear expectations that he will receive the services which are needed in his case."[68]

But circulars seldom fall into the hands of the general public many of whom were to remain convinced that all the services mentioned in Section 2 of the Chronically Sick and Disabled Persons Act were to be provided free and without any form of means-testing. In fact parliamentary procedure had forced the parliamentary draftsmen to leave provision open-ended.[69]

It is not difficult to see how such widespread misunderstanding of the implications of the Chronically Sick and Disabled Persons Act came about. It is quite clear from subsequent speeches made by Mr Morris, outside the House of Commons, that he had hoped that the services for the disabled outlined in Section 2 of the Act would have been theirs as of right and free of charge. Public speeches by other prominent Members of Parliament served to reinforce these hopes and the media tended to follow their lead. Almost overnight hopes became translated into fact in the minds of many of the general public and the assumption that local authorities had no statutory right to ask disabled clients for financial contributions was to persist for some time. Social workers reported having copies of the 1970 Act thrust into their faces as late as 1973 with the result that carefully nurtured casework relations foundered on the refusal of disabled clients and their relatives to believe, for example, that adaptations were not necessarily provided free of all charges to the client.

By not clarifying the issue of payment the Chronically Sick and Disabled Persons Act 1970 did many disabled persons no small disservice, for disillusion was proportionate to those "clear expectations" to which Mr Morris had referred in Parliament. The situation was not made any easier by the fact that both clients and social workers were all too frequently kept in the dark about the policy of their own social services committee. They knew that some public money was available but they did not know how much. If clients were asked to contribute to an adaptation they had no way of knowing if they had been fairly assessed.[70]

Whereas the National Assistance Act 1948 had faced up squarely to the limitations imposed by the lack of local authority resources, the Chronically Sick and Disabled Persons Act entirely evaded the issue of finance, leaving it to the realities of the situation to be expounded in circulars of guidance. Guidance by the Minister (later the Secretary of State) was a feature of both the 1948 Act and the 1970 Act.[71]

The question of payment by clients was not the only problem evaded by the Chronically Sick and Disabled Persons Act. Blaxter, in a recently published study, draws attention to the difficulties in determining eligibility arising from the loose formulation of the 1970 Act :

"the loose formulation of the Chronically Sick and Disabled Persons Act made the services very vulnerable to different pressures. Widening groups in 'need' was leading to problems of defining eligibility."[72]

Were the services offered to the disabled still to be determined by Section 29 of the National Assistance Act (not repealed) and therefore to be made available only to people who were "substantially and permanently handicapped" or were they also to serve people with fluctuating degrees of sickness and disability? Blaxter also points out that the Seebohm Report "enlarged the concept of the potential clients for the services", but the difficulties in extending these services were further compounded by the fact that

"legislators, social work administrators, social workers themselves, referring agents and clients, may all see eligibility differently . . ."[73]

Clearly the Chronically Sick and Disabled Persons Act, by its very title, must have been intended to transcend the limitations imposed by the 1948 Act. Yet it did not commit local authorities to any statutory provision for persons with disabilities which are not static, nor to providing services for less severely disabled people who might have benefited equally, or even more, from some of the services recommended in Section 2.–(1), and who either did not receive an aid to daily living or did not receive one in time to prevent deterioration.

In the Greater London area the study that follows will show that in 1974–75 a great many aids and simple adaptations were in fact being issued in the majority of boroughs to people with comparatively minor handicaps. In 1976, when cuts in expenditure had to be made, the very generous policy of some boroughs was changed. Increasingly rigid criteria were applied so that the issue of aids for minor handicaps ceased and aids were issued only to disabled people "at risk" and, in one borough, issued only to people "at risk of their lives". This is a retrograde step which, although strictly within the letter of the *National Assistance Act 1948*, contravenes the spirit of the later Act of 1970.

5. *The Housing Needs of Disabled People: Section 3 of the Act*

Section 3 of the Chronically Sick and Disabled Persons Act 1970 requires local authority housing departments "to have regard for the special needs of the Chronically Sick and Disabled" and to submit proposals about what they intended to provide in the way of new purpose-built dwellings for the disabled to the then Minister of Housing and Local Government. Adaptations were not mentioned in this section of the Act.[74]

Further legislation was however to be more specific about adaptations and Sections 105 and 56 of the *Housing Act 1974* were to prove of considerable relevance to adapting property for the disabled, Section 105 in the public sector and Section 56 in the private sector. The interviews for this study were begun before the publication of the *Housing Act 1974* but by the end of the study in the summer of 1976, the influence of the act was beginning to be apparent. Other legislation which overtook the researcher included the *Housing Rents and Subsidies Act 1975* which made further regulations affecting the financing of adaptations in both sectors and legislation in July 1977 to increase the amounts of the grants that had been recommended in 1975.

A consultative paper, published in November 1976 by the Department of the Environment,[75] suggested that total responsibility for major adaptations in the public sector should ultimately be transferred from the social services departments to the local authority housing departments. These suggestions became recommendations in a joint circular issued on 27 August 1978. Although not mandatory it assumes that "authorities will want to adopt a positive approach to the new divisions of responsibility proposed.[76]

NOTES

1. The National Insurance Act 1911, Section 8a.
2. *Ibid.*, Sections 23–29.
3. Levy, H., *National Health Insurance: a critical study* (Cambridge, 1944), p. 195.
4. The amount of money available for "additional benefits" varied in different parts of the country and with different approved societies.

5. The Royal Surgical Aid Society, 77th annual report, 1940, p. 45.

6. "A miner, aged 30, thanked the Society in 1939 for an artificial arm for which he had been waiting fifteen years. . . . A deckhand pensioner expressed his gratitude for now being able to do with his artificial leg what he had not been able to do for six years." Quoted by Levy, H., *op. cit.*, p. 199.

7. For a more detailed definition of equipment, aids and appliances see Chapter Six, pages 122 and 130.

8 Items of "equipment" commonly supplied included crutches and hoists; spinal carriages and wheelchairs were more often than not either hired or provided by one of over three hundred charities interested in helping disabled children and adults.

9. This principle was in fact frequently breached in practice as, under Section 16 of the Act, the Minister was encouraged to give preference to disabled people returning from the Second World War when selecting candidates for vocational training and industrial rehabilitation. Nevertheless the idea of thinking of disabled people as a "general class' of society was to exert a considerable influence on future legislation.

10. The Disabled Persons (Employment) Act 1944, Section I.–(1).

11. Ministry of Health Circular 48/47.

12. The National Assistance Act 1948, Preamble.

13. Ministry of Health Circular 32/51, Part II, Appendix II, Note on Clause 1.–(3).

14. Ministry of Health Circular 118/48, Section 72.

15. Ministry of Health Circular 118/48, para. 56.

16. The Blind Persons Acts 1920 and 1938.

17. Ministry of Health Circular 32/51.

18. Ibid. Appendix I.

19. *Ibid.* Part II, Clause 3. *The Register.* It is desired that the register should be known as the Register of Handicapped Persons (General Classes).

20. Circular 16/58, para. 3.

21. Circular 15/60, para. 2.

22. See e.g. Sainsbury, Sally, *Registered as Disabled* (London, 1970), Appendix III, p. 199, "Variations between Local Authorities in their Provision for Physically Handicapped Persons," and also p. 32 above.

23. The Education Act 1944 and The Disabled Persons (Employment) Act 1944. The extension of the latter act in 1958 made the provision of sheltered employment and special training a mandatory duty of local authorities.

24. Services for the General Classes of handicapped reflect the strong emphasis placed on handicraft in previous legislation for the blind.

25. The Central Council for Education and Training in Social Work drew attention to the fact that many disabled persons were still confusing the two registers in 1974. See CCETSW Paper 9 (London, 1974), p. 47.

26. For further details on the keeping of the Register see Circular 32/51, Appendix II, Part II, Notes on Schemes for Handicapped Persons (General Classes), pages 16 and 17.

27. These five classes remained unchanged until 1974 when, after Circular 17/74, they were superseded by three new classes based not on employability but on the degree of handicap. These three classes were: (i) very severe handicap; (ii) severe and appreciable handicap and (iii) all other persons. They reflect the changing attitudes of the Seventies towards the needs of the handicapped as well as the desirability of streamlining administrative processes in the face of the general shortage of administrative and clerical staff to deal with the increasing number of disabled persons identified.

28. Information officers at centres which local authorities were permitted to form under Section 8 of the Local Government Act, 1948, were asked to make sure that enquiries by or on behalf of disabled people were followed up by a visit to that person's home.

29. The report of a survey conducted for the Office of Population Censuses and Surveys showed that 82 per cent of the sample have not heard of the register and that of these 60 per cent would not have registered had they known of its existence either because they wished to conceal the extent of their handicap or because they felt they had no need of any welfare services. See Harris, Amelia, *The Handicapped and Impaired in Great Britain*, Vol. I (HMSO, 1971) for the OPCS.

30. Circular 32/51, Appendix Part II, Note on Part I, clause 3.

31. Ministry of Health Circular 70/48. Relieving officers could gain a certificate of knowledge of the Poor Law.

32. Ministry of Health Circular 32/51, Appendix II, Part II, Note on Clause 12(3).

33. *Ibid.*, Appendix II, Part I, para. 4(4), p. 12.

34. See the references to training in Younghusband, Eileen, *Report on the Employment and Training of Social Workers* (Carnegie UK, Trust, 1947), and Smith, Marjorie, *Professional Education for Social Work in Britain*, (London, 1953).

35. 31/51, Appendix II, Part II, para. 12.–(4).

36. See Circular 32/51, Appendix II, Part I, para. 12.–(2).

37. Many of them, by the late Fifties, had been on Younghusband Courses which stressed the value of casework within the family setting.

38. For a discussion of the way in which welfare officers perceived their role see Sainsbury, Sally, *op. cit.*, Appendix I, "The Role of the Welfare Officer". Workloads varied greatly but the average in a London borough in 1968 was estimated to be around 350 clients to each welfare officer. Visits tended to "cluster" around times of crisis, particularly if a transfer to Part III

accommodation appeared imminent. In some boroughs attempts were made to visit those in most need at intervals of six weeks.

39. This clause links up with Section 12 of the National Health Service Act, 1946, in its emphasis on the need to obtain help with preventive and remedial treatment.

40. See Chapter Three, The Financing of the Chronically Sick and Disabled Persons Act, 1970, p. 55.

41. See Buckle, Judith, *The Handicapped and Impaired in Great Britain*, Vol. II, "Work and Housing of Impaired Persons in Great Britain" (HMSO, 1971), p. 89, Table 83.

42. See also Chapter Four: the Financing of Aids and Adaptations in the Greater London boroughs.

43. See the *Mental Health Act,* Section 8.–(2).

44. Ministry of Health Circular 15/60, paras 1, 2, 4.

45. The Seventies were to see a complete reversal of this attitude, and in 1972, the handicapped were reported as being "overwhelmingly critical of the lack of status granted them by the community and their helpers in particular", CCETSW, *op. cit.,* para. 35, p. 15.

46. Ministry of Health, Circular 87/48.

47. Dr Shirley Summerskill, Second Reading of the Chronically Sick and Disabled Persons Bill. Parliamentary Debates, *House of Commons Official Report*, Vol. 792, Col. 1901.

48. See Townsend, P., *The Last Refuge: A Survey of Residential Homes and Institutions for the Aged in England and Wales* (London, 1962); and from the USA, Goffman, E., *Asylum* (published in England in Pelican Books, 1971).

49. Home helps for the younger physically handicapped were not made mandatory until the Health Services and Public Health Act, 1968, Section 13.

50. See Townsend, P., *op. cit.,* page 429.

51 See Shenfield, Barbara, *Social Policies for Old Age: A Review of Social Provision for Old Age in Great Britain,* (London, 1957), p. 170.

52. Symons, Jean, *Care with Dignity* (London, 1972).

53. See *The Sunday Times,* 3.5.75.

54. Pressure groups such as the Disability Alliance began to express concern in 1977 at the way in which local authorities have cut back the number of hours offered by home helps and also the number of meals on wheels, many of which have also increased in price.

55. *Report of the Committee on Local Authority and Allied Social Services* (Cmnd. 3703, HMSO, 1968), para. 325.

56. *Op. cit.,* para. 332.

57. See Parliamentary Debates, *House of Commons Official Report*, Vol. 792. The Second Reading of the Chronically Sick and Disabled Persons Bill, 5 December 1969, Col. 1915. Also footnote 25 on p. 28 above.

58. DHSS Circular 45/71, para. 8(iv).

59. See Jerman, Betty, *Do Something! a Guide to Self-Help Organisations* (London, 1971). This lists 60 such organisations of which 21 were connected with disability. These included the Disablement Income Group, the Multiple-Sclerosis Society and the Spastics Society. Such societies continue to proliferate.

60. *Op. cit.,* Section 1.

61. Mr Alfred Morris, M.P., later to become, in 1974, the first Minister for the Disabled.

62. Quoted in Fact Sheet 9 issued by Action Research for the Crippled Child in 1974.

63. "The best way of getting something done" said one client, "is to threaten to go on 'Nationwide' ". This is a popular television programme that includes the ventilation of social injustices and social grievances. A Radio 4 programme concerned entirely with the problems of the Disabled entitled "Does he take sugar?" has also gained a wide following.

64. Sections 8 (1) and 8 (2) (a) and (b).

65. Secton 5 (1) and Circular 32/51 Note on Clause 5 (5).

66. The drain on local authority social services resources that on-going telephone rentals was to prove is discussed in Chapter Four, pp. 81 and 82. Before the Act telephone charges were occasionally met by central government for housebound people at risk. See DHSS, *Supplementary Benefits Handbook* (1970), para. 65.

67. DHSS Circular 12/70.

68. See *Parliamentary Report (Commons)* of Standing Committee C, Chronically Sick and Disabled Persons Act, Session 1969–70, Col. 150.

69. Parliamentary procedure forbids any discussion of finance until the adoption of a Financial Resolution which in the case of this Bill was not until 3 February 1970, the final date on which the Standing Committee met.

70. Section 2.–(1)(e) of the Chronically Sick and Disabled Persons Act echoes, almost word for word, the first lines of Section 5(5) of the outline scheme appended to Circular 32/51 of the National Assistance Act. But it omits all references to payment. See p. 41 of this chapter.

71. See The Chronically Sick and Disabled Persons Act 1970, Section 2.–(1).

72. See Blaxter, Mildred, *The Meaning of Disability* (London, 1976), p. 87.

73. *Ibid.,* page 36.

74. For further discussion of the Housing Needs of Disabled People see Chapters Twelve and Thirteen.

75. DOE, *Adaptations to Housing for People who are Physically Handicapped.* (HMSO, 1976).

76. Joint Circular DOE 59/78; DHSS, LAC 78(14); Welsh Office 104/78.

CHAPTER THREE

THE FINANCING OF THE CHRONICALLY SICK
AND DISABLED PERSONS ACT 1970

1. *Introduction*

The Chronically Sick and Disabled Persons Act got off to an awkward start. The timing cut right across the rhythm of the financial year and, because priority was being given to the formation of the new local authority social services departments, it became a temporary casualty of local government reorganisation. Although eagerly awaited by disabled persons, it was also premature insofar as it was passed before the completion of the government survey on the adult chronically sick and handicapped,[1] already referred to in the previous chapter. Hard evidence would be needed if services for the disabled were to compete against other demands for expenditure in a time of economic stringency. From the outset Dr Dunwoody, the Joint Under-Secretary of State for Health and the Social Services, warned the House that government resources were limited :

> "In many ways, a decisive consideration is the problem of resources. Hon. Members need no telling of the Government's determination to get our economy right . . . though the local health and welfare authorities are no less likely than the Government to continue saying that the social services must command priority, the financial resources cannot be stretched indefinitely. If more is spent in one direction there may be less to spend in another."[2]

Whilst welcoming the bill in principle – and what Parliamentarian could do otherwise – Mr Dunwoody made it clear that :

> ". . . it would not be in the interest of the services or of the sick and handicapped themselves to rush into premature conclusions based on partial results."[3]

The attention of the House had already been drawn[4] to the state of flux in which local authority social services were liable to find themselves as the result of legislation arising out of the recent Seebohm Report. Only a few weeks previously, an important report on housing management policy had been published dealing among other matters with the "weight to be attached to the claims of the sick and handicapped to housing".[5] Implications would be discussed with local authorities and departments. A valuable report on voluntary services had recently been published on behalf of the National Council of Social Work and the National Institute of Social Work. As a result structural improvement would be introduced throughout the services reported on. A Government Green Paper on the organisation of the health services was due to appear in the near future.[6] Under all these circumstances it was thought the Treasury might have difficulty in arriving at a balanced judgement about any increases in expenditure that the Chronically Sick and Disabled Persons Act might involve. The Rate Support Grant had already been fixed for the year 1971–72 before the Bill – a Private Member's bill which had secured first place in the ballot – came before the House on 26 November 1970 and the Joint Under Secretary of State was mustering every possible excuse in advance to explain why no extra money would be forthcoming from the Exchequer.[7]

What was to be the standard reaction of directors of local authority social services was also anticipated in Parliament. In a speech made during the Second Reading of the bill a worried Member said :

"One thing which appears to me to be a criticism of the Bill is the fact that throughout its length there is no reference to money . . . We are contemplating a Bill which merely confers powers on Government Departments without any definite instructions that they may use them, and at the same time imposes on local authorities a mandatory duty involving the expenditure of an unknown amount of money. Because I am enthusiastic about the principle behind the Bill, I feel a little apprehensive. I was once a member of a local authority, so I can guess what they will feel . . . they may be a little less enthusiastic about it than I should like them to be."[8]

Clearly finance for any expanded services would have to be found by the local authorities themselves. Here again the Chronically Sick and Disabled Persons Act was to suffer from bad timing for the very things which saved it from oblivion – the appointed days[9] – were completely out of step with the local authority financial year. Although this begins on 1 April and ends on 31 March there are two peak times during the year for local authorities, the first, early in November, when the extent of the Rate Support Grant from central government is made known, and the second in March when final cuts in the estimates have to be made to produce an acceptable rate to set before the local electorate. As the Act was not passed until 30 May 1970 the need for local authorities to make special financial provisions to extend services for the disabled under sections of a new act not due to become operative until 30 August 1970 and 29 November 1970 had not been foreseen; nor were any such provisions forthcoming. The most that could be hoped for was that money already allocated to departments "having functions under Section 29 of the National Assistance Act 1948" could be made to stretch until the new financial year began on 1 April 1971, particularly as it was to those departments that the Act had been obliged specifically to address itself.[10]

The appointed day for the establishment of social services departments under the Local Authority Social Services Act 1970 came at an even worse time, on 1 January 1970, when the last cuts in the provisional estimates for 1971–72 were going up to Finance and General Purposes Committees for scrutiny, revision, coordination and approval. In this respect, although both Acts were passed on the same day, the timing of the Local Authority Social Services Act cut right across the timing of the Chronically Sick and Disabled Persons Act. Legally, the situation was tidied up by a conditional amendment in the Local Authority Social Services Act requiring the newly created Local Authority Social Services Departments to subsume the duties of local authorities under Section 29 of the National Assistance Act 1948. Officially there was no gap, but the reality was to prove different; indeed, the Secretary of State concluded Circular 45/71 by saying:

"once the Social Services Departments have settled down . . . the problem of lack of coordination between local authority departments concerned with the needs of the handicapped should diminish."[11]

In the meantime although expectations of improved services had been raised the needs of the disabled continue to be looked after in the same way as before by local authority welfare departments.

2. *The Social Services Budget 1971–72*

From 1 April 1971, the greater part of the money for services for the disabled has had to be found from the social services budget, including those enumerated in Section 2 of the Chronically Sick and Disabled Persons Act, 1970. This is the section which makes mandatory continued help with the provision of aids to daily living for people in need who are substantially and permanently handicapped;[12] and which also makes the first reference to the mandatory duty of local authorities to help with arrangements for adaptations in the home.[13] In addition this section imposes a duty on local authorities to give some measure of assistance in providing holidays, meals on wheels, television and telephones, none of which had been the previous responsibility of welfare departments,[14] and all of which would have considerably more popular (and therefore political) appeal than the provision of aids and adaptations.

Section 2 of the Chronically Sick and Disabled Persons Act became mandatory on 29 August 1970. This allowed local authority health and welfare departments and their committees, either jointly or separately, to draw up rough provisional estimates of what they thought had been essential in the past rather than what might be essential in the future and to get some form of limited approval for them from the borough treasurer before they themselves were superseded. Some, but by no means all, of the councillors sitting on welfare committees would be asked to continue as members of the new committees : these would also draw heavily on councillors serving on health and children's committees. Thus it came about that the last stages of the estimates of expenditure under Section 29 of the National Assistance Act 1948 and the estimates for the mandatory extension of services under Section 2 of the Chronically Sick and Disabled Persons Act 1970 were presented by new directors of new departments to members of re-constituted committees, many of whom had had no previous experience of legislation for the disabled and no particular knowledge of past or present policies towards them.

In the ensuing scramble it is not surprising that budget allocations for services for the disabled, including aids and adaptations, received less attention than the raising of money for services connected with setting up the new social services departments themselves; and also that long identification with other services on the part of some of the members of the new social services committees may further have influenced priorities.

According to Ripley, writing shortly before the passage of the Local Authorities Social Services Act, each local authority department had :

> "a traditional status and claim in the annual round of bargaining which [was] only modified by the rise and fall of the comparative political strengths of their respective chairmen or major shifts in central government policy."[15]

The Local Authorities Social Services Act 1970 certainly reflected such a shift in central government policy, but one which came too late in the financial year to have much influence on local political attitudes. As far as finding money for the disabled was concerned, the problems of the financial year 1969–70 were well summed up by a senior officer as "scratching around for money, first for the welfare department and then for the social services department, first in one place, then in another; begging a bit off the contingency fund there, getting a slice of a supplementary somewhere else. It was possible but it was not easy, the money was very difficult to get." The difficulties of 1969–70 were inevitably carried over into the financial year 1970–71 when they were to be further compounded by a letter from the Secretary of State on 10 May 1971[16] announcing that the appointed day for the implementation of Section 1 of the Chronically Sick and Disabled Persons Act would be 1 October 1971. This Section required local authorities to inform themselves of the numbers of substantially and permanently handicapped persons in their area, and then to go on to publicise the existing, extended and new services available. This would obviously be costly.

3. *The Effect of Section 1 of the Chronically Sick and Disabled Persons Act on the Financing of Services for the Disabled*

On 4 May 1971, six days before the appointed day for the implementation of Section 1 was announced, the long-promised results of the national survey[17] were finally published. Copies of the report were hurriedly sent out by the three Departments involved with providing aids and adaptations under cover of a joint circular.[18] The survey had thrown up evidence of widely differing needs in different regions of the country and comments were accordingly invited from relevant local authority associations on how local authorities could most quickly gather information about the scale of local, as distinct from national, needs. These comments formed the basis of the circular of guidance of 16 September issued on the authority of the Conservative Minister for Social Services. This said :

> "One way of obtaining this information would be through local sample surveys. This would still leave local authorities with the ultimate task of identifying everyone who both needs and wants a service. The completion of this task should in any case be the authority's aim and there will be certain authorities who will feel able to embark at an early date on a programme of identifying all those people or have already done so whether by individual enquiries to each household in the authority's area (personal enquiry, or initial postal enquiry with personal follow-up where appropriate) or by bringing together information at present scattered amongst the whole range of statutory and voluntary services and agencies to whom handicapped individuals are known."[19]

Already the original intention of Part I of the Act to seek out each and every one of the disabled had been diluted by the substitution of "sample" surveys. The circular making the now familiar and routine acknowledgement of the limited financial resources of many local authorities goes on to caution them against allowing "the cost and effort of making enquiries of each household" to nullify the whole purpose of the task :

"In these circumstances it may be desirable to begin by sample surveys to build up an assessment of total demands for services and their variety; to develop the services shown to be required; and only when this has been begun to start to identify the disabled in the area who need and want services."[20]

Whichever method local authorities decided to adopt, a small sample survey or a full survey,[21] or if they decided not to make a survey at all, more money still would be needed for the social services budget, because services had also to be publicised.

The duty to publicise services for the disabled under Part I of the Act was more easily fulfilled. All local authorities mounted some form of publicity campaign, although, like the surveys, they varied greatly in scope and in the amount of money spent on them. Some local authorities were content with leaflets pushed through randomly selected letter-boxes by volunteers, often children. Others produced well-designed, illustrated booklets for people already identified as disabled. In some, posters went up in strategic places such as doctors' surgeries, Rotary clubs and "Bingo" halls asking the general public to help in the search for disabled people not yet known to the local authority. One borough organised a Christmas Day "phone-in" manned by a team of concerned social workers. Pages were taken in local newspapers and some authorities, where stations existed, took time on local radio programmes. The result of the various forms of publicity, especially if they were also backed up by efficiently conducted surveys, was precisely what Section 1 of the Act intended — the identification of numbers of previously unknown disabled with previously unmet needs, including disabled people who would benefit from aids and adaptations.

Unfortunately there was a backlash. A major result of the publicity, and of many of the surveys, was to raise false hopes about what local authority social services departments might be realistically expected to provide. Although many social services departments made gallant attempts to match expenditure with expressed need, the development of services for the disabled has at no time kept pace with the unprecedented and ever-increasing demand which had been triggered off by Section 1 of the Act.

4. *The Provision of Aids and Adaptations under Section 2 of the Chronically Sick and Disabled Persons Act*

The provision of aids and adaptations, it must be remembered, forms only a part of the many services that it is suggested local authorities ought to provide for the disabled. The circular 45/71 does however give them due attention in paragraph 9 as "being among the implications" of the OPCS report. Paragraph 9 (x) states :

"There is a need for the greater provision of simple personal aids and domestic equipment for the disabled, together with more careful and continuing instruction in their use."

which clearly suggests a policy involving increased expenditure both on aids and on staff to deal with the after-care of clients receiving them. There is also a clear recognition earlier in the same paragraph in 9 (x) that

"In many cases the dwellings of disabled people need special adaptations to make them more convenient or to enable them to be used more fully. Fittings and the lay-out of rooms as well as of access to them need to be considered."

Adaptations however get a further mention in a full paragraph of their own, paragraph 27 which, under the heading *Adaptations to Dwellings*, refers to co-operation between the Department of Health and Social Security and the Department of the Environment "in planning a study on the housing needs of the handicapped . . . which it is hoped . . . will include consideration of the extent to which adaptations can be helpful.' Paragraph 27 ends by saying

"the possibility of carrying out adaptations can only be assessed with regard to individual needs and individual dwellings".

Taken in conjunction with 9 (ix) above this clearly implies a hope that local authority social services departments will assist with adapting property for disabled people on an *ad hoc* basis.

In fact the level of local authority provision in the subsequent financial year, 1972–73, remained generally very low as the annual returns to the Department of Health and Social Security bear witness.[22] Figures showing that a county council had provided only eight adaptations in all, three in the public sector and, in the private sector five, of which none cost more than £150 are not untypical. Or of a county borough providing a total of six, with two in the public sector, two costing less than £150 in the private sector and two costing more. One possible reason for such an extremely low level of activity – apart from the generally low order of priority that adaptations had received after the National Assistance Act 1948 – may lie with the study mentioned in paragraph 27 of Circular 45/71. Until the two central government departments engaged in evaluating the usefulness of adaptations had made their findings known, many social services committees, already hard-pressed to find money for other services for the disabled, may well have felt justified in marking time until they received guidance from central government. This guidance was not to be forthcoming until May 1974. This circular,[23] issued on 7 May 1974 under the title *Housing for People who are Physically Handicapped* stated in paragraph 7 :

"For many handicapped people, it is better to adapt their existing homes, if suitable for adaptation than to rehouse them in purpose-built accommodation. This means, above all, that they do not have to move away from the house and area they are used to living in and can continue to rely on established links with relatives and friends."

This pronouncement left local authority social services departments in no doubt as to their moral obligation to adapt whenever possible. Unfortunately the obligation was also a financial one. Whereas purpose-built dwellings for the disabled were matters for local authority housing departments financial help for adapting existing properties in both the public and private sectors, had to come out of current allocations in the social services budget. The debate on the Housing Bill 1974, which Circular 74/74 preceded by a matter of only a few days, did little to alleviate what was to become, for some social services departments, a very heavy financial burden indeed although some help in the private sector – and under strictly limited conditions – was introduced at the House of Lords stage.[24] This will be discussed in detail in Chapter Thirteen.

5. Establishing Local Priorities

When resources are scarce the ways in which priorities are established become increasingly important. Some priorities are more easily defined than others. One director of social services, when presented by officers of his own research and development division with data showing a vast increase in domiciliary services for the elderly and the disabled was able to recommend that the committee close two residential homes and discontinue the practice of taking up places in residential care across borough boundaries. Another director, confronted in 1974 with a list of more than two hundred elderly and disabled people waiting to go into Part III accommodation, saw the length of the waiting list both as a disgrace and as a challenge and was able to use it to convince his committee that the allocation for both domiciliary and residential care must be substantially increased for the subsequent financial year. In both these examples the same categories of people, the elderly and the disabled, were affected by the changes made. It is when changes that benefit one category of clients can only be made at the expense of other categories that difficulties ensue and these may be highly sensitive politically. Is the council to provide, for example, an increasing number of telephones for the disabled or to increase financial provision for a completely different category of client?

In 1972 the Conservative Secretary of State for Social Services

55

invited local authorities to submit plans of what they intended to do about the social services in the next ten years. The Department's guidelines[25] were based on what at first sight may seem to be the remarkably generous assumption that there could be an annual rate of increase in expenditure of ten per cent in real terms. Even more substantial increases were recommended for some services; for example, meals on wheels and the home help service, both used a great deal by disabled people, were to increase by over 250 per cent in the next decade. Nothing however was said about increases in expenditure on aids and adaptations although all the directors of social services interviewed in the course of this study were to say how much they would have welcomed some kind of directive in these first years.

The expansive days of confident optimism were short-lived. As a consequence of the sharp increase in oil prices in November 1973 and the disastrous effects these had on the national economy, cuts in planned expenditure had to be made and a circular about the Rate Support Grant issued in December 1973[26] went so far as to suggest a priority rating for different categories of client rather than merely laying down guidelines. These were :

(a) children at risk;
(b) the very elderly or severely handicapped living alone;
(c) the mentally handicapped or mentally ill in urgent need of residential or day care, or domiciliary support;
(d) vulnerable individuals, or families with vulnerable members, who are at imminent risk of breakdown under severe stress imposed on them by handicap, illness, homelessness or poverty.

Different social services committees would certainly single out different degrees of priority depending on the influence of local pressure groups, the power of individual members to sway the committee and, frequently, on the persuasive powers of directors of social services departments themselves. A circular issued in 1974 again stressed the needs to "moderate the present momentum of development with the minimum effect on those requiring the service" but left the responsibility of decision to "individual local authorities in the light of local circumstances".[27] But isolated cases that receive a lot of attention from the media can influence the amount of money spent on certain categories of client both locally and nationally. A much publicised case of child neglect – the Maria Colwell case, in 1974[28] – led one director of social services to comment "Everything's children in this year's budget".

By 1976 the needs to make cuts in local authority expenditure was to force the establishment of priorities and in the foreword to a consultative document published by the Department of Health and

Social Security in 1976[29] the Secretary of State acknowledged the unavoidable reality that the demand for the health and personal social services "will always outstrip our capacity to meet it." However in Chapter VI this document faces up, for the first time, to what exactly is required in the way of detailed information when planning services for the physically handicapped and, in the context of "helping them to lead as full a life as possible", a direct reference to the degree of expenditure required on aids and adaptations and certain other services provided under Section 2 of the Chronically Sick and Disabled Persons Act is made for the first time :

"Given the great contribution they make to the mobility and quality of life of physically handicapped people, we suggest that a high rate of expansion (9 per cent a year) would be justified."

The consultative document made it quite clear that, even in a time of economic stringency, the provision of aids and adaptations could not be allowed to fall off and that, on the contrary, a continued increase in real terms was to be maintained. It also recognised the fact that those local authorities which had been laggard about providing aids and adaptations would need to increase provision by more than nine per cent in the next few years and that this would cost more money than their social services budgets would be able to afford. Expansion of services in these circumstances "might be a suitable subject for joint finance," using health service money to buttress social services expenditure.[30]

Statistics published by the Disability Alliance Group covering the period of this study, 1974–75 and 1975–76, show that of the 107 local authorities listed, 65 showed a decrease in real terms in spending on aids and adaptations as between the two financial years ranging from 0.3 to 70.5 per cent, the average fall being 24.9 per cent; while 41 local authorities (one showed no change) increased their expenditure by percentages between 0.7 and 114.7, with an average rise of 26.4 per cent.[31] This is a very wide band round the 9 per cent suggested in the consultative document.

6. *The Role of Central Government in Financing the Chronically Sick and Disabled Persons Act*

(a) *The Rate Support Grant*
The role of central government has long been the dual one of providing local authorities with cash to spend, through the Rate Support Grant, the level of which is announced each year around November, and of suggesting to them, without wishing to appear to be interfering, and in the broadest possible terms, some of the ways in which they might spend it.[32] The amount of the Support Grant

varies from year to year according to the way in which the Treasury anticipates the spending needs of local authorities in the context of national economic trends. It includes an element of rate equalisation which means in effect that it varies between one local authority and another in order to spread its benefits where social need is greatest. In 1974–75 it was over 62 per cent, with the remainder being made up out of the local rates, but by 1977–78 this had dropped to just over 60 per cent. Even a decrease of half of one per cent in the Rate Support Grant results in severe cut-backs in planned local authority spending, although the amount spent on personal social services had continued to increase by just over 2 per cent in the three years 1974–75 to 1977–78 and is expected to continue at this rate in 1978–79.[33]

When the Chronically Sick and Disabled Persons Act was first passed, central government was content to shelter behind its traditional role as spectator/counsellor and made no suggestions whatsoever about what proportion of public money might be allocated for extending services. Sir Keith Joseph, speaking for a Conservative administration soon after the passing of the Act, said that he expected expenditure on the disabled to rise by 25 per cent between 1972 and 1974 but this could be met by contributions from the Rate Support Grant. "However", he was careful to add, "no part of this sum is specifically ear-marked for the disabled." Two years later he was to remark, in answer to parliamentary questions concerning the lack of effective provision by numerous local authorities, that the Rate Support Grant had been increased sufficiently to allow for the necessary expansion of services. In fact between 1972 and 1975 the Rate Support Grant was sufficient to allow local authority social services departments to achieve a growth, in real terms, ranging from 15 per cent in 1971–72 to 12 per cent in 1975–76.[34] Under such circumstances a strict adherence to the Redcliffe-Maude principles of local autonomy[35] might appear justifiable. In times of national economic crisis, however, a doctrine of "laissez faire" becomes less tenable. Cuts in the Rate Support Grant make the allocation of local priorities increasingly difficult and – as we have seen in the previous section – increasingly liable to receive suggestions, although not downright directions, from central government departments about priorities of need and also about ways of cutting existing services.

One of the cuts advocated was in the salaries of local authority staff which, according to the White Paper of January 1977 constituted "a quarter of all public expenditure on the main environmental and social services programmes." One result of this was that, by 1975–76, many vacancies for social services staff were to be frozen while new posts, created specifically to deal with the needs of the rising number of disabled clients identified, were to remain unadvertised and unfilled. This is just one example of the way in which

58

central government, although it cannot exert any direct control over the money received by local authorities in the form of local rates from local rate payers, can nevertheless bring indirect pressure to bear on the current expenditure of local authorities.

Over capital expenditure the control of central government is virtually absolute through its powers to grant or withhold loan sanction for all capital projects. To soften the immediate impact of the cuts on current expenditure local authorities were allowed, in 1975–76, to transfer money already in capital funds to current expenditure in the subsequent financial year.[36]

Concern that adequate services for the disabled may not survive continued expenditure cuts has led to some Members of Parliament reviving discussion about the possibility of a specific grant for the disabled which would state categorically what proportion of the Rate Support Grant must be devoted to their provision. The restoration of specific grants would seem to many to be a retrograde step but it is arguable that unless special safeguards exist it will be the weakest who go to the wall in a scramble for available funds.[37]

Another source of funding by central government – cash benefits provided for certain categories of the disabled as Social Security – has so far had no effect on the current expenditure of local authorities although, should they be substantially increased in the future, some social services committees might feel able to spend less of the money received from the Rate Support Grant on services for the disabled.[38]

(b) *Grants to Local authority housing authorities*
Other grants from central government which help to make life easier for the disabled are given to local housing authorities. At first these were mainly concerned with subsidies for new, purpose-built housing such as bungalows but then, after the publication of the joint circular, *Housing for the Physically Handicapped* in May 1974, subsidies were also offered to encourage the building of special types of housing for people confined to wheelchairs. The circular also introduced the totally new concept of "Mobility Housing". This term refers to a design which would be equally suitable for a family with no special problems or for a family with a handicapped member and could therefore be allocated to meet the varying housing areas as they arose. The main features of Mobility Housing are that the dwelling should be on the ground floor, without front doorsteps and with easy access for wheelchairs, wider than normal doorways and enough circulation space in bedrooms, kitchens and bathrooms to make it possible for people in wheelchairs to use them. The design might also include one inner wall that could be easily removable to add to the circulation space if necessary.

The nature of the subsidies offered which were called "The Yardstick Allowances for Mobility and Wheelchair Housing" were described in detail in another joint circular, called *Wheelchair and Mobility Housing: Standards and Costs* issued seventeen months later on 2 October 1975.[39] An allowance of £50 per dwelling could be claimed for each dwelling designated as Mobility Housing. This was in addition to the basic yardstick allowances applicable to all new council housing and any other allowances that might be available under a previous circular.[40] The financial inducements to build Wheelchair Housing varied with the number of "bedspaces" included in the design from £700 per dwelling for a single storey unit for a person living alone, to £650 per dwelling in a two-storey unit for families using seven bedspaces.

In addition to financial help with these dwellings central government also offered a grant of £150 for a hard-standing serving either kind of housing, or £400 for a car-port designed for wheelchair housing.

The circular describing these subsidies accompanied by a special occasional paper on design,[41] was sent to directors of social services and administrators of regional and area health authorities as well as to housing managers but the idea of Mobility Housing was nevertheless slow to percolate through the various systems.[42] Domiciliary occupational therapists, alerted by their professional journal, were among the first employees of social services departments to realise the value of this kind of council property as an alternative to adaptations and were amongst the first social services employees to urge their directors to negotiate fixed percentages of all new local authority housing projects to be offered to disabled clients.

The building of new council dwellings suitable for disabled clients living in property unsuited to adaptation would eventually be of considerable help to social services departments by providing suitable alternative accommodation of which, in the majority of boroughs, very little existed, and by providing it at no cost to the social services. But when it came to converting or modernising existing council properties – assuming permission could be obtained under section 105 of the 1974 Housing Act – the local authority housing managers had to find the money to do so out of their own Housing Revenue Accounts. Consequently very few local housing authorities, throughout the country, were prepared to help with the financing of even the most minor adaptations for disabled council tenants already in residence. Bills for all adaptations in the public sector were almost invariably met in full out of social services budgets.

The possibility of exchequer subsidies for anything but new buildings did not show up clearly in the drafting of the Housing Act 1974 but the *Housing Rents and Subsidies Act 1975* by amending Section 79 (4) of the previous act made it possible for local housing authorities to apply for improvement grants outside the Housing Revenue Account up to the same limits as those in the private sector. This was to have a potential effect on policy towards adaptations for the disabled, in that it would provide both disabled clients and social services departments with an element of choice.

(c) *Grant to Housing Associations*
A developing source of adaptations and conversions is provided by the housing associations. Indeed one of the chief aims of the 1974 Housing Act was "to extend the functions of the Housing Corporation and provide for the registration of, and the giving of financial assistance to, certain housing associations." The Housing Corporation, which is financed largely out of central government funds, has the power completely to finance the projects it approves and also to lend money towards approved projects.

Its main object, like that of the whole of the 1974 Act, is to rehabilitate badly run-down areas rather than to convert, adapt or put up new buildings. Unfortunately, although a large percentage of disabled clients live in such areas, the kind of dwelling in need of rehabilitation – the steep terraced house with steps down to the basement and up to the front door – is the least suitable for adaptation. Housing associations have been encouraged by the Corporation to adapt property for resident disabled tenants whenever this can form a feasible part of the rehabilitative process. More often than not rehousing may be the only alternative and one that is not always available for offer.

One of the Corporation's main functions, in addition to rehabilitation, is to complement in the public sector the work done by local authority housing authorities. Often an offer of a suitable dwelling from a housing association may be the only hope of escape for a disabled person imprisoned in sub-standard, ill-maintained accommodation rented from private landlords who have resisted attempts to force them to rehabilitate the property themselves and have also refused to give local authority social services departments permission to adapt the property at their expense.

Fortunately for the disabled not all the Corporation's money goes towards rehabilitating property. Variable proportions of its budget also go towards new building,[43] including new building for the disabled. By February 1978 a spokesman for the Corporation said that "something of the order of 7,500 'Mobility' dwellings and around 700 wheelchair units were in the pipe-line even if not all the keys were as yet actually in the doors." These units had been provided, either by housing associations whose work concentrated on various kinds of handicap, or as "in-fills" in other projects. A few sheltered housing schemes for the younger physically handicapped who would have to learn to live without relying on aging parents had also been launched. All these units were part of fair-rent schemes.[44]

Between its inception in 1964 and 31 March 1976, the Housing Corporation had received capital advances of £369 million of which over £335 million had come from the Secretary of State for the Environment and the remainder from the Secretaries of State for Scotland and Wales. Over 200,000 housing associations had been registered. In addition to commanding such a large amount of central government money the Corporation also scrutinises any requests made by housing associations to local authorities. This means that not only does the Corporation protect local authorities from exploitation by the less worthy enterprises but, that it could, if it so wished, also exercise control over the money local authorities would be allowed to lend. Joint projects financed by money from long-standing reputable charities, central government money and local authority money are not infrequent. New housing associations, if they can show good cause, may also be jointly financed by local authority money and exchequer grants through the Corporation.

Between 1974 and 1976, the time when senior officers in the social services departments of the Greater London boroughs were being interviewed for this study, few of them knew whether any housing associations existed in their area, let alone whether those that did were helping with the housing problems of disabled clients. "Habinteg", a housing association actively helping disabled persons, was operating in four boroughs at the time but was known to senior officers of the social services departments in only two of them. Another researcher who was interviewing housing authority staff noted a similar lack of awareness in many boroughs of the contribution that housing associations could make.[45] The 1974 Housing Act as a whole took a long time to make any noticeable impact on local authorities which may explain to a certain extent why there was so little apparent interaction between them and the Housing Corporation and why senior officers in social services departments were not actively bringing pressure to bear on their opposite numbers in local housing authorities to explore the possibilities that housing associations might offer.

The formation in late November 1977 of a special unit within the Housing Corporation itself to deal with housing projects for people with special needs reflects both the growth of the housing association movement and the ways in which housing associations themselves have widened their scope. Among a lengthening list of the different categories of people with special needs – a list that includes homeless single young people as well as the elderly who are perhaps most traditionally associated in the public mind with housing associations – the physically handicapped take their due place. Whenever feasible the majority of physically handicapped people will be housed in a normal community. Discussion has begun over the possibility, at least in the Greater London area, of making it Corporation policy to insist on a percentage of mobility or wheelchair housing in all housing associations plans for new buildings.

Housing Associations enjoy, in the private sector, the same eligibility for additional exchequer subsidies such as renovation grants, yardstick allowances and mobility and wheelchair allowances as local housing authorities do in the public sector.

(d) *Contributions to the Family Fund*
The Family Fund, which came into being on 1 April 1973, represented a new departure in the way in which central government money is allocated and administered. It was

> "The creation by government of an alternative source ... to supplement statutory provision and reduce the inequalities inherent in the unevenness of local government administration."[46]

A sum of £3 million was ear-marked by the Department of Health and Social Security in November 1972, to assist families having the care of a handicapped child "with very severe congenital disability". In introducing the scheme to the House of Commons Sir Keith Joseph, the Secretary of State for Health and Social Security, said :

> "In many cases the parents need more help in shouldering the various burdens which caring for these children entails ... It is not intended that this money should be by way of compensation for being disabled,[47] but rather that it should serve to complement the services already being provided by statutory and voluntary bodies to help the families concerned."

The Trustees of the Joseph Rowntree Memorial Trust, who agreed to administer the fund, were somewhat influenced in their decision by the observation of the then Under Secretary of State (Mr Michael Alison) that the new fund would have "value ... in teaching us more about handicapped children and the problems that they face." Indeed the first decision made by the Trust was to offer a Research Fellowship to the Department of Social Administration and Social Work in the University of York where a specialist unit was set up. The Trust refused financial help from the Department of Health and Social Security for this, preferring to regard the project, at least in the initial stages of the Fund's existence, "as part of its own research programme which it might well have wished to sponsor regardless of its own part in the administration of the Family Fund." The need for an objective analysis of the implications of the establishment of such a Fund was thought to be all the more essential as no precedent existed at that time for a private Trust administering a sum of central government money as large as £3 million. The research unit also undertook to supply the Trustees, their advisory panel and the administrators with computerised administrative statistics. The expense of collecting and sifting this data was to be borne by the Department of Health and Social Security as were all day-by-day expenses incurred solely for the purposes of the Family Fund. The Trustees thus secured a considerable measure of independence both in the field of research and in decisions on policy including the right to establish the Fund's own criteria of need. Of these the relief of stress within families with a severely handicapped child has remained the primary objective.[48]

Variations in the amount of help given by different local authorities were quick to reveal themselves, including variations in the provision of aids and adaptations. Initially, the policy of the Fund towards helping with the cost of aids and adaptations was a very generous one :

"Right from the start of the Fund families asked for help with aids and adaptations to property. The Fund's initial policy was that council tenants should be helped by their local authority, but that private tenants and owner occupiers could be assisted by the Family Fund if their local authority was unable to help the family at all (for whatever reason), was only able to help towards part of the cost of the work, or if undue delay would occur in a case of urgent need."[49]

Among the *aids* frequently provided were washing machines and tumble-driers for families with handicapped children who were also incontinent.[50]

Help with *adaptations* included the installation of central heating for children with circulatory problems, the provision of patios and play-room extensions to adaptations already paid for by local authorities and wall-to-wall carpeting for children who could only drag themselves along the floor once they had left their wheelchairs.[51]

A disturbing short-fall in local authority awareness of the number of families with a severely handicapped child in their area was revealed by a Family Fund Research Paper based on a sample survey of 33 families, living in five Northern and Midland areas, who had received help from the Fund in the early months of 1975. The survey, and the follow-up later in the year, revealed

"that for 75 per cent of the families in our sample, contact with Social Services Departments was non-existent to minimal and usually initiated by the families themselves in response to particular needs or crises."[52]

64

In the light of information such as this the Family Fund can hardly be considered to be complementing, rather than supplementing, the statutory services. It would also appear to have become something larger than the "centrally-directed 'mini-service' parallel to that locally directed by statutory authorities" which is how Lewis Waddilove, the Director of the Trust, had envisaged it in 1973.

The complexity of the negotiations with local authorities about adaptations and the strain these imposed on the Fund's administrative staff – together with a growing feeling that some local authorities were exploiting the Fund – had led, in early 1975, to a hardening of policy :

"The development of financial constraint and a belief that local authorities were beginning to off-load their responsibilities led the Fund in 1975 to revise its policy so that it virtually ceased giving help with aids and adaptations to families."[53]

The administrators did however reserve the right to help if a local authority were prepared to make a substantial contribution, and the imminence of cuts in local expenditure in the financial year 1975–76 led the Trustees, at the end of 1976, to revise their policy towards major adaptations once again. With their own backlog of applications cleared, they decided to review each new application on its merits and if the family satisfied the Fund's criteria of eligibility and if the local authority social services department were prepared to make some contribution then the Fund would help. It would either match that contribution or in some cases contribute a major share of the cost.

By the end of the financial year 1975–76, 5.4 per cent of families with a handicapped child had asked for – and 3.1 per cent had received – help with major adaptations in their homes from the Fund. It is probable that the percentage of families helped with adaptations will continue to increase.

During 1 April 1973 and the 1 April 1977 the Family Fund has received over £11 million from the Department of Health and Social Security of which £10.3 million has been used for grants to families which meet the Fund's own criteria of need and the rest has gone on administration.

One of the main advantages of the Family Fund is that the guidelines laid down in 1972–73 insisted on considerable independence and flexibility of policy – the Fund has, for example, extended its help to families with a child with a very severe handicap that is not necessarily congenital, such as for example, children very severely injured in road accidents, and also, in certain circumstances, it continues to help families after the child has passed the age of sixteen. But this very flexibility carries with it those inherent dangers of exploitation

65

c

of which the Trustees very soon became aware.

The existence of the Trust as a dual source of finance has implications for social policy at a national level, providing

"a new mechanism to overcome the rigidity and slow response often inseparable from a service shaped by regulation and circular"[54]

and possibly also a precedent for other categories of people in need, such as the elderly or the handicapped adult. An over-reliance by local authorities on an agent of central government could be as damaging to local initiative as the over-reliance on the voluntary associations which had impeded the implementation of Section 29 of the National Assistance Act 1948.

On the other hand for some families in need of help the alternative might be no provision at all.

(e) *Contributions by Central Government to Voluntary Associations*
Most of the voluntary associations helping with services for the disabled were already being largely financed by local authorities, with help from central government, before 1970 and had been acting as the agents of local authorities since the National Assistance Act 1948. A growing recognition of their importance at the national level is reflected by a rise in central government grants from £19 million to £35 million over the three year period covered by this study – from £19 million in 1974–75 to £35 million in 1976–77.[55] And also by "the setting up under a Conservative government and the continuation under a Labour one of the Voluntary Services Unit." The VSU, as it is called, "is intended to act as a link between voluntary organisations and government departments" and, where it is appropriate for central government to do so, "stimulate the use of volunteers". It also "functions as a financier of last resort within Whitehall with limited funds to assist national organisations or projects whose work spans the interest of several departments or which are directly related to a single department."[56]

The Report of the Wolfenden Committee put in a strong plea for an increase in the statutory contributions by central government which it saw as "the central strategic makers of social policy." It drew attention to the need for a "collaborative social plan which will make the optimum and maximum use of resources," instead of dissipating resources and duplicating services.

Some local authorities had reduced or discontinued their grants to the local branches of at least one major national voluntary organisation in 1976 because they duplicated services now provided by the social services department.[57]

66

(f) *The Urban Programme*
Contributions in the form of Urban Aid to help ease the special problems of the inner cities were originally part of a programme funded by the Home Office out of the Community Services vote.[58] Between 1974–76 services for the disabled benefited under this scheme in four Inner London boroughs. One borough obtained funds for the salary of a handyman. In another, Urban Aid provided the salaries for three assistant technicians each with a tail-lift van in which to deliver aids to clients – which in the private sector they also immediately installed. A third borough received money for the salary of a community social worker whose commitments included organising help for the disabled in the form of street groups and steering volunteers towards doing practical tasks for them that were outside the services provided by home helps. A fourth, with a predominantly Jewish population and a higher than average proportion of elderly people, received money for a van for "kosher" meals on wheels.

(g) *Joint Care and Finance*
The first mention of proposals to allow

"a limited amount of money to flow from health to local authorities [which] should enable them jointly to find mutually desirable projects"

came in the opening speech of Mrs Barbara Castle, then still Secretary of State for the Social Services, at a Seminar on Disablement which was held at Sunningdale in February 1976. The use of health service money was at first to be confined to laggard social services departments whose provision of services for the handicapped in their areas fell far behind identified needs. The suggested contribution of health authorities was 60 per cent of the expenditure on joint projects over an interim period of three years after which the local authorities would be required to assume full responsibility for any future provision.

A consultative paper was issued which made it quite clear that, even in a time of economic stringency, the provision of aids and adaptations could not be allowed to fall off and that, on the contrary, a continued increase in real terms was to be maintained. Joint care and planning teams were set up to discuss projects which were at first limited to current expenditure.[59] This might, in some areas, include joint payment of the salaries of occupational therapists. Early in 1977 more flexible conditions were introduced and it became possible to apply for joint finance for projects, such as a joint store for aids, that involved capital expenditure.[60]

The introduction of joint care and finance was a new and exceptional way of bending and shifting the distribution of limited amounts

67

of central government finance. It was not however always welcomed by social services committees some of whom were reluctant to commit themselves to joint projects representing as much as 3 per cent of their total budgets for which they might ultimately have to assume full responsibility.[61]

7. *The Social Services Vote: Allocations for Aids and Adaptations*

Under the present system accounting for the social services budget is highly complicated inasmuch as it concerns the installation of aids and the provision of both minor and major adaptations. Periodic bills are submitted by other local authority departments "against the social services vote". What appear at the time to be non-existent costs because they are temporarily invisible become substantial when the bills, costed in a variety of ways, appear. Budgeting is made all the more difficult in the case of major adaptations as accounts are seldom rendered the same year as they are begun. Some aids to daily living may also be supplied under the annual grants made to various voluntary organisations although since 1976 the local branches of the Red Cross Society, although continuing to supply aids to nursing patients at home, have discontinued supplies of aids to daily living.

Against these large bills for services the amounts received from clients as a result of the application of a means test in connection with adaptations have to be offset. Also the very small contribution which clients may insist on contributing voluntarily towards the cost of aids. Money received from central government in connection with improvement grants and claimed retrospectively has also had to be taken into consideration since 1974, when costing major adaptations in the private sector.

Planning for future allocations for aids and adaptations should be calculated on anticipated needs and not only on known expenditure in the past, but unfortunately the need to make overall cuts in local authority expenditure has effectively put paid to any forward planning of the kind envisaged in the Ten Year Plans that local authorities were asked to submit to the Department of Health and Social Security in 1972.[62] However, the true cost of aids and adaptations can only be arrived at if the cost of the staff involved in their provision is included : this has been rising steadily since 1972.

8. *National Statistics*

The only continuing source of information about expenditure on aids and adaptations in national terms is provided by the Chartered Institute of Public Finance and Accountancy and the Society of

County Treasurers (formerly the Institute of Municipal Treasurers and Accountants, or IMTA).[63] Their annual statistics give the estimated, but not actual, cost of aids and adaptations by all local authorities for each financial year and present them per 1,000 population as a whole. Taken in conjunction with the statistics published annually by the Department of Health and Social Security,[64] which gives the numbers of aids and adaptations issued, they give a reasonably reliable indication both of activity and expenditure and a means of comparing one region with another. On the other hand it is unwise to assume that more aids and more adaptations, together with a higher level of expenditure on them, is necessarily a qualitative as well as quantitative index of concern. Examples can be found where the same amount of money spent on fewer aids represents a more professional service to disabled clients. There are also instances where local authorities have spent more money on more aids only because in the past the services they have provided have been deplorably inadequate. Some local authorities deliberately stepped up expenditure in 1974–75 and 1975–76 in order to ride out the gathering financial storm by "living off the cupboard".

Statistics of this kind are useful as far as they go but are not a substitute for the kind of information which can be gathered locally. What, for example, were the expectations of the directors of social services concerned? Did they envisage a budget for aids and adaptations of the order of £18,000 or of £80,000? How nearly did the estimates which were approved approximate to those that were originally submitted? How many supplementary grants were made that do not appear in the published estimates – and for how much? Were these made on an *ad hoc* basis or in blocks? The director of one Greater London borough reported that he had kept his sights low when submitting estimates so as not to antagonise other departments because he knew he could raise three times as much through supplementaries once he and his committee "got down to cases."

It was partly in order to find answers to questions such as these that the study was undertaken. It was also useful to get a separate breakdown of how much money went on aids and how much on adaptations as this is not done in the statistics presented by the Institute. Nor do these statistics show which boroughs budget for aids and telephones together, so that large sums apparently devoted to aids and adaptations may in fact include large, on-going costs for telephone rentals, whilst no account is kept of the equally large sums going on the salaries of specialist staff.

In the section that follows the ways in which the Greater London boroughs were financing the provision of aids from 1974–75 to 1976–77 are given in more detail than is possible on the basis of the statistics examined above. Table 1 which follows was originally pub-

Table 1 – Provision of Telephones in the Greater London area
Extract from The Guardian – 12 March 1974

GLC Area: *Payment of Telephone rental* per 1,000 population*
National average: 0.26 per 1,000 – GLC average: 0.52 per 1,000

Inner London		Outer London	
Average	0.89	Average	0.30
Camden	2.42	Hounslow	0.65
Tower Hamlets	1.73	Merton (2)	0.63
Wandsworth	1.07	Kingston	0.48
Lewisham	0.98	Richmond	0.44
Kensington (1)	0.95	Ealing	0.44
Southwark	0.80	Haringey	0.39
Hackney	0.75	Newham	0.35
Greenwich	0.70	Harrow	0.33
Islington	0.59	Barking	0.32
Lambeth	0.54	Bexley	0.30
Westminster	0.50	Brent	0.29
Hammersmith	0.13	Redbridge	0.29
		Havering	0.24
		Sutton	0.22
		Barnet	0.20
		Croydon	0.18
		Enfield	0.18
		Hillingdon	0.17
		Bromley	0.11
		Waltham Forest	0.10

GLC Area: *Provisions of Telephones* per 1,000 population
National average: 0.36 per 1,000 – GLC average: 0.67 per 1,000*

Inner London		Outer London	
Average	1.10	Average	0.41
Wandsworth	2.55	Haringey	0.81
Camden	1.74	Brent	0.76
Lewisham	1.66	Barking	0.68
Islingtom	1.32	Merton (2)	0.66
Tower Hamlets	1.21	Richmond	0.60
Westminster	1.06	Sutton	0.55
Lambeth	0.91	Havering	0.54
Kensington (1)	0.71	Hounslow	0.54
Greenwich	0.53	Ealing	0.49
Hackney	0.47	Harrow	0.44
Hammersmith	0.37	Redbridge	0.43
Southwark	0.37	Hillingdon	0.35
		Newham	0.33
		Bexley	0.31
		Kingston	0.31
		Barnet	0.25
		Waltham Forest	0.24
		Croydon	0.20
		Enfield	0.18
		Bromley	0.12

(1) Scaled up from 9 months figure.
(2) Scaled up from 7 months figure.
  * The original table gave details per 100,000 population, these have been given in the table above per 1,000 to conform with basic statistics in Appendix.

Table 1 – Provision of Aids and Adaptations to Property in the Greater London Area Extract from the Guardian 12 March 1974

GLC Area: *General Aids Issued* per 1,000 population*
National average: 2.70 per 1,000 – GLC average: 4.20 per 1,000*

Inner London		Outer London	
Average	5.10	Average	3.70
Tower Hamlets	12.70	Merton (2)	8.30
Hammersmith	10.00	Redbridge	8.20
Greenwich	9.90	Hounslow	7.20
Wandsworth	6.30	Newham	5.60
Camden	5.40	Waltham Forest	4.70
Southwark	4.40	Kingston	4.00
Hackney	3.90	Hillingdon (3)	3.80
Lambeth	3.90	Havering	3.80
Lewisham	2.20	Sutton (3)	3.60
Kensington (1)	2.10	Bexley	2.80
Westminster	1.90	Harrow	2.70
Islington	1.70	Enfield	2.60
		Ealing	2.60
		Barnet	2.50
		Barking	2.30
		Haringey	2.10
		Croydon	2.00
		Brent	1.60
		Richmond	1.40
		Bromley	NA

GLC Area: *Adaptations to Property* per 1,000 population
National average: 0.62 per 1,000 – GLC average: 0.99 per 1,000*

Inner London		Outer London	
Average	1.01	Average	0.97
Tower Hamlets	2.22	Merton (2)	4.60
Lewisham	1.92	Hillingdon	2.68
Southwark	1.53	Kingston	2.14
Camden	1.38	Brent	1.66
Lambeth	1.30	Barking	1.43
Wandsworth	1.10	Hounslow	1.18
Hammersmith	0.61	Bromley	1.10
Islington	0.47	Barnet	0.98
Hackney	0.40	Sutton	0.93
Westminster	0.37	Newham	0.88
Greenwich	0.35	Waltham Forest	0.84
Kensington (1)	0.06	Croydon	0.71
		Harrow	0.70
		Haringey	0.54
		Havering	0.54
		Enfield	0.47
		Richmond	0.40
		Ealing	0.34
		Redbridge	0.20
		Bexley	0.15

(1) Scaled up from 9 months figure.
(2) Scaled up from 7 months figure.
(3) Based on estimated figure.
* The original table gave details per 100,000 population, these have been given in the table above per 1,000.

lished in *The Guardian* in March 1974, and caused a considerable stir amongst the fieldwork staff of social services departments. Few of them had previously known that statistics of this kind were being kept for the Department of Health and Social Security or that it was possible to compare "the batting averages" – as they came to be known – of one borough with another. The *Guardian* article puts some of the achievements of the Greater London boroughs – the provision of telephones, aids and adaptations – within the context both of the national average and of the average of the Greater London area itself. As far as aids are concerned it is noticeable that ten out of the 32 boroughs fall below the national average for aids, and 12 below that for adaptations. Figures for the City of London, which was involved at that time with the handover by the Medical Officer of Health to the first Director of Social Services, are not given.

Even so the average provision by the Greater London boroughs for both aids and adaptations is well above the national average with 4.2 per 1,000 of the population for aids in the Greater London area as against 2.7 per 1,000 nationally; and for adaptations, 0.99 per 1,000 as against 0.62 per 1,000. One reason why these averages are substantially higher than the national figure may be that many of the boroughs in Greater London inherited a well-established tradition of providing aids and, to a lesser extent, adaptations, from the old London County Council and some of the neighbouring counties. Another reason may be that the boroughs have their own powerful association in the London Boroughs Association and that this has done a good deal to raise as well as unify standards. It must however be remembered that for the rest of the country the financial year 1973–74 was the last year before the re-organisation not just of the personal social services but of local government as a whole and that many social services departments were being obliged to plan for new units of government which had still to come into being on 1 April 1974. The existing boroughs outside the Greater London area were therefore being confronted with an upheaval similar to that which followed hard on the Local Authorities Social Services Act, 1970 and this was to be their second major upheaval in two years. This should be borne in mind when looking at Table 1. This table nevertheless makes a valuable and necessary link between the situation in the country as a whole and the more detailed study of the way in which aids and adaptations were financed in the Greater London boroughs – the subject of the next chapter.

NOTES

1. Harris, A., *op. cit.*
2. See *HC Debates*, 1969–70, Cols. 1914–15.
3. *Ibid.*, col. 1917.
4. *Ibid.*, col. 1913.
5. Ministry of Housing and Local Government, *The Ninth Report of the Housing Management*

Sub-Committee of the Central Housing Committee. Council Housing, Purposes, Procedures and Priorities, (HMSO, 1969). "The Cullingworth Report".

6. DHSS, *The Future Structure of the National Health Service* (HMSO, 1970).

7. The House might wish to be careful not to obstruct the general approach indicated by the Seebohm Committee "by putting statutory labels on a group of people and conferring statutory advantages unless they can be fully justified", *HC Debates, loc. cit.,* Col. 1914.

8. *Loc. cit.,* Col. 1922, Mr A. H. Macdonald, M.P.

9. Only two sections of the Act, Section 1 (local surveys) and Section 21 (car badges) were not immediately subject to appointed day orders

10. See the Chronically Sick and Disabled Persons Act, 1970, Section 1.

11. Department of Health and Social Security Circular 45/71 of 16 September 1971, para. 28 "Conclusions".

12. The Chronically Sick and Disabled Persons Act, Section 2.–(1) (a).

13. *Ibid.,* Section 2.–(1) (e).

14. *Ibid.,* Section 2.–(1) (f) (g) (h).

15. Ripley, B. J., *Administration in Local Authorities* (London, 1970). p. 241.

16. DHSS Local Authority Circular 18/71 of 10 May 1971.

17. Harris, Amelia, *op. cit.*

18. DHSS, Circular 27/71; DOE, Circular 1DP/733/1971; DEP. Circular 1DP/733/1971, all, dated 4 May 1971, and entitled *The Chronically Sick and Disabled Persons Act 1970.*

19. See DHSS Circular 45/71, *Services for Handicapped People Living in the Community,* para. 11.

20. *Ibid.,* para. 11.

21. According to a report by the Social Services Unit and Social Services Research Group of the University of Birmingham, sent to the Department of Health and Social Security in 1976, 18 out of the 174 authorities existing before 1974 had not undertaken surveys of any kind. See also Bowl, R., "Survey of Surveys" in *New Society,* 28 October 1976.

22. See the Department of Social Security, Statistics and Research Division 6, *Local Authority Social Services Departments Aids to Households,* September 1973. Although the returns from one London borough fell below even the meagre totals quoted above the general level of provision of the Greater London area as a whole was well above the national average.

23. Joint Circular DOE 74/74 (Welsh Office, 120/74).

24. *The Housing Act 1974,* Section 56.–(2) (a).

25. DHSS Circular 35/72. Local Authority Social Services: *Ten Year Development Plans* (issued jointly with six other departments).

26. DOE Circular 77/73 issued jointly with five other departments to local authorities which says "the very high rate of growth must be limited", and DOE 157/73 which calls for a 10 per cent reduction of all goods and services at November 1973 prices.

27. Joint Circular DOE 19/74, DHSS LAC 11/74, Home Office 16/74 and Welsh Office 35/74; *Rate Support Expenditure and Rate Calls in 1975,* para. 20, "Personal Social Services".

28. See *Report of the Committee of Inquiry into the Care and Supervision Provided in Relation to Maria Colwell* (HMSO, 1974).

29. DHSS, *Priorities for Health and Personal Social Services in England. A Consultative Document* (HMSO, 1976).

30. *Ibid.,* p. 48. See Section 6 (g) below.

31. See Wright, Fay, *Public Expenditure Cuts Affecting Services for Disabled People,* pp. 14–15 (London, March 1977).

32. As late as 1976, Circular LAC (76)6 suggested, but did not insist, that local authorities might wish to cut back on residential care in order to have more money available for field and domiciliary services.

33. The White Paper, *Public Expenditure to 1978–79,* Cmnd 5879 (HMSO, 1975), projected a 2.7 per cent increase in personal social services, but the White Paper of 1976 (Cmnd 6393) cut this to 2.0 per cent, and that of 1977 (Cmnd 6721) assumed virtually no growth in local authority expenditure. A very small margin of increase was allowed in social services budgets. See *The Government's Expenditure Plans,* Vols I & II, Cmnd 6721 (HMSO, January 1977). The most recent White Paper on *Public Expenditure, 1979–80,* Cmnd 7049, Vol. II (HMSO, 1978), relies on joint finance to give a little flexibility.

34. Mrs Barbara Castle speaking to officials of the Association of Local Government Organisations in November 1975. She went on, however, to warn them that "next year they would not have it so good".

35. See the *Report of the Royal Commission on Local Government in England 1966–69, Volume I, "The Redcliffe-Maude Report",* (Cmnd 4040, 1966). On p. 31 the Report says: "if local government is to achieve its full potential, it will need a deliberate determination on the part of Ministers and Parliament, supported by the press, radio and television, both to make local authorities responsible for any services which ought to be provided locally and to allow local authorities to settle local issues themselves. It will need an equally deliberate determination on the part of local government collectively to see that this is done".

36. This policy has continued. See DHSS Consultative Document, *The Way Forward, Priorities in Health and Social Services,* a continuation of the consultative document of 1976, which was published in 1977, and LASS (77) 19.

37. Mr Jack Ashley, M.P., speaking at a seminar organised by the Disability Alliance in 1977.

C*

38. Increased cash benefits, much advocated by certain pressure groups, such as the Disabled Income Group, also run the risk of being eroded by inflation.

39. Joint Circular DOE 92/75 and Welsh Office 163/75.

40. DOE Circular 61/75 and Welsh Office 109/75. Appendices 2, 3 and 6 which are subject to regional variations.

41. DOE, HDD Occasional Paper 2/75.

42. At the time of this study senior officers of social services departments in the Greater London area interviewed as late as six months after the issue of Circular 74/74 had not heard of the concept of Mobility Housing although head occupational therapists in some London boroughs were already discussing possible percentages some months before Circular 92/75 was issued. These varied from as little as 3 per cent to 15 per cent and many were agreed on by 1976.

43. Projects to be approved in the London area from 31 March 1978 to 1 April 1979 are New Build 3,500, Rehabilitation 5,700.

44. The cost of every fair-rent scheme is subsidised by a government grant (Housing Association grant) often equivalent to 70–80 per cent of the total.

45. See Tester, Susan, *Housing for Disabled People in Greater London* (University of London, 1975), p. 21, for a list of the best known housing associations in the Greater London area.

46. Waddilove, Lewis E., Director of the Joseph Rowntree Memorial Trust, "The Family Fund", *The Year Book of Social Policy in Great Britain 1973*, ed. Jones, Kathleen (London, 1974), p. 205.

47. The fight for compensation of the parents of children damaged by the drug thalidomide was much in the public mind at the time.

48. The Fund has never operated a Means Test of any kind. However, by 1977, an analysis of applications and re-applications by over 30,000 families revealed that the amounts of the grants awarded varied with social class. Findings such as this could influence the future policy of the fund and it is neither possible nor desirable for the Research Unit to preserve a hermetically sealed objectivity.

49. *Housing Handicapped Children and Their Families*, Family Fund Research Paper FF 1/77, Department of Social Administration, University of York (York, 1977).

50. Even those Greater London boroughs which fully accepted their mandatory responsibilities towards providing financial help with adaptations looked on such machines as "luxuries" or "extras", the expense of which could not be justified out of the social services budget irrespective of whether the borough provided a laundry service for the incontinent. Any suggestion that they might count as "additional facilities", "designed for the greater comfort" of the child and the "greater convenience" of the family would not have been welcomed by any social services committee. Senior staff interviewed felt help from the Family Fund to be the most appropriate source.

51. The above examples of help by the Family Fund were the most frequently mentioned in interviews with the staff of the Greater London boroughs. In one borough carpeting for a similar purpose had been paid for, not by the Fund, but by a well-established charity that helps invalid children at home.

52. See, Family Fund Research Unit, Paper FF/57/4/76. *Some Practical Consequences of Caring for Handicapped Children at Home.* (University of York, 1976).

More research needs to be done on the ways in which families become known to the social services. In the Greater London area the most frequent sources of referral were either head-teachers or social workers for children's charities. Many social services departments appear to have ignored DHSS Circular 45/71, para. 22, *Priority Groups*, which puts the needs of families with a severely handicapped child second only to those of elderly persons living alone.

53. During the first three years the sum of £6 million was contributed by the Department and, in addition, the Department also paid all the costs of administration. In 1976, when the project came up for review, an annual sum of £0.2 million (£200,000) was decided on to cover the administrative costs and was to be met by central government. This left the Fund with £2.5 million for grants to families in 1976–77 and £1.8 million in 1977–78 from the total contribution made each year by the Department of Health and Social Security. For the financial year 1978–79 the expected contribution is £2.2 million of which £0.4 million will go on administrative costs and £1.8 million to families with a severely handicapped child.

54. Waddilove, Lewis E., in Jones, Kathleen, *op. cit.*, p. 205. Interestingly it is this Trust which together with the United Kingdom Carnegie Trust, initiated and sponsored the inquiry into the role of voluntary organisations in the last quarter of the 20th Century which began on 1 October 1974 and which was published in November 1977 as *The Future of Voluntary Organisations, Report of the Wolfenden Committee* (London, 1977). This report is discussed in the following section.

55. The grants made by local authorities to voluntary organisations showed wide variations. In the Greater London area Islington, in 1976–77, made a grant of £805,000 which worked out at £7.22 per head of the population. Camden provided £6.46 per head, Wandsworth £1.74 and Hammersmith £1.24 per head. Among the Outer London boroughs the figure for Brent was £1.00 and for Croydon £0.49. See *The Future of Voluntary Organisations*, Appendix 6B, p. 257.

56. See Appendix 4, "Government Departments, a Note for the Wolfenden Committee", *ibid.* p. 214.

57. See note 55 above.

58. The urban programme has recently been transferred to the Department of the Environment.

59. See DHSS, LAC (76)6, HC (76) 18.

60. See Joint Circular HC 77/17 and LAC 77/10.

61. See DHSS, LASSL (77) 13, *Forward Planning of Local Authority Social Services*, which says that a growth rate of 2 per cent could do no more than maintain and not improve the standards. It was however hoped that although no money could be made available for improving services, "a small margin together with joint finance from the health authorities", would allow some progress in building community services as an alternative to hospital care.

62. DHSS Circular 35/72, *Local Authority Social Services Department. 10 year Development Plans.*

63. *Social Services Statistics: Estimates 1974–75* (CIPF and SCT). An abstract of some of these statistics is reproduced in Table 1 of the Appendix.

64. *Local Authority Social Services Departments: Aids to Households.* Department of Health and Social Security, Department of Health and Social Security Statistics and Research Division, 6. Table R1.

75

CHAPTER FOUR

THE FINANCING OF AIDS AND ADAPTATIONS
IN THE GREATER LONDON BOROUGHS

1. *Introduction*

In 1974, when this study was started, there was not much in the way of statistics readily available on the actual expenditure on aids and adaptations over the preceding three years. The social services departments of only six Inner and ten Outer London boroughs sent in figures either for aids and adaptations together, or, which is much more useful, aids and adaptations separately. These figures are to be found in Table 2 on page 77. Where figures for 1971–72 have been given, the 1974–75 figure is also expressed as a percentage increase. All show a steady increase ranging from 133 per cent to 1,633 per cent. Three others showed an increase of more than five hundred per cent.

During 1975 to 1976 the officers interviewed frequently spoke of a triple increase in their social services budgets as a whole, typical figures quoted being £4,500,000 in 1974–75 as compared with only £1,700,000 in 1971–72 (Outer London borough) and over £8 million in 1974–75 as compared with £2,500,000 in 1971–72 (Inner London borough). Increases on a similar scale were also to be found in money allocated for aids and adaptations. All but one of the boroughs that submitted figures had done at least one major adaptation costing more than £500 but any comparison between figures for 1971–72 and 1975–76 need to take into account the effect of inflation on the cost of building materials and building labour. Prices for individual aids also rose. The figures given in Table 2 were supplied by the finance officers of fifteen Greater London boroughs and were said to represent actual expenditure including, where starred, money raised by Supplementary Grants.

Represented as a percentage of the social services budgets as a whole the money spent on aids and adaptations is small. Only nine of the sixteen boroughs submitting figures on aids and adaptations also gave figures for the total social services budget in 1974–75. These are shown in Table 3 (page 80). Of these the lowest percentage devoted to aids and adaptations is 0.28 per cent, the highest 1.86 per cent and

Table 2 – Increases in Expenditure on Aids and Adaptations – 1971-76

Inner London Boroughs – based on figures provided by social services departments

Population of borough in 1974	1971-2 (1)	1972-3 (2)	1973-4 (3)	1974-5 (4)	1975-6 (5)	Percentage increase 1974-5 over 1971
1. 182,000 Aids	Figures not available					—
Adaptations						
2. 292,000 Aids	6,000	8,090	34,220	52,470	—	—
Adaptations						
3. 254,000 Aids	6,826	8,343	12,317	18,000		
Adaptations	1,013	10,626	14,164	28,000		
	7,839	18,969	26,481	46,000*	—	486.8%
4. 242,000 Aids	8,650	4,800	9,530	12,590		
Adaptations		7,140	7,920	10,430		
		11,940	17,450	23,020*	—	166.1%
5. 214,000 Aids	6,000	12,000	7,000	7,500		
Adaptations			7,000	8,000		
			14,000	15,500	—	158.3%
6. 148,000 Aids	8,500					—
Adaptations					25,000	

Table 2 – continued
Outer London Boroughs

Population of borough in 1974		1971–2 (1)	1972–3 (2)	1973–4 (3)	1974–5 (4)	1975–6 (5)	Percentage increase 1974–5 over 1971 (6)
1. 233,000	Aids	5,106	14,969	18,762	36,125	—	1,632.8
	Adaptations	5,895	28,049	98,516	164,500 (200,625**)	—	—
2. 235,000	Aids	—	4,300	6,150	9,070	11,800	—
	Adaptations	—	9,000	15,000	44,000	48,000 (59,800)	
3. 226,000	Aids	15,000	25,000	30,000	36,000*		133.3%
	Adaptations						
4. 217,000	Aids	—	4,500	5,500	10,000		644.4%
	Adaptations	Nil	4,500	17,500	33,500		
5. 265,000	Aids	9,800	11,000	8,700	13,000	—	226.5%
	Adaptations		15,500	19,300	19,000 (32,000)	—	
6. 170,000	Aids	1,775	3,500	5,250	11,200		571.5%
	Adaptations	2,871	3,000 (6,500)	12,000 (17,250)	20,000 (31,200*)		
7. 306,000	Aids	3,000	3,700	4,000	7,000		268.4%
	Adaptations	5,250	12,150 (15,850)	18,900 (22,900)	23,390 (30,390)		
8. 275,000	Aids	11,700	15,000	11,500	15,000	—	145.7%
	Adaptations			12,500 (24,000)	13,750 (28,750*)	—	
9. 333,000	Aids	500	5,500	8,000	26,000*	—	593.3%
	Adaptations	3,250	2,920 (8,420)	8,000 (16,000)		—	
10. 136,000	Aids	3,856	6,742	9,451	13,880	17,000	315.2%
	Adaptations	812	2,022 (8,764)	6,492 (15,943)	5,500 (19,380)	6,160 (23,160)	

* Part of expenditure borne by housing departments in the public sector.

** The exceptionally high figure of £164,500 for adaptations is because this borough had persuaded its housing department to pay for all adaptations made to council stock since 1973. The breakdown between adaptations to private property (against the social services vote) and to council property (against the housing vote) was £66,363 on private and £32,153 on council property in 1973–74, and £104,402 and £60,098 respectively in 1974–75.

By the end of 1975 two other boroughs had decided that housing was the more appropriate department for financing adaptations into its own properties. In one of them the housing department paid up to 75 per cent of the cost depending on a sliding scale. In the other the whole cost was paid but no adaptations above £500 had ever been attempted.

the average 0.88 per cent. As a standard of comparison the figures for another service widely used by disabled people are also given – the use of the home help service for the disabled (excluding the elderly). These are noticeably higher with the lowest percentage 5.6, the highest 20.1 per cent and the average 11.7 per cent. But the variation between authorities even in this long established service remains wide.

Estimated expenditure on particular services at the beginning of each financial year is published annually by the Chartered Institute of Public Accountants[1] and the Society of County Treasurers. Estimates for aids and adaptations, meals on wheels, home helps, clubs and centres for the disabled and elderly frail are to be found in the Appendix, Table 1. These figures show how difficult it is to separate the disabled as a group from the elderly frail in need of similar services. Indeed only four of the Greater London boroughs attempted to do so at the time of the study when budgeting for aids and adaptations and then only because they had received a separate allocation of money for the elderly aged 75 and over. The estimates in this table nevertheless allow the amount of money spent on aids and adaptations to be put in the wider perspective both of the provision of other services for the disabled and between one Greater London borough and another.

Estimated expenditure on aids and adaptations in the Greater London boroughs in 1974 varied from 36.6 per thousand population to 483.0. The borough with the highest expenditure was therefore spending more than thirteen times more per head than the borough spending the least. Four boroughs spent less than £50 per 1,000 population. Eleven boroughs spent more than £50 but less than £100. Ten spent between £100 and £200. Three spent more than £200; one more than £300 and only two spent more than £400. The City of London, which has many more disabled workers than it has disabled residents, spent £76.

As too little money had been allocated in the first two years after the passing of the Chronically Sick and Disabled Persons Act 1970 a backlog of aids and adaptations had already begun to accumulate by 1973–74. Indications of the amounts of money actually needed to cope with these backlogs were given verbally by some directors of social services. The two examples that follow are typical of the problems posed by an unanticipated increase in the number of disabled clients identified as being in need of services. In the late summer of 1973 one director of a large Outer London borough asked for a block supplementary grant of £94,000. He got £66,000 of which £44,000 was for aids and £22,000 for adaptations. By the end of six months all this additional money had been used up and for the remainder of the financial year the committee made no further block grants, although further small supplementary grants were made on an *ad hoc* basis during the remainder of the financial year. In the

Table 3 – Percentages of the total Social Services Budget, 1974–75

Population of borough in 1974	(1) Total social services budget £	(2) Aids and Adaptations	(3) (2) as % of (1)	(4) Home Helps £	(5) (4) as % of (1)	£ Expend. per 1,000 pop. on (2)	£ Expend. per 1,000 pop. on (4)
Inner London Boroughs							
1. 182,000	6,511,390	77,750	1.19	367,010	5.64	430	2,020
2. 292,000	8,339,750	52,470	0.63	616,900	7.4	180	2,110
3. 254,000	8,460,220	46,000	0.54	816,620	9.6	180	3,210
4. 242,000	8,057,750	23,020	0.28	885,900	11.0	100	3,660
5. 214,000	4,446,020	15,500	0.34	627,280	14.1	70	2,930
6. 148,000*							
Outer London Boroughs							
1. 233,000*							
2. 235,000	2,858,520	53,070	1.86	397,330	13.9	230	1,690
3. 226,000*							
4. 217,000	1,994,700	33,506	1.68	400,450	20.1	150	1,850
5. 265,000	3,168,260	32,000	1.01	410,840	12.9	120	1,550
6. 170,000*							
7. 306,000	2,538,290	30,390	1.20	262,690	10.3	100	860
8. 275,000*							
9. 333,000							
10. 136,000*							

* These boroughs did not give figures for their (total social services) budget in 1974–75.

next financial year, 1975–76, the allocation for aids was £56,000 but that sum had to include all the on-going expenses for telephone rentals as well as the cost of installing new telephones and special telephone equipment. No further supplementaries, the committee warned, would be forthcoming.

Another borough which made the needs of disabled clients, and not available finance, the only acceptable criterion for providing aids and adaptations was given a special advance, in the autumn of 1973, against the money that was to be allocated for 1974–75. All of this had been spent by 1 June 1974 which left nine months of the financial year still to go. Further supplementary grants were then given for cases of exceptional need and urgency but a very conscious system of rationing of aids had to be operated for the rest of 1975 and no major adaptations could even be started. In 1975–76 the social services committee refused to approve more than £12,000 for aids but allowed £50,000 for adaptations. Criteria were to remain rigorous, accounting kept meticulously up to date and although new needs were being identified at a rate of some 200 a month the social services department was warned that there would be no more supplementary grants forthcoming.

These, and other examples, show that tables of social services estimates as set out in Table 1 of the Appendix, although a reliable guide to the sums originally approved by local authority finance committees, cannot take into account backstage manoeuvrings of this kind. Not all directors of social services were however as successful in obtaining additional sums of money as those quoted above. The majority had to make do as best they could within allocations for aids and adaptations which they knew from the start to be inadequate, eked out by only the most meagre supplementaries for cases of special need granted on an *ad hoc* basis. A director who fought pertinaciously for three years to get the allocation increased from £8,500 in 1971–72 to £25,000 (exclusive of money for telephones) in 1975–76 pointed out that a minimum of £60,000 was needed to meet identified needs at current prices.

2. *Provision of Telephones*

Figures for the provision of telephones have been given advisedly and are to be found in Column 89 of Table 1 in the Appendix. Telephone provision is frequently used by pressure groups as an index of overall interest in the disabled; but it was a sensitive issue politically and it does not follow that a borough which is generous in its provision of telephones is equally generous in its provision for aids and adaptations. Many social services committees rushed to provide telephones in considerable numbers between the financial years 1972–3 and 1974–75, but rental costs became a heavy on-going commitment and

81

a steady drain on available finance. In some of the Greater London boroughs money for telephones was actually included in the aids and adaptations budget to the severe detriment of provision for aids and adaptations.[2]

The Greater London area as a whole supplied more telephones in both 1972–73 and 1973–74 than any other region : average rates of 67 per 100,000 in 1972–73 and 90 per 10,000 in 1973–74 compared with a national average of 36 and 47. That telephones are desirable for the disabled is not disputed, nor that they can be a lifeline to the household. But they rank lower than aids and adaptations as a means of keeping disabled people out of residential care. They were in fact among the first items to be cut, in the majority of Greater London boroughs, first by applying the criteria drawn up by the London Boroughs Association more rigorously; later, in 1975–76, by cutting down on the numbers of new telephones provided and then in 1976–77, while ongoing commitments to paying rentals continued to be honoured, by suspending all future provision no matter how great the need might be. Three directors reported that they had been obliged to refuse help with further provision. Two, by moving to a system of area budgeting (discussed in Chapter Five, page 117), expected to see a marked decrease in the number of telephones installed annually.

3. *The Financing of Aids*

The financing of aids is relatively straightforward as the London Boroughs Association recommended in 1973 that all aids to daily living should be free and on loan, no matter what their cost. The practice of making small hiring charges had already been discontinued in 1963 by the welfare and public health departments of the London County Council.[3] In spite of vast increases in the number and kinds of aids now supplied, to reimpose any kind of means testing on the issue of aids even at a time of extreme financial stringency would not only appear to be a retrograde step but unduly costly in terms of administration. In 1975–76 only two of the Greater London boroughs continued to sell aids to clients and their relatives. These were sold at cost price against the personal receipt of the fieldworkers involved and also against regulations forbidding them to receive money. Official receipts were obtained later from finance officers who shared the view that clients wishing to demonstrate their independence had a right to do so. (The most popular aids to be bought outright were non-slip bathmats at just under £1). In these two boroughs contributions to aids were also openly solicited – a practice which, although entirely in keeping with the traditions of welfare departments in the Fifties, somewhat contravened the spirit if not the letter of the

Chronically Sick and Disabled Persons Act 1970. No figures are available about the total sum collected from clients in any one financial year but it cannot have been large enough to affect the provision of aids in general.[4]

The head occupational therapist in a third borough would have liked to run an "aids shop"[5] where aids could be purchased outright at cost price and under professional guidance. This she felt would have cut down the length of the waiting list for people who genuinely could not afford to buy aids, but the policy of the social services committee prevented her from doing so. She would also have liked to see a reversion to hiring charges disguised as a "minimum voluntary contribution" and argued that the money collected, now that the issuing of aids had become big business, would be far from the trivial sums raised formerly.

It should be emphasised that this is an isolated point of view and one that social services committees in the Greater London boroughs appeared unlikely to adopt, irrespective of their political composition, even in the most stringent economic conditions and even though there is nothing written into the Chronically Sick and Disabled Persons Act that forbids local authorities to accept payment for aids.[6] Another item with some bearing on the financing of aids was the estimated value of aids that had been recalled, cleaned and recycled.[7]

Although the principle that aids were issued free and on loan was upheld in all but the three boroughs referred to above, there was considerable variation in practice over aids requiring expensive installation or which were in themselves expensive. One borough took any aid to committee that, together with the costs of installation, cost over £500. (In the first instance it was a "Terry" lift). If the committee agreed to the aid being issued then the social services department undertook to pay not less than 50 per cent of the combined cost irrespective of the client's ability to pay, and the director made sure that this principle was written into the minutes of the crucial meeting at which it had been discussed. Stair-lifts and hydraulic lifts were classified as aids in some boroughs and as adaptations in others, a confusion which is discussed further in Chapter Eleven. In all but five boroughs however, aids such as stair-lifts continued to be lent free – if indeed they were provided at all – to clients who were then only assessed on the cost of installing them, if they were assessed at all. What is unfortunately not known is how many such aids had been issued in these boroughs or with what frequency.[8]

The statistics compiled annually by the Department of Health and Social Security do not give any indication of the cost of personal aids issued by local authority social services departments nor do they divide aids into minor aids and major aids as is done for adaptations in the private sector. To ask for returns on the number of aids costing over £150 (exclusive of installation) would be one way of monitoring the provision of costly aids such as stair-lifts. But in a time of inflation any definition based on cost would have to be used most carefully for drawing comparisons in subsequent years. Considerable resistance might also be expected to the use of inadequate staff resources to collect still more data not all of which would necessarily be reliable.

Apart from the figures provided in Table 2 on page 77 no statistics are available for expenditure on aids alone, only for joint expenditure on aids and adaptations.

4. *The Financing of Adaptations*

The figures in Table 3 on page 80 show how little was spent in 1971–72 on aids. One borough spent only £500 and another only £1,013 while the total expenditure for both aids and adaptations together did not exceed £6,000 in six of the 16 boroughs providing statistics. This confirms the strong impression gained from the archives of the former London County Council that adaptations had not really begun to get off the mark before the Greater London Act of 1963,[9] or indeed until after the passing of the Chronically Sick and Disabled Persons Act 1970. The response, for example, of a highly placed officer in the welfare department in 1957 to a builder who wrote asking if adaptations costing under £5 could be put on a day-work basis instead of three builders being asked to submit tenders is revealing :

"this department has not had a great deal of experience in placing orders for work of adaptations ... One of the biggest difficulties is that there are very few firms who have been working for the Council in the homes of disabled people as long as you have and it would be undesirable to place work on a day basis with any firm which is not a local one."

No files for the welfare department of the Greater London Council, which came into being in 1965, were available for scrutiny, but officials who served in the welfare department at that time, from 1965–1970 – some of them now highly placed as directors and assistant directors in social services departments – recalled "schemes" that gave a noticeable impetus to the provision of clubs and centres for the disabled but no significant increase in the priority awarded to the provision of either aids or adaptations. This may be one reason for the low rates of provision in the majority of the Greater London boroughs during the first year after the Act as shown in the annual tables of the Department of Health and Social Security in terms of numbers and in Appendix, Table 1, in terms of costs.

Information about the financing of aids and adaptations in one of the new Inner London boroughs between the reorganisation of London government in 1965 and of the personal social services in 1971 is contained in a survey commissioned by the Social Services Council of the new borough of Tower Hamlets.[10] This survey, although able to give a clear picture of the number of pieces of "nursing equipment" issued free on loan in 1966–67 by the Health Department, is much more vague about the aids to daily living issued by the welfare department which it treats together with adaptations. From the context of a paragraph headed "Aids and Adaptations" it is difficult to determine whether aids to daily living were issued on free loan or subject to assessment. The paragraph begins :

"Where necessary, special appliances and aids were supplied and adaptations carried out to facilitate movement within the handicapped person's home. Such aids ranged from pick-up sticks, grabrails, bath and toilet seats, etc., to structural works of access."

and ends

"Charges made to the recipient depended on assessment of means using those scales adopted by the Ministry of Social Security in respect of supplementary benefits. Structural adaptations were contracted out to private firms."[11]

As it was also "the policy of the department that recipients of aids should be registered handicapped as laid down by the National Assistance Act 1948", such aids and adaptations would in any case be available only to one-fifth of the disabled population as identified by the survey.[12]

The confusion over aids that do not need installation and aids that need installing and are therefore assessed as adaptations was found still to persist in some Greater London boroughs when interviews for the present research was begun in late 1974.[13]

By 1974–75 however there was a marked increase in the money allocated for adaptations as distinct from joint expenditure with aids. The table that follows, Table 4, was drawn up by the Disability Alliance. It gives the estimated cost of adaptations in all of the Greater London boroughs, except the City of London, in terms of per 1,000 of the population and is to be found on page 86. This table is valuable in that it shows the variations of expenditure on adaptations alone, that is divorced from aids, as between one Greater London borough and another, which no other published statistics indicate, and also because it includes any additional money raised by supplementaries. What it does not show is how this money was spent. No breakdowns of expenditure are given of what proportion of

Table 4 – Assistance with Adaptations in the Greater London Boroughs – 1974–75 per 1,000 of the population (excluding the City of London).

Inner London

	Number of Households assisted per 1,000 population	Expenditure per 1,000 population (£)
		£
Wandsworth	3.69	291
Lambeth	2.06	65
Camden	1.93	86
Southwark	1.90	34
Tower Hamlets	1.85	NA
Hammersmith	1.60	60
Lewisham	1.39	98
Greenwich	1.23	190
Kensington	0.73	9
Westminster	0.59	34
Islington	0.19	NA
Hackney	0.04	NA

Outer London

	Number of households assisted per 1,000 population	Expenditure per 1,000 population (£)
		£
Merton	5.03	104
Hillingdon	3.57	448
Barking	2.71	150
Kingston	2.41	21
Brent	1.95	55
Richmond	1.82	145
Harrow	1.65	166
Waltham Forest	1.62	7
Bromley	1.60	89
Barnet	1.56	60
Sutton	1.23	110
Ealing	1.11	85
Hounslow	1.07	71
Haringey	0.87	56
Enfield	0.80	68
Croydon	0.70	27
Havering	0.49	—
Redbridge	0.40	64
Bexley	0.38	NA
Newham	0.22	19

Figures by courtesy of the Disability Alliance.

expenditure went on providing a large number of minor adaptations and how much, if any, of the money went on the provision of major adaptations costing, for example, over £2,000. Nor of the sums spent in the public and private sectors.

5. The public sector: financial responsibility of local housing authorities

Until the passing of the Housing Act 1974 the guidelines followed by the majority of the Greater London boroughs were those laid down in the Cullingworth Committee on "Council Housing, Purposes, Procedures and Priorities" which reported in 1969, only a few weeks before the Chronically Sick and Disabled Persons Bill received its Second Reading.[14] In the section on housing for the disabled[15] the report quotes a speech by Mr J. P. Dixon, the Director of Housing for Newcastle-on-Tyne, in which the financial responsibility of both housing departments and social services departments towards adaptations for the disabled is clearly defined. Local authority housing authorities are to be responsible for the cost of all adaptations to new property that are made at the drawing-board stage. Anything that is added later to meet a specific disability is to be paid for by the local authority social services departments.

In a speech which anticipates the concept of "mobility housing" that was to be put forward by the Department of the Environment in 1974[16] Mr Dixon says:

"The cost of ensuring that at least a percentage of all ground floor flats or bungalows are built in such a way as to be particularly suitable for physically handicapped persons is minimal. The provision of wide door openings, space for a wheelchair alongside the toilet, low electric light switches, provision for a low level sink, waist high electric outlet sockets, shallow ramps instead of steps, etc., only represent a fractional increase in initial building costs, but the same items cost quite staggering sums of money if they have to be provided at a later date. It does not seem unreasonable to expect the housing authority to meet the cost of this kind of provision, leaving the welfare authority to bear the cost of any additional aids or adaptations necessary to meet the special needs of a particular handicap."

Mr Dixon's speech referred only to new council property and projects and there was no reference in the report to adaptations to old properties that are being modernised or converted. For any adaptations made on behalf of disabled clients to old, existing properties the financial responsibility fell, by implication, on the social services departments concerned, as did the cost of any adaptations made after a new building had begun but was still not completed.

And, as Mr Dixon pointed out, calling a halt in a routine building programme in order to insert an adaptation can be prohibitively expensive.

By the autumn of 1974, when the first interviews for this study on aids and adaptations took place, only one local housing authority in the Greater London area had assumed full responsibility for all adaptations – both major and minor – in council property.[17] By the end of the interview period one other housing department had agreed to pay two-thirds of the cost and in 1977–78 a third had agreed to pay the two-thirds which, it had been discovered, could now be reclaimed in the form of retrospective exchequer grants. In another borough the director of social services had agreed with the housing director to operate a sliding scale of charges. This took a considerable burden off the social services committee for large adaptations but left them to pay the whole, or a large percentage, of the cost of adpatations under £50.

Similar adjustments over cost were made between some social services departments in the Greater London area and the GLC. In the majority of the London boroughs the whole cost of minor and major adaptations to old property owned by the GLC was borne by the relevant social services departments. Four boroughs reported contributions from the GLC as a result of independently conducted negotiations with the GLC districts involved;[18] and one borough had come to an arrangement to pay only 50 per cent of the cost of adaptations to new GLC property, parts of which were being purpose-adapted in the final building phase. The consultative document in recognising these disparities points out that there is a clear need for discussion between central government and local authorities about alternative ways of financing major adaptations.

Those directors of housing who were willing to assume some responsibility for adaptations to council property saw an advantage in building up a pool of dwellings suitable for disabled persons. Adaptations, providing the existing housing stock lent itself to structural alterations, were seen as a desirable alternative to re-housing. If suitable stock of housing did not exist – and if there were not enough new purpose-built dwellings in the pipeline – then adaptation was the only alternative to a move that would have to be across borough boundaries.

Interestingly the Greater London area, according to a report by the then Central Council for the Disabled,[19]

"had the highest level of adaptations in 1973–74 in relation to its estimated numbers of handicapped people as well as the highest levels of proposed new purpose-built dwellings."

From this statement it would seem that a good deal of attention had been paid both to the recommendations of the Cullingworth Report 1969 and to Section 3 of the Chronically Sick and Disabled Persons Act.

Any such generalisation, however, masks considerable variations in the policy of individual boroughs. Researchers for the Greater London Council pointed out, in another study[20] that it would be unwise to assume that a low level of re-housing pre-supposes a high level of adaptations – it could merely reflect a low interest in all kinds of provision for the disabled, or, as has already been pointed out, a prevalence of below average housing stock or stock that is unsuitable for adaptation.

The housing legislation of 1974 and 1975 opened up a rich vein of possible subsidies in the public sector for mobility and wheelchair housing but the influence of local authority social services departments on the policy of their local authority housing departments depended on the quality of liaison between different levels of the staff of both departments and of some other relevant departments as well. The most profitable discussions were frequently informal. In three London boroughs where the occupational therapists had built up a good working relationship with research officers of the housing department, technicians from the engineers' department and surveyors from the architects department a fixed percentage of all new housing units had already been allocated for the disabled by the end of 1975. By the end of 1976 the percentages set aside for the disabled varied from 3 per cent (in two boroughs) through 10 per cent (in four), 12 per cent (in one) and 15 per cent (in two). These fixed percentages represent the result of applying an important principle – joint planning between borough housing authorities and borough social services departments.

All too often attempts by social services departments to implement declared policies, either of re-housing or adaptation, are slowed down or rendered untenable by matters outside the direct control of either directors of social services or social services committees. Nor is co-ordinating existing services sufficient. There is need for housing and social services budgets to be programmed together in the light of the known housing needs of the disabled but the researcher did not find any hard evidence that this was being done in any of the Greater London boroughs. References were made to programmed budgeting in four boroughs but this appeared to have been confined to the input from social services departments and to have no influence on the policy of other departments. Even in boroughs committed to a policy of corporate management it was not possible to extract chapter and verse about any budgeting that affected more than one department where the needs of the disabled were concerned.

By the end of 1976 the existence of adequate stocks of housing suitable for disabled people was undoubtedly beginning to influence the policy of social services committees towards major adaptations in the public sector. Evidence was forthcoming in four boroughs of a swing away from providing major adaptations – the cost of which in those boroughs came entirely out of the social services vote – towards what was virtually compulsory re-housing for all disabled tenants who lived in council property and who needed a major adaptation to that property if they were to lead more normal and more mobile lives. It should be noted that even compulsory re-housing depends on good liaison between the two departments concerned.

6. *Financing adaptations in the private sector*

Before the Housing Act 1974 only one Greater London borough accepted full financial responsibility for all adaptations in both the public and private sectors alike, once need had been established. In all the other London boroughs adaptations in the private sector were done free of all charge to the client only if they cost less than whatever ceiling had been set by particular local authority social services committees.[21] This system had the virtue of simplicity but it also meant that clients might be penalised simply because of the financial policy of the borough in which they lived.

After 1974 the introduction of exchequer grants towards major adaptations for disabled people living in the private sector resulted in complicated procedures that led to long delays between application and completion even for owner-occupiers. These are discussed in detail in Chapter Thirteen. The plight of disabled tenants living in privately rented accommodation remained largely unchanged by the new legislation, as landlords remained equally unwilling to pay the difference between the money provided by the new grants and the total cost. Once again, unless the social services department were prepared to foot the landlord's part of the bill, no major adaptations would be possible.

By the beginning of 1977–78 a second social services department had agreed that all major adaptations would be done at no charge to the disabled client but in all other social services departments cuts in local authority expenditure had resulted in fewer major adaptations being undertaken in the private sector.

7. *Contributions by the Client towards the Cost of Adaptations*

With the exception of the two boroughs mentioned above all the social services departments in the Greater London boroughs assessed clients for contributions towards some part of the total cost of a major adaptation. Some also insisted on assessing the ability of clients to contribute towards costs in the public sector as well. The definition of what is an aid can therefore be crucial in terms of whether or not a client must pay the whole or part of the expenses involved in installing such relatively inexpensive items as bannister rails as well as costly items like ceiling track hoists, hydraulic lifts and stair-lifts. Local authorities also differ in whether they assess for everything that they themselves define as an adaptation or whether they establish ceilings below which adaptations are free.

The ceilings below which adaptations were provided free in the Greater London boroughs in 1974–75 and above which clients would be expected to contribute towards the total cost are shown in Table 5 on page 92. These ceilings should not be confused with the ceilings of authorisation, that is the sums of money for which various grades of social service staff are permitted to sign and which are shown in Table 14. Nor do they have anything to do with the sums of money, such as post office savings, that it is common practice to disregard up to the sum of £400. The figures in the table refer only to the sums of money which social services committees were willing to spend on free adaptations.

In one borough all adaptations costing less than £200 were paid for out of the social services budget in both the public and private sectors. Should the accepted estimate for an adaptation exceed £200 then, before any work on it could go ahead, the client would be asked to complete an elaborate form on which he would be asked to give such details as his net weekly earnings, the net weekly earnings of other members of the household, the weekly contributions of other members of the household towards household expenses and any rent from lodgers. In addition questions would be asked about sick pay from unions or Friendly Societies, compensation for disability, sickness and injury benefit, superannuation and pensions. Clients might be obliged to give the number of their post office savings account and the numbers of their national savings certificates and also the name of their bank and the number of their deposit account, the name of their building society and the number of their account with the society and to specify any other investments.

Against this the finance officer responsible for assessment might offset some of the money the client – if an owner-occupier – spends on mortgage repayments, general and water rates and ground rent and, if divorced or separated, maintenance payments. An allowance for normal household and living expenses is made to all clients. It is not surprising that it takes a good deal of time for some disabled clients to muster all the required details. Or that others, confronted with such a total invasion of privacy, withdraw their application for assistance with an adaptation.

The sums chosen as the points above which financial assessment

Table 5 – Financial sanctions for aids and appliances: ceilings authorised by different grades of staff

	C	P	C	P	C	P	C	P	C	P	C	P	C	P	C	P	C	P	C	P	C	P
Number of Boroughs																						
	25		30		50		90		100		150		200		250		300		350		500	

Amount (£), below which Adaptations are free

 Council Private

began varied from as little as £5 in both the private and public sectors (raised in 1976–77 to £50) in one borough to as high as £300 in two others. The prevalence of certain ceilings shows up in Table 5 above. The sum of £200 is the most frequent choice for both the public and private sectors.

The choice of ceiling was not related to the total amount of money a social services committee was prepared to authorise for adaptations in 1974–76. In one of the boroughs that did not assess at all, as a matter of principle, twelve adaptations costing between £1,000 and £5,000 each were completed in 1976. In another borough which insisted on clients contributing to any adaptation costing more than £25, no adaptation costing as much as £500 had ever been attempted. Figures were not available for this study on the amount of money actually raised by contributions from clients, but it is probable that the majority of disabled clients living in the public sector would have been receiving supplementary benefit and therefore have been exempted. Whether owner-occupiers are assessed or not will depend on whether or not they are eligible for improvement grants. This is discussed in Chapter Thirteen, which also discusses the difficulties of the disabled tenants of private landlords when applying for adaptations. Frequently the council will be asked to assume full financial responsibility for any adaptations done in privately

92

rented property and social services committees will vary in their willingness to comply.

To assist assessment in the Greater London area, the London Boroughs Association issued a somewhat lengthy document containing guidelines on such problems as the percentage of the income of a disabled person – or of a family with a disabled member – that might be disregarded. None of the administrators belonging to the social services departments felt able to allow the researcher to read this document, which was loosely referred to as the "LBA Scale". One reason for this may have been that in all but two of the boroughs the calculations were in fact done by finance officers based on what used formerly to be called the borough treasurers' department. Directors of social services and other senior officials interviewed all laboured the point that the scale was heavily weighted in favour of the client. Three social services departments used their own scale of assessment which they described as modified versions of the LBA Scale.

Latitude about whether or not to ignore the result of assessments was occasionally permitted. In one social services department discretion rested entirely in the hands of an adaptations officer at consultant level with long years of experience in the welfare department of the former London County Council. His summing up of what he called "honest ability to pay" was then accepted without question by the committee, although in the opinion of one of his colleagues he was "notoriously" soft-hearted. In another borough it was a sub-committee of the social services committee which took *ad hoc* decisions on whether or not to assess, having first demanded very full reports from the social workers.

It was not possible to gather any information about the harshness or otherwise of assessments made in other boroughs, but some indication of the varying attitudes of social services departments towards assessment may be gained by looking at where the officers responsible for making the calculations were based. In two boroughs they were on detachment to the social services department, and made personal calls on the clients in order to help them fill in the official form. These two finance officers were not available for interview but indicated that they were thought to be generous in what they disregarded for heavy clothing and heating expenses and for payment for essential services such as window cleaning or cutting the grass.

Where finance officers were based on departments other than the social services departments the business of assessment was more likely, in the first instance at any rate, to be conducted by post. The home would then only be visited if clients failed to reply. Many clients felt unable to cope with the complexity of the forms sent them.

Finance officers with no experience of fieldwork were said by one administrator to be "trained not to upset the disabled clients" but that they were also "expected to remain aware of their accountability to the treasurer". From interviews with occupational therapists it was clear that the best results, from the clients' point of view, were likely to be obtained if a fieldworker filled in the forms for new clients and then got them to sign it. One occupational therapist said that she always put up a good case for expenses for professional hair-dressing and cosmetics as a necessary boost to the morale of female clients, in addition to a possible need for additional warm clothing and extra heating.[22] For this there is a precedent in the Department of Health and Social Security Joint Circular 12/70 of 17 August 1970[23] which says :

> "Whenever clients of an authority are required to make a payment for a service or facility . . . and the authority in exercising its discretion in such matters takes account of the cash resources and requirements of such a person, authorities are invited to take into consideration any claim by a chronically sick and disabled person that he does, by reason of disability, incur abnormal expenditure and to make sure that clients know this and that they will do so."

Procedures also varied between fieldworkers on whether or not to take into account the income of other members of the disabled person's family. In the case of a congenitally handicapped child, the financial responsibility of the parents was never in dispute, but how much of their income should other relatives be expected to contribute? Should two brothers, aged 17 and 23 and still living at home, be compelled to contribute anything beyond their share of the rent? One case, that of a handicapped person aged 33, emerged as a subject of dispute during the second phase of the research when an intensive study of clients was being made. This concerned the liability of a family with an unmarried daughter, who had once gone to work by public transport. Around the age of twenty, symptoms of a degenerative disease began to show up but after a spell in hospital she had returned to work in an "Invacar" provided free by the Department of Health and Social Security. A further onset of the disease in her early thirties led to her having to give up work altogether and she became totally wheelchair bound both indoors and outdoors. Expensive adaptations were needed to accommodate her wheelchair, including knocking down an internal wall, but her father and brothers flatly refused to reveal their incomes because it was the daughter who needed the alterations and she was in receipt of supplementary benefit.[24]

The senior social worker dealing with the case ruled that unless all details of the family were known no help with the adaptations would be forthcoming. However a colleague working in another area of the same borough and confronted with a similar case had been instructed by her Senior to disregard the income of family members and to submit a return saying "nil contribution". The first social worker, reluctant to go over the head of her own senior shelved the case but the client then wrote to the local Member of Parliament who took it up with the director of social services. At its next meeting the social services committee agreed that all the necessary adaptations would be done free, but the director saw to it that the minutes recorded that this was an exceptional case and not to be regarded as a precedent.[25]

Figures on how much money has been credited to local authority social services departments in the Greater London area, as the result of assessing clients for contributions towards adaptations, were not available. Nor were figures available for the cash contributions that clients in some boroughs make voluntarily towards the cost of an adaptation, nor of the cash collected for aids purchased outright by clients from local authority stores, at cost price. It is however unlikely that, once the cost of administering means tests and keeping records of small cash transactions are offset against the cash gains, the total of contributions by clients forms anything but a small percentage of the overall budget for the social services.

8. *Changes in the financial policy of social services departments*

There was evidence by the end of 1975–76 that a number of local authority social services departments were less ready not only to contribute towards the cost of major adaptations in the private sector but also less ready to contribute towards any major adaptations at all. There was a noticeable trend towards spending their full allocation for adaptations in the social services budget on as many minor adaptations as possible rather than on tying up large sums in just a few major adaptations, and to consider cases in exceptional need of a major adaptation on an "ad hoc" basis, if at all. This shift of emphasis did not at first effect the amount allocated for adaptations in the budget – all it did was to alter the way in which available finance was used. But by the end of 1976 there was a noticeable decrease, in real terms, in the amount of money available for either major or minor adaptations.

9. *Future Provision in a Time of Economic Stringency*

In the Greater London boroughs the financial years 1973–74 and 1974–75 were peak years in spending on aids and adaptations in real terms. Unharassed by the need to re-organise, many of the Greater

London boroughs "rolled" their budgets forward whilst they still had the opportunity. But already by November 1974 the need to make cuts was being broached.[26] One director interviewed in the December of that year had already persuaded the finance committee not to make cuts in any services for the disabled by comparing the state of the nation's economy with that of a nation at war. In World War Two, he said, the top priorities had been food, shelter, clothing and medical attention, and it had been the duty of society to see that those that could not forage for themselves were provided for. The same priorities still prevailed in times of economic crisis and the same categories – young children, the sick, the elderly and the disabled – must take financial precedence over any others. Another director of social services reported that he had been far less successful. His committee had insisted that aids and adaptations should only be provided to clients who were not only "at risk" but "at risk of their lives". Even so the number of clients on the waiting list, together with an expected increase of at least a thousand new needs, meant that, even when applying this rigorous criterion, more aids would certainly be issued. In this borough money allocated for adaptations was switched to aids in order to allow essential aids to be issued in the numbers required.

By 1976–77 the "no growth" budget had arrived. Figures produced by the Disability Alliance in March 1977 suggest that many social services departments may have been unsuccessful in maintaining services essential to the disabled or may have reduced services such as meals on wheels rather than put up the price.[27] Indeed cuts in the provision of aids and adaptations had already been made in 1975–76 in 19 Greater London boroughs, as shown in Table 6 below.

Table 6 – Aids and Adaptations: Percentage Decrease in Real Expenditure per 1,000 population between 1974–75 and 1975–76*

Borough	Per cent decrease	Borough	Per cent decrease
1. Greenwich	3.6	10. Harrow	24.1
2. Redbridge	6.8	11. Bromley	26.4
3. Enfield	7.7	12. Lambeth	26.7
4. Kingston-upon-Thames	8.1	13. Haringey	31.2
5. Westminster	10.7	14. Brent	34.6
6. Croydon	11.4	15. City of London	46.3
7. Hackney	14.5	16. Wandsworth	50.4
8. Kensington & Chelsea	16.1	17. Barking	51.9
9. Richmond-upon-Thames	6.4	18. Sutton	52.6
		19. Hillingdon	52.9

* Figures provided in March 1977 by the Disability Alliance.

The situation is worse than it seems because the price of building materials and labour have risen by more than the rate of inflation.

Also small jobs, such as minor adaptations, cost proportionately more than big building projects. Yet it is on a very large number of small jobs that the bulk of social services money for adaptations is spent.

By the end of 1975–76 some social services departments in the Greater London area were becoming increasingly unable – and unwilling – to shoulder the whole burden of expense for adaptations. After the consultative paper of November 1976 still more social services departments were content to mark time on major adaptations until the result of consultation came to be translated into the circular of guidance which appeared on the 29 August 1978.[28] This simplifies the procedures for claiming subsidies and seeks to transfer the responsibility for "structural adaptations to local authority housing departments in both the public and private sectors.[29]

10. The Need for Monitoring and Evaluation by Local Authority Social Service Departments

The implications and effects of the transfer of powers recommended by the joint circular will need careful monitoring and evaluation to ensure that the interests of disabled clients continue to take priority over the problems inherent in overhauling the machinery of local government. The response of housing associations to the suggestion in the circular that they "should come to suitable arrangements with social services authorities, consulting as necessary with housing authorities" will also need to be examined. It is essential that recommendations designed to prevent the overlapping of functions between the agencies involved, including the area health authorities, should result in increasing cooperation and that uncertainties which in the past could lead to delay, and even to the denial of "the help which disabled people have the right to expect", should be replaced by a deliberate and corporate policy towards all their housing needs. The circular also asks local authorities once again "to publicise the working arrangements finally drawn up so that individual disabled people know where to seek help." That too is a job for the research division of social services authorities.

Another subject for research is the effect of increased cash benefits, e.g. the mobility allowance introduced in 1976, on the continued willingness of local government to provide services in kind. It would be difficult to include an element in any cash benefit that could be expected to cover the cost of all but the simplest aids to mobility or very inexpensive minor adaptations. A decreasing reliance on local authority provision is the price which many disabled people might be willing to pay for increased freedom of choice. Social services authorities might still wish to provide the professional guidance of occupational therapists free of charge to the client and so continue

97

to exercise the functions required of them under Section 2 of the Chronically Sick and Disabled Persons Act 1970.

NOTES

1. This took over in 1973 from the Institute of Municipal Treasurers and Accountants (IMTA).

2. In one borough, although the block grant provision had risen from £14,200 in 1972–73 to £86,750 in 1974–75, less than £25,000 was spent on aids and adaptations in the latter year. Subsequently, in 1975–76, when separate allocation was made for telephones and for aids and adaptations, £45,000 was budgeted for aids and adaptations together, but £60,000 was still spent on telephones.

3. In November 1963 the chief welfare officer asked for aids costing up to £3 to be written off "unless the recipient is clearly willing to purchase outright". Hiring charges, based on the cost of the aid rather than on the client's ability to pay, were abolished in welfare departments the following month, December 1963, and the public health departments, which had operated a different scale of hiring charges, were asked to come into line. At the same time the Red Cross and St John Ambulance Brigade were asked to cease from levying or soliciting contributions for aids lent. The reasons given for this change in policy were that (1) the majority of clients had such low incomes that they were exempt from paying anyway, (2) the income from those who did pay amounted to only £420 in 1961–62, considerably less than the amount it had cost to collect contributions and (3) "the emphasis seems at times to lean more to recovering of charges than to welfare needs.", (See the archives of the LCC).

4. In one of these boroughs contributions went into a small "miscellaneous" fund and were used to purchase small items such as a special pastry blender or a tin-opener for a left-handed client bought locally. This cut down delays imposed by regular administrative processes but used up the time of the professional workers who did the shopping. The practice of inviting contributions was justified by the individuals concerned in operating it as being "good" for the client. It was "good" not to let disabled people feel dependent. No evidence was produced to show that the social services committee had endorsed a policy of expecting payment and it seemed, in 1974–75, to be a legacy of the old days of "welfare officers".

5. This should not be confused with shops to dispose of goods made by the disabled (c.f. Lord Roberts Workshops for the Blind). Only one borough maintained such a shop as an outlet for the work of the housebound-physically handicapped although in three boroughs occupational therapists had found private shops willing to sell things made by clients.

6. See Chapter Two, page 42.

7. See Chapter Ten, pages 211/18.

8. See also *DHSS Statistics of the Personal Social Services*, Report of the Working Party of the Social Services Research Group (London, 1975).

9. See the archives of the Greater London Council, Welfare policy files on Aids and Adaptation, 1955–65.

10. See Skinner, F., ed. *Physical Disability and Community Care*, Tower Hamlets Council of Social Services (London, 1969). This survey mentions 26 different kinds of "nursing equipment" ranging from 2 hoists through 185 commodes to 392 fireguards, and a grand total of 773.

11. *Ibid.*, p. 21.

12. The number of persons identified as disabled in 1968 in Tower Hamlets was estimated as 11,371 of which 2,131 were registered at 31 March 1968. Over 8,000 were therefore unknown to the welfare department. Not all of those who were registered would have necessarily received a service.

13. See Chapter Eleven, Section 1, pp. 222/30.

14. Dr Dunwoody referred to the report during the debate. See Chapter Three, pp. 48 and 49.

15. *Op. cit.,* Section 9.

16. See Circular DOE 74/74. *Housing for people who are physically handicapped* (May 1974), para. 10.

17. Expenditure on adaptations to council property at the request of the social services department was carefully budgeted for and monitored by a finance officer based on the housing department, and was entered separately in the Housing Assessment section for forward planning. This practice still continues in 1978–79, and at no time have the social services department been asked to contribute towards the cost. In this the borough has anticipated and contributed to the policy outlined in the consultative paper of 1976.

18. The GLC was reorganising its districts at the time of this study and was short of senior officers in many of them. A joint working party with representatives of the London Boroughs Association was set up in 1976 in an attempt to rationalise procedure, but its findings had not been published by May 1977.

19. Central Council for the Disabled, Working Party on Housing, *Towards a Policy for the Disabled*, p. 9 (CCD, London, 1976). Since a merger in 1977 the Council is now known as "The Royal Association for Disability and Rehabilitation".

20. Miners and Plank, *Housing for the Disabled in Greater London* (GLC, 1975).

21. See Table 5 on p. 92 above.

22. Formerly such matters were considered to be more properly the concern of officers from the Department of Health and Social Security who visited to assess for supplementary benefit allowances.

23. This was the first circular issued after the passage of the Chronically Sick and Disabled Persons Act. It gave as examples of abnormal expenditure, "clothes, linen, domestic equipment or travel", but went on to point out that there can be no common measure – "Individual circumstances will of course vary between wide extremes".

24. They also genuinely believed that they were legally entitled to free adaptations under Section 2 of the Chronically Sick and Disabled Persons Act 1970.

25. DHSS Joint Circular 12/70 upheld the right of local authorities to exercise their own discretion about waiving charges. See above, Chapter Two, p. 43, where para. 40 is quoted.

26. C.f. Circular DOE 77/73 on the Rate Support Grant.

27. The Disability Alliance pamphlet (Wright, Fay, *op. cit.*) insists that there has been a reduction in real terms of the number of meals on wheels served in four of the Greater London boroughs by 7.5, 14.6, 18.5, and 18.5 per cent, while eleven Greater London boroughs are said to have cut back the number of hours of service given by home helps by percentages varying from a decrease of 0.3 per cent to 20.9 per cent.

28. Joint Circular LAC (78) 14 (DHSS); 59/78 (DOE), and 104/78 (Welsh Office).

29. For the research that contributed to the new procedures see Chapter Eleven, p. 255.

CHAPTER FIVE

THE STRUCTURE OF THE SOCIAL
SERVICES DEPARTMENT

A preliminary description of the structure of a social services department is essential if procedures for the supply of aids and adaptations are to be readily understood. Other local authority departments, such as the borough architects department and the technical services department help at times with adaptations but the time taken by their staff, and any expenses they incur, are charged to the budget of the social services departments.

The basic structure of the social services departments tends to follow a "hierarchical" system, often with a very long chain of command, although some follow a "geographical" system[1] under which more autonomy is given to the areas into which all boroughs are divided. Two of the London boroughs approximated to the "geographical" model at the time of this study but the degree of autonomy did not affect the patterns of staffing in the area offices. The City of London, the smallest of the boroughs, had not appointed its Director of Social Services until shortly before the interviews and was still somewhat influenced by the pattern that had obtained under its Chief Medical Officer of Health. The remaining thirty boroughs followed the hierarchical pattern but with distinct local variations.

For this reason it is not possible to present one model of a "typical" social services department. Indeed the only mandatory employee that all of them have in common is the director of social services himself. This is a mandatory appointment under the Act. The director is responsible to the local authority's social services committee "for the purposes of their social services functions".[2] The Act further insists that, having appointed their director, the local authority must go on to "secure the provision of adequate staff for assisting him in the exercise of his functions". It is at this point that variations of responsibility, duty, salary and nomenclature begin, both in the secretariat and in the field.

The directors of social services head two different kinds of staff, those who deal with clients, either in their homes, at day centres or residential homes, and those who help them administer the services. The number of staff for whom they are responsible is considerable, varying in 1974 from 29 in the City of London (a special case as so few of the population are resident) to 2122 in Lambeth.[3] The average number of staff for Inner London boroughs, excluding the City, was 1568, and for Outer London boroughs was 824.

The breakdown of staff for Lewisham – an Inner London borough with a population of over a quarter of a million, a high standard of services and a social services budget of £8½ million – shows that of the 2001 employed 273 were social workers (including assistants and trainees) supervised by 21 senior staff. There were 460 home helps, with 21 people organising them, and there were 59 staff working in Day Centres and Training Centres. Drivers, vanmen, cleaners, caretakers, warehousemen and handymen numbered 112, classified as "other staff" and, excluding the people delivering meals on wheels, more than 65 per cent of all staff were engaged in providing some form of domiciliary or day care. To back up these services, and also the residential services, there were 210 clerical and administrative staff, just about 10 per cent of the total. The majority of these were based on the secretariat, a small proportion in area offices and a few in residential homes. If one excludes residential homes for children then the percentage of staff working in residential homes for the younger physically handicapped, the adult physically handicapped and the elderly came to 29 per cent of the overall total.

The provision of aids and adaptations depends in the first instance on the fieldworkers in the area offices. It is they who decide what aids and adaptations a client needs in order to continue to live at home. Their requests then go on to officers in the secretariat who are directly concerned with the administration of the more costly aids. In order to begin where the requests originate we will first examine the structure of a typical area office. The key grade for consultants is Principal Officer (PO); then come Senior Officers (SO), administrative and professional staff (AP) and clerical staff, which includes typists (Clerical). This grading is applied equally to fieldworkers and officers of the secretariat at equivalent levels of responsibility which means that the staff of area offices are as aware of their exact place in the hierarchy as are those of the secretariat.

Fieldwork: The Area Offices

The area offices grew out of recommendations in the Seebohm Report for community based social services[4] but moving social workers out into area offices could not be achieved by waving a magic wand. Suitable buildings had first to be acquired. There was also resistance on the part of some directors to dispersing fieldwork staff until they had achieved some sort of identity within the larger framework of the social services department as a whole. By the end of this study in June 1976, five social services departments still had two or more teams based in the same buildings as the secretariat, three had only recently re-housed teams and four had decided that the social work team servicing the area surrounding the secretariat building should be based upon it. One social services department kept a team in the same building as the secretariat even though the area it served did not coincide topographically. The justification was that clients living in that area were better served by public transport if they went to the secretariat building.

Social workers based on area offices quickly discovered what this new accessibility meant in terms of work. Not only could they get to their clients more quickly but their clients could get to them. This they did in such overwhelming and unanticipated numbers that, at times, services ground to a standstill or were arbitrarily halted by the social workers themselves. In some areas offices were closed to all but the most urgent cases on certain days of the week, or at certain stated times, while social workers attempted to catch up with the backlog of cases. Disabled people suffered less from such shut-downs than other clients as the majority of them did not go in person to the area offices. If they did, they were more likely to be seen by a social worker than people with less obvious problems. But of those disabled on the lengthy waiting list for people of all categories who needed a fieldworker to visit them in their own homes those disabled who were housebound were particularly vulnerable to delay.

The number of area offices in any one borough depended on the size and density of its population and also on its composition. In the Greater London area the smallest number of area teams was three (in one Outer London borough), and the highest number ten (in one Inner London borough). The number of social workers allocated to each area also varied according to the expected number of clients, as did administrative and clerical back-up at the local level.[5] No area office was operating at full strength in 1974–75. There was an overall shortage of trained social workers, and on over-reliance on untrained ancillary staff.

The way in which area offices were run depended on a number of factors such as the personality of the principal area officer, the degree of militancy amongst the social workers, the overall political complexion of the social workers and whether they saw themselves as operating in "contingency" situations or favoured a "casework" approach. For example, some areas had an "Intake" team to deal with all new referrals in the first instance whilst others continued with the system favoured by the majority of the former welfare departments and children's departments of having a duty officer of the day, backed up by one or more trained social workers and auxiliaries. The hypothetical model that follows (Table 7) assumes an "Intake" team because a number of areas were experimenting with this system of internal organisation during the time of the study and its popularity with social worker was increasing.

The number of fieldwork staff in an area office shown on Table 7 on page 104 – three seniors plus 27 social workers, assistant social workers and auxiliaries – represents what directors of social services in the Inner London boroughs had come to consider the minimum numbers practicable to serve between 25,000 and 30,000 people. It is almost four times as great as the minimum figure recommended by the Seebohm Committee for a population of upwards of 50,000 although the number of trained and experienced social workers shown in Table 7 – twelve – works out at only twice as many as Seebohm's minimum. All the directors interviewed felt it would be impracticable to cut back on fieldwork staff[6] and regretted having to freeze vacancies.

Of the trained social workers few would have had much knowledge or experience of working with physically handicapped people as, until 1970, the disabled had been largely the province of welfare officers. After 1970, when the new local authority social services departments absorbed the old welfare departments relatively few welfare officers were promoted to become senior social workers[7] with the result that inexperienced social workers and untrained social work assistants were more likely to be supervised by people who had previously specialised in, for example, the children's services. In such circumstances, unless there was an occupational therapist attached to the office, there might be no person trained to advise on cases of physical handicap.

The area occupational therapist is shown, in Table 7, on page 104, in square brackets. This is because not all area offices had an occupational therapist. Policies over their employment varied. Not all boroughs felt an occupational therapist for each area was needed; two Outer London boroughs were content to employ just one as a centrally-based consultant and two did not think it necessary to employ any in 1975. Other boroughs at that time were aiming at an establishment for one, or more, domiciliary occupational therapists in each area but the posts frequently remained unfilled for long periods. This was partly because there was an overall shortage of domiciliary occupational therapists and also because, unlike the hospitals and district health authorities who were obliged to adhere to a strict scale of salaries, local authorities were able, if they so wished, to call them by a different title, such as "rehabilitation officer" and offer rather more money.[8] Because of the shortage, local

Table 7 – Typical Staffing of an Area Office (Social Services)

Secretariat

Director . . . Soc. Services Comm.

Assistant Directors
Fieldwork/Casework   (Others)

Controller
Deputy Controller

Consultants. Prin. Officer level

Elderly & Disabled	Children	Mental Health

Controls 3 to 10 Area Offices

Area Office

Area Team Manager

Three Senior Social Workers

Long-term "generic" → *Team*	Long-term "generic" → *Team*	Intake → *Team*	[Domiciliary OT attached to Area Office]

2 qualified social workers
2 unqualified social workers (experienced)
1 trainee (in-training)
1 student (if lucky)
3 or more ancilliary or assistant social workers (untrained)

Administrative Support
1 Admin. Officer (AP 3)
1 Clerical Officer (Grade 1/2)
1 part-time typist

Use of Secretariat Typing Pool   (up to 3 weeks' delay)
(dictaphone service)

Secretariat Administrative Support.

including Typing Pool

104

authorities not only wooed occupational therapists away from the hospitals but also from each other.[9]

By 1975 the majority of the Greater London boroughs who had employed only one occupational therapist, if any, to cover perhaps as many as six areas had come to rely so heavily on their professional skills in assessing the need for aids and adaptations that complements of at least one, and possibly two, for each area were being aimed at. Some boroughs also advertised for "floating" occupational therapists to work mainly with clients in day centres. By the end of 1975, 12 of the boroughs were also employing head occupational therapists who supervised and gave professional identity to area occupational therapists who, left on their own, often felt cut off from their profession. They also supervised the ordering and issuing of aids, determined what kinds of aids should always be kept in stock and initiated and monitored the progress of adaptations.

The Seebohm Report is all too frequently thought of as having recommended the abolition of all specialism in favour of "general purposes and family" social workers. This is not true. It saw specialists, in the interim period while the new social services departments settled down, as continuing to share professional expertise acquired in other settings. But in looking to the future the report urged the creation of new specialist posts in the hope that specialisation would lead to new initiatives and new patterns of organisation.[10]

One such pattern was seen to be emerging in a number of the Greater London boroughs. This was the formation of specialist rehabilitation teams and they were to exert a major influence both on the quantity and the quality of aids and adaptations provided and also on the speed with which they were ordered, issued and delivered and adaptations completed. The workers required to staff these teams had usually been advertised for as a group and had included some new posts and/or posts that had been up-graded to meet the additional responsibilities called for by the identification of so many disabled people.

By the spring of 1975 there were eight such rehabilitation teams in the Greater London area, each led by a head occupational therapist (See Table 8, page 107). By the beginning of 1976 six more had been formed, making a total of 14 out of a possible 33 teams of this kind. The structure of the teams and the grades and salaries of individual members within them varied widely from borough to borough.

Not all directors of social services thought it necessary to extract special rehabilitation teams from the main body of their fieldwork services. Some saw such separation as contrary to the whole spirit of the Seebohm Report. One borough held steadfastly to the pattern it had evolved in the days when it operated a joint department of health and welfare and used the term "generic" to describe a team of specialist officers of all kinds who together offered a comprehensive

D*

service to the disabled beyond the skills of so-called "general purposes" social workers. This team was made up of state-registered nurses, state enrolled nurses, specialist officers for the blind, deaf and dumb, an occupational therapist, an adaptations officer with knowledge of the building trade, a technician, an administrative officer, a registry clerk, a clerk, a typist and a receptionist. All work with the physically handicapped in this particular borough came direct to this team from the area offices and the casework files remained with the team the whole time even after they had ceased to be active. This encapsulation had been criticised by an outside team of management consultants but the principal specialist officer defended its rationale by referring to a study done by a team of researchers from the National Institute for Social Work on the preferences of social workers in four area offices in Southampton.[11]

The pattern of organisation of this specialist services unit, unique in the Greater London area but still extant in some parts of Great Britain, kept its emphasis on health and remained heavily biased towards a clinical approach to disability even although the nurses were obliged to merge their former professional identity into the new one of specialist officer. The pattern of organisation is shown in Table 9, page 108.

The Specialist Services Unit shown in Table 8 had the advantage of enjoying an excellent team spirit and also benefited from the pooling of a variety of skills and experience. But it was under-staffed on the administrative side. More clerical help was needed because of the amount of work involved in keeping files which would, in other boroughs, have been dealt with by clerks in the separate area offices and in keeping statistics which in other boroughs would be kept by a member of staff centred in the secretariat. The main disadvantage was that, except for those clients in need of continual specialist attention, the physically handicapped were hermetically sealed off from the main stream of family casework. This meant that families with a physically handicapped member who might well have recurring problems remained unknown to area social workers. The unit was also under-staffed compared with area teams carrying all-purpose case-loads and their work loads were disproportionately heavy. The ration for specialist service officers dealing with the "general classes" of disabled was one officer to 452 clients with more than sixty cases active at any one time.

Another borough which had no establishment for an occupational therapist in 1972 re-organised its services for the disabled completely in 1975. The new structure was similar to that described above in Table 9 except that each member of the unit acted purely as a consultant to area social workers who remained in charge of the case. Although these consultants visited clients whenever necessary, they did not hold caseloads at any time. In this way they differed from

Table 8 – A Typical Rehabilitation Team

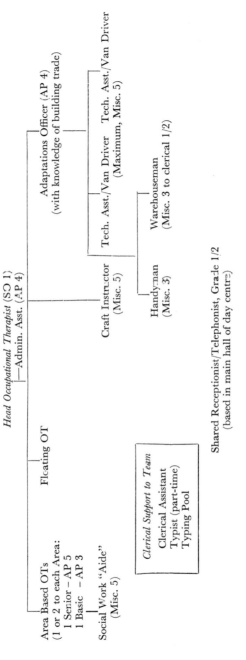

Head Occupational Therapist (SO 1)
—Admin. Asst. (AP 4)

Area Based OTs
(1 or 2 to each Area:
1 Senior – AP 5
1 Basic – AP 3

Social Work "Aide"
(Misc. 5)

Floating OT

Adaptations Officer (AP 4)
(with knowledge of building trade)

Craft Instructor
(Misc. 5)

Handyman
(Misc. 3)

Tech. Asst./Van Driver   Tech. Asst./Van Driver
(Maximum, Misc. 5)

Warehouseman
(Misc. 3 to clerical 1/2)

Clerical Support to Team

Clerical Assistant
Typist (part-time)
Typing Pool

Shared Receptionist/Telephonist, Grade 1/2
(based in main hall of day centre)

Table 9 – A Specialist Services Unit

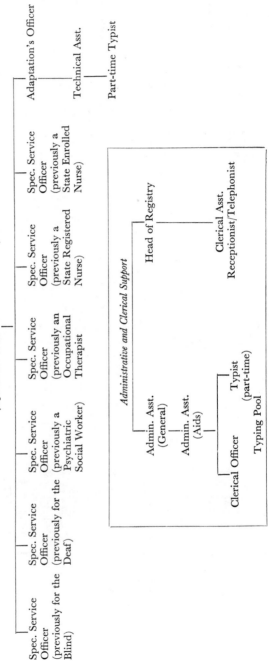

the members of all other specialist teams including those led by head occupational therapists, in that the emphasis remained firmly on the social workers of the area, and the thorny problem of "handing back" cases did not – in theory – exist.

Teams extracted to work specifically with the physically handicapped enjoyed considerable autonomy and their leaders often worked direct to assistant directors, whose confidence they had earned by reason of their professional skills. This could result in the elimination of as many as three stages in the former hierarchical pattern of decision-making and always cut down on some of the delaying processes.

The Secretariat

The work of staff based on the secretariat is of the utmost importance to the efficient provision of aids and adaptations because it is they who control the flow of finance.[12] They can either speed up or slow down the pace with which requests for aids are authorised by means of established "ceilings" up to which staff at various levels of the hierarchy are permitted to authorise expenditure without going back to the social services committee. They can decide whether to take controversial cases to committees on *ad hoc* basis or, if the allocation of money looks like running out, whether to go to committee for a supplementary grant for a whole block of cases. Or they can decide to impose conscious and deliberate rationing on the number and kinds of aids supplied, and adaptations begun, as a way of slowing down the stream of provision, and at times they may even shut the sluice gates altogether. This is most likely to happen towards the end of the financial year although some secretariat staff, usually those rather low down in the hierarchy, are also inclined to look on quarterly totals as a time for calling a temporary halt.

More bewildering to fieldworkers are the forms of unconscious rationing which staff at various levels in the secretariat may employ. This is most likely to happen if the personal views of an aids clerk are at variance with, and less generous than, those of the social services committee by whom she is employed. The keys of a store-cupboard temporarily mislaid, or a stocktaking lasting several days and used as an excuse to stop issuing aids, may serve to illustrate how power is often vested much lower down the hierarchy than is always realised. Policy shaped at a high level is only as effective as the way it is carried out in the lower reaches of the hierarchy. Decisions about how much money to spend on a particular aid, whether aids are bought judiciously in bulk, which manufacturers offer the best value for money, are frequently taken by aids clerks based on the secretariat. With the exception of the specialist teams with their own clerks attached to them, it is a clerk in the secretariat who will be the most likely person required to know about the speed and reliability of manufacturers' delivery dates. Clerks control the issue of aids and, unless there is a transport officer, will frequently arrange for the collection and delivery of aids. The progress of adaptations is also monitored, more often than not, by clerical staff based centrally on the secretariat. The grades of the staff who do this work, and the responsibility they are asked to undertake, are therefore of crucial importance to the efficient and speedy provision of aids and adaptations.

Beginning at the top there is the director of social services whose salary will be fixed according to the population of the borough he serves. If the population is around a quarter of a million, he will have a deputy director immediately under him who will also have specialist responsibilities for a particular branch of the organisation. Then come the assistant directors – between three and six of them – whose titles will vary from borough to borough, but will include duties associated with such posts as Assistant Director (Finance), Assistant Director (Finance and Administration), Assistant Director (Fieldwork), Assistant Director (Community Affairs), Assistant Director (Residential and Day Care), Assistant Director (Domiciliary and Day Care), Assistant Director (Day Care), Assistant Director (Residential Care), Assistant Director (Casework) and Assistant Director (Research and Development). There was no way for the researcher to know in advance under which of these umbrellas the responsibility for aids and adaptations would be found. In two boroughs, aids came under a different assistant director from the one responsible for adaptations. In a third borough, adaptations for the elderly handicapped came under the assistant director for community affairs whilst adaptations for the disabled under 65 years old were the province of the assistant director for domiciliary and day care. In one borough aids were firmly ensconced in the day care section but adaptations to private homes came under the asssistant director for residential care for no other reason than that one of his administrative assistants had once worked in the borough surveyors' department before transferring to the new social services department in 1971 and "knew the approved builders". In another borough adaptations were administered by a former social worker who was also the Court Officer for juvenile delinquents. Explanations were always readily forthcoming as to why the provision for aids and adaptations had been fitted into the organisation in a particular way, but it was not always easy to find a really satisfactory rationale.

The disabled client may need the services of a fieldworker, either for a limited space of time or on a long term basis or not at all. If clubs are used or there is a need to enter sheltered employment, then the clubs and centres, together with transport to get him there

110

will be administered by officers responsible for day care based on the secretariat. Should the client qualify for financial assistance towards a telephone then the domiciliary section of the secretariat might well be called into action. Should the client wish to travel independently then it will again be the responsibility of the domiciliary section to provide the concessionary bus fares, the car badges for disabled drivers and perhaps transport for a subsidised holiday. Transport for evening classes, however, might come under the aegis of community care. All these needs should be met but, in the context of the Chronically Sick and Disabled Persons Act, 1970, with its emphasis on the total needs of disabled people, the methods of provision seem unduly fragmented, however efficiently each of them works in its own limited context. On the face of it the organisation of the majority of the social services department in the majority of the Greater London boroughs still looks backwards to the days of health and welfare departments rather than forward to the newer concepts of care that deal with the total needs of an individual and his family set, within the community as a whole.

Table 10 which follows has been constructed to illustrate a basic pattern of organisation which attempts to make the best of both worlds, the old and the new. The long-established post of Assistant Director (Residential and Day Care) remains but two new managerial posts have been created at the third tier level, one called Manager (Day Centre) and the other Manager (Residential Homes). These posts are exclusively managerial and carry with them no responsibility for advising fieldworkers. Details about other staff are given in the table only if their functions touch on the provision of aids and adaptations. Examples of such offices are purchasing officers, transport officers and finance officers based on the social services secretariat.

The bulk of the work of writing out orders for aids and telephoning to manufacturers would fall on the clerical officer. It should be noted that the aids and adaptations officer comes lower in the hierarchy than advisable although it is unlikely that he will be dealing direct with builders or be required to have much knowledge of the building trade. His main work will consist in referring requests for adaptations upwards to a higher authority, according to a set scale of financial ceilings and in chasing up direct labour in other departments. Should requests about installations and adaptations fail to achieve results within six weeks referral to the manager (day care) for more definite inter-departmental action might then be necessary.

In four boroughs following much the same overall structure of residential and domiciliary care, the aids and adaptations officers were placed much higher up the ladder, either in third tier management or with the consultant rank of principal officer. They had gained

111

Table 10 – The Secretariat

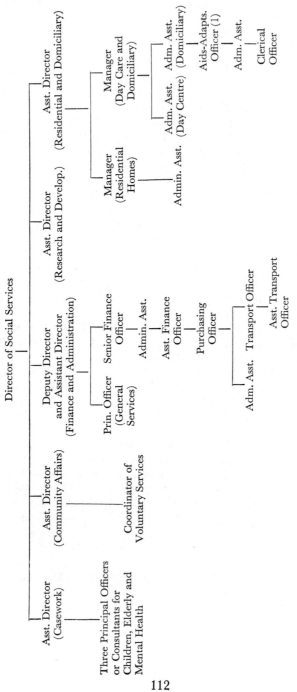

Director of Social Services

Asst. Director (Casework)

Three Principal Officers or Consultants for Children, Elderly and Mental Health

Asst. Director (Community Affairs)

Coordinator of Voluntary Services

Deputy Director and Assistant Director (Finance and Administration)

Prin. Officer (General Services)

Senior Finance Officer

Admin. Asst.

Asst. Finance Officer

Purchasing Officer

Adm. Asst.

Transport Officer

Asst. Transport Officer

Asst. Director (Research and Develop.)

Asst. Director (Residential and Domiciliary)

Manager (Day Care and Domiciliary)

Manager (Residential Homes)

Admin. Asst.

Adm. Asst. (Day Centre)

Adm. Asst. (Domiciliary)

Aids-Adapts. Officer (1)

Adm. Asst.

Clerical Officer

(General clerical back-up – typing pool; telephonist/receptionist)

1. Aids and Adaptations officer orders Aids.

112

considerable experience in old welfare departments and felt, in consequence, that they could supply the answers to any questions asked them by social workers about aids and adaptations. Two saw no need for any domiciliary occupational therapists except in a hospital or health authority setting and those who were prepared to tolerate them expressed regret that they were not consulted by them more often. Significantly no borough employing an aids and adaptations officer at consultant level also employed a head occupational therapist. A head occupational therapist would duplicate or usurp such functions as keeping abreast of the aids market and controlling the contents of the storeroom.

Eleven of the Greater London boroughs followed much the same pattern as that in Table 10 with all the control over the ordering, issue and delivery of aids and the management of stock aids, automatic re-ordering of stock and supervision of the stores and storemen centralised in the secretariat in the person of an officer graded as a clerk or, at the highest, AP 1. In five of these the assistant directors wore both a residential and a domiciliary hat. In the remaining six, responsibility was split between such diverse disciplines as finance, community and casework.

The next table, Table 11, still shows the manager (day care) as the key figure but this time he is backed up by a team of occupational therapists which includes not only a head occupational therapist, based on the secretariat, but a deputy head occupational therapist, based on a day centre, one occupational therapist for each area office and two "floating" occupational therapists, one with special responsibility for mental health and the other looking after the interests of disabled school leavers.

As the implementation of policy about aids and adaptations is only possible within the restrictions of the available money a social services committee is prepared to vote, it is arguable that the most appropriate person to head a division in which aids and adaptations are to be dealt with might be an assistant director (finance). But because finance officers tend to put finance before clients in the same way as fieldworkers tend to put clients before finance, a division headed by an assistant director (finance) would need someone at the third tier level who was strongly orientated towards the client – in fact a head occupational therapist.

The last table, Table 12, shows a much shorter and much more simple chain of command than Tables 10 and 11, and is based on the concept of a rehabilitation team, self-contained and independent, but reaching out to the social workers in the area offices and up towards the assistant director (finance). The assistant director (finance) will be asked to approve a budget drawn up, not by an officer of the secretariat, but by a head occupational therapist who works both in the field and in the secretariat and whose duties include liaison with

Table 11 – The Domiciliary Services

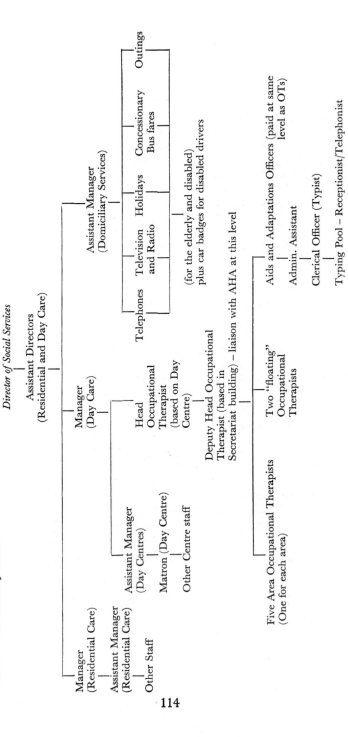

hospital and other health authority staff.

It will be apparent from these tables, that, no matter what the level of decision about aids and adaptations may be, the actual ordering is done very low down the ladder, generally by the Clerical 3 grades who consequently need to acquire considerable knowledge of the aids market. This important work had become fixed at the Clerical 3 level or below at the time when the social services departments were created in 1970. Few planners at that time predicted the constantly increasing demand for aids that the Chronically Sick and Disabled Persons Act, passed in the same year, would generate.

One of the most effective sub-divisions discovered during the course of this study in 1976 was a small, compact team under a finance officer (SC 1) who was assisted by an administrator (AP 5), an assistant administrator (AP 3) who looked after the provision of telephones and two clerks (Clerical 2 and Clerical 3), one of whom looked after the provision of holidays for both the elderly and the physically handicapped and the other radios, television and refrigerators. A third clerk, graded only at Clerical 2, was entirely responsible for ordering and issuing aids, for overseeing their delivery and also, when necessary, their installation. This post of aids clerk had grown with the identification of need but attempts by the senior officer to get it up-graded had been unsuccessful because of the economic situations.[13] The administrator (AP 5) immediately below the finance officer did much of the work that in some boroughs was done by a head occupational therapist, namely, advance planning for the budget, overall supervision of the way the money allocated is spent, supervising the control of stock, etc. The salary grade of AP 5 was the equivalent of that of some head occupational therapists and the responsibilities might therefore be considered commensurate. But what the administrator could not do was to give professional identity to those domiciliary occupational therapists who felt isolated in the areas, nor apportion their work loads. For this reason, the unit although efficient, lacked the careful balance between different kinds of expertise that can be seen in Table 8.

The area-based occupational therapists had repeatedly asked for a head occupational therapist, some had left and some vacancies remained unfilled but as this was also true of occupational therapists in other boroughs it is not possible to deduce any need to restructure the unit from their behaviour. Blau's theory of "spontaneous" innovations is relevant. These, he says, are not the result of individual whim. On the contrary they can only occur when existing procedures become disturbing, and "unless organisational need is experienced as disturbing by operating officials" then it is the clients who will ultimately suffer.[14]

Many of the patterns of organisation discussed in this chapter had evolved as it became more and more obvious that existing procedures

115

Table 12 – A Rehabilitation Team in an Outer London borough

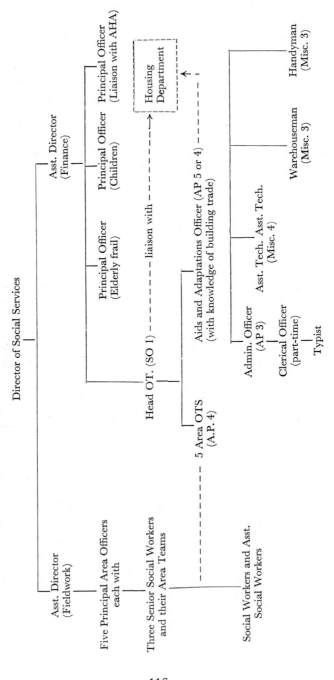

could no longer cope with the built-up pressures of demand released by the Chronically Sick and Disabled Persons Act. Some boroughs had called in help from outside agencies to suggest ways of re-organising their secretariats. Two had employed people from the Institute of Management Studies, two had been helped by the University of Brunel and three by staff and students of the local Polytechnics. Resistance to changes imposed from outside was apparent in the delaying tactics in some boroughs of the working parties set up to consider the new proposals. However three boroughs went over to area budgeting between 1975 and 1977 as a result of management studies which recognised the desire on the part of field-workers for more direct participation in the control of the money spent on services to clients. (The two "geographical" departments had given the area managers considerable autonomy from the time the area offices were created, in 1971).

Area budgeting, as far as aids and adaptations were concerned was, however, still on trial in two boroughs and in a third some unease had been expressed over the ceiling of £300 "for any one adaptation in any one year to any one client." At 1976 prices this meant that any major adaptation would have to proceed in piecemeal fashion and the £300 ceiling would also exclude the purchase and installation of a number of aids.

In another borough it was considered inexpedient to attempt area budgeting for adaptations but a sum of £2,000 was allocated to each of its three areas for aids. Because it was also recognised that demand for aids might vary from area to area money from a centrally-controlled "float" of £1,000 was made available as needed. Even so the sum allocated for aids in the financial year 1976–77 was only £9,000. Indeed another director spoke frankly about area budgeting as the most effective means of cutting expenditure on all personal aids and on telephones in particular. Once area managers have to find the money for them out of their own area resources, he said, they made certain that their fieldworkers apply all the criteria laid down by the London Boroughs Association before putting in an adaptation.

In another borough which operated area budgeting agreement about responsibility for ordering aids and where they were to be stored had not been resolved by the time this research ended. This borough had formerly allowed its areas to order aids as they saw fit but this was now recognised as uneconomic. The imminent appoint-ment of a head occupational therapist was seen by a working party set up to discuss the whole question of aids and adaptations as a threat to area autonomy.

As far as could be determined the system of area budgeting in the few Greater London boroughs that are experimenting with it does little to alter the prevailing hierarchical patterns of organisation, and

117

control by the centre, at least as far as the provision of aids and adaptations is concerned, is likely to continue in the majority of boroughs if only to ensure uniform standards of appropriateness and quality.

Many services supplied by social services departments involve the use of staff from other departments. The installation of many aids, and the provision of adaptations, is frequently dependent on direct labour controlled by other local authority departments. It is therefore important that the director of the social services, the newest arrival on the local authority scene, is on amicable terms with the heads of such departments as engineering, architecture, technical services, building works, or whatever their current titles may be.

A number of assistant directors of research and development departments were turning their attention to problems of reorganisation at the time of this study. Some felt that only a thorough-going upheaval and the creation of entirely new divisions such as, for example, a family case-work division, could approximate to what the Seebohm committee had in mind. Others were content to advocate piecemeal changes by creating new consultant posts for large groups, such as "the over-eighties" or "the adolescents" just one level below that of an assistant director, and heading a division that still spanned both residential and day care. In still other boroughs specialist posts for fieldworkers were being created at a newly constituted rank somewhere between that of qualified social worker and all-purpose, supervisory senior social worker. These new posts reflected not only a growing concern about the need for more specialist supervision for unqualified social workers but often an attempt to scale down the vastness of the new social services departments to a more manageable size.

With the exception of two boroughs, none of these new specialist posts carried as their sole responsibility the efficient initiation, expansion, organisation and supervision of services for the disabled. More often than not, they were combined with similar duties connected with the welfare of the elderly. This combination of duties was not always a matter of overt policy but rather a simple question of the number of posts at a particular level that were on the establishment. On the other hand, in some boroughs where deliberate efforts were being made to co-ordinate services for the elderly and the physically handicapped, the clerks were still obliged to enter applications for an aid or adaptation for the elderly under a different code from a similar application on behalf of a physically handicapped person and the computer continued to separate what the policy-makers had attempted to join.

But as far as the structure of the social services departments is concerned it is interesting and informative to look at the use made by social workers of existing consultants. If these are based on the secretariat, social workers from the areas often find themselves unable to make time to visit them. On the other hand, if the consultants visit area offices to hold "surgeries" at stated intervals, urgent cases may prevent social workers from being in the area offices. There is evidence to suggest that, despite the willingness of the consultants to help and advise fieldworkers, contact is devitalised either by geographical distance, rank or the fact that many of the consultants hail from an early, pre-Seebohm era.

One of the ways of making sure that such expertise is not under-used would be to call case-conferences frequently, especially when the opinions of fieldworkers over, for example, the need for a major adaptation, clash with the views of highly placed officers in the secretariat.

Although one assistant director was opposed to what he saw as a "Parkinsonian" expansion of staff at the lower end of the hierarchy, the one point on which all the other senior officers interviewed agreed was that much more clerical back-up was needed for the services for the disabled and that more typists were needed both in the pool and attached to individual units.[15]

This chapter has shown how both the fieldwork staff and the secretariat staff of social services departments fit in to a hierarchical structure headed by directors with considerable power vested in them by the social services committees to whom they are responsible. It has also shown that, as the installation of many aids and the provision of adaptations more often than not involves the assistance of the staff of other local authority departments, it is most desirable that a policy of mutual respect and cooperation operates at all levels of the several departments involved in the work. This will be just as essential when local authority housing departments take over some of the administrative duties now performed by social services staff.[16] This obvious truth is stated because, even in those boroughs that paid lip service to corporate management, relationships between the staff of different borough departments often appeared to be lukewarm and tentative.

A good working relationship with the head of the housing department merits high priority. Good liaison with area health authority staff is equally important if only to resolve some of the problems inherent in the financing of aids that lie in the "grey areas" which are discussed on page 127 of the next chapter. It should also be remembered that area health authorities have the power to purchase on behalf of social services (welfare) departments at contract prices and that since 1976 the introduction of joint finance has further highlighted the importance of good relationships between health authorities and social services departments.

Co-operation with voluntary organisations has become still more important as community services increase. The specialist "community officer", based on the social services departments and with duties that include recruiting and briefing volunteers to help, is a comparatively new post and, in the Greater London area, was to be found in only three boroughs at the time of this study. It is not shown on any of the tables, because there is still a good deal of debate about what the function of such a community officer should be and where he should be based, but a "coordinator of voluntary services" appears in Table 10.

Criticism is constantly levelled at the increased "bureaucratisation" of social work that has occurred since the new social services departments were established. This overlooks the essentially caring work done by the majority of the members of the secretariat on behalf of the clients for whom they help to provide services. It is a mistake to confuse "organisation" with "bureaucratisation" for some of the patterns of organisation that have evolved in the Greater London boroughs, notably those of the rehabilitation teams, allow all the staff concerned with the provision of aids and adaptations a degree of involvement which can only be of benefit to disabled clients.

NOTES

1. The terms "hierarchical" and "geographical" were used by the University of Brunel's Institute of Organisation and Social Studies (BIOSS) in its study, *Social Services Departments* (London, 1974). It reports that "seven hundred staff from 120 of the 174 authorities accepted the need for a hierarchical structure". See p. 27.

2. Key posts in the new departments of social services were frequently created with specific members of the old Welfare, Health and Children's Departments in mind. These departments were disbanded but many senior staff took their attitudes – and their administrative habits – across with them. This meant that, in addition to an unduly large number of "consultant" posts at Principal Officer level and above some of the new directors were hampered from the outset in their attempts to re-think policies in terms of more recently defined concepts of "need".

3. *The Annual Abstract of Statistics for Greater London*, Vol. 9, 1974.

4. This must not be confused with "community" work. Being based on an area office does not mean that social workers are "community workers"; they are case-workers working from an office as their base.

5. The Seebohm Report suggested one area office to a population of about 50,000 to 100,000 and a minimum of at least 10–12 social workers to each area office. *Op. cit.*, para. 59. However, Circular 45/71 in Section 6, *Staffing*, thought that the average county borough would need a range of 21–33 social work staff (including trainees and assistants) per 100,000. "Some Inner London boroughs have figures well above this range and undoubtedly require these higher staff ratios because of the concentration of problems in heavily populated areas." For these a range of 50–60 fieldwork staff was to be aimed at. The figures for Lewisham, given above on page 51–3 were, in 1974, still well below those suggested in the circular.

6. See Chapter Eight, p. 156, Section 2, *The Intake Team*. During 1975 there were two strikes by social workers and auxiliary staff in Inner London boroughs, both officially sponsored by NALGO. See Chapter Eight, p. 167.

7 Reasons for this includes lack of graduate qualifications; too little experience of casework and the fact that they were excluded from membership of the British Association of Social Workers. Many did get higher positions in the secretariat.

8. No mention of occupational therapists was included in the "Scheme of Conditions of Service" (Eighth edition, 1975) published by the National Council for Local Authorities' Administrative Professional, Technical and Clerical Services. Directors of Social Services were therefore in some dilemma as to whether to pay them at the same rate as untrained, unqualified social workers, and subject to the same salary bar, or to devise some means by which they could be paid as professionals at a grade commensurate with the three years' professional training that they had received. At the time of the study head occupational therapists in some boroughs were being paid at salary grades ranging from the top of the Administrative and Professional grade (AP 5) to that of Senior Officer

(SO 1 and SO 2). In some boroughs occupational therapists had gone i nto senior management posts as Principal Officers and in two boroughs, they had become assistant directors of social services. After the revised Whitley scale came into force, although salaries in the lower grades of occupational therapist still remained marginally higher than that of their health service counterparts, head occupational therapists in social services departments found themselves financially less well off than if they were to transfer to district health authorities. None of those interviewed felt that it would be proper for them to "change loyalties".

9 The rationale for employing domiciliary occupational therapists in local authority social services departments is given in Chapter X of the Seebohm Report, para. 325. Previously occupational therapists had always worked in a medical context – either in hospitals or under a MOH in local authority health departments. By 1975 the British Association of Occupational Therapists (BAOT) had been obliged to reword its requirements so that "access to a medical practitioner" was as acceptable as working under one. The superior salaries offered by some local authorities became a bitterly divisive issue.

10. The report of the working party of the Central Council for Education and Training in Social Work stressed the need for specialists with knowledge of the problems of the disabled to the extent that it considered it "imperative" to ask for a re-consideration of the structure of LASS Departments. CCETSW, op. cit., paper 9, p. 35.

11. See Neill, June, Fruin, D., and Goldberg, E. Matilda in "Reactions to Integration", Social Work Today, Vol. 4, No. 15, 1 November 1973. This study showed that work with the elderly and the disabled was given a very low priority on a scale of preferences compared with work with children and families although they constituted 62 per cent of all refusals. By inference, the principal specialist officer felt, social workers in area offices might be unhappy at having to include the significant number of physically handicapped clients in their caseloads, would tend to give a low degree of priority to those for whom they were required to provide a service and consequently fail to develop or improve the skills necessary to deal competently with the disabled and their families.

12. See Chapter Nine – "Getting the Aids to the Clients (2)", p. 178.

13. Only three years previously, a clerk similarly graded as Clerical 2 would have been expected to deal with all the services detailed except holidays and outings and probably issue concessionary bus fares as well. The issuing of concessionary bus fares is still frequently added to the duties of either an aids clerk or a clerk whose duty it is, among others, to monitor the progress of adaptations. Blau, P.M. *The Dynamics of Bureaucracy: A Study of Interpersonal Relations in Two Agencies* (Chicago, 1963), p. 213.

14. See also *The Remedial Professions, op. cit.,* p. 40, par. 16, which said in 1973 that "proper clerical, secretarial and *portering* support must also be provided". (Researcher's italics).

15. See Joint Circular DOE 59/78.

16. See Joint Circular DOE 59/78.

CHAPTER SIX

APPLIANCES, AIDS TO HOME NURSING,
AIDS TO DAILY LIVING, EQUIPMENT.
SOME DEFINITIONS WITH COMMENT

Appliances are prescribed by consultants in the National Health Service and are thus chargeable to the Service. Aids to home nursing, though not prescribed by consultants, are also a health need and therefore charged to the National Health Service. Aids to daily living are a welfare, not a health need, and are thus charged to social services departments.

This theoretical distinction is not always clearcut in practice. There is a large area of overlap – "a grey area" – between aids to home nursing and aids to daily living. This can lead to disputes about who should be providing what and which service should be paying for it. Such disputes can lead to delays in meeting the needs of disabled people or even in needs not being met at all. Disabled people in need of appliances and nursing aids tend to fare better than those in need of aids to daily living. This study deals only with the provision of aids to daily living which are the responsibility of London social services departments. Unfortunately many people working with the physically handicapped use the terms wrongly and interchangeably and a brief description of appliances follows in order to make sure that the reader knows what is not included.

Appliances are supplied to patients who are in hospital or attending hospital as out-patients. A medical consultant who prescribes them must first satisfy himself that they are needed for reasons that are not solely cosmetic. They are then ordered by the hospitals direct from companies with whom the Department of Health and Social Security has negotiated contracts.[1] They are measured for, fitted by and issued by specialist fitters sent to the hospitals by these contractors or by trained technical staff at Department of Health and Social Security Appliance Centres.[2] Technical officers of the Department of Health and Social Security may control quality by inspecting manufacture at the contractor's premises. The quality[3] and the kind of appliances are therefore controlled at source, and the risk of their being unsuitable to the patient's clinical condition is theoretically minimal.

Appliances include false limbs, prostheses such as false noses, ears and breasts, artificial eyes, surgical footwear and trusses. Most of them are issued free of charge. But payment by the patient is required for abdominal supports, elastic stockings, anklets, knee caps and thigh pieces; charges are also made for bespoke and stock wigs.[4] Certain clients e.g. those on supplementary benefit and others exempted from prescription charges[5] are also exempted from making any payment for any appliances.

Since 1972 some aids to mobility, namely invalid tricycles, "Invacars", and "wheelchairs for permanent use" may be supplied on the request of "any doctor giving General Medical Services in the National Health Service or a Local Authority employed Doctor", unless the doctor himself considers assessment by a medical consultant to be essential in cases of very severe disability.[6]

A letter was sent by the Department of Health and Social Security to all general medical practitioners on 18 August 1972 stating that "by agreement" they "may also refer a patient to the local authority" for "help in describing a patient's particular disabilities and home circumstances". In practice this has meant that general medical practitioners have come to rely heavily on the time and services of occupational therapists and social workers employed by local authority social services departments. The same letter also stated that "the arrangements under which local authorities supply wheelchairs for temporary use will continue".

At the time, in 1971, when local welfare services were brought into the new local authority social services departments the number and quality of wheelchairs in stock for temporary use varied from borough to borough. They were there to lend to disabled and elderly people coming to stay with relatives for specific family occasions such as weddings and christenings and for brief visits from elderly and possibly handicapped relatives who would enjoy being wheeled into the local parks. Stocks might also be kept for use by physically handicapped residents going on holidays organised and subsidised by the boroughs, and for other specially planned occasions such as Christmas shopping expeditions and parties. Such loans were meant to be short-term, for clearly defined purposes and for clearly defined periods of time.

By 1974–75 many directors of social services departments were becoming aware that this system of lending wheelchairs for temporary use needed review. Far too many wheelchairs were, in practice, being lent for considerably longer periods and to clients whose clinical condition necessitated chairs for permanent use and who were waiting for chairs from the Department of Health and Social Security appliance centres. Without these temporary loans they would be housebound. On the other hand, their provision masked their need for chairs more carefully designed to meet their special needs. Loans of social service department chairs for so-called temporary use frequently exceeded six months in twenty-five of the 32 boroughs and the City. Ten boroughs reported "temporary" loans of over one year and five of more than three years.[7] Because all clients needing wheelchairs for any but the most temporary occasions had medically diagnosed conditions, the provision of such chairs was considered by many directors of social services to be more properly a matter for the area health authorities. It was also arguable that responsibility for wheelchairs on short term loan might also be removed from social services departments to avoid a clumsy overlap in administration.

By the end of 1975, three social services departments had discontinued supplying wheelchairs as a matter of policy. Two boroughs had issued none since the local authority social services departments had come into being and three had consistently referred clients to health departments or voluntary agencies.[8] The remaining twenty-eight were continuing to lend chairs but were not replacing those in need of expensive repairs or maintenance and had begun to call in chairs after stated periods of time in the hope that the inconvenience to the user would lead to speedier delivery of a chair supplied by the National Health Service which would be more suited to the patient's clinical needs. For those clients in genuine need of a wheelchair on a short term loan this is nevertheless an alarming situation particularly as many health authorities have also reduced their stock.

During the summer of 1975 the long delays experienced by many disabled people in obtaining medically prescribed wheelchairs from Department of Health and Social Security appliance centres was a matter of considerable concern. These delays were variously blamed on the Three Day Week,[9] which had restricted supplies of essential materials to manufacturers under contract to the Department and also on the expansion of the private market for the same manufacturers as a result of the war in the Middle East. That delays also occurred in the latter part of 1973 – six months before the research reported in this study began – was confirmed by the results of an investigation undertaken on behalf of the Disablement Services Branch of the Department of Health and Social Security. Although not published until 1977[10] this report was based on material collected from appliance centres in June 1973 and on interviews conducted in the following six months. Its findings are very similar to the verbal reports offered by many senior staff in social services departments and occupational therapists throughout 1975 and 1976 in the Greater London area.

Section 2 of the report, page 4, mentions delays which merit serious concern :

124

"The survey showed clearly that there were often considerable delays in supplying wheelchairs; for instance, over a fifth (22 per cent) of chairs took at least eight weeks to be delivered. In the circumstances, the DHSS might usefully examine why these delays occur to discover what steps can be taken to shorten the waiting period."

In two centres, both of which had distribution problems, "well over a quarter of wheelchairs took at least eight weeks to be delivered." This confirms the experience of clients living in those Greater London boroughs served by one such centre in 1976. Service in these areas is known to have improved by 1976 except for special orders for custom-built chairs. For these every appliance centre is obliged to wait until the manufacturer finds it convenient to make and deliver the chair.

The investigation also showed that many more disabled clients had received a second wheelchair than verbal reports in 1975 to 1976 had implied.

Aids

No signature by a medical consultant or a general practitioner is needed before the issue of an aid. Thus, except in the case of wheelchairs, the distinction between aids and adaptations is simple and absolute. The distinction between *aids for home nursing*[11] and *aids for daily living*,[12] is much less clear. Its origin was in the separation of the functions of health and welfare into two different local authority departments under two different chief executives. As definition determines who has to pay the bill attempts at clarification have been frequent but to date no guidance from the Department of Health and Social Security has been forthcoming. It has been left to local authorites and area health authorities to make local decisions about payment for certain items.

Aids to Daily Living include certain small aids such as special can-openers and tap-turners, suction pads to keep kitchen equipment from slipping, teapot tippers, hot water bottle fillers, special knives and razors with long handles, nose-blowers, toilet paper suction holders, stocking aids, elastic shoe-laces and pick-up sticks which are clearly designed to help handicapped people to be independent and to live as normal a life as possible. So are some of the larger and more expensive aids like chairs with ejector seats and other chairs specially designed for arthritics and specially constructed kitchen equipment which provides people in wheelchairs with an independence they could not otherwise hope to achieve. Aids of this kind are clearly classified as *aids to daily living*, and as such chargeable against the social services departments' votes.

Bath aids, of which there are many varieties, have also been classified as aids to daily living by the mutual consent of all the Greater London boroughs. One assistant director of social services, formerly a chief nursing officer, expressed doubts about the advisability and safety of their being used without a nurse or nursing auxiliary in attendance. Similar doubts were expressed to the author by some occupational therapists and social workers. Bath aids, which include non-slip bath mats, bath seats, stools and boards and various kinds of handrails which can be fitted on to taps, make up the largest group of aids kept in stock. They are always bought in bulk and often automatically re-ordered at fixed intervals. Bath boards and stools are also the aids most frequently manufactured by the boroughs themselves in their training centres, day centres and sheltered workshops.

A request for a bath aid[13] is commonly believed to be the most frequent way in which disabled clients make their first approach to the Personal Social Services. Such clients may often be needing other help. This suggests that classification as an aid to daily living is appropriate, though the desirability of nursing supervision in their use would be a justification for the alternative definition.

Aids to Home Nursing. Whether the nursing is done by a district nurse or a relative an aid to home nursing would seem at first sight to be easy to identify. Rubber sheeting, a commode or chemical toilet, a bed cradle to keep blankets off a damaged limb, bedrests to support patients in the sitting position, a simple hoist to help them get into a sitting position, a bedtable to swing across the bed at mealtimes, a bookrest to help the convalescent read, a walking frame to help with the first steps when he starts to be up and about again ... it is not difficult to compile such a list. What is difficult is to distinguish between commodes used as a sickroom aid and commodes used to help a patient retain independence in daily living. If a battery-operated ripple mattress is used to prevent bedsores and constant lifting in the case of terminal illness then it is clearly an aid to home nursing, but how is a similar ripple mattress to be classified when it is issued to a client with a severe degenerative disease who may yet live for some months or even years? It is on the answer to such questions that the source of finance depends – whether the aid should be paid for by central government or local government. Nevertheless only two senior officers of the Greater London social services departments wished for a circular of guidance from the Department of Health and Social Security to help with the making of such decisions; one small authority accepted the decision of the community physician without any discussion; the twenty-nine remaining boroughs, including the City of London, continued to want as flexible approach as possible[14] so that decisions could be made after discussions between local authority staff and members of the Area Health Authority about certain "blocks" of aids, e.g. beds,[15] hoists and *ad hoc* decisions about other aids in specific circumstances and for "one-off" aids.

One borough, influenced by staff coming over from the former welfare department, continued to operate a simple criterion that had been in use since 1965 :

"As long as a district nurse is visiting the home the 'Aid' is an 'Aid to Home Nursing'. The moment she leaves the Aid becomes an 'Aid to Daily Living'. The Welfare Department will then pay for the Aid in cash or by replacement in kind."

In this borough a relative operating an aid counted as a "nurse" and only aids that could be operated by the patients themselves – and then only when a district nurse had ceased to visit – were classified as aids to daily living. In all the other boroughs a relative-operated hoist would have been classified as an "aid to daily living" or argued over as "grey".

"The grey areas" include every type of bed (divans, hospital type beds, beds with cot sides, low beds and high beds and very expensive electrically operated beds which can be adjusted at the touch of a switch), also mattresses (hard, soft and "ripple") and any make of portable hoist. Commodes and chemical toilets can also be subjects of prolonged disputes.[16]

All the social services departments in the Greater London boroughs used as guidelines lists based on those drawn up by health and welfare departments before 1965. Many of these lists had not been revised after the re-organisation of the National Health Service and the establishment of social services departments despite the vast increase in the number, variety and quality of aids available.[17] These lists, one usually headed "Nursing Aids" and the other often headed "Welfare Aids", are not unform throughout the Greater London boroughs and have as many variants as the staff concerned in drawing them up. Nor are such lists always uniform within the new boundaries of the area health authorities as some boroughs have more than one area health authority district within their boundaries and hospitals may serve more than one borough.[18]

Hospital Provision of Aids. In boroughs served by hospitals with catchment areas that included more than one health district there were local variations in the number and kind of aids supplied and paid for by the health service and those ordered by hospital staff but charged to the social services departments. In one borough served by two different hospitals from two different districts, one district was paying for the kind of aid that the other hospital had successfully succeeded in establishing as the responsibility of the personal social services. Such variations suggest that the whole question of financial responsibility for some aids to home nursing and some aids now classified as aids to daily living needs examination at a high level.

The most disputed issue at the time of this study was the provision of walking frames for patients discharged from hospital. The most common procedure in 1973–74 was for a member of the hospital staff to telephone the social services department to give the date of discharge to the patient's own home and to ask for a social worker to visit, measure the patient for a walking frame and see that one was supplied from the social services department stores or specially ordered.[19] This worked reasonably well if the patient was already on the caseload of an identifiable social worker and if a good stock of walking frames of different kinds and sizes had been maintained. But it was not unknown for newly discharged patients to wait as long as three weeks without a walking frame before a social worker found time to make a preliminary home visit. By the beginning of 1975 most hospitals were sending patients home with walking frames on loan until the social services department replaced them either in cash or kind. One director of social services had cut administrative cost to the bone by keeping a large supply of walking frames purchased by his department "at the hospital end". This also ensured that patients returned home with walking frames suited to their clinical condition, which they had already learnt to use in hospital and to which they were accustomed. Undoubtedly some of these aids to daily living might from time to time be used as short-term aids for home nursing. The director was fully aware of this, but argued that on their return to the hospital they might well end up as long term aids to daily living. "It would", he said, "all come out in the wash" and "was greatly to the benefit of the hospital and social service staff as well as to the most important person of all, the client".

This approach did not, however, meet with the approval of the majority of directors and administrative officers who were unwilling to use social services money for health service responsibilities at any time. In three other boroughs however social workers refused to issue walking frames unless the patient had been properly measured for them at a hospital or by a general practitioner and they had been prescribed as necessary. They argued that the indiscriminate issue of walking frames could be damaging to the patient both physically and psychologically. If they had to be prescribed by a general practitioner then they should be classified as appliances and paid for either directly by hospitals or out of health service money under the same rules already governing payment on the part of clients receiving appliances. On the other hand domiciliary occupational therapists expressed doubt about the ability of doctors to prescribe walking frames accurately as nothing in their training had prepared them for this kind of "nuts and bolts" prescribing. Some general practitioners, who were reluctant to prescribe wheelchairs without the help of domiciliary occupational therapists because they did not find the manual of instruction from the Department an adequate substitute for experience, might well be equally reluctant to measure for walking frames.

With the exception of walking frames, aids for daily living ordered by hospital staff were seldom subject to dispute. Directors of social services, aware both of the limited expertise of the majority of generic social workers and of the importance of good liaison with the hospitals, made it their policy, throughout the Greater London boroughs, to issue such aids without question and with maximum speed. This policy decision was, however, frequently questioned by the domiciliary occupational therapists employed by social services departments who felt that hospital-based members of their profession, divorced from the need to find the money to pay for them, were inclined to send clients home either with too many aids, with aids unsuited to their home environment or with "lists as long as your arm". Three head occupational therapists and two senior occupational therapists, employed by local authorities, confessed to "dumping aids back on the hospital"; every domiciliary occupational therapist interviewed felt steps should be taken to avoid raising false hopes in clients by making unrealistic lists of aids and all the domiciliary occupational therapists saw hospital-issued aids as one of the more conspicuous examples of waste, especially if there were no domiciliary occupational therapist or social worker following up the case to ensure their safe and continuing use.[20]

There was some evidence, on the other hand, of duplication with patients recently discharged from hospital receiving the same aids – or different aids – from hospitals, district nurses and social services departments. This confusion somewhat undermined the confidence of patients in the value of clinical prescription.

By the end of 1975, two directors of social services had simplified administrative procedure by allowing the head occupational therapist in the teaching hospitals serving their borough to order aids at their discretion and without prior consultation up to a ceiling of £70 in the one borough and £50 in the other. The head occupational therapist with discretionary powers up to £70 was further empowered to keep a permanent and renewable stock of as many kinds of aids to daily living, chargeable against the social

129

services department vote, as she considered necessary and in quantities best calculated to ensure speedy delivery without obsolescence. This control of stock by a very senior hospital based occupational therapist had the additional value of ensuring that the quality of the aids kept in stock by the social services department of the boroughs served by the hospital was also kept up-to-date. Most aids to daily living, irrespective of who ordered them, were supplied by commercial manufacturers. The sources of supply and the different methods of storing them are discussed in the next chapter.

One more term – equipment – needs to be explained, as the latest leaflet[21] issued for the disabled re-introduces a term that had fallen into disuse or been used very loosely.

Equipment

The first mention of equipment comes in the National Insurance (Industrial Injuries) Act 1946 which granted permissive powers to the Minister to secure the provision and maintenance of "equipment and appliances", but did not define them. The health departments of the old Metropolitan boroughs tended to list aids for home nursing under the title of Medical Loan Equipment, a nomenclature that was also used by branches of the British Red Cross Society and the St John's Ambulance Brigade. Over the years the word "equipment" thus acquired health rather than medical connotations.

The recent Department of Health and Social Security leaflet attempted to define it as follows :

"Equipment is mainly distinguishable by size (not usually portable) and is a term used to describe any standard article prescribed to assist functional ability, or a standard article specially adapted to fit the requirement of an individual".

The emphasis both on function and on modification of a standard article for what is presumably a long-term need implies that equipment, as defined in 1976, is more likely to apply to the kind of provision made by local authority social services departments – that is to aids to daily living – than to short-term articles lent to assist patients being nursed at home.

On page 2 of the leaflet the association with local authority social services departments is further re-inforced by a reference to the invaluable booklets called "Equipment for the Disabled"[22] first published in 1966 by the National Fund for Research into Crippling Diseases and still edited at Mary Marlborough Lodge, Nuffield Orthopaedic Centre, Oxford, although later titles in the series refer to work undertaken on behalf of the Department of Health and Social Security.

The titles of the booklets so far published include "Clothing and Dressing for Adults", "Disabled Mother", "Disabled Child" and "Leisure and Gardening", all of which suggest that the overall title of "Equipment" is slanted towards aids to daily living and provision by social services departments. On the other hand the first booklet published – now in its fourth edition – is called "Wheelchairs and Outdoor Transport". Wheelchairs are a National Health Service responsibility. The term "equipment" therefore remains ambiguous.

The kinds of non-portable aids that suggest themselves are electrically-operated ceiling track hoists and specially installed baths with chairs that can be swung over and into them. These are obviously non portable and equally obviously aids to daily living. The riddle "when is a hoist not a hoist" which perplexes so many administrators need not be further complicated by answering "when it is equipment". A hoist may be either an aid to home nursing or an aid to daily living.

Because of this ambiguity the word "equipment" will be avoided in all subsequent chapters.

NOTES

1. See *Provision of Medical and Surgical Appliances*, (National Health Services (Welsh Office) 1974), known as "The Orange Book" and *Surgical Appliances Contract 1976* (DHSS (DSB 4A) 1976) known as "The Yellow Book".

2. Four Appliance Centres serve the Greater London Area, situated at Balham, Euston Road, Ealing and Kingston.

3. Paragraphs 61 and 62 of "The Orange Book" refer specifically to the Quality of Appliances to be provided which "are required to be of best workmanship and design and functionally efficient; only suitable materials of good quality should be used in their manufacture".

4. Under the terms of the National Health Service (Charges) Regulations Act, April 1st 1971. In January 1976 an abdominal support cost £2.00 and a bespoke wig £7.50.

5. Other people exempt from charges are old age pensioners, war pensioners and children still at school. People on low incomes may also receive discretionary help towards the cost.

6. On August 18th 1972 a letter, often called "the doctor's letter" went out from the Chief Medical Officer of the DHSS to all registered general medical practitioners advising them on how to assess patients for wheelchairs. A booklet was available on application about what models were available and where to send patients if they felt they lacked the necessary knowledge and qualifications to decide for themselves which wheelchair would be more suitable and what modifications might be needed.

7. The record length of loan was of the same chair being lent to the same client for fifteen years and through three periods of reorganisation of health, welfare and social services. This borough had 104 wheelchairs in stock of which 49 had punctured tyres or were otherwise in need of repair.

8. Only one borough reported that it had never issued wheelchairs for temporary use. Nor had the area health authority, now in a roughly equivalent district. Both had relied on the Red Cross, although clients had complained of how old some Red Cross wheelchairs were and how uncomfortable.

9. Legislation for the Three Day Week was announced on 14 December 1973 and took effect from midnight on 31 December. It ended at midnight on 7 March. (Evidence suggests that it became expedient to blame shortages on it in excess of the real shortages it occasioned.)

10. Fenwick, D., *Wheelchairs and their users: a survey among users of National Health wheelchairs in England and Wales, to establish their characteristics and attitudes to the operation of the wheelchair service.* OPCS (HMSO, 1977).

11. Also frequently referred to simply as "Nursing aids" (not to be confused with auxiliary aides) "bedroom aids" and "sickroom aids" by staff who used to work in health and welfare departments.

12. Usually called ADLs in health and welfare departments, which also helps to distinguish them from social work "aides" who are in fact "social work assistants".

13. Bath aids may be issued unnecessarily, sometimes through hospitals, to people with no baths; often to people who would prefer to "wash down" because they have dizzy spells, lack the

131

confidence to bath alone or cannot afford enough hot water to fill the bath above the level of a bath stool. They may also be issued as a palliative to the consciences of social workers who have failed to understand the underlying problems that led to the request in the first instance, and by untrained workers who lack the professional confidence to say "No" or the courage not to provide a client with something tangible. On the other hand where a hot bath can be a means of easing pain, as with certain kinds of arthritis, their issue is valuable and necessary. Nevertheless one assistant director said he would like to "declare an amnesty on all unused bath aids" so that relatives could hand them in at the nearest police station.

14.   At one such discussion a high official in a social services department succeeded in "swapping" an agreed number of ripple mattresses plus batteries, costing around £38.00 each, against over £200 fees at £3.50 a time, submitted by GPs who had examined physically handicapped patients to determine whether they were able to go on a local authority subsidised holiday. Another officer had persuaded the AHA to take responsibility for issuing and paying for all beds against the understanding that all hoists would be regarded as aids to daily living chargeable to the SSD vote. The DHSS has since issued guidance about payment of doctors' fees but in a borough with two separate AHA districts within its boundaries the AHA in July 1976, was paying them in the northern district whilst the SSD continued to pay them in the southern half of the borough.

15.   One head occupational therapist persuaded a local hospital to buy beds at the lower contracted price charged to health authorities and to store them free. The cost was, however, met from the social services budget.

16.   One unfortunate client had to use a bedpan for six months before it was decided that a commode would be an aid to daily living and not an aid to home nursing.

17.   An examination of LCC welfare files in the fifties and sixties pinpoints the first reference to whether an aid was a nursing aid or an aid to daily living in a memorandum from the Department of Public Health dated 23 August 1956 about which vote should pay for a "Lazy Tongs". Three weeks later an "Easicarrie" hoist, then the only welfare aid also on the list of nursing aids, became an issue to be resolved by amicable discussion between the two departments concerned.

18.   The "firm view" expressed in The Green Paper, *The Future Structure of the National Health Service* (HMSO, 1970) that "The new area health authorities must serve the same areas for which the new local authorities will be providing social services" did not become reality and the hope that even in London, " . . . no borough will be divided for health purposes" was not always fulfilled.

19.   Procedures of ordering can also differ according to who is doing the ordering. In one borough anything ordered by the hospital occupational therapist was immediately granted while the medical social worker who was now, since 1974, in the employ of the social services department had to go through the same lengthy chain of command as an inexperienced and untrained social worker. The speed with which an aid for a patient discharged from hospital reached that patient was therefore determined by whoever happened to order it.

20.   One hospital-based occupational therapist admitted to sending "lists that might seem outrageous" as the only way of goading social workers into making a much-needed home visit This highlights the shortage of social workers interested in, or feeling confident about, working with physically handicapped clients.

21.   Aids for the Disabled (DHSS, 1976), p. 1.

22.   "Equipment for the Disabled" can be obtained from 2 Faredown Drive, Portslade, Brighton BN4 2BB.

CHAPTER SEVEN

AIDS : SOURCES OF SUPPLY; SAFETY OF AIDS; STORAGE

Since the greatly enhanced demand generated as a result of the Chronically Sick and Disabled Persons Act 1970, commercial manufacturers have had a strong impact on the number and type of aids provided. In addition, the strengthening of pressure groups and a growth in the formation of new local and national associations for people suffering from specific diseases have increased client awareness of what is available.

As one ex-welfare worker turned administrator said "clients are not *innocuous* any more, they know what they want and won't settle for less". One warehouseman criticised social workers for taking clients to the Disabled Living Foundation[1] where they "filled their heads with all sorts of ideas as well as the ones they went there with in the first place". Yet another warehouseman, whose views on social policy differed from those of the social services committee who employed him said "I always forget to order geriatric chairs because whenever I had them in stock these young occupational therapists would come and see them and take them straight to their clients". Such remarks indicate the importance of all levels of staff coming to terms with changing definitions of "need". On the other hand it would be equally unreasonable if public money were to be spent on what clients "want" or "fancy" unless their choice is also the most suitable for overcoming or minimising their disability.

Every director of social services interviewed insisted that the identified need of the client determined the kind and cost of the aid supplied. A more expensive aid would not be supplied if a cheaper and equally appropriate model would meet that need equally well. In theory the psychological importance of the cosmetic quality of an aid was recognised but all too often the attractiveness of the aids provided depended on the knowledge and attitudes of the fieldworkers recommending them and the clerks and warehousemen ordering them. Decisions about cosmetic quality, particularly if extra expenditure is involved, need to be made at a level high enough to carry weight – by a consultant aids and adaptations officer or a head occupational therapist. Old out-dated and ugly aids had been called in by occupational therapists in three boroughs, and by an aids clerk in a fourth; in order to replace them with more attractive, up-to-date models. In two boroughs occupational therapists said that if "grotty" aids came in for repair they seized the chance to replace them with better ones. It is fortunate that the competitiveness of the commercial market means that the cosmetic qualities of aids receive due attention from the manufacturers, whether or not social services departments insist on their improvement.

1. *The Commercial Market*

The availability of large sums of public money with which to buy aids had led to a greatly expanded market for them. The rapid proliferation of commercial suppliers has undoubtedly complicated the problem of procurement. In the Fifties and Sixties there were relatively few commercial firms producing aids, Occupational therapists often made the more simple aids themselves, improvising such things as tea-tippers and bottle holders; other simple inexpensive aids such as suction egg cups, angled cutlery and knitting gadgets could be obtained from Government Training Centres.[2] By the 1970s even the simplest aids tended to be commercially produced. Expressed demand is now high enough to ensure that the commercial market is profitable although it still remains for the most part small and specialised. Many small manufacturers make up aids to their own design and it can be difficult for buyers to choose between them except on grounds of cost or – and this is an important factor – delivery dates. Some of the larger firms now employ travelling salesmen who visit social services departments in order to publicise their more costly aids and to introduce new designs. Occupational therapists and aids clerks complained at times of having been subjected to "hard selling". One large agent which distributed aids for a number of small firms hired coaches to take local authority occupational therapists and aids clerks from London to Harrogate for a trade exhibition in 1974. Annual trade exhibitions, paid for in part by the manufacturers who take stands and in part by the Department of Health and Social Security, are a good way of disseminating the latest information about the aids available and the open competition at such exhibitions can be assumed to have some affect on keeping prices down. Nevertheless it would appear that many of the prices remain unduly high given the cost of the labour and materials involved, simply because there are still comparatively few manufacturers interested in making aids. Some manufacturers of standard equipment are however beginning to enter the aids market and are adapting their machinery at times when the market for routine goods is low to do special "runs" of articles suitable for the disabled. These include special cut-away sinks and modified gas or electric ovens. These always cost more than standard versions of the same items.

In order to provide disabled people with some form of independent guidance on what aids to choose the Consumers' Association published a book in 1974 which covers a wide variety of aids such as aids for bathing, dressing, cooking, eating, drinking, lifting, walking, cleaning floors, etc., with clear diagrams. The forewords points out :

"The aids market is small and constantly changing; what is available now may not be made in six months time but new ideas may have been developed."

Many of the people in local authority social services departments who order aids from commercial sources have developed a high degree of sensitivity to the changes in the market and have become adept at "shopping around" for the best value in terms of both delivery dates as well as price. On the other hand, firms which are willing to hold over their bills until the beginning of the next financial year, or who are willing to lend equipment until the money is forthcoming to buy it, gain an edge on their competitors. Firms who are good about replacing faulty equipment without argument are also considered favourably, provided the faults are not too frequent. Most firms make substantial reductions if aids are bought in bulk but this carries with it a danger of built-in obsolescence both of design and the materials used.

A number of commercial aids are imported from foreign countries, especially Sweden and Germany. They are usually supplied by wholesalers in the Midlands who then have to make costly deliveries to clients living elsewhere. Because of balance of payment difficulties and the falling value of the pound there has been a recent tendency to try to "Buy British". But many of the people involved in recommending and ordering aids had little knowledge of similar aids being made in Britain although in at least one such case a comparable aid was being manufactured within the boundaries of the borough in which they were working. Local Polytechnics have at times produced cheaper alternatives to foreign aids but care has to be taken to avoid infringing patents.

2. Aids made in borough workshops

Many boroughs have long used sheltered workshops as a source of supply for aids. Bedblocks, for example, are frequently made by mentally handicapped people attending day centres and also wedge-shaped removable wooden ramps for wheelchairs. Some borough workshops are able to produce more complicated items. One of the most famous of these, the St Pancras workshops, has been supplying a number of boroughs, including the borough of Camden in which it is now situated, for over thirty years and has lent its name to articles such as the St Pancras pick-up stick.

At the time of this study it was sending wooden items of high quality and finish to five other boroughs and five area health authorities at very competitive prices. These included kitchen stools, kitchen trolleys, bathseats, bath stools, bathboards and geriatric chairs. It also produces wooden parts for some of the "Possum" units (patient-operated electronic selector mechanisms) which are manufactured under licence for the Department of Health and Social Security. Unfortunately this workshop has no facilities for working in metal or plastic and demand for many of the items that were once popular has fallen off as clients begin to insist on bathseats with aluminium frames and trolleys made of metal and plastic which are at once lighter and more "contemporary" in taste. Such workshops are however still useful for "one-off" aids made to suit special individual needs.

Only three Greater London boroughs had workshops for making metal goods as well as wooden ones. The London Borough of Merton, for example, kept a store of gas-piping of many different lengths together with similar pipes set at a variety of angles ready to join up to provide handrails and bannisters with awkward bends. This meant that any such needs could be dealt with rapidly and also that the cost of materials, labour and installation were greatly reduced. Only semi-skilled labour was required but if necessary the instructor in metal work could also undertake highly skilled work.[3] Large numbers of metal toilet surrounds and simple walking frames were also being made under his tutelage in 1975 and any surplus stock was sold to neighbouring boroughs.

Only one borough had workshops equipped for working with plastic although two more were contemplating the necessary equipment at the time of the study.

Work on a more modest scale is done in the sheltered workshops of many other boroughs, more often than not by mentally-handicapped adults. Wooden bedblocks are among the simplest items made but bed-tables, trolleys and removable wooden ramps are also part of their routine production. Wooden bath stools with cork seats, ordered in bulk by the welfare departments of the Sixties are no longer in demand as the cork stains and they are therefore not re-usable by other clients.

With the exception of portable ramps, most of the wooden aids, however well made, have gone out of fashion. In addition the cost of instructors who have the qualities needed to supervise mentally handicapped pupils, together with the fact that output cannot hope to

136

average that of normal workers in factories, makes the manufacture of even the simplest aids uneconomic. Three boroughs continued to maintain such workshops in the belief that their value in terms of therapeutic help to the people making them outweighed economic considerations. Two boroughs felt that, with the increased availability of commercial aids, it was pointless not to buy more durable, although more expensive, aids direct from manufacturers. In the remaining boroughs the number of such aids made in sheltered workshops and the number of places where they made them varied widely according to different policies and the availability of suitable instructors. There was a shortage of instructors throughout the Greater London area but the social services departments of the Inner London boroughs, who could still count on the services of instructors provided by the Inner London Education Authority in some of their day centres, appeared to be at an advantage compared with most of the Outer London boroughs.

One of the problems of asking disabled people, especially people with mental handicaps, to make aids for other disabled people is how much they can be paid without losing benefits from the Department of Health and Social Security; and also how much to pay them in comparison with commercial employment. One County borough, adjacent to Greater London, has solved the problem by taking the cost of the raw materials and the manufacturers' price, deducting the former from the latter and paying the person making the aid the difference, whether it is made in a sheltered workshop or in the client's own home. When payment is made on a weekly basis, however, and not for individual articles, relatives have been known to protest about "slave labour". Rates of payment at adult training centres, sheltered workshops and day centres coming under social services departments are fixed by the local authority concerned. Since these centres are run on a non-commercial basis, and do not necessarily demand of those attending a full day's work or a standard output, the payments vary a good deal. Hospital day centres for the mentally handicapped may also undertake work as a means of education and training under sub-contracts arranged by the local authority but again the rates paid vary very considerably because of the rehabilitative nature of the work. Only one example of piece-work done at home was found during the study. This was for pillow-cases to fit odd-shaped cushions and pillows supplied commercially for clients with special need for support but supplied without spare pillow-cases or washable covers.[4] Rates for piece-work vary. In one borough the worker was paid the difference between the cost of the materials used and the estimated commercial price. In the majority of boroughs it is believed that the rates are considerably lower than for any commercially made equivalent.

137

Keeping the sheltered workshops in production, as distinct from workshops where trained technicians make special aids, involves decisions about policy which are not easy to make. These decisions are made still more difficult by the obvious pleasure clients might take in the more sophisticated, up-dated, chromium and plastic aids available from commercial manufacturers. Who is to benefit? The handicapped person making an aid or the handicapped person receiving it?

The one great advantage of aids made in borough workshops over commercially manufactured aids is that their availability and safety can be controlled at source. No such control can be exercised over commercial aids which are not made under contract to local authority social services departments or, as in the case of appliances supplied by the National Health Service, under licence to the Department of Health and Social Security.

3. *Other Sources of Supply*

(a) *Aids made by employees of social services departments*
Occupational therapists have always been good at making simple one-off aids but lack the ability to handle certain materials in the way that technicians can. Ideally the best source of the one-off aid is a qualified technician based on a social services department or a sound practical man, possibly paid at a "Miscellaneous" grade,[5] who will bring imagination as well as common sense to the task of providing a special aid for a special circumstance. A gadget to hold a milk bottle so that a quadriplegic mother could feed her new-born child was one of the examples quoted. Another was a specially made bath hammock for a spinal bifida child who was also blind. This left the mother's arms free and minimised the child's fear of the water. Aids and adaptations officers have been known to take prototypes to manufacturers and also to badger them into modifying existing aids.[6] Only four of the Greater London boroughs employed such people at the time of this study. Yet with his own van, his own bag of tools and a good workbench at a day centre, a technical assistant of this kind can also be invaluable for delivering aids, for instructing clients in their use and for repairing aids. Technical assistants can contribute greatly to the quality of life of the disabled people living in the boroughs that employ them and indirectly to the lives of other disabled people throughout the country who enjoy the benefit of their inventions.

(b) *Aids made by educational institutions*
A general need to economise has led those social services departments who do not employ skilled technicians of their own to ask Universi-

ties, Polytechnics and Colleges of Further Education to make one-off aids and prototypes of new inventions. No commercial firms are willing to make one-off aids, nor will they make prototypes unless a specified number of orders can be guaranteed.

For "one-off" aids institutions such as the Royal College of Art, the Queen Mary College of Engineering and all the London Polytechnics have long given freely of their services when approached, e.g. the Royal College of Art makes special toilet seats for spinal bifida boys and girls; the Department of Engineering at Queen Mary College, which made the prototype of the "Comet" chairs used by thalidomide children, has also made a special bath and is anxious to turn its attention to "one-off" aids as well as prototypes. It welcomes all requests, as do Polytechnics, but there may be difficulties about sorting out whether the social services department or the outside institution pays for the cost of the materials. Labour has always been given free, but a proposal by one college that the salary of an extra technician should be paid jointly by the university and the social services department met with so much opposition from the borough engineers' department – said to be union-inspired – that this appointment, along with another proposal for a joint appointment with a teaching hospital, had to be shelved.

An organisation called "Remap", described as consisting of "retired mechanical engineers with a toolshed at the bottom of the garden", also welcomes enquiries about "one-off" aids and prototypes for newly developed aids with limited markets. Three of the Inner London boroughs had already made use of its services at the time of my visit.

(c) *Aids supplied by Voluntary Societies*
Aids supplied by societies like the Red Cross and St John's Ambulance Brigade tended to be aids to home nursing on short-term loan rather than aids to daily living and many of these had become obsolete.[7] In 1976 the British Red Cross Society decided that the time had come to discontinue the practice of acting as agent for local authority social services departments and those government training centres from which they could still get supplies. This was partly because commercial manufacturers now produced similar aids at competitive prices which were more to the taste of clients and partly because of the disproportionately high costs of administration and distribution. There were also difficulties in getting enough volunteers to look after the store cupboards.

It is significant that the four London boroughs that had no complaints about the quality of the aids issued by the Red Cross had a population that included a large number of comfortably off middle-class, middle-aged women willing to sell flags to raise money and to take their turn at minding the stores. With the growing tendency for middle-class women to undertake paid work this source of voluntary help is diminishing.[8]

The quality of the aids provided by the Red Cross varied considerably between the branches. One occupational therapist complained of a mahogany commode with collapsing arms that had been sent to a client who had lost the use of her own arms; and some of the wheelchairs supplied were reminiscent of the wheelchair commented on by Amelia Harris – "someone left it to the Parish and the Vicar gave it to us". Nevertheless, the local branches of the British Red Cross Society and of the St John's Ambulance Association continued to provide valuable stop-gap services for clients in need of permanent aids to daily living and were noticeably quicker at delivering aids than many local authority social services departments. Their van men also tended to imply that a cash contribution to their society would not be out of order.

Groups such as Rotary clubs and The Round Table frequently raised funds to provide some of the more expensive aids to daily living. "Whip-rounds" took place and examples were given of electric beds bought for specific persons whose cases had become known to them, possibly through local hospital staff, and of comfortable chairs for arthritics to use at day centres. Wheelchairs for temporary use at day centres or for shopping expeditions and outings were another frequent gift but one made all too often without seeking professional advice. Six "Snowdon" chairs were not being used at one day centre – these had been a private bequest – because the central steering pillar precluded their use by disabled people with some kinds of paralysis in their lower limbs.

Another source of aids is the London taxi-drivers. These are widely known for the annual trip they give to the severely disabled people living at the "Star and Garter" home at Richmond but not as widely known for the fund-raising activities they organise to buy aids for schools for children with multiple handicaps in four East End boroughs. These and other examples of private and corporate generosity which form only a fractional percentage of the aids provided today complement the provision of aids from public funds.

4. *Storage of Aids*

All but the specially designed "one-off" aids may need to be stored for varying lengths of time and often in considerable numbers. Storage presents problems of location and expense. Aids were discovered stored in places as varied as a derelict swimming pool, a slaughterhouse no longer in use and, more conveniently, in the vast basements of Town Halls abandoned at the time when London government was re-organised in 1965. Such premises cost varying amounts for staff, heat, light, roof repairs and general maintenance. The abandoned Town Halls, which frequently house the secretariat as well as the aids, are probably the roomiest and most readily available places for storage. Day centres, especially those that were formally workhouses, are a spacious second choice. One borough had recently purchased two Nissen-type huts to house stores that had already outgrown the space provided before the Chronically Sick and Disabled Persons Act. None of the boroughs at the time they were visited, even those with purpose-built stores for aids, had enough storage space available to satisfy either the director or its occupational therapists. Ideally a centrally-based and separate store is required (which might or might not be at a day centre or residential centre) for aids to daily living. Only eleven boroughs had achieved this, if one discounts a special lavatory for the disabled which, never used after construction, was purpose adapted to provide the smallest storage space of any inspected. Six other boroughs had made plans for a purpose-built store for aids to daily living, but these had been shelved because of anticipated cuts in capital expenditure.

By the time of this study the demand for aids arising as a result of the Chronically Sick and Disabled Persons Act 1970, had clearly outgrown existing storage space. In two boroughs all that was available to the social services departments was a small section of a central warehouse used by a number of other borough departments. In these a small corner had been found for aids which had been crammed in wherever possible. Special can-openers and elastic shoe-laces were stored in commodes, geriatric chairs were stacked high with inflatable rubber rings and raised toilet seats and walking frames hung from the ceiling.

Twenty-two social services departments had succeeded in getting their own, independent stores, but even in these aids tended to get mixed up with other things supplied by the social services such as giant tins of custard powder for residential homes and stacks of "welfare" foods.

In one borough aids were stored "anywhere, all over the place wherever we can find room" and it was common practice to lend new geriatric chairs to day centres and area office waiting rooms as a means of storing them. This in itself led to increased demand for them.

Five occupational therapists had attempted to tidy up the aid stores before a visit was made in connection with this study. They expressed horror at some of the unusable equipment they had found. Much of this had been returned by relatives of clients who had died, but some was debris from the days of the joint health and welfare departments. Eleven obsolete urinals were observed in one store and

141

in another a skeleton was discovered in an old cupboard.[9] An administrator in the domiciliary section of another department had long been wanting to reduce the aids stores to some kind of order but found this could only be done by a full audit. She was not interested in how many screws and feet of wire were missing but wanted to "take stock" in the wider sense of meeting clients' needs. No steps had been taken to rationalise storage before she was interviewed. Only one borough refused to allow the stores to be seen, the assistant director admitting frankly that it was "nothing to be proud of". In another borough the "man with the only key" had gone off to deliver an aid that had been required urgently, although normal deliveries were done at regular and stated times two mornings a week, during which times the store was inaccessible until he returned. One store, in adapted outbuildings in the grounds of a residential home, was looked after most efficiently by the widow of a former cook who lived in a tied cottage and prided herself on arranging for aids to reach clients within 24 hours of her being asked for them.

Only ten of the thirty-two boroughs and the City of London had achieved separate storage space for the exclusive use of aids. Six stores had been purpose-built and incorporated into new day centres but already, according to the occupational therapists who supervised them, demand had outstripped storage capacity.

The largest and best organised store was arranged rather like a super-market. There was adequate shelf space and small articles were kept separately in plastic vegetable racks. Everything that could be hung on a wall or ceiling, e.g. Zimmer walking frames and raised toilet seats, was suspended safely from special hooks – falling aids appeared in some boroughs to be an occupational hazard – and the task of stock-taking was made a comparatively easy one. The more untidy the aids stores were the more likely they were to be harbouring obsolete and useless items in space that was badly needed for items in constant demand. The need to provide expensive storage space is however having a beneficial affect on policy about buying aids which tend to be ordered less haphazardly than in the past.

Attempts were being made in some boroughs to determine the optimum number of aids of certain kinds that ought to be kept in stock and the number below which they should not be allowed to fall. Large aids such as hoists, for which many manufacturers offer special prices if twelve or more are bought at a time, take up a good deal of storage space and the numbers bought cannot necessarily be adjusted to anticipated demand within the next few months.

Three social services departments had drawn up two separate lists of aids, an A List and a B List. On the A List were aids commonly in demand which were not allowed to fall below an agreed number. On the B list were aids less frequently needed and perhaps more costly, of which only a few would be kept in store and the rest ordered as required. Typical A lists included bathing aids, aids for eating and toileting and for doing simple household tasks. The B lists dealt with such things as portable hoists and geriatric chairs. Aids that would have to be ordered specially would include heavy duty patient lifters and chairs with ejector seats adjusted to the weight of a particular client. Such lists, in addition to easing some of the pressure on storage space, made for much simpler administration. Social workers could take aids on the A list from the stores without needing a counter-signature from a higher authority, but aids on the B list could only be authorised by senior social workers and occupational therapists. The ordering of aids on the B list also required sanction from a head occupational therapist or an aids and adaptations officer of a similar grade.

Storing aids in area offices was not generally popular at the time of this study, although some area offices were said to carry minimal supplies of small aids like pick-up sticks and elastic bootlaces.[10] The main reason given for the resistance by area staff to carrying larger supplies of aids appeared to be that there would be additional paperwork.

Every occupational therapist kept a limited store of aids in the back of the car. These usually included a couple of raised toilet seats of different thicknesses, well-known types of bathrail which fit on to taps, a collapsible – and adjustable – walking stick and a patent can-opener for arthritics. To their annoyance they were seldom allowed to issue these aids without going through the routine ordering processes but even so carrying samples to the clients served to cut down on delay. One borough had a demonstration van which visited clients, centres and clubs with samples of aids. Again these could not be issued on demand, but the aids clerk did her best to see that supplies were kept in stock and topped up for rapid disbursement.

Policy about where to store aids, how many aids should be kept in stock, which aids should be bought in bulk and which automatically re-ordered if stocks went below an agreed quantity, varied from borough to borough as did the respective duties of clerks and storemen. In some boroughs storemen took over many duties, such as arranging for transport and delivery and the automatic re-ordering of aids that in other boroughs were the responsibility of clerks and assistant administrators. The kind of duties required of storemen was frequently an indication of the importance attached to the prompt provision of appropriate aids. In some boroughs where no establishment existed to increase clerical staff it was possible to expand the service by up-grading the job of storeman. Alternatively, by employing storemen as "miscellaneous" staff, it became possible to write job descriptions for them that covered gaps in the service.

One such example is provided by a physically healthy craft instructor who combined helping to load heavy aids on to vans with repairing aids in a day centre under the omnibus title of "assistant to the storeman". The duties of storemen are listed in Table 13 opposite.

5. *The Duties and Responsibilities of Storemen*

At the time of the study the duties and responsibilities of storemen varied greatly from one Greater London borough to the next and from caretaker pure and simple to fully-fledged administrator. Two boroughs had no caretaker for their stores at all and "stock" aids were issued as required over the counter by receptionists in their Town Halls who "told someone" when an aid was out of stock. In two other boroughs with stores based on day centres the clerk to the rehabilitation teams, which were also based there, attempted to add stock-taking and the issuing of aids to her other duties. At the other extreme was the storeman who was graded as administrative staff with a part time clerical assistant who kept up-to-date records of stock, booked aids in and out and automatically re-ordered them when the number remaining in the stores fell below the prescribed minimum. Some storemen were required to send release of payment slips to the finance department and to keep a running total of quarterly expenditure. Thirteen storemen had no other duties than that of caretaker. Three of these had assistants called porters to help them lift heavy aids in order to conform with union requirements and there was also the craft instructor already mentioned. Seven stores were equipped with tools and work-benches so that storemen could make simple repairs to aids, but only two of these had an electric vice. Only two stores had equipment to work with any materials except wood. Eight storemen were responsible for arranging transport for the aids they issued, but only five were expected to deliver aids themselves. This meant closing the aids store while they were away. Only one of the storemen who was also required to deliver aids had an assistant, and then only part time.

Altogether eight storemen did simple repairs to aids and seven storemen or their assistants were willing to clean them. Cleaning aids that had been re-called to store presented a major problem which is discussed further in Chapter 9.

The table that follows sets out these varied duties.

It is clear that changes in policy about the storage and ordering of aids must affect the functions of the storemen employed in the various boroughs. In some it was thought advisable to transfer some of their responsibilities to the secretariat but in others an up-grading of the storeman's job was considered likely to be more effective.

Table 13 – Functions of Storemen

Caretaking	28
with assistant (porter)	3
with assistant (clerical)	2
Ordering Stock aids	5
Choosing manufacturer	2
Keeping records	2
Cleaning aids	7
Repairing aids – wood	8
metal	2
plastic	0
Making simple aids	5
Arranging transport for delivery	8
Delivering aids	5
Installing simple aids	4

6. Social Services Departments storing aids as agents of the Area Health Authorities

The joint storage of what used to be called "welfare aids" and what used to be called "medical loan equipment" or "aids to home nursing" was inherited by boroughs that had once had joint health and welfare departments. Although the new area health authorities came into official being on 1 April 1974, many social services departments were continuing to store aids on their behalf in the winter of 1974. By 1975 however all but two had succeeded in off-loading any aids that could not be charged to the social services vote, one only a week before the aids store was visited and exactly one year after the area health authorities came into being on 1 April 1974. One social services department, according to the storeman, had used the expected visit of the researcher as a way of precipitating the final clear-out. Only two social services departments, both in Outer London boroughs and with the vast basements of their Town Halls at their disposal, continued to view their role as agents for the area health authorities with equanimity. Senior officials in these boroughs argued that as the same aid could be either an aid to daily living or an aid to home nursing there was a good deal to be said for storing them together and sorting out payment after they had been issued.

Joint storage of aids was however seen as something to be avoided by all other boroughs in the Greater London area. Shortage of storage space and the difficulty of expanding existing stores to meet the increased demand for aids to daily living was the main reason given – it was assumed that the level of aids for nursing patients at home remained fairly constant in spite of increasingly swift discharges from hospitals – but difficulties were also said to arise about the quality of the aids issued by the respective authorities. Pads for the incontinent were those most frequently cited as an example, those

145

issued by the area health authority being considered in all cases inferior to the brands supplied by local authority social services departments. By the time the study finished, when money for aids looked certain to be reduced all round, a certain amount of rethinking had begun to take place and, reinforced by the introduction of joint finance in 1976, the possibility of joint storage for aids began once again to seem attractive. No moves towards this had been made in the Greater London area but, in the country as a whole, the possibility of regional control over aids of both kinds was gaining credence. In one area outside London a voluntary association had assumed the responsibility of acting as tri-partite agent for a county, a city (a county borough in itself) and an area health authority and was eventually expected to extend its purchasing power to take in the whole area constituting the regional health authority.

The financing of this service was fixed experimentally in 1977 in the ratio of 60 :40 after an analysis of the kinds of aids issued in the previous year and the speed with which they had been returned to stock for re-cycling. As aids to daily living had generally remained out of circulation for long periods the social services departments agreed to pay 60 per cent of the annual cost against the 40 per cent paid for by the health authority. Any voluntary contributions that came in were banked as a bonus. Hiring charges were also made to clients for aids that had not been prescribed by a doctor or an appropriate employee of one or other of the authorities involved and these, together with the voluntary contributions, brought in £12,000 a year in addition to the £60,000 already allocated.

The extension of such a scheme has considerable implications for Greater London. From the client's point of view the existence of one store and a philosophy of "supply first and argue later" offers certain obvious attractions. The idea of Regional Supply Depots certainly needs ventilating but it could be unfortunate if the shortage of money, of which all local authority social services departments are acutely aware, contributed to over-hasty decisions. The needs of clients might still be better suited by a 6 :4 division of expenses on a local basis. Indeed this might prove a much more satisfactory way of dealing with the "grey areas" than by further arguments about the definition of aids.

7. Safety of Aids

With the exception of those aids manufactured in their own workshops, most social services departments are ill-equipped to control at source the quality and safety of the aids they issue. One occupational therapist reported that a bath-board supplied by a commercial manufacturer proved to have been made of unseasoned wood and had broken under a person who weighed less than eight stone. Such accidents are not in the interests of manufacturers and it was not difficult to prevail upon the one responsible for this accident to recall the whole batch. Inspection of commercial aids at source is possible only to a very limited degree because they are not made under contract to local authority social services departments nor, as in the case of appliances,[11] are they made under contract to the Department of Health and Social Security. The freedom of the aids market makes possible a much greater flexibility of design but also poses problems of control over both the quality and the safety of commercially manufactured aids. There is no special British Standard for aids comparable, for example, with the awards made by the magazine *Good Housekeeping* for good and safe designs in normal household equipment, tested by staff in their Institute kitchens. The British Standards Institution (BSI) produces standards for various products but the mark of its approval is sought voluntarily by manufacturers who are at liberty to decide whether or not it is to their advantage to try to get the official seal of approval. If they are not disposed to bother they can quite legally sell their products even if they fail to comply with officially approved standards.

Under the Consumer Protection Act, as amended in 1971, the Department of Prices and Consumer Protection took over most aspects of safety from the Home Office. It was found that during the preceding fourteen years regulations had been drawn up for only nine specific products, none of them used only by disabled people. The purpose of the Act as amended is to prevent the sale of dangerous goods before they cause an accident but as the Trading Department's decreasing number of inspectors are stretched by mandatory duties under legislation such as the Weights and Measures Act and the Trades Description Act, many goods escape inspection. There have also been very few prosecutions to serve as warnings to manufacturers as trading officers prefer to advise and warn in the hope that this will be sufficient to bring about the withdrawal of dangerous goods.

The disabled must therefore look for protection to the professional expertise of the employees of social services departments who decide on what aids they should have and on the capabilities of those who install them.

Specially employed staff in the Department of Health and Social Security have made frequent tests on electrical aids on which they have reported annually. Recently the Department also involved itself with the safety of various kinds of lifts used by disabled people. After a series of disconcerting accidents the Department

"initiated an engineering investigation of all known stairlifts marketed in the United Kingdom and an enquiry into the experi-

147

ence of selected social services departments and their clients in using their equipment."[12]

As a result of two serious accidents which happened before the report of these investigations was ready for publication the Department took, in April 1977, the unprecedented step of issuing a letter of guidance on the basic requirements of all stairlifts and home lifts and listed points that must be checked to ensure that they have been safely installed. Such lifts are usually installed by engineers sent by the manufacturer but the clear implication of the letter is that a cross check should also be made by a borough employee.

Similar investigations are being made into showers after disabled people, unable to move quickly out of the way, have been reported to have been severely scalded by certain types of "instant" shower in which thermostatic devices for controlling the temperature of the hot water have failed. It is expected that a letter of advice on similar lines to the one on home lifts will be issued. In the meantime manufacturers are not required by law to guarantee the safety of the disabled consumer.

Risks arise not only from the use of faulty aids or aids that have been badly installed but also from the misuse by clients of aids that are intrinsically of safe design. Where aids are very expensive and assembly may be complicated it is customary for the manufacturers to send their own instructor/technicians at the time of delivery but the majority of aids are delivered by borough vanmen. Social workers and occupational therapists have such heavy work-loads that many days may elapse before they can visit the client to show him how to assemble and use the aid or a social work assistant may visit them who lacks the necessary knowledge to give adequate instruction.

Some clients with physical handicaps may lack the mental ability or the power of concentration to use even the most simple aids correctly all the time and some may just be too careless. For such clients it is difficult to provide safeguards.

Before 1970 it was the custom of welfare departments to insist that clients signed a form indemnifying the council against blame at the time the aid was delivered, whether or not the client had received instruction in its use and entirely without any safeguards to the client.[13] By 1974 only five boroughs were continuing this practice. In the other boroughs there was a growing tendency to seek comprehensive insurance. There should however be a moral obligation to do everything possible to prevent accident as well as to compensate clients or their relatives after accidents have happened.

8. *Research into the design of aids*

Under Section 22 of the Chronically Sick and Disabled Persons Act 1970 the Secretary of State is required

148

"each year to lay before Parliament a report on the progress made during that year on research and development work . . . in relation to equipment that might increase the range of activities and independence or well-being of disabled persons, and in particular such equipment that might improve the indoor and outdoor mobility of such persons."

Since 1972 reports on work being done on these lines have been printed annually. Much of this work is concerned with scientific and medical investigations into prosthetics and orthotics, and with the improvement of appliances such as artificial limbs, but research is not limited to such projects. A grant to the Institute of Consumer Ergonomics, for example, which is attached to the University of Loughborough has made it possible to set up a large-scale investigation into the design of aids for toileting and feeding with special reference to both hygiene and safety. Its report, which is expected early in 1979 should have beneficial effects on the daily life of a very large proportion of disabled people.

It might seem that the existence of stores full to overflowing with aids, the numbers of which have been carefully adjusted to anticipated demand, would result in a swift matching of aids to clients, followed by rapid authorisation, issue and delivery. Unfortunately this was seldom found to be the case for the reasons set out in subsequent chapters.

NOTES

1. The Disabled Living Foundation is a non-profit making organisation which, since 1973, has kept a permanent exhibition of up-to-date commercial aids at its premises at 346 Kensington High Street. It sends out monthly literature to all boroughs, charging them a subscription for this service.
2. When two of these centres closed in 1962 there was a backlog of six months for raised toilet seats. These cost 22 shillings as against £6.10 shillings on the commercial market. An enterprising welfare officer persuaded Wormwood Scrubs to make some for the LCC and also some bath boards and stools at 25 shillings and 7/6 respectively with guaranteed delivery within 7 to 10 days. In 1976 the only article manufactured in any prison workshop to help disabled people is a car for handicapped children called a "Hobcar". Information about this may be obtained from "Prindus", c/o The Home Office.
3. In the main the job descriptions of instructors do not include the making or repairing of aids although occasionally an instructor has been known to make a one-off aid "as a favour" or to repair aids if paid overtime. This falls entirely outside the duties for which they are employed in the majority of boroughs.
4. In another borough members of the St. Raphael's Society made pillow cases of this kind out of old sheets.
5. This may mean that the employee has not passed certain examinations that allow him to be called a technician. On the other hand, it will also mean that he does not qualify for Union membership and is thus unshackled by the restrictions that this can entail.
6. Examples of these are the "Croydon" alarm system and the "Surrey" toilet frames. Although these are reproduced commercially the prototypes were designed by an employee of the Croydon social services department.
7. Local branches of the British Red Cross Society continue to act as agents for area health authorities for the distribution of what is called "Medical Loan Equipment" (otherwise aids to nursing patients at home). According to a "financial spokesman" the Society still received subsidies to local branches from "about a dozen" London boroughs in 1977.
8. One borough reported a similar difficulty in getting uniformed volunteers to serve meals on wheels as many of the members of the Womens Royal Voluntary Service were now well over sixty and possibly even receiving meals on wheels themselves.

9. It was seriously suggested that this might be given to the area health authority in exchange for a couple of ripple beds as skeletons are not only costly these days but also hard to obtain.

10. Only one borough reported that its area offices preferred to store aids locally. See Chapter Five, p. 117.

11. See p. 46, para. 7, *Technical Inspection*, of the Surgical Appliances Contract 1976 which insists that contractors and sub-contractors allow technical officers employed by the DHSS to have access to their premises "at all reasonable times"; para. 8(i) which insists on the immediate reporting of any defects, including those discovered in the course of repair work; and para. 8(ii) which insists that appliances sent for repair by hospitals must be inspected as a whole "to ensure that dangerous defects do not exist whether or not covered by the order".

12. DHSS Local Authority Social Services Letter. LASSL (77) 11. 15 April 1977. *Stair Lifts and Vertical Passenger Home Lifts.*

13. The need for indemnity arose because welfare departments had allowed relatives of clients to fit aids and install gadgets instead of insisting on borough workmen supervised by borough staff. This cut out delay, but may have increased the risk to clients.

CHAPTER EIGHT

GETTING THE AIDS TO THE CLIENT (1):
REFERRAL; ALLOCATION; THE WAITING LIST;
ASSESSMENT

It might seem that the existence of stores full to overflowing with
aids, the numbers of which have been carefully adjusted to anticipated demand, would result in a swift matching of aids to clients,
followed by rapid authorisation, issue and delivery. Unfortunately
this was seldom found to be the case and a great many applications
by, or on behalf of, clients were subject to a number of procedural
steps.

The FIRST STEP – becoming known to the social services

If an aid to daily living is available in a store and a client needs such
an aid it might be supposed that provision would be made in three
or four days. This seldom happens even if a client is already known
to the social services in the area in which he lives. For the new client,
a lengthy period may elapse before need is verified and an aid is
provided on loan.

There are three main ways in which a client's name is first drawn
to the attention of the area office – a personal visit, a telephone call
or a letter. Various research teams have established that a personal
visit produces the quickest results and the letter, contrary to expectations of the writers, is less effective than either a visit or a telephone
call. The processes initiated by a personal visit will be described first.

(a) *Reception*
Normally the first person seen by a visitor to an office of the social
services department is a receptionist. This is the case whether it is in
a building also housing the secretariat or a local area office to which a
team of social workers has moved. As clients may be ill-informed
about available services, and frequently require an entirely different
service from the one they have called about, the receptionist should
ideally be selected and trained to receive with understanding,
patience and tact. She must also be able to answer straight-forward
requests for information or know where to send people for such

information. As many of the enquirers are diffident, harassed, emotionally disturbed, under stress, aggressive and so on, the receptionist should also have the ability to put them at their ease if they seem to need to see a duty officer or a member of an intake team.[1]

This ideal is seldom achieved in practice. As a great many receptionists are also required to operate telephone switchboards, visitors may not receive undisturbed attention.[2] Some clients may become impatient and leave before receiving the interviews for which they had hoped.

An additional duty of the receptionist-telephonist may be to keep some form of Day-Book. As what is entered in it varies from area to area in the same borough, as well as from borough to borough, no valid inference can be drawn from such books about the proportion of disabled clients who come in person to area offices. Nor is there any way of determining what proportion of callers are referred to other local authority departments, e.g. housing information services, or to outside agencies offering appropriate services, e.g. Citizens Advice Bureaux.[3]

Although all social services departments and area offices had made careful arrangements about access, including ramps for wheelchairs, the number of disabled people thought to use these facilities was felt to be disproportionately small; in two boroughs specially adapted toilets in area offices were said to have been used less than six times a year.

It is probable that the majority of disabled people find it easier either to ask a friend or relative to call on their behalf or to make the first contact in some other way.

(b) *Requests by telephone*

The majority of requests come over the telephone, both from clients themselves and from people ringing on their behalf. Calls may be noted either by a social worker on duty for the day, after which they then go through the same processes as requests made by letter, or dealt with by a member of an intake team.[4]

Many callers fail to get through at all. Outside lines are frequently tied up. When social workers are in their offices they are often telephoning out on behalf of their clients. Calls put through on inside lines fare little better.

When social workers are out of their offices they all tend to be out at the same time, either out of the building visiting clients during the hours when they are most likely to be at home or with a client in an interview room. At such times area offices echo and re-echo to the sound of unanswered phones. A telephonist who is also the receptionist cannot hope to run an efficient message-taking service as well, if only because, after she has rung round several rooms, frustrated clients, many of whom ring from coin boxes, are likely to cut themselves off. More clerical help might lead to more messages being taken, thus freeing the lines more quickly but more lines would prove impossible for one receptionist-telephonist to manage unaided.

In theory, people with urgent requests will continue to ring until they get through to the right person. In practice, the times when they can get to a telephone may be limited. This applies as much to a hospital sister ringing about the aids needed by a disabled patient who is about to be discharged as to a working relative making a lunch call from a telephone box. District nurses, health visitors and geriatric visitors, considered to be the largest source of requests for aids and adaptations, touch down in their offices for only limited period each day. They are, however, the least likely to give up – even if it means a personal visit to an area office.

There are, however, exceptions. When the ordering of aids is dealt with by a centralised section of the secretariat rather than a local area office, district nurses, health visitors, hospital-based medical social workers, hospital-based occupational therapists and local GPs quickly learn to by-pass the local area office. This has the advantage, for the client, of the aid being ordered promptly, and unless it is above a certain fixed sum, without question. It has a disadvantage in that the client may require other forms of help in overcoming handicap in addition to an aid but the need may never become known to the area office of the social services.

(c) *The letter of request*
(i) Letters from disabled people asking for advice, a service or an aid or adaptation are usually addressed to the Director of Social Services in the mistaken belief that he will give them his personal attention and so speed up subsequent processes. Some letters, particularly those written by older people, may be written to "The Welfare". They are sorted according to the social work area in which the writers live and delivered by internal messenger to the appropriate area offices, usually within 24 hours. Here it falls to an assistant administrative officer or a clerical officer to give them an order of priority, if any. Letters suggesting obvious urgency may be shown to the Area team manager (also called Principal Area Officer or Area Team Leader) the same day but the majority may well have to wait until the next weekly meeting between the area team manager and the senior social workers.

At this meeting some of the results will be disregarded on the grounds that social workers are already carrying heavy caseloads. No form of acknowledgement, apology or regret will necessarily be sent to the writer.[5] Some requests will be diverted to an intake team, if one is operating. The remainder will wait until the seniors hold their meetings with social workers, which may be in the same week or at fortnightly or even monthly intervals.

In areas where it is customary for all requests arising from disability to be handled by an occupational therapist "anything smelling of an aid" will be on her desk within 24 hours after which the priority it receives will depend upon her workload and her judgement, possibly after consultation with a head occupational therapist.

(ii) Letters from relatives, friends and neighbours on behalf of a disabled person may follow the same pattern. If these do not appear urgent, they may go to the bottom of the pile because "they have managed all right up to now".

(iii) Letters from hospital consultants who write about aids tend to get a prompt acknowledgement as a matter of policy but the speed with which their requests are met will depend on a number of other factors including the availability of the aid and its cost.

(iv) In cases of severe disablement as a result, for example, of a road crash, a fall from a roof by a building worker or a very severe attack of poliomyelitis, hospital staff may notify area team managers months in advance of the kind of aids and adaptations such clients will need on discharge. As no fixed date of discharge can be given so far ahead such notifications, though important for planning purposes, frequently lose their sense of urgency and little advance work may be done on them especially if the client is in a specialised hospital outside the borough.

(v) Letters from GPs may be just scribbled notes, often posted on by the patients themselves, such as "Mrs X wants a bath aid". Often no indication is given of the kind of aid considered necessary or the nature of the disability. Where aids are known to be expensive, e.g. a stair lift, the doctor may go into more detail. Acknowledgement will usually be prompt but follow-up not necessarily so.[6]

(vi) Letters from senior officers in other local authority departments and from outside agencies tend to be acknowledged but the clients on whose behalf they write cannot necessarily expect any form of priority as much will depend on the current availability of finance.

A study of all referrals to the borough's three area offices in 1974–75 was carried out by the Research Section of the Royal Borough of Kensington and Chelsea. It discovered that 90 per cent of referrals by other agencies were by telephone or letter but that many of the letters were notifications rather than requests. If positive action on behalf of a client were required then "the best measure of activity involves personal callers and telephone calls".[7] This study confirms similar findings in a study done in 1973 in an area office in Southampton which, after analysing the time taken to follow up requests made in different ways, said "speed of action is clearly related to

154

methods of referral." "Referrers who want to ensure speedy action" should "telephone or send the client along to the office."[8]

A personal visit is more likely to result in a reasonably quick service because it is more likely to lead automatically to a preliminary interview either with one of the duty officers for the day or with a member of an intake team. There is no guarantee that the social worker conducting this interview will be either qualified or experienced but at least notes of any practical assistance required, such as an aid, will be taken and a file opened. This means that the client who has made a personal visit to the correct office may be one jump ahead of clients who have telephoned or written letters. On the other hand the personal visitor may not manage to get past the receptionist.

(d) *The function of receptionists*
The receptionist, who is the first point of contact with the social services department, wields a power that is seldom commensurate with either her skill or training. As early as 1963 Blau[9] was pointing out that, as well as deriving satisfaction from helping people, they were also using their powers to apply sanctions to aggressive clients and in furthering the cause of clients whom they personally felt to be deserving of special treatment. In England, Hall, when embarking on his study of reception practices in four children's departments in 1969 and 1970 was to discover that the American findings were also relevant in the rather less formally structured organisations familiar to British readers. In an article published in 1970, he pointed out that the reception function, although seldom geared to the needs of client was by no means passive.

> "The performance of the reception function far from being a passive administrative expedient was found to have a profound influence upon the way the agency operates, the services it pro vides and to whom they are provided."[10]

Hall was later to introduce the term "client-bombardment", a term that is now much used by the social workers whom he alerted to the problems of reception and which is echoed by the Northern Area Team in Kensington and Chelsea in their desire to see a receptionist at the social services enquiry desk who was "able to deflect inappropriate referrals". The team felt that this task of identifying appropriate referrals

> "would require a great deal of skill as the functions and brief of the social services are so wide . . . The use of a trained worker who would be under a social worker's supervision rather than a receptionist is one possibility."

In those areas using intake teams, rather than one social worker on

155

duty for the day, the receptionist was likely to leave the initial screening of the clients to a member of the team. Between 1974 and 1976 at least one area team in each area was trying out an intake team but no social services department was using intake teams in every area.

2. *The Intake Team*

The intake team stands half way between the system of duty officers, common to ex-welfare departments, and the more intensive – and extended – approach of long-term casework teams.

Whereas a duty officer would feel unable to leave the building except in cases of extreme urgency, the worker in an intake team who conducts a preliminary interview can, if essential, deal with a case as a contingency situation; offer any practical assistance that is required, help with an application for a constant attendance allowance, a request for a rent rebate, or a telephone; make a home visit if thought to be necessary and then either close the case or, if there are obvious deep-seated problems, hand it over to a long-term caseworker. Where practical assistance means the provision of simple aids such as certain kinds of bath aids these will be ordered on an official form and supplied as quickly as the prevailing administrative processes – and the state of the aids store – permits. In such circumstances the client will have become "known to the social services" and remain listed on an area office index but will not remain active on any caseload or come up for periodic review.

Intake teams work to an experienced senior social worker and usually consist of at least two other qualified social workers and a heavy tail of social work assistants to do the running around. In the whole of the Greater London area only two areas included occupational therapists on intake duty and these areas were in two different boroughs. Both areas had two occupational therapists and in one area each did two days on intake and three off. In the other they did alternative weeks on and off but stood in for each other if an urgent call from a long-term client came in.

These occupational therapists working as part of an intake team kept the cases they dealt with on intake, closing them when they thought fit. On-going social work problems were referred to social workers once problems needing the expertise of the occupational therapist, such as the right kind of aid, had been solved. Frequently the shortage of social workers led to such cases then being suspended.

The work of the intake team has become an increasingly popular, and necessary, subject for research on both sides of the Atlantic. Smith and Ames,[11] writing on the importance of what they call "the bureaucracy of access" refer to the studies by Zimmerman, published between 1966 and 1969.[12] Here again, as with the untrained receptionist, the power wielded by the initial interviewer may not work in the client's favour. Summarising Zimmerman's findings, Smith and Ames say that Zimmerman :

> "points to the organisational constraints which intake workers experience. In practice intake workers construct the eligibility of their clients in such a way as to control the practicabilities of their own day-to-day work situation. The processal character of client entry into the department, the highly routinised character of reception events and, above all, the overriding dependence upon documentary materials, together with the importance of generating these materials to demonstrate competent performance on the part of the professionals, all mitigate against an approach in which client considerations predominate."

The power is all the more alarming in that it is largely unconscious. The study in the Northern Area Office does however recognise the dangers implicit in the creation of an intake team which

> "may have an impact in that formal policy statements are thereby made operative by a small group of full-time gate-keepers."

Under this system, when pressures of referral intensify,

> "marginal cases may get reduced attention or be dealt with less soon after the day of referral."[13]

How much need remains unmet will however depend, in the first instance, on how the social services department as a whole sees the limit of its responsibilities and, in the second instance, on developing some uniform system for assessing need "which overcomes the differences in perception of need between different social workers". A clear policy centred on professional judgement is essential but even so it is almost impossible to monitor shifting trends in the way in which need is perceived.

3. Sources of Referral

The various ways in which clients become "known to the social services" are frequently described as "referrals". Often these take the form of a request for a specified service, such as a home help, holiday or aid. Few details about the sources of requests for aids are available in the centralised sections of the secretariat and none had been put on computer by the time of this study. The "Front Sheets" of the files made up by Intake teams and Duty officers vary from area to area and from borough to borough but most were said to have been re-designed by 1975 to include a list of possible sources of referral against which a tick could be put.[14]

During the course of this study appropriate senior officers, administrative officers and clerks engaged in ordering aids were each asked how they rated twelve different professions as sources of referral. Where occupational therapists were in post, they were asked as well. The same questions were asked in each of the Greater London boroughs and the answers were unanimous in claiming that the majority of requests for aids – or for any service for the disabled – were medical. The next most important source of referral was believed to be home helps, who were ideally placed to notice rapid degeneration of a client.[15] There was also considerable belief that the majority of so-called initial self-referrals were not in fact self-referrals at all but made at the suggestion of another party, frequently a general practitioner, a neighbour or a relative.[16]

At the time of the study, head occupational therapists were beginning systematically to collect data about the number of referrals from different area offices but not of the sources of referral. With the appointment of more domiciliary occupational therapists and more head occupational therapists more data may become available.

To have attempted to determine the incidence of referrals involving physical handicap in the Greater London boroughs at the time of this study would have meant exceeding the brief. It was however known that methods of recording referrals varied greatly not only from borough to borough but also from area to area. Neill, in her study in Southampton, also reports on the variety of uses to which an official referral form might be put, including their use as "message papers on clients who were already on the area caseload". Approximately 75 out of every 1,000 referrals were also likely to be lost.

Interest in the source of referrals showed up in isolated pockets of research as early as 1972 when Loewenstein found that 21.8 per cent of all referrals in an Inner London borough were self-referrals, 9.4 came from relatives and friends, 41.4 per cent were referrals by other agencies of which the majority were from other local authority departments including the health department and 13 per cent by medical practitioners. The proportion of referrals due to problems of physical handicap is not however given.[17]

Two studies by research staff from the National Institute of Social Workers in the County Borough of Southampton in 1972 and in 1975 show that in 1975 although the sample differed slightly from that of 1972 "the main reason for contact was again physical handicap". The figures given were 46 per cent in 1972 and 45 per cent in 1975 with over half the referrals coming from a third party, either the health department (still under the local authority in 1972) or a medical practitioner. So-called self-referrals were found almost always to have originated in suggestions by agencies, doctors or friends.[18] A third study, in 1976[19] looked at all the referrals in one friends.[18] A third study, in 1976[19], looked at all the referrals in one area office and also compared current practices with those observed in 1972 and 1973. It identified changes in the uses of a social work area office – there was a noticeable trend towards using them as centres of information – and indicated ways in which both the services and the expectations of clients were changing. Certain kinds and sources of referral however did not change significantly.[20]

The proportion of referrals involving the physically handicapped, together with the frail elderly, remained constant as the highest of all client groups with 614 or about 30 per cent of all referrals. When analysed by age it was found that

"Three quarters of those aged 64–75 living in family groups came into contact with the area office because of needs arising from frailty or disability"

while

"Almost half the middle-aged presented problems of physical disability which included serious illness such as terminal cancer or progressive diseases such as multiple sclerosis."

The sources of referral for all types of client showed an increase since the previous year in the number of self referrals and referrals on the advice of friends and relatives. Nearly a half of all referrals were now made through informal channels but, at the same time, 21 per cent of all referrals on behalf of the physically handicapped and the frail elderly were still made by health personnel. These figures, the 1976 Southampton study points out, were much the same in 13 other studies including those of teams in Buckinghamshire, Cambridge, Cornwall and Gloucestershire and three Greater London boroughs.[21] Readers are however warned that it could be "hazardous" to compare the Southampton findings with other statistics involving the frail elderly as the area office on which their findings are based only recorded the frail elderly with identified social work problems. This is borne out by the variations between the three areas in the Kensington and Chelsea study which reveal not only the differences in the hinterground of each area, and to a more limited extent its accessibility, but also considerable differences of technique in record-keeping.[22]

What the Southampton study calls "the service package" for the frail elderly and physically handicapped is made up as follows :

"84 per cent received some form of practical help, the highest

159

percentage of any client group. These services ranged from aids and adaptations (received by 36 per cent of cases), meals on wheels (23 per cent) and home helps (22 per cent) to a mere handful who had had a holiday arranged or who were referred to a voluntary visitor (3 per cent)."

This amount of practical assistance needed is very much what the previous samples had led one to expect. The report then goes on to say :

"For the more vulnerable and severely disabled longer term cases regular surveillance (41 per cent), support (33 per cent) and some form of counselling (33 per cent) were also part of the social work intervention."

The majority of the work with the severely disabled was done by the domiciliary occupational therapists who worked part-time for a long-term team consisting of 5 social workers, one half-time social worker and one senior social worker.

Unknown numbers of disabled people were still receiving the services of a home help and similarly unknown numbers of clients using aids and benefiting from adaptations. Clearly the habit of reviewing such clients was not built into this Southampton system.

The report does not indicate whether the 36 per cent who received aids and adaptations during the study year had received them quickly; nor if there were any cases requiring adaptations still outstanding. By implication the waiting list had not reached the overwhelming proportions that characterised some of the Greater London boroughs during a co-incident period of time.

The SECOND STEP – Allocation to a Social Worker

1. *Allocation to a Social Worker*

Those requests for aids that have not been winnowed away by area team managers, rejected by senior social workers, off-loaded on to other agencies or closed by intake teams, now find their way to the meetings of senior social workers and their teams. It was normal practice for seniors to outline the cases up for allocation and then invite members of their team to offer themselves for cases that interested them. Considerable doubts about this method of allocation were expressed by consultant staff interviewed as there was a general reluctance to take on handicapped clients. Few social workers showed any interest in working with disabled people and their families possibly because the majority of them felt they lacked the necessary

160

skills; and also perhaps because of the present reluctance of young workers "to work with clients who present problems outside the sociological context", and certainly because many senior workers who had formerly been able to "strike a spark" had left the field for administrative posts.[23] Mixed caseloads were not including physically handicapped people in anything like the percentage of the numbers referred and there was a tendency for such cases to remain unallocated[24] or for them to be given to untrained social workers and social work assistants.[25]

In two London boroughs which were visited twice in the course of the study, once in the autumn of 1974 and once in the spring of 1976, consultants for the handicapped had been responsible for changing the methods of allocation in these boroughs. Senior social workers were taking a much more active part at allocation meetings and were now directing cases to individual members of their teams. Their object was not only to see that everyone carried a fully mixed caseload but also to make sure that no single team member carried too many cases demanding intensive work at any one time.[26] In both of these boroughs cases were starred from five stars down to one star. Those with one star, the cases for periodic review, were retained by the senior social workers and became their sole responsibility. This relieved the social workers from feelings of guilt about failure to review clients and made room in their in-trays for work demanding a more rapid turn-over and for cases demanding intensive work over short periods. Neither of these boroughs employed occupational therapists.[27]

Allocation direct to occupational therapists varied from borough to borough and from area to area. Some areas invited occupational therapists to the seniors' meetings, but whether every case involving aids would necessarily be allocated to them varied with local practice. In some areas the role of the occupational therapists was seen as purely consultative, in others the "generic" principle prevailed over specialisation to the extent that occupational therapists complained that cases were deliberately withheld from them and that they were not even informed when clients were registered as physically handicapped. It was felt that the decision about whether an occupational therapist, a social worker or an ancillary social worker should make the first visit ought to rest with the professional, i.e. the occupational therapist, in order to minimise the possibility of damage to the client due to inexpert diagnosis in the first instance.

(i) *The Waiting List*
Between the allocation of a case to a specific fieldworker and the first visit to a client's home there falls a shadow – the Waiting List. Social services lack the resources to meet the demands made on them. Few

161

figures were forthcoming about the number of people who were waiting for a first home visit or for the average time they had to wait but
an average of six months for all but the most urgent cases is probable
in many boroughs.[28] Centrally-based administrators did not know
if staff in area offices had been asked to collate information about
waiting lists; figures had certainly not been asked for, or offered to
the secretariat. There were, however, frequent references by newly
appointed occupational therapists to the impossibility of catching up
with the backlogs they had inherited. Occupational therapists who
had been longer in post used such terms as "stagnant pools that will
never be drained". One occupational therapist said that she could
do no more than "keep a finger in the dyke", a metaphor that illus-
trates how threatened many people who work with the disabled felt
as a result of ever accumulating pressures.

Every director and assistant director interviewed was aware of the
overwhelming nature of the problem. They commented on the positive correlation between the success of well-conducted surveys[29] and
the impossibility of meeting all the needs they had uncovered. At the
time of the study only two boroughs had gone beyond a sample
survey. In these, trained social workers, specially seconded for the
job, were still working patiently ward by ward in an attempt to piece
together an overall picture of authenticated needs, but their directors
were under no illusions about the possibility of meeting any but the
most urgent cases that were continually being brought to light. The
thousands of false hopes that had been raised when inexperienced
and badly briefed volunteers had been involved in surveys often
served to compound and obscure problems of genuine need and
consequently further contributed to delays in identifying priorities of
need. Although new patterns of administration had been created in
some boroughs and new appointments made in all of them, demand
was more than even extended departments could cope with. As one
director said "the time has come to cry 'Halt' ". He felt that social
services departments could not be expected to seek out one single
new need until they had managed to provide an adequate service for
people on the waiting list. There was no shortage of money available
for aids and adaptations in this borough, the social services committee had always given the disabled a high priority and, even when
cuts in public spending became essential, the money available for aids
was still readily forthcoming, yet the waiting list grew steadily longer.

The effect of a lengthy waiting list on both clients and staff in
another borough with an equally proud record show how the initial
mood of optimism created by the appointment of a Rehabilitation
Team which also had special responsibility for aids and adaptations
changed to one of frustration and despair. Other boroughs which
had succeeded in identifying as many disabled people as possible

were meeting with similar difficulties and were similarly forced to decide between using untrained social work assistants to make the maximum number of visits possible or keeping up the high standard of professional care. In May 1974, in the borough chosen for an intensive study of the waiting list, a highly experienced head occupational therapist was appointed to lead a team of three domiciliary occupational therapists, an aids and adaptations officer (paid as AP 4), a half-time administrator (paid as AP 2) and a part-time clerical officer (paid at what was then called Clerical One).

Before the setting up of the team only one of the occupational therapists had served any length of time in the borough. She had dealt almost entirely with the mentally handicapped, both those in residential homes and those in the community. This, with admirable single-mindedness, she continued to do, although her new responsibilities now included the physically handicapped of two areas as well. Neither of the two other occupational therapists had any previous knowledge of the borough. Although there had been an establishment for three occupational therapists ever since the social services department had come into being, two of the posts had been filled only spasmodically and with long gaps in between.

During the first six weeks the head occupational therapist concentrated on visiting the area heads and social workers in order to hear their point of view and to describe the basic services to the physically handicapped that she saw as necessary. This initial period led to the domiciliary occupational therapists feeling well integrated with the social worker teams although they were based elsewhere, on a complex of day centres for the elderly, physically handicapped and mentally handicapped.[30]

By 31 December 1974 the head occupational therapist, the three area occupational therapists and the occupational therapist who also worked with mentally handicapped clients[31] had, between them, visited 1149 new referrals in their own homes. They had also made 756 "tie-up" visits, many of them to cases previously known to the and general practitioners, and a further 418 visits to hospitals, clinics and general practitioners. One month later, on 1 February 1975, the number of clients on the waiting list was 521 and as new cases were still flowing in from area intake teams and duty officers at a rate of between twenty and thirty a week the head occupational therapist spent a good deal of thought and time on helping her area occupational therapists to establish the urgency of needs and in distributing priorities between new cases, cases needing review and cases on a continually lengthening waiting list of those who still had to be seen for the first time.

By the end of February 1975, the average length of time between referral and first visit was six to sixteen weeks, of which only twenty-four hours was accounted for by the time taken for a request to reach the occupational therapist from area intake teams and duty officers. Attempts to send out letters to individual clients explaining why an immediate visit might not be possible were discontinued as, far from diminishing the frustration felt by the recipients, they appeared to the occupational therapists to reinforce a conviction that nobody was really bothering about them. Telephone calls, which could be very time-consuming, were dropped for similar reasons and all efforts were concentrated on making as many home visits as possible without reducing the quality of the assistance offered and the professionalism of the assessments made.

In spite of this the number of clients on the waiting list six months later had risen to 867, whilst the waiting period had risen from a minimum of six weeks on 1 February 1975 to a minimum of nine months by 31 July 1975. The number of clients on the waiting list had therefore increased by 62 per cent and the maximum time spent waiting by 250 per cent.

At this point the head occupational therapist demanded more staff. In a report to the social services committee made in August 1975 she pointed out that the length of the waiting list was demoralising for the existing staff as well as for clients and by June 1976 establishments for three more domiciliary occupational therapists had been created and advertised. Two of these posts were the re-allocated social worker posts already referred to and the third was to provide additional help in day centres and to "float" where demand was at its highest. In the meantime the professional skills of the four occupational therapists then available were now concentrated on the four areas which threw up the greatest number of demands. In the two remaining areas only cases of the highest urgency would be accepted by the occupational therapists, although clients could have their names put down on the waiting list on the firm understanding that no visit from an occupational therapist could be guaranteed. The practice of sending out letters of explanation was re-established but in the form of a standardised explanation without any reference to individual requests.

New criteria of urgency were drawn up as follows :

a. *Mobility*
   Where there is severe risk of falls (not due to blackouts) in negotiating steps or stairs in order to reach necessary parts of the house, e.g. access to the toilet.
b. *Toilet*
   Where there is great difficulty in managing toilet when living alone for all or part of the day.

c. *Bath*

Only if necessary for medical reasons, e.g. in severe cases of psoriasis or where saline bathing had been prescribed.

d. In some cases a *move of house* will present new or additional problems for a long established disabled person. If problems do occur, as indicated above, these cases may be regarded as priority.

e. *Sudden handicap in the younger age group living alone* could present problems in addition to those listed above. Clients in this category would be those suffering from a traumatic paraplegia, a stroke with resultant hemiplegia, those discharged from hospital following major surgery, e.g. amputation of a limb.

When all other cases of referral are discouraged in this way, there is a danger that subsequent figures will mask the true situation. At no time was it suggested that these clients who were being virtually rejected by occupational therapists were not in need of practical assistance and also of professional assessment and guidance.

The curtailment of services was undertaken with the sole object of reducing the numbers on the waiting list whilst still offering a fully professional service to those disabled people most in need of it. These included disabled people of all ages who were at risk and lived alone and people to whom access to existing amenities was no longer possible. The criteria laid down, although rigid, did not therefore exclude the possibility of extensive adaptations to property as well as the provision of aids. Indeed the social services committee, long accustomed to giving the disabled a high priority, continued to increase the budgetary allocation for aids and adaptations and also to give supplementary grants when essential. The over-stretched occupational therapists, unlike many social workers in 1974–75, willingly worked unpaid over-time, frequently making evening calls in order to assess disabled people in the context of the whole family. The only solution appeared to be to appoint still more domiciliary occupational therapists but although two more posts were advertised the rehabilitation team had still not reached the desired strength by the end of 1976.

One reason for this was that the acute shortage of occupational therapists meant that potential applicants could pick and choose where they wished to work and even at what salary. Inner London boroughs were not a first choice for occupational therapists for a variety of reasons. In this particular borough, because of the need to cut public expenditure, the social services committee of the borough studied felt unable to raise the salaries of its occupational therapists and therefore continued to advertise the posts as AP 3. This was a realistic salary in 1973–74 but was out of step with the AP 4 and AP 5 being offered by neighbouring Inner London boroughs and by some of the Outer London boroughs.[32] Many boroughs kept expenditure within bounds by employing fewer domiciliary occupational therapists at higher salaries. This it was felt ensured keeping the ones they had to at least the agreed complement.

The highest establishment for domiciliary occupational therapists in the Greater London area in 1975–76 was in an Outer London borough. It was for one head occupational therapist and sixteen area occupational therapists, two for each of eight areas. Fourteen of these posts were filled at the time of the study by occupational therapists paid at AP 4. The lowest establishment, other than the two boroughs who saw no necessity to employ educational therapists at all, was one – in another Outer London borough. When asked whether there was a long waiting list in this borough, the senior administrative officer replied that there had never been and never would be because he had made sure that the criteria for receiving aids and adaptations were so rigid that demand could not exceed supply. This borough had conducted only a very small token survey in 1972 and had never at any time been inundated by increases in identified needs. Somewhat surprisingly, it was nevertheless spending only one tenth less, in 1974–75 on aids and adaptation per 1,000 population, than the borough in which there was such a long waiting list.

A satisfactory compromise between professionalism and the over-use of inexperienced social work assistants would seem to offer the most practical solution. By the end of 1976, four boroughs had begun to encourage social work assistants interested in the disabled to work directly to their area occupational therapists. This involved the occupational therapists in the considerable work of briefing and follow-up, but produced a much speedier and on the whole satisfactory service for the majority of disabled clients. With the less complicated cases, such as simple requests for aids, dealt with quickly by their social work assistants, the occupational therapists were freed to concentrate on the more obviously complicated cases although occasionally it was said, their assistants might lack the skill required to pick up hidden needs.

One third line manager, formerly an occupational therapist herself, said "middle-aged women with commonsense, the ability to use a screw-driver and no desire to take a diploma in social work, are the backbone of the social services department." Another senior officer said "the social work assistants act as extra eyes, ears and legs. Without them the waiting list for aids would be even longer."[33]

(ii) *The use of untrained social workers and ancillary staff*
A senior officer in one of the Greater London boroughs said "We can't spare trained social workers to work with the disabled". One of

the few area team managers interviewed, asked why no social workers from his borough had attended a seminar on the management of arthritis, replied "But the invitation was for trained social workers only; we do not use trained social workers for the physically handicapped."[34] Other officers interviewed were less forthright although regrets expressed by directors and assistant directors about the shortage of experienced social workers implied, in the context of questions about the provision of aids and adaptations, a reluctant and all too frequent reliance on ancillaries. Carefully phrased questions about the content of induction and orientation courses reinforced these implications. One assistant director said that home helps showed far more interest in talks given for them about the physically handicapped because "unlike social workers, home helps actually work with disabled people". An assistant director (training) confessed that the only way to get a good attendance by social workers for any lecture on the physically handicapped was to mask it by titles like "Families with special problems of stress" – "otherwise that's the day of the course that they get 'flu' "!

There is therefore a vicious circle – social workers might become more interested in working with the disabled and their families if they acquired the requisite skills, but their preferences lead them away from acquiring these skills and so they remain uninterested and unwilling to take on cases of physical handicap.[35] A few social workers and social work assistants may hope to qualify, after in-training or secondment, for the new CCETSW diplomas, but the brunt of work with the physically handicapped, even in boroughs with an establishment of domiciliary occupational therapists, will continue to be borne by untrained social work assistants. Many of these are worried by their lack of experience and expertise and share with trained social workers misgivings about visiting clients with problems that they feel ill-equipped to deal with. Strikes in two Inner London boroughs in 1975 stressed a felt need for guidance from people with professional skills. In one of these boroughs all social workers and assistant social workers refused to take on any disabled clients until the social services committee agreed to create and advertise posts for four domiciliary occupational therapists on analogy with those on the strength of a neighbouring borough. In the other only one area office was involved. Here assistant social workers refused to work with the disabled until a long-standing vacancy for a senior social worker was filled. There was no occupational therapist attached to the area office and they felt they had no source of expert advice or supervision for cases and lacked the knowledge to deal with even the simplest issue of an aid. Both these strikes had the official backing of the union of National and Local Government officials.

Although senior officers in social services departments in the

Greater London boroughs were for the most part non-committal about the use of inexperienced staff for work with the physically handicapped, clients were not. All the clients in the small group interviewed in the second phase of this study were quick to volunteer comments about the quality of social work staff sent to visit them. Comments like "The one that came later wasn't the college one" and "She'd been to college but I mean to say she didn't know anything about life did she, hadn't brought up a family", show an awareness of the fact that some social workers were graduates. Another client asked if it were known whether or not the young lady ever passed her diploma. "She was so anxious to get my adaptation finished in case it went against her in her exam". Occupational therapists, however young, tended to be recognised as professionals more readily than trained social workers probably because their profession was already known to clients who had attended out-patients clinics, and possibly because some clients drew comfort from the fact that they had been trained at least for a short time within the discipline and structure of a hospital. For some disabled clients this association with hospitals offered a degree of security that was not felt in the presence of social workers. Clients were also remarkably quick to spot ancillary workers who were seen, more often than not, in the role of messengers from superior professionals who never came themselves, and were only very occasionally, if they were not young, taken for trained social workers.

The studies of consumer reaction in Southampton point to increasing client awareness as to whether or not they were being given professional help. This arose in part out of a marked increase in the level of expectation between 1972 and 1975 of what the social services should provide.[36] Expectation was lowest among the elderly and physically handicapped who formed almost half the sample in both years and about whom the report drew the conclusion that

"Because the elderly need so much practical help, their care is often entrusted to the social workers with the least skill and experience, such as welfare assistants."[37]

Clients in this age group were the least likely to expect casework relationships and usually saw a service as completed once a request, whether for a home help, meals on wheels, a holiday or an aid, was complied with. Because their demands on the whole were limited to the practical they were the most satisfied consumer group, but this did not mean that there were no complaints – 34 per cent of them complained in 1972. The most frequent complaint was that they were not visited often enough. In 1975 this group made fewer complaints, only 23 per cent, than the rest "but they made just as many suggestions."

Spontaneous criticism of the youth and immaturity of social workers and of a general lack of specialism, especially in work with the physically handicapped, were frequent complaints from clients of all age groups. The report says that, by 1975

"There was a shift in consumers' perceptions of social workers towards specialist knowledge and training rather than the practical knowledge and basic education emphasised in 1972."

One physically handicapped male, aged 54, said :

"There should be specialised training and not all lumped together. It's such a wide field. Again I don't think they can do everything."

One young physically handicapped person said :

"They should stick to what they are trained for, elderly or disabled or specifically children, not go from one to another."

In 1975 twice as many customers emphasised the need for training and specialist knowledge although experience of life and its problems was still valued. Such strongly held – and strongly expressed – views emphasise the need for a much more rapid implementation of the findings of the working party established in November 1972 by the Central Council for the Education and Training of Social Workers.

This report, which is called *Social Work: People with handicaps need better training*[38] was published in August 1974 and examines the problems of providing suitably trained workers at a variety of levels as seen by professionals from a variety of disciplines including local authority administrators, college lecturers, medical practitioners, social workers and social work assistants. It also recognises how many disabled people would themselves like to be involved with planning and decision-making about training workers and also in some of the training programmes including student placements that involved "round-the-clock-contact" with a family with a disabled member.[39]

The working party felt strongly that all fieldworkers should be provided, during their training,

"with basic knowledge about handicaps and the challenges and problems they present for individuals, their families and the community."

This should include up-to date knowledge of the various benefits in cash and kind available, including knowledge on how to instruct clients in the use of the simpler aids.[40]

It was also important that there should be

169

"opportunities for advanced studies for a small number of experienced staff"[41]

to replace the specialists who were becoming increasingly lost to the field since the reorganisation of local authority social services departments.

But the working party did not under-estimate the vital role played by some social work assistants :

"The interest shown by many of these non-professional staff in meeting some of the needs of the handicapped has to be kept alive."

One way of doing this might be through providing courses varying in aim, content and duration among which there would be some

"for workers in post who have had no adequate preparation for this kind of work."[42]

Such courses would involve day release as well as supervision by both academic and social work staff.

Nothing much appears to have developed in the way of advanced training since the report appeared in 1974 but pilot studies in six local authorities begun in 1975 show that, given the willingness of directors of social services to second social work assistants and the co-operation of colleges of further education to plan new courses focused on the problems of disability, such courses could prove of considerable value.[43] They would also provide the possibility of professional advancement for the less academically minded.

Apart from the problems involved in secondment, when there is already an acute shortage of trained workers, and of finance, at a time when many vacancies for professional workers have been frozen, it is possible that many untrained fieldworkers might not wish to be bothered with day release. The majority of social work assistants interested in working with the disabled were middle-aged, married women who had no interest in advancement within a career structure and no desire to be bothered with examinations or certificates. Indeed, they might be positively discouraged from working for occupational therapists if formal in-training were to be insisted on.

These studies also revealed a growing awareness of the part that might be played by the community. There was, it was felt, a place for self-help organisations and for volunteers but not for untrained social work assistants as emissaries of the social work profession. Nevertheless there remains a manifest need to employ social work assistants to back up the professional services of trained social workers and domiciliary occupational therapists by making preliminary visits, delivering small aids and checking on the safety of aids. What should not be done by untrained staff is any kind of clinical assessment and the step

170

that follows, the third step, although it may well succeed a visit by a social work assistant, should not be replaced by attempts at assessment made by non-professionals.

The THIRD STEP – The first home visit: assessment

The first visit to a client at home is crucial to all else that follows. In the Greater London area it must nevertheless be inferred that with the exception of three boroughs where the head occupational therapist saw visiting the disabled in terms of a "closed shop" and one borough with a specialist service unit,[44] the member of staff making that crucial home visit will in all probability be an untrained, unqualified and possibly inexperienced assistant social worker or an ancillary social work assistant. What assessment are they expected to make, and in what depth?

A straightforward, commonsense definition of what assessment is supposed to mean since the passing of the Chronically Sick and Disabled Persons Act 1970 is given in the first joint circular to follow it :

"the task of assessment should be undertaken as a normal part of the authority's social work service, i.e. it should be an occasion for considering all relevant needs and not merely those needs to which the Section [Section 2 (1) of the Chronically Sick and Disabled Persons Act] refers; and a judgement whether these needs or others are of prior importance should be drawn from a complete and not partial picture of the situation."[45]

Such a definition implies a high degree of skill and experience on the part of the person making the assessment, but local authority social services departments are sadly lacking in staff with the necessary qualifications either to suggest ways of reducing handicap or to make sensitive assessment of need.

Ideally the best person to make a total assessment of need would be a qualified, experienced generic social worker, of which there are relatively few. In such circumstances occupational therapists would then only be called in to give specialist advice, including advice on the most suitable kinds of aids and adaptations, in the way that general practitioners call in consultants. In practice the occupational therapist is being forced to become a generic social worker or perhaps even a new form of social worker altogether. The majority of occupational therapists found it simpler to make themselves authorities on things such as heating and constant attendance allowances than to try to involve social workers. When skilled staff are scarce, duplication of effort needs to be avoided. But at the same time occupational therapists may need to concentrate on physical assessments which social workers are not trained to do if they are to visit the maximum number of clients in need of their specialist skills.

Assessments sometimes take place outside the client's home e.g. a domiciliary occupational therapist may accompany her client to a hospital wheelchair clinic or an Appliance and Artificial Limb Centre. Some boroughs have incorporated special aids to daily living (ADL) units rooms in day centres, where clients may well benefit from practice in using a washing machine, a special kind of sink, a split-level cooker or a new kind of wall-positioned hot water boiler, provided similar models exist in their own homes, or can be installed under home conditions. The ability or otherwise, of a client to get in and out of beds of different heights can also be assessed at an ADL unit but the positioning of the bed at home has still to be determined. Can it be reached on the client's "good" side? Can it be put in the middle of a bedroom or bed-sitter? If so, can other necessary aids for getting in and out of bed still be used? Can the height of the present bed be adjusted by the use of bed-blocks or by sawing off bits of legs? Is the mattress lumpy, unhygienic, possibly even infested? Even the use of an aid as simple as a stocking gutter may depend on having somewhere to sit that is convenient and at the right height for dressing. The folly of issuing clients with bath aids without first assessing if they have baths, feel able to pay for sufficient hot water or feel much safer "washing down" still occurs all too frequently. These are details which occupational therapists are trained to pick up, but which are not always realised by social workers or by hospital staff unacquainted with the home conditions of their patients.

For these reasons the first visit to a client should be in his or her own home. It should be used to assess the total situation and should concern itself with how long, and by what methods, the client can be kept out of residential care. In such a context it matters very little what size of pearl button arthritic or weakened fingers can manage to do up on a shirt or blouse. There are many accepted garments today that do not have buttons at all, and there are "Zip-aids" to help with zip fasteners and strips of adhesive fastening that do away with the need for any other kind of closure.

During the course of the study ex-welfare officers were heard to volunteer the information that they could "do" eight or ten full assessments a day and consequently could not understand why occupational therapists were unable to undertake an equal number of visits. Qualified occupational therapists who had formerly worked in welfare departments under the title of welfare officers were also heard at times to express similar views, but they were in a minority. Obviously some assessments of need will take a shorter time than others. A client with fairly severe arthritis might need small aids, such as tap-turners and a special tin-opener, and perhaps a self-operated hoist and an ejector chair. Before the latter could be ordered the client would need to be weighed in order to ensure correct springing in the seat. If a good relationship with the client is also to be established it is unlikely that a first visit could take less than an hour. The assessment of clients with severe degenerative diseases of the nervous system might well take longer, especially as these have to be done in a way that will minimise rather than increase anxiety. Professional skill is needed to assess even apparently small needs. One client sent home from hospital needed only a bath stool, but the social work assistant sent to measure for it immediately offered a stocking gutter and a long-handled comb as well, although it was medically of vital importance for the client to continue to make all the movements of everyday life as often as possible. As a result of this over-pampering with aids, this client's muscles seized up for good greatly to the concern of the medical staff who had been treating her. For similar reasons – and also for psychological reasons – it may at times be wise to encourage clients to do without aids, and adaptations, for as long as possible. Perhaps one of the greatest advantages of employing professionals to make skilled assessments is that professionals are more likely to have the knowledge, and therefore the courage, to withhold services and to say a firm "No".[46]

The majority of assessments, however, lead to requests for aids, the authorisation of the requests and the ordering, issuing and delivery of aids to the client's home. These processes are discussed in detail in the next chapter.

NOTES

1. Two directors and one assistant director wanted to see the receptionist upgraded from Clerical 1/2 to AP/4, the grade of the qualified and experienced social worker, and specially trained to conduct preliminary interviews and relieved of the need to deal with a switchboard. Such receptionists would be able to allocate priorities and pass clients on to the most appropriate case-workers, thus by-passing some of the work done by duty officers and intake teams.
2. When the receptionist deals with more than one municipal department, the task of re-directing clients is often made easier; on the other hand the strain on the switchboard can be correspondingly increased especially when there are not enough internal lines free or enough lines for incoming calls.
3. In one borough a research project which monitored referrals in 1974–75 revealed 16 official and 17 voluntary agencies to which clients were referred.
4. A great deal of social work is done over the telephone, involving long periods of "hanging on" for information needed by clients from the local offices of the DHSS, Department of Employment, Gas and Electricity Boards, etc.
5. The Disabled Living Foundation reported that disabled people who had been to their permanent exhibition and who had been advised by them to ask their local social services department for advice on the suitability of an aid for their home conditions frequently complained that neither an acknowledgement of a letter nor any help was forthcoming. Routine acknowledgements on behalf of the directors are seldom sent out on grounds of expense.
6. In a borough which considers a stair-lift an aid not an adaptation a request from a doctor on behalf of a patient suffering from severe angina was sympathetically received as "a means of saving life." Nevertheless, the stair-lift itself took over nine months before installation was completed.
7. See *Report on New Referrals to the Social Work Division Northern Area Office 1974–75*. (Internal publication, 1975), Appendix D4, p. 5.
8. See Neill, June E., *A Study of Referrals*, the National Institute for Social Work Research Unit, internal publication, (1974), p. 18.
9. *Op. cit.*, p. 87.
10. See Hall, A. S. "Client Reception in a Social Services Agency", *Public Administration*,

Vol. 49, pp. 25–42 (London, 1970) later to be elaborated in *The Point of Entry: A Study of Client Reception in the Social Services* (London, 1975).

11. See Smith, G. and Ames, Janet, in "Area Teams in Social Work Practice: a Programme for Research," *British Journal of Social Work, Vol. 6, No. 1* (London, 1977), p. 47.

12. Zimmerman, D. H. "Tasks and Troubles: The Practical Bases of Work Activities in a Public Assistance Organisation," Chapter 8, in Hansen, D. A. (ed.), *Explorations in Sociology and Counselling* (Boston, 1966). Zimmerman, D. H. "Record Keeping and the Intake Process in a Public Welfare Agency", Chapter 11, in Wheeler, S. (ed.), *On Record: Files and Dossiers in American Life* (New York, 1969).

13. *Op. cit.*, paragraph 8.6.

14. For the interested student who meets the required standards of confidentiality such case files would throw a valuable insight into, among other things, the changing expectations that clients have of what a service should provide. The case histories of clients long known to the social services, and the health and welfare departments before them, could also yield information. Many an initial self-referral is followed by referrals from neighbours, gasmen, milkmen, coalmen and even sanitation officers as the years go by.

15. In some boroughs home helps attended special lectures on the needs of the disabled given by occupational therapists and Aids and Adaptations Officers. Evidence suggests that the majority of home helps liked going to such lectures as indications of a degree of professionalism on their part.

16. Of 390 cases from ten area offices in one London borough the source of referral was known for only 49. Of these, 42 were from hospitals (29) health visitors (8) school health visitors (2) and general practitioners (3).

17. See Loewenstein, Carole, "An Intake Team in Action in a Social Services Department in an Inner London Borough", *British Journal of Social Work*, Vol. IV, No. 2 (1974).

18. See McKay, A., *et al.,* "Consumers and Social Services Departments", *Social Work To-day*, Vol. 4, No. 1, 15 November 1973, and Glampson, A., *et al.,* "Post-Seebohm Social Services (2): The Consumers' viewpoint". *Ibid.,* Vol. 8, No. 6, 9 November 1976.

19. See Goldberg, E. Matilda, *et al.,* "Towards Accountability in Social Work: One Year's Intake in an Area Office". *British Journal of Social Work*, Vol. 7, No. 3, Autumn 1977.

20. *Ibid.* Referrals were up one-fifth on those of the previous year but of these more than half were re-applications by known clients. This reflected a deliberate policy of closing cases earlier that was also the practice in the Northern Office in Kensington and Chelsea.

21. The three boroughs were Camden, Kensington and Chelsea and Kingston-upon-Thames (internal publications).

22. The Northern area office which followed much the same practice as the Southampton area office showed that 21 per cent of referrals concerned problems associated with the elderly and 12 per cent with physical handicap, making a total of 34 per cent. In the Southern area the percentage for the elderly was over 50 per cent with the physically handicapped who were not elderly accounting for only 4 out of 123 clients; in the Central area the figures were 27.5 per cent (elderly) and 20 per cent (physically handicapped) making a combined total of 47.5 per cent compared with the 30 per cent in the Southampton study.

23. See CCETSW, Paper 9, *op. cit.*, page 35.

24. See Neill, June E., *et al.:* "Reactions to Integration", and Chapter Five, p. 121 n. 11.

25. The most recent of the Southampton studies reported that in 1976, the physically disabled under 65, except for the mentally handicapped, were the group in which the highest number of unqualified staff were involved. This was, however, also the group which was most likely to expect and receive only practical assistance. *Op. cit.*, p. 272. See also C (iii) of this chapter.

26. Allocation in the majority of boroughs was frequently postponed. Studies in Kingston-upon-Thames showed that the reason for this in 90 per cent of cases was shortage of staff. "It was found that around 60 per cent was carried forward each week (i.e. pending a decision or action to be taken), and that this proportion grew over the weeks studied . . . mainly because the group leaders considered that their staff already had the maximum numbers of cases they could cope with . . . " See *Clearing House*, No. 4, 1975.

27. In boroughs employing Head occupational therapists cases involving the physically handicapped are allotted with the same objects of balancing case-loads and removing guilt feelings but Head occupational therapists do not themselves carry caseloads.

28. One Head occupational therapist said that each area office could put up a thousand cases with genuine but not urgent needs.

29. See Section 1 of the Chronically Sick and Disabled Persons Act 1970, and DHSS Circular 45/71, para. 11.

30. The good relations established then were to pay off two years later when, under pressure from area social workers, two social work posts that fell vacant were advertised as posts for two more domiciliary occupational therapists. This brought the total establishment for domiciliary occupational therapists up to one head occupational therapist and one occupational therapist for each of the six areas.

31. The occupational therapists throughout the Greater London boroughs reported anxiety about the neglect of the mentally handicapped, as the result of the demand made on them for aids and adaptations, the result of the Chronically Sick and Disabled Persons Act 1970. By the end of 1975 many were saying that this neglect has also led to less job satisfaction.

32. The willingness of some Greater London boroughs to pay domiciliary occupational therapists

more than their colleagues in hospitals and district health authorities was to prove professionally divisive. A marked bitterness on the part of some hospital-based occupational therapists persisted well into 1976, over a year after a new Whitley scale had brought their salaries more into line with those of borough employees. The use by domiciliary occupational therapists of such names as rehabilitation officer in order that payment could exceed the Whitley scale was also a source of contention.

33. The 1973 report on *The Remedial Professions* had noted in para. 13, "the employment of 'aides' (sometimes called 'helpers') to qualified therapists is increasing throughout the country, although there is no common standard on the degree of help they are allowed to give, or the extent to which they can act on their own. Nevertheless they make an essential contribution to the remedial services of which full advantage is not being taken". And in para. 39 the Report suggests that "certain tasks might safely be delegated to aides".

Until the length of the waiting lists for aids and adaptations assumed menacing proportions it was customary to use scarce auxiliary social work staff for a variety of purposes. Before "attachment to occupational therapists could be made extra ancillary posts had to be established to cover the gaps left in more generalised service but between 1974 and 1976 the first priority was to secure a sufficient number of occupational therapists.

34. Elderly arthritics form the highest category of the disabled population and receive the highest percentage of aids but once they have been given an aid their cases, except for the most severely affected, are either closed or suspended between reviews.

35. C.f. Neill, June E., *et al.*, "Reactions to Integration" (1973). This study of preferences asks: "Is social work with the elderly and physically handicapped taught with as much imagination and conviction as is social work with children and families?" *op. cit.*

36. See McKay, A. *et al., op. cit.*, Glampson, A. *et al., op. cit.*

37. The term "welfare assistant" here means the same as social work assistant in the Greater London area.

38. CCETSW Paper 5 (London, 1974),

39. *Ibid,,* paras 36, 10 and 88.

40. *Ibid.,* para. 64.

41. *Ibid.,* para. 9? (f).

42. *Ibid.,* para. 93.

43. Plans for a special option in the course for the Certificate for Social Work can be found in CCETSW Paper No. 9 (London, 1976).

44. By the end of 1976 a second borough had decided to detach a specialist service unit to act as consultants for social workers. This borough hoped to have one occupational therapist as part of this unit.

45. Circular 12/70 (Department of Health and Social Security) issued jointly with Circular 13/70 (Department of Education and Science) Circular 65/70 (Ministry of Housing and Local Government) and Circular ROADS No. 24/70 (Ministry of Transport) on August 17th 1970, four months after the Act went on to the Statutes. Para. 7, Section 2, of the Act includes provisions for help with practical assistance in the home and also adaptation.

46. Financial assessment is done when necessary by officers of the borough finance department. See Chapter Four, pp. 91-94.

CHAPTER NINE

GETTING THE AIDS TO THE CLIENT (2):
INDENTING, AUTHORISING, ORDERING, DELIVERING
AND INSTALLING AIDS

If the home visit shows that the aid asked for was necessary, or that a
different aid would be more appropriate, then the next step is to
indent for the aid. Sometimes more than one aid will have been
considered necessary, in which case they will be asked for simul-
taneously.

The FOURTH STEP – The Indent

All the boroughs in the Greater London area used stock forms for
requesting aids and all save one issued these forms in triplicate with
each copy a different colour.[1] In the borough that did not use tripli-
cates, the aids were requested on a Roneo-ed piece of paper, too
thick for carbon copies to be easily made from it. This form went off
to the clerk who ordered the aids and, unless the fieldworker had
made careful notes, "chasing up" the ordering of the aid, which was
often necessary, could be difficult.

What happened to the different coloured copies in the other
boroughs varied from borough to borough, but one copy always
ended up with an officer in the finance department so that its cost
could be entered against the money allocated for aids when payment
was authorised. One copy was used to initiate ordering processes and
one was usually retained by the fieldworker concerned and placed
on the client's file. Those boroughs which had adopted tear-off slips
at the bottom of the forms were able to simplify such processes as
ordering transport and getting receipts from clients. They might also
have used them as a simple way of keeping the fieldworkers informed
about the stages reached.

Several social services departments had either recently redesigned
the forms used to request aids or were considering doing so. The new
forms tended to have been designed with an eye on the annual
statistics required by the Department of Health and Social Security,
e.g. age of client, if living alone, etc., which was sensible although not
all supplied the information needed. Few forms had been re-designed

with the deliberate intention of stream-lining the processes involved in getting the aids to the waiting clients, although one social services department had designed a form which could be used jointly with the head occupational therapist of a large teaching hospital in order to speed up the delivery of aids for patients awaiting discharge from hospital.

A typical form might well ask for the following details :

NAME OF CLIENT

SEX

MARRIED/WIDOWED/SINGLE

NATURE OF DISABILITY

REGISTERED AS PHYSICALLY HANDICAPPED   YES/NO

AIDS REQUIRED

AGE   under 16   16/65
(please tick)
                         ☐   ☐

                       over 65   over 75

                         ☐   ☐

KIND OF ACCOMMODATION (Please underline)
Council   GLC
Privately rented   Owner occupier

CLIENT LIVES (Please underline)
Alone   With relatives

These details might be of little interest to clerks ordering aids, although of value for statistics and planning. Clerks may notice that a client lives alone and so might arrange a convenient time for delivering an aid, e.g. when a visitor or home help would be available to answer the door, but for the most part the name and address of the client and the aid requested is the limit of their concern. A well-designed form might also include a space in which the fieldworker could give details about the best days and times for delivery.[2] This happened in only two boroughs.

Many forms will already have received a signature of authorisation (e.g. relatively inexpensive aids authorised by a senior social worker) before reaching the clerk. In such cases, ordering can begin at once. But if further authorisation is needed the Fifth Step must be taken before the clerk may order an aid.

The FIFTH STEP – Authorisation

Before an aid is ordered, even if it is in stock, it may be necessary first of all to find out how much it costs and then to seek authorisation for its issue from a superior officer either in the field or in the secretariat. The different levels of expenditure that can be authorised by different levels of the hierarchy without referral to the social services committee are known as "ceilings of authorisation". They are a system of procedural checks and balances that have been built into local government administration and whilst ensuring that public money is not spent without due consideration they are a major cause of delay. They impose a kind of rationing by slow-down which, especially where adaptations are concerned, contributed to holding down expenditure in any one financial year. Even the less costly aids are subjected to similar procedures of internal review. One borough expected an area team manager to countersign for a senior social worker for anything costing over £25, a figure recently raised early in the financial year 1973–74 from £5, and raised again in 1975–76 to £50. By the year 1975–76 the average ceiling below which a senior social worker was allowed to sign was £100, and most domiciliary occupational therapists had secured the right to sign for the same amount. A majority of head occupational therapists could sign for anything up to £500, as could aids and adaptations officer at consultant level.

The ceilings authorised for different grades are shown in Table 14 on pages 180–81. The low sums at which some boroughs go to committee are in heavy contrast with the discretionary powers allowed directors of social services departments in other boroughs. In order to make savings in the cost of administration one borough wrote off any adaptation costing less than £5 but took any adaptation over that amount to committee.[3] That as low a figure as £5 was chosen as the point at which to go to committee is of interest as 1974–75 was the peak year for local authority social services spending in most of the Greater London boroughs.

The ceilings of authorisation for adaptations were the same as those for aids in all except one borough and although only a very few aids, such as special beds, would have cost over £1,000 in themselves some boroughs included the cost of installing the aid along with the price of the aid and assessed for both together. This meant that certain kinds of stair-lifts, lifts and electric ceiling track hoists involved a total cost of more than £1,000. In such cases permission to buy and install the aid would have to be sought at one of the appropriate levels as indicated in Table 14.

The minimum of delay in the issuing of aids, while ensuring a responsible attitude towards the expenditure of public money, might be achieved as follows :

1. Small "stock" aids in constant supply to be signed for by social workers and assistant social workers and (exceptionally) store-keepers.
2. Aids up to £100 to be signed for by a senior social worker or area occupational therapist.
   [Counter-signature by area team manager eliminated]
3. Aids costing between £100–£500 signed for by either
   (a) a head occupational therapist or
   (b) an aids and adaptations officer of principal officer rank, or
   (c) a third-line manager
4. Any aid which costs more than £500 or which, together with the costs of installation costs more than £500, to go up to the assistant director, who may
5. request a personal authorisation from the director or
6. take the request to committee.

For *Adaptations*, a reasonable sum for authorisation by assistant directors and/or directors would be £2,000.

No assistant director should have the power to turn down any application that has gone far enough up the hierarchy to reach him without calling a case conference and/or taking the case to committee. It goes without saying that a decision to take a case to the social services committee should be taken as quickly as possible so that the necessary reports can be prepared in time to catch the first available committee cycle. Otherwise an additional delay, on top of all the previous delays, of as much as six weeks will be unavoidable.

Throughout 1974–76 there was considerable pressure on directors of social services to raise the amounts at which different grades of staff could authorise expenditure on aids and adaptations partly because in a time of inflation the cost of individual aids had made the lower ceiling administratively impracticable and partly because the fieldworkers concerned felt it was time that social services committees showed a reasonable confidence in their professional competence. For similar reasons, the level of discretionary powers afforded directors of social services also reflected a scaling upwards. By 1975–76, three directors had been granted total discretionary powers, a fourth had discretion up to £3,000 and a fifth up to £5,000. None of these however envisage using their powers for anything exceeding £3,000, and most of them "would at least have a word" with the chairman of the social services committee" on matters involving sums

179

Table 14 – Financial Sanction for Aids and Adaptations
Ceilings Authorised by Different Grades of Staff. £'s

Borough	S.S.W. and S.S.O.	Area O T	Area Team Manager	A.P. 3	A.P. 5	S.O. 1	Principal Officer	Assistant Director	Director	Committee	Notes
1						over 500	----→	----→	----→	over 500	
2		500					Aids 500 Adapts. 300	over 500 over 300			
3									Total discretion		
4	Any Aid on Standard List						200. All aids over 200	Over 200 under 500	----→	over 500	
5	Any Aid on Standard List			Adapts. 50				Adapts. over 50			
6		Aids 200		Aids over 200					as necessary	All Adapts.	
7	All Aids on Standard List. Other Aids 30				----→				Total discretion but reports ----→	everything of interest*	*To Sub-Committee
8			50 ----→								
9						----→		----→			
10											
11	100	100						over 100	Total discretion		
12			50	25				1,500		Sees all over 200	
13											
14	100					100–250	----→	250		Sub-Committee 250	
15						100		1,500	3,000		
16	100*										*Aids and Adapts. Officer

180

17	75	250	250		
18	50		Aids 100 Adapts. 500		
19	100*				*Specialist Service Officer
20	10		Aids 50 - - - - → 50 Adapts. 500 - - - - → 500		
21			Sees everything over 10	300	
22		400 (Head OT and SO 1)		Total discretion within budget	
23	100	500 (Head OT)	500 - - - - - - - - →		
24	100	100	400		
25	1,000		1,000		
26		over 1,000 - - - - →	over 1,000 - - - - →	Up to 500*	Signed by Chairman
27		25 (Head OT)	All over 25	Aids and Adapts. powers fully delegated	
28	All Standard Aids on List		750	Yes	
29		250 (Head OT)		Over 250*	But always approved
30		150	1,000	Over 1,000	
31	100 - - - - - - - →		300	Over 300	
32			100	250	Yes
33	30	50	5,000		

181

a good deal lower. A sixth director had total discretion within the budget and had been told that no supplementary grants would be forthcoming.

Even in those Greater London boroughs which operated the fewest (and therefore the highest) ceilings of authorisation, delays for any aid or adaptation costing more than £100 were seldom less than one month even when it had not been considered necessary to take the case on to committee.

All delays of any kind are costly in terms of the frustration of administrators, fieldwork staff and clients alike; they also cost hard cash. The price of building materials keeps going up while officials ponder their decisions. In boroughs with a bad name for being slow to gain committee approval after estimates have been submitted, fewer builders will be willing to tender. The result is that where demand for services is higher than supply, those who do submit estimates price them unreasonably high in the knowledge that social services departments not using direct labour are compelled to accept. If public money is to be saved the process of decision-making needs to be speeded up. This is far more pressing than evaluating proposals at various stages in the hierarchy. Three boroughs had been forced to adopt a system of interim payments "to keep the builders happy". A fourth had resorted to a variety of subterfuges that ought not to have been necessary.[4] The quicker an adaptation or a costly installation of an aid is authorised the better for all concerned.

The SIXTH STEP – Ordering the Aid

Once an aid has been authorised the process of ordering can go ahead. If the aid is one that is already in stock the person in charge of the stores will be given written instructions to release it. If it has to come from a manufacturer, the ordering officer will need to have a clear idea of what is required.

Describing an aid on an order form is not easy. Domiciliary occupational therapists and aids and adaptations officers at consultant level will have made it their business to keep abreast of the commercial market and will know the trade names of aids and the names of the firms manufacturing them. Assistant social workers, social workers and even seniors may have little knowledge of what is available. They may never have visited the permanent exhibition at the Disabled Living Foundation or even local demonstrations run from time to time by manufacturers in day centres or Town Halls. The literature, which is issued monthly by the Disabled Living Foundation and to which every Greater London borough subscribes,[5] was rarely to be found in an area office. The special books on Equipment for the Disabled, from Mary Marlborough Lodge[6] have always been kept centrally, and are thus more likely to be known to clerks in the secretariat. All the clerks interviewed were knowledgeable about manufacturers, comparative prices and the speed and reliability of delivery dates. On one occasion it was the clerk who told a team meeting of occupational therapists that she had seen a device at the Disabled Living Foundation for turning patients that cost £40. This knowledge obviated the need to purchase a special kind of bed costing several hundreds of pounds. This degree of interest and involvement on the part of clerical staff was in no way exceptional.

An analysis of all the aids to daily living issued by an Inner London borough during a three-month period shows that just over 66 per cent of them were bath aids, most of which came direct from stock. These and other aids kept in stock, such as pick-up sticks, trolleys and high-seat chairs, are marked with an asterisk on Table 15 that follows on pages 184–85.

The issue of two beds is interesting as in some boroughs all beds are considered a health responsibility even if a disability is chronic rather than temporary. Those issued by this social services department went to clients with a severe degenerative disease who were being looked after by relatives.

The number of aids to mobility and aids to help in the performance of simple household tasks reflects a higher than average proportion of aged people in the borough's population and a high incidence of arthritis. Of the 39 clients in the sample just over 60 per cent were over 65 with eleven clients over 75. Just over half suffered from either rheumatoid or osteo-arthritis.

This borough was one of two to issue refrigerators as aids to daily living for severely disabled people who live alone and cannot do their own shopping. These do not show up in the period analysed, possibly because it was winter.

Responsibility for ordering aids, and seeing that they reach the client, belonged, in the borough chosen for the analysis, to a small sub-section of the domiciliary section of a fieldwork management division. The actual ordering was done by an officer graded as Clerical Three. This officer also dealt with the installation of aids and any minor adaptations to property that installation might involve.[7] All requests received, whether on a stock form or by a telephone call from another agency, were entered in some form of Day Book or Day Ledger. Although the ledger kept in the borough chosen was in no way a model of clarity, the number of aids issued were among the three highest for the Greater London area. The speed with which they were delivered also compared favourably with that of the majority of boroughs for reasons which are discussed in the next section.

Table 15 – Breakdown of 631 Aids ordered for 397 clients by an Inner London borough during the period 1 January to 31 March 1976 (excluding aids for the blind and deaf)

Kind of Aid	Number issued	Percentage of total of aids issued
Bath aids		
* Non-slip bath mats	77	
Non-slip strips	4	
* Bath boards	46	
* "Economic" bath rail	29	
Bath rails (other)	53	
* Bath seats	81	
Bath hammock	1	
** Grab rails	70	
Sponges	3	
* Long-handled brush	2	
	366	58.0
Showers		
Cabinet shower	1	
Spray shower (telephone)	5	
Shower curtains (set)	1	
	7	1.1
Toilet aids		
*Raised toilet seats	38	
* Screw down toilet frames	12	
Drop down arm for toilet	1	
	51	8.1
Lifting aids		
Monkey poles	7	
Rope ladders	4	
* Hoists (Mecalift)	3	
Hoists (Wessex)	1	
Hoists (Trapeze)	1	
Heavy-duty patient lifter	1	
	17	2.7
Bed Aids		
Beds	2	
Bed cradles	3	
Back rests	6	
* Bed blocks	7	
* Bed tables	2	
Bed boards	1	
* Foam rings	2	
	23	3.6
Mobility Aids		
* Walking sticks	12	
"Glide abouts"	1	
* Walking frames	11	
Tripods	5	
* "Ewall" trolleys	14	
* Portable wooden ramp	2	
	45	7.1

Kind of Aid	Number issued	Percentage of total of aids issued
Sitting Aids		
* High seat chairs	22	
Geriatric	2	
Ejector chairs	2	
* Stools (high)	8	
* Stools (foot)	2	
* Leg rests	4	
* Chair blocks	4	
	44	7.0
Aids to help arthritics etc.		
* Elastic shoe laces	1	
Tap turners	2	
Knitting aids	1	
Hot water bottle filler	1	
* Teapot tippers	3	
* Spike boards	1	
* Tin openers (1 wall fitted)	12	
* Bottle openers	6	
* Stocking gutters	4	
* Sock aids	1	
* Suction egg cups	1	
* Nelson knives	1	
* Special plate	1	
* Plate mat	1	
* Pick-up sticks	10	
* "Helping Hands"	2	
Twixtik	1	
* Zip aids	2	
Razor attachments	3	
* Potato peelers (left-handed)	2	
* Dusters	2	
* Shoe horns	3	
Strainers	3	
Pastry blenders	1	
Key holders	1	
	66	10.5
Miscellaneous aids		
Strip light for kitchen	1	
Extension leads for power points	2	
"Entry phones"	3	
Sheepskin heel protectors, pr	1	
Tack-down carpet	1	
Fracture board	1	
Gas lighter	2	
Rubazote	1	
	12	1.9

* The aids starred were bought in bulk and stocked in varying quantities in the stores.
** Grab-rails, although considered to be adaptations in this borough, were nevertheless counted as aids to daily living for administrative convenience.

The clerk entered the aids required against the surname of the client, along with the date on which the request had been received, but there were no columns or headings and the information was haphazardly set out. This made retrieval time-consuming for the researcher as it was not possible to see at a glance whether an aid had been delivered, or when, although the information was there. A typical entry for a client with multiple handicaps needing more than one aid might read;

SMITH 1.1.75. EBR. n/s/b b/b/s   Surrey LO 12345 4.2.76.
Grabrail   Undoit/Strongbow.   P/u stick   LO 56789 7.2.76.

This, translated, meant that the client needed an "Economic" bath rail, a non-slip bathmat and bath seat, a special kind of screw-down toilet rail, a grab rail, a special kind of can-opener, a special bottle opener and a pick-up stick. The initials LO meant that two of these articles required installation by staff from the borough engineers' department under a system known as "local orders" and the dates following them indicate the date on which the clerk received written confirmation from the borough engineers' department that the installation had been completed.

The choice of the last quarter of the financial year for this analysis may seem unwise but clear-sighted budgeting had left enough money for purchases in March[8] and the staffing situation was good in both the social services department chosen and rather better than usual in the borough engineers' department. As the installation of aids in council property could only be carried out by technical officers on the staff of the borough engineer, it was important to find a period when neither department was experiencing more than routine difficulties with staff.[9]

The SEVENTH STEP – Delivering Aids

Seeing that aids actually reach their destination often requires a good deal of organisation, especially when other borough departments are involved. The simplest way of getting an aid to a client, if it is small enough to go in a car, is for an occupational therapist or social worker to collect it and deliver it in person. This may not be as easy as it sounds for stores are not always open, especially if the storeman is also a driver or a handyman, and many aids bought in bulk may go first to the aids section of the secretariat which, in a large borough, may be some miles away from the area to which they are working. In such cases other means of delivery must be found.

The great advantage of occupational therapists delivering aids themselves is that they can make sure that the aid delivered is the correct one and that it is safe. They can also instruct the client in its

186

correct use at a time when the client is most likely to be interested in trying it out and most in need of encouragement.

Social work assistants were frequently used to deliver aids and one borough which had been required to prune the number of vans allocated to its social services department as a measure of economy had come to rely on them to deliver all but the most cumbersome aids. They could also be expected to check the aids they delivered and do their best to advise and instruct clients about how to use them.

The least satisfactory method of delivery was by transport ordered from a centralised borough pool. For this a minimum of 24 hours advance notice had to be given and there was no guarantee that the aids could be fitted in on established runs for at least a week. One senior official in the "Supplies" section of a social services department reported that he frequently had to rent a private "Rent-a-Van" for aids needing urgent delivery. Recourse to private "Rent-a-Van" companies was also mentioned by officials in two other boroughs as a means of reducing backlogs in delivering aids even when transport was centred on the social services department.

Twenty-one social services departments had their own pool of transport vehicles. These were serviced centrally by employees of the borough engineers or technical services departments but it was seldom possible for a van in need of servicing and repair to be replaced by one from the general pool. Nor were replacements made for drivers on sick leave or holiday. A number of vans allocated to the social services departments were off the road for such reasons. The social services departments with the largest fleet of vans nevertheless allotted only one day a week for the delivery of aids in spite of repeated protests by its head occupational therapist. On the other hand the borough issuing the maximum number of aids in the Greater London area was also dependent on social services department transport, but was nevertheless able to guarantee a daily delivery to all areas, often at less than 24 hours notice. Two other social services departments claimed to have no problems about daily delivery but so few aids were issued that there were no problems about fitting them in on daily runs connected with a variety of services. Two boroughs could rely on delivery by a social services department van for three stated days a week; one had the use of a van and driver on two mornings and two afternoons a week and in another borough deliveries could be planned, given 24 hours notice, by three vans which between them visited all areas of the borough daily.

Although it seems reasonable to rationalise transport by making the maximum possible use of vans visiting any one area on any one day – and to fill them to capacity – there is no doubt that this can result in delay in delivering aids. There is only so much space available on each vehicle and a transport officer may lack sufficient background information to determine priorities or to decide between one request for transport and another. There is also a risk of small aids, such as walking sticks, being overlooked on the first run because they have slipped down behind bulkier objects.[10]

Another problem arises if a client is out or if there is no one in the house able to answer the door at the time of delivery. The impersonal delivery service provided by vanmen who have no duties beyond the need to knock at a door needs to have built-in administrative safeguards. Some vanmen in some boroughs were prepared to obtain a signed form of receipt but others were not. Only two social services departments felt confident that the receipt form could be used to ensure that, if an aid had been out on a van and not been delivered, delivery on the next run to the area concerned would be automatic. Lack of feed-back about delivery meant lack of follow-up in most boroughs with resultant delays that were neither predictable nor controllable under the existing system.[11]

Somewhat better results were obtained when the vanmen making the deliveries had some degree of personal involvement with the clients, e.g. the same vans and vanmen delivered nothing except aids on certain specified days. In some boroughs vans, but not drivers, were put at the disposal of storemen, handymen and technical assistants. Planned deliveries, in one borough, were made by four handymen[12] who between them had three goods vans at their disposal to serve four areas. In two boroughs, storemen had the exclusive use of a van for two days a week and in two more for three days a week. Only one storeman had a van for his exclusive use at all times and he had also achieved the right to park it in the same compound as his storehouse, instead of having to return it nightly to a central garage.

Only one social services department had its own vehicles. They had been built to the department's specifications and were multi-purpose. One borough had succeeded in buying two tail-lift vans for delivering aids out of funds supplied by Urban Aid but another borough had its application for a similar van turned down in favour of a second van to deliver kosher meals-on-wheels to areas with a predominantly elderly isolated and Jewish population.

Regulations forbid vans or ambulances carrying passengers, e.g. on a daily run to a day centre, to carry anything else such as aids. This prohibition was usually adhered to as van-drivers were very well aware of rules and regulations of all kinds and had a very strong Trade Union. Indeed only three boroughs claimed to have had no difficulties with the Union and of these three two could "see them coming". Not all the problems were to do with delivering aids and some of those that were seemed reasonable from the drivers' point of view. Drivers were not prepared to load or unload heavy aids without adequate assistance and they were not prepared to carry aids up stairs. As far as they were concerned the delivery of aid stopped at the front door. From the point of view of disabled clients, especially those living alone, those refusals on the part of drivers to take a lightweight toilet frame into a bathroom or put a set of hand-rails in some place safer than a narrow pasage-way seemed unreasonable, inconsiderate and dangerous. Not all drivers refused to perform these helpful tasks but there was growing evidence that this majority refused to do anything that slowed down the run. An officer in the one "services" section summed up the situation by saying : "Individually most of the drivers are decent chaps but collectively they can be a major headache".

By far the most efficient delivery services were achieved by involved members of the social services department driving their own transport, purchased under Assisted Purchase schemes. Two social services departments were employing technical assistants and handymen who were buying estate cars under such schemes. They also received mileage allowances.[13]

Apart from circumventing difficulties with the unions the use of privately owned transport helped to speed up deliveries and prevented a backlog of aids building up from week to week. It could also mean that the people delivering aids were able, if necessary, to install them – at least in the private sector.

The EIGHTH STEP: Installing aids; delays in installation

(i) *Installation*
Not all aids need installing. Aids such as hoists, monkey-poles and some kinds of bath rail will have to be installed in a place and way which will make it convenient, comfortable and safe for clients and their relatives to use them. Bannister rails and grab-rails in toilets, which most boroughs treat as aids, always need installation and, because so many of them are issued, are frequently subject to long periods of delay between delivery and installation. Senior officers in five boroughs freely admitted to backlogs of about six months. In another a handyman was aiming to put in 80 grab-rails a week but as soon as he was taken off to install something else, such as a hoist, he said he was immediately thirty short of his weekly target.

In order to tackle the problem of installation, eight boroughs had created new posts for handymen and assistant technicians based on social services departments. In three of these the need was recognised as so great that the money for their salaries, transport and tools had been granted as part of Urban Aid. Senior officers of another six boroughs considered handymen and technical assistants as one of the most urgent of many needs, but in one of these the application had

189

been turned down outright by a council committed to a policy of using direct labour and in another three, although an establishment was approved in principle, the vacancies were immediately frozen because of limited resources. One borough with a long tradition of employing nothing but direct labour waived the rules when the gravity of the situation became apparent. Once it was appreciated that every client waiting for a grab-rail was at risk, the social services department was allowed to make the maximum possible use of a small private contractor. The man chosen had a handicapped child himself and willingly worked long hours of overtime, and even at weekends, in an attempt to reduce the backlog. On the other hand, a newly appointed director of social services in an Outer London borough used his first meeting with the director of technical services to issue a challenge that was to result in one of the speediest services for the whole of the Greater London area. Technicians with their own vans were allotted to work exclusively on work asked for by social services departments. The vans were equipped with radio telephones and it was possible to install aids within 24 hours of the first request and to install them at a time when the client was not only at home but also had someone in the house who could answer the door if necessary. This service was exceptional.

Only one other borough had followed a similar system of detaching technical officers – in this case a surveyor, an electrical engineer and a draftsman – to work exclusively on requests from social services departments for installations. It must be noted that in neither of the boroughs were the two technical officers actually attached to the social services departments who had no control over where they worked, or when, or of the progress of installations and no way, at the time of the study, of controlling the order of priority in which the works of installation were done. Two other boroughs detailed one of their handymen to set aside part of their time for work on installing aids, but this amounted to only two hours a week of help in each of four areas in the one instance and five afternoons in the other.

Decisions about what work to do, and where and when, remained firmly in the hands of the departments concerned. There was consequently no possibility of control over either priority or progress by anyone from the social services department.

The wider issues of using direct labour as a means, for example, of providing steady employment, are outside the scope of this study. Senior officers in the social services departments of the Greater London boroughs felt able however to express widely divergent views on the effectiveness or otherwise of using direct labour as a means of speeding up installations and works of minor adaptations. One of the problems posed was the overall shortage of direct labour available to take on work requested by social services departments. Whereas the social services departments had been able to respond to the increased demand for aids and adaptations by increasing their establishment few directors of other borough departments, already unable to fulfil many of the normal vacancies, had been quick to anticipate the additional demands that would be made on them as a result of the Chronically Sick and Disabled Persons Act 1970. In such circumstances large backlogs of work for the social services departments became inevitable in the majority of the Greater London boroughs.

At the time of the study four of the Greater London boroughs used nothing but direct labour in both the public and private sectors. Two further boroughs normally used direct labour in both sectors but it was pointed out by their directors that the council owned so much of the property in their boroughs – and what little privately rented property there was had compulsory purchase orders on it – that they had virtually no private sector to operate in. One borough used direct labour for everything under £150 but was compelled by its social services committee to go out to private enterprise for anything over £150. In two boroughs agreement had been reached to allow "small" private builders to undertake adaptations and installations costing less than £50. In another borough the borough architect, who had complete control of the disposal of the direct labour force, did not take over until after the cost involved was likely to exceed £400. One borough, with a long history of direct labour,[14] conducted its own control experiment to find out if direct labour was cheaper than using private contractors. It found that in every case the cost of using direct labour, as charged against the social services vote, was at least twice as expensive as estimates by private contractors and also no quicker. As a result of the investigation the social services committee authorised the use of a private contractor who worked for a negotiated price. The director already referred to, who had gone over from private labour to direct labour, thought that using direct labour had proved marginally more expensive than private contractors, but, as hidden costs such as storing such things as grab-rails and bannister rails for lengthy periods of time had been cut to a minimum under the new system, the use of direct labour in this borough may in fact have proved very little more expensive than the use of private contractors. He felt the saving to clients in terms of frustration and physical distress was considerable.

Had direct labour proved to be any cheaper from the point of view of social services departments than private labour it might have been arguable that it had to be used. For at least the smaller routine jobs such as installing grab rails the study revealed that it was in fact more costly. Grab-rails which cost £2.50 from a commercial supplier at the time of the study never cost less than £7.50 – an increase of over 200 per cent – when installed by direct labour and frequently cost £9.50. In one borough where there was a delay of six months, the flat rate was £15.00.

Three social services departments did not have to make a choice between direct labour and private contractors as their borough did not employ a direct labour force. The director of one of these said he "lived from hand to mouth and from private contractor to private contractor", but in the other two boroughs the absence of direct labour was considered a positive advantage by one senior official interviewed. The remaining boroughs used a mix of direct labour, approved builders and private contractors. The composition of the mix varied; it was determined by a number of factors including agreed financial limitations, whether the time of the year was busy or slack for direct labour, and the willingness of private contractors to submit reasonable estimates. There was a marked tendency for boroughs to use approved private builders in the private sector and direct labour in the public sector, although occasionally private builders were brought in to the public sector if there had been an exceptionally lengthy period of delay.[15] The direct labour force used for work connected with aids and adaptations was drawn from a variety of departments, among them being those of borough architects, engineers, directors of technical services and of planning and development. Staff from housing maintenance were also used. Private builders were selected in all but two boroughs from a list approved by one or other of these many departments and they were required to work to plans drawn up by borough surveyors and draftsmen and under the supervision of a borough clerk of works. In only one borough were clients encouraged to invite tenders from builders of their own choice, and then only in the private sector.

With the one exception quoted above – the borough with radio-telephones in its vans – it was generally believed by officers of the social services departments that the use of direct labour for installing aids and doing minor adaptations was less satisfactory, more costly and more prone to delays.

The extent of the problem throughout the Greater London area of how to get aids installed swiftly and efficiently can be gauged by the fact that in one borough three handymen were being asked to install eight grab-rails a day, that is 120 a week between them. Because of other demands made on their time, which included the installation of other aids which were urgently required, such as bath-rails, hand-rails in passages, bannisters and screw-down toilet frames, they had not once succeeded in reaching the set target.

In the private sector things were marginally better in that handymen and assistant technicians on the strength of social services departments who were barred by the attitudes of trades union representatives from working in the public sector were accordingly able to concentrate on installing aids and doing minor adaptations in privately owned property. With the exception of the one borough already quoted above, and two boroughs which employed no direct labour in any capacity, all aids installed in council property had to be done by employees based on the borough engineers' department, the architects' department, technical services department or departments with similar functions although called by a different name. Installations in property owned by the GLC were either done by the GLC's own technicians or, after agreement with GLC surveyors, by direct labour employed by the borough in which the property was situated.

In those Greater London boroughs which employed head occupational therapists at the time of the study, the establishment of good relationships between them and direct labour was considered to be a primary task. Only two were satisfied that liaison and mutual confidence had reached a level at which problems arising out of inter-departmental boundaries had ceased to exist and delay over work done by technical officers minimised. Problems continued to arise, however, when the actual installation was carried out by contractors and small builders on the approved lists of these departments. Technical officers do not go round installing grab-rails and screwing down toilet frames themselves. They may, however, should installation present a particularly tricky problem, be asked to advise. Generally speaking it will be the person to whom they farm out the work who will take the responsibility of deciding if a wall or floor will safely bear the weight of an aid – and of the person using it. Similarly, the decision as to when the work of installation begins, although ostensibly that of the borough's technical officers, is also likely to be made by the approved contractor. He would seldom allow such work to stand in the way of more lucrative offers either from other borough departments or from private clients. Installing aids all too often is something that gets "fitted in", frequently haphazardly, so that not only is delay increased, but the difficulty of keeping track of progress is maximised – particularly as the social services department, which has the responsibility for meeting the needs of its clients, has no control over the progress of the work of installation that has been requested whether direct labour is used exclusively or a mix of private contractors controlled by direct labour.

The need to establish a system of priorities – and special procedures – for installing aids in the homes of patients discharged from hospital showed up during the course of the study as something that needed a good deal of attention. For the most part requests for aids to be installed for people discharged from hospital who lived in council property landed in the same in-trays as any other installation ordered and were done in the same strict order of rotation. Should

G

a case be urgent a request to jump the queue might be telephoned across by a clerk in the social services secretariat to a technical officer or surveyor in another borough department but without any written follow-up to make sure that the urgency of the message was appreciated or that the message itself reached the person concerned.

A system of starring requests for installation or of writing emergency requests on forms of a different colour might be one way of overcoming such delays, but it has always to be remembered that no system of priorities will work well unless the staff of both departments involved are confident that it is not being abused. Requests by a social worker who marked everything "very urgent" went irremediably to the bottom of the pile in the office of one borough architect.

One solution to the problem arising out of hospital discharge – and these are frequently premature and sudden because of pressure of beds – is for the hospitals to use their own technicians. Only one hospital in the Greater London area was prepared to do this and at least two hospitals were without technicians having advertised unsuccessfully for them. An effective solution in two boroughs was provided by a joint appointment by the area health authority and the social services department. This combined in one person responsibilities that must otherwise have been divided between three separate and distinct systems – the hospital, the social services department and the borough department that employs the technicians – so that delays in communication are eliminated and access to stock aids immediate.

Head occupational therapists in social services departments are less blessed. All they can do is indicate their preferences and ask for an installation to be given priority. After that there is a complete break in the chain of command when the request leaves the social services department and becomes the responsibility of officers trained in other disciplines and based on other borough departments. The moment of this break occurs when the clerk who writes out a request, in triplicate, for an installation, takes up a specially numbered order pad marked "Local Orders" (usually referred to as LOs). From there on all the routine work associated with carrying them out ceases to be the responsibility of the social services department. At some later date, sometimes many months later, the LOs will turn up in finance departments where, with the exception of one, in which the housing department bears the whole of the cost of work done in the public sector, either a percentage of the total cost or the whole cost of the installation will be charged against the social services vote.

Details of local orders are however retained in the social services department – in the case of the borough sampled merely as an entry in the Day Ledger. The clerk who has ordered the aids and asked for them to be installed will usually have the additional duty of "chasing up" installations that have taken an unduly long time to complete. In order to preserve good inter-departmental relations, enquiries about their progress seldom begins until at least a month has passed, and then usually only if clients have been complaining about delay or the staff of other agencies have been vociferous on their behalf. Clerks may assume too readily that it is the clients whose needs are the most urgent who are the most likely to complain. Some boroughs admitted to relying largely on what they called "client initiative" to monitor the progress of work being done but this is to ignore the depressing effects of continued delay which are as likely to lead to apathy and inaction as to aggression and complaint.

At first sight the obvious solution would be to attach technical officers to social services departments for which they would then work full time. A partial solution, but one which has received a certain amount of opposition from trade unionists, has been to attach assistant technicians without paper qualifications to undertake the simpler installations and work of minor adaptations unsupervised by qualified technical officers. It has been argued that the safety of disabled clients should only be entrusted to qualified technical officers most of whom prefer to be based on borough departments other than the social services departments. In one borough, the head of the technical services department raised no objection to the social services department employing its own handymen "provided they did not bore any holes in a wall or floor in any property belonging to the council". This at once eliminated the possibility of them installing a single grab-rail, screw-down toilet seat or bannister in the public sector. In the private sector, disabled clients were presumably considered to be entitled to make their own decisions about any risk involved. The safety of clients is no light matter and a number of senior officers were beginning to feel dubious at the time of the study about the possible hazards involved in employing only partially qualified staff to install aids. Nevertheless eleven boroughs were employing a new breed of auxiliary called "technical assistant". To evade misunderstanding with the unions these were graded as "miscellaneous" staff, that is staff "whose duties are neither wholly manual nor wholly clerical". The flexibility of this "miscellaneous" grade has already been mentioned in connection with the duties of storemen but it is unfortunate that evasions of this kind should be necessary. Clients need aids and certain aids need installing. There is a job to be done and it ought to be possible to employ people to do it without the need to disguise their function.

One of the advantages of employing assistant technicians of this kind is that they are based firmly on social services departments. This eliminates the somewhat fatuous exercise usually referred to as 'chasing" in which a clerk is obliged to telephone staff in other

195

borough departments at fixed intervals to enquire politely about the progress of any work in hand. Monthly intervals were generally felt to suggest importunacy and most social services departments arranged for telephone calls to be made at six weekly intervals.

The chief advantage of employing assistant technicians was that – at least in the private sector – they were able to combine in one person the functions of delivery, installation and possibly even the next step, instruction in the use of aids, thus eliminating the need for steps eight, nine and ten.

(ii) *Delays in between delivery and installation*
In order to discover more about the kind of aids that needed installation, the sort of delays that occurred and some details about the clients on whose behalf the aids were ordered, another look was taken at pages of the day ledger for 1 January 1976 to 1 March 1976 from which the 631 aids listed on pages 184–85 had been extracted. It was found that these aids had been delivered to 397 clients of whom 193 (48.6 per cent) had received aids from stock which did not need installation – and also some installations in the private sector – in less than one week. The remaining 204 clients had had to wait for longer than one week and of these 158 (51.4 per cent of the total) had been obliged to wait for more than four weeks. This left just 46 clients (11.6 of the total) who had waited more than one week but less than four weeks for their aids to be delivered and, if need be, installed.

In order to find out more about the clients, for example whether they lived in council property, GLC property or in the privately owned or privately rented sectors, it was necessary to go back to the original forms on which the request for an aid had been made. Details of the age and sex of the client and the nature of their physical disability were also extracted and whether they lived alone. It was found that, of the original sample of 46, three had died before their aid was delivered, one had gone into Part III accommodation and one into hospital for terminal care. Three clients had been classified as frail elderly rather than as physically handicapped but one of these was suffering from diabetes and so counted as chronically sick. This left a final sample of 39 clients who had waited more than one week and less than four before being able to use one or more of the aids ordered for them. One of the 39 was, it was discovered, waiting for a minor adaptation – a half-step to an old-fashioned, enthroned toilet. Two of the 39 were not known to the offices of the areas in which they lived having been referred by hospital staff directly to the clerk in the secretariat. A third had not been picked up by the area occupational therapist until four months after discharge from hospital.

Distribution among the borough's five areas was 3, 9, 9, 11, 8. The low figure in the one area was attributed by the clerk to the fact that it had been without an occupational therapist for seven months but, without looking at possible variations in the client population, this could not be confirmed. Nor was there any way – except through examining the confidential files of the clients, which were kept in the area offices – of discovering how long the clients who died, or had been moved into residential care, had waited before they had been assessed for the aids that came too late.

Although permission had been granted, before the sample was extracted, by the assistant director and the area managers to visit any clients who expressed a willingness to be interviewed, this permission was later withheld on the grounds that social workers were opposed to an independent researcher seeing their confidential files. This was a disappointment as clearly the sample posed a number of questions, some of them unexpected, which need an answer. It should however be remembered that aids and adaptations – and other domiciliary services – may at times result in people with physical handicaps being kept in their own homes longer than they themselves would wish and that domiciliary care may cease, at some point, to be the best solution to particular problems.

Of the 39 left in the sample eleven were over 75 years of age, fourteen were over 65 and only 14 were below retiring age. One of these was an infant. Rheumatoid or osteo-arthritis was the main reason for handicap in 25 out of 39 cases and this again raises the fundamental question as to whether some of the clients suffering from arthritis were fit, for example, to bathe alone and whether they were in need of nursing care. One client had indeed already been in possession of a pick-up stick, prescribed by a district nurse, at the time a duplicate was delivered by the social services department. It would have been useful to know if any aids had been supplied at some time by the health authority and at what point the client's condition was recognised as "chronically sick" with the provision of aids – should any eventually be supplied – becoming a responsibility of the social services rather than the health authority. And also if a district nurse was still visiting any of these clients regularly.

These questions must remain unanswered in this survey although the researcher was assured that there would be a follow-up of the clients listed in two of the five areas concerned.

NOTES

1. A harassed clerk in a centralised section complained that the areas had been given so much autonomy that not only the format of the forms differed from one area to another but also the colours of the triplicate copies. This made the job of sending the request one step further that much more difficult.
2. Disabled people are often out at day centres and at times have to go to the out-patients' departments of hospitals. Those with aids to mobility may go out as often and spontaneously as people without handicaps.
3. When £5 no longer covered the cost of installing grab-rails in toilets it wrote these off as specific items but it still assessed for bannister rails and took them up to committee as well.

4. Typical of these subterfuges was a submission to the social services committee for an extra £417 "for locating drains". As the drainage plan for the estate was available in the local library the researcher queried the request and was told that it was really a payment to a builder who had been getting restive. "Councillors", it was said, "never bother to go underground to look so it is always safe to say it's drains".

5. All the Greater London boroughs subscribed to the monthly bulletin of the Disabled Living Foundation. Only one took enough copies for each Area to have one.

6. *Equipment for the Disabled*. A series of illustrated booklets for professional workers including photograph/diagram, description, dimensions, manufacturer/supplier, price area, export availability guidelines to assist selection. Compiled at Marlborough Lodge, Nuffield Orthopaedic Centre, Oxford (Oxford Regional Health Authority on behalf of the DHSS). UK Price £1.50 each booklet.

7. Twelve other boroughs used a similar pattern of procedure. Few boroughs kept ledgers in a form that could be used for anything but the immediate purpose of ordering aids on an *ad hoc* basis, Where other staff recognised the potential value of these records, e.g. for estimating demand and for maintaining levels of stock, the clerks made entries in a form that could be easily interpreted. In two boroughs, cards were filed under aids as well as clients and a "Kalamazoo" system helped to maintain stock at agreed levels and to re-order aids if supplies fell too low.

8. In the last quarter of 1975–76 the average monthly expenditure on aids increased from £60–£90 to £900–£1,500. Most of this money went on aids for stock. There was no evidence to suggest that aids had been rationed or held back during the first three quarters of the financial year and though the issue of 631 aids in the last quarter is above the quarterly average of 503, the fact that there were occupational therapists in post in all except one area during the period studied almost certainly contributed to the increased demand for aids.

9. By July 1976 the staffing situation in the borough engineers' department had deteriorated with correspondingly longer delays over installing aids.

10. In one borough evidence was produced of a walking stick that was not discovered until it had been on a van for four weeks, by which time no knowledge of the name or address of the client for whom it had been intended was forthcoming; nor were any suggestions made as to how these might be tracked down by referring back to indents. The client, it was assumed, would eventually "kick up a fuss to someone" and the whole process of delivery would then start again from scratch.

11. Social services departments vans take cots to temporary foster mothers, furniture to homeless families rehoused in borough accommodation, supplies of tinned goods such as mashed potato and custard powder to day centres, meals-on-wheels kitchens and residential homes; also supplies of toilet paper and soap bought in bulk. Small aids such as suction egg cups and pick-up sticks can easily get mislaid or wrongly delivered.

12. Handymen not on the staff of the social service department, but employed as private individuals, provided their own transport in all cases.

13. Assisted Purchase schemes were also used by technical officers in other borough departments.

14. Table 2 in the Appendix is of historical interest on this point. It is reproduced from the archives of the LCC.

15. One social services department which used direct labour in the public sector had not been able to provide deaf clients with flashing light signals for over nine months. This was because the vacancies for technical officers with qualifications in electrical engineering had not been filled. Eventually it had to press to use private electricians to deal with the backlog.

198

CHAPTER TEN

THE FOLLOW-UP; CLOSURE OF CASES; RECALL OF AIDS

The NINTH STEP: Instruction in the Use of an Aid

The provision of an aid should not stop at delivery or installation. There is one more vital step in the process and that is the instruction of the client in the safe and confident use of the aid. For this the optimum moment is as soon as possible after delivery and installation. In view of known confusions arising out of inadequate arrangements for delivering aids, it is also necessary to check that the aid received is the one meant for the client. Even mixing up two walking sticks on a van could result in damage to the clients involved, if the sticks delivered were of the wrong height. Collapsible walking sticks need expert adjustment.

With the completion of this ninth step, the aids can truly be said to have reached the clients. They may have taken as little as one week or as long as six weeks – or even six months – from the time they were first asked for until the day they were ready to be used safely.[1]

The table that follows, Table 16 on page 200, is based on questions asked in interviews with domiciliary occupational therapists, aids and adaptations officers, assistant technicians, handymen and aids clerks. Very little documentary evidence in the form of records kept in the area offices of the Greater London boroughs or the confidential files of clients was available to the researcher at the time of this study and in the majority of the boroughs, unless there was an intake team, requests for an aid – whether written, telephoned or made in person – were unlikely to be met under three weeks and then only if the aids required were in stock and did not need installation.[2]

Three weeks was also the average time taken by a member of an intake team to visit, assess and indent for an aid.

If the request for an aid involved a visit by staff other than intake, the time taken up to the first home visit would be one month on average, but a maximum of ten months was not exceptional. On the other hand some urgent cases took only one day.

The time taken in getting authorisation from senior social workers

Table 16 – Estimated Periods of Delay (Minimum, Average or Maximum) from Referral to Follow-Up Visit for Aids other than Emergency Requirements (figures based on verbal answers by staff of the social services secretariat and by domiciliary occupational therapists).

Steps	Processes	Minimum			Average			Maximum		
		Days	Weeks	Months	Days	Weeks	Months	Days	Weeks	Months
1–2	Referral to Allocation	3	–	–	–	3	–	–	6	–
2–3	Allocation to Assessment	–	3	–	–	–	1	–	–	10
3–4	Assessment to Indent	2	–	–	3	–	–	–	1	–
4–5	Indent to Authorisation (non-stock aids)	2	–	–	–	4	–	–	–	3
5–6	Authorisation to Order	1	–	–	–	3	–	–	6	–
6–7	Order to Issue	1	–	–	3	–	–	–	–	4
7–8	Issue to Delivery	1	–	–	–	1	–	–	1½	–
	Total Time, steps 1–8	10	3	–	6	11	1	–	14½	17
			4½ weeks			4 months			20 months 1½ weeks	
8–9	Delivery to Installation	1	–	–	3	–	–	–	–	4
	Total time, steps 1–9		4½ weeks			4 months 3 days			24 months 1½ weeks	
9–10	Installation to Instruction in Safe Use	3	–	–	–	3	–	–	–	3*
	Total time, steps 1–10		5 weeks			4 months 3½ weeks			27 months 1½ weeks	

* If any follow-up at all.

200

for inexpensive stock aids varied from one day to one week but for more expensive aids, whether kept in stock or not, authorisation at principal officer level could take up to six weeks and, if reports to committee were involved and a committee cycle missed, up to six months. Further delays occurred over aids not in stock when manufacturers fell behind with delivery dates or aids had to be ordered from abroad.

From authorisation to ordering varied from one day through three weeks to six weeks depending on the pressure of work on the aids clerk, the stage reached in the financial year and attitudes to rationing aids.

Delivery of aids varied from one day to ten depending on the availability of transport to the area in which the client lived.

If the aid had to be installed this might, if only simple installation were required, be done in the private sector on the same day as delivered by a storeman/driver/handyman. In those social services departments employing assistant technicians, installation even of complicated aids was likely to be done within a month. Private builders employed in both the private and public sectors were more often a source of delay than of speedy installation.

In the public sector delays over installation often depended on the availability of technical officers. There were large backlogs.

Sophisticated aids that had to be installed by the manufacturer's own representatives were subject to their own special form of delay especially if one representative covered large areas of the United Kingdom.

Follow-up visits were often done by social work assistants not all of whom were necessarily competent to do so. Where done by trained staff the time between delivery and follow-up visit tended to be longer or not to take place at all. The majority of clients received no follow-up visit of any kind.

In one borough the head occupational therapist reported that clients registered in 1972 – before any occupational therapists had been appointed – had already waited three and a half years for a home visit and would continue to wait unless they became emergencies. Only clients who had been put on the waiting list by the occupational therapists themselves were being dealt with. This expedient was endorsed by occupational therapists in other boroughs and was thought to be common practice. Even patients who had been recently discharged from hospital and who were in urgent need might well have to wait for at least three weeks. For this reason there is much to be said in favour of the practice of hospital staff sending patients home with the aids they need and billing the social services department later.

201

(b) *Closing cases*

Once they have received the aids needed to reduce handicap and have become accustomed to using them the majority of physically handicapped clients do not require further social work support. Nor do all of them want it. But some cases have to be closed prematurely because of more urgent calls on professional time.

An Outer London borough with an above average number of domiciliary occupational therapists on the strength of its social services department analysed, in 1974, the level of provision of their services to disabled clients and gave details not only of cases that had been closed prematurely but of the reasons why extra visits would have been desirable. The sample taken was restricted to seven occupational therapists and one occupational therapy aide" who had been working with the department for more than six months. Each of these eight people were asked for a sample of one in ten of their closed cases but it is not stated whether these cases were chosen at random or whether they represented a higher than usual level of involvement on the part of the staff reporting on what was felt to be premature closure. The results of the sample are given in Table 17 on opposite page – from which it can be seen that 180 clients needed further follow up visits merely to check on how they were managing with a recently installed aid or adaptation as against only 20 who needed to be visited in connection with re-housing and 50 who required intensive rehabilitation. "The rising pressure of work", says the report, "made it difficult and sometimes impossible, for occupational therapists to undertake in full the wide range of rehabilitation work for which they had been trained." Furthermore "bread and butter" visits, mainly concerned with adaptations, took up a disproportionate amount of their time and it may be inferred that this led, as in other boroughs, to a decrease in job satisfaction.[3]

For some clients the closure of a case, whether or not it is premature, is a traumatic experience. To tide such clients over, some boroughs make use of social work assistants who are asked to make a number of "tailing off" calls, such as calling on someone who had recovered from a stroke to take them for a daily walk beginning with the pillar box and increasing in length until it was felt they were confident enough to "go it alone". Frequently the clients concerned do not know that their case has been closed and continue to wait hopefully for visits.

No client should ever be left feeling suspended. If it is not possible to review cases periodically then social workers should encourage clients to get in touch with their area office and they should also make sure that the clients know how to do this.[4] Unfortunately those clients who "do not like to be a bother" are often those who may be most in need of some continuity of service. This is especially true of elderly clients.

Table 17 – Additional Work not carried out by Occupational Therapists because of limited time

| | | Estimated Number of Clients in Need Number of Clients requiring extra visits | | | |
	1–5 Visits	6–10 Visits	16–20 Visits	21–25 Visits	Total
1. Deteriorating condition – more regular follow-up required.	110	10			120
2. Aids or adaptations installed – checks needed to see how client is managing. Training in use of aids (some aids are issued direct from hospital, and not checked in the client's home).	80	20			100
3. Support and Training for client's family on personal care of client: bathing, dressing and washing techniques.	40	10	20	10	80
4. Client suspicious of help – better relationship needs building up so that the client's true difficulties become apparent, and a more accurate assessment is made.	30	10			40
5. Mobility training, etc. required	90	10		20	120
6. Support in daily living activities required. This includes encouragement to client to be more independent, and training in cooking, washing and dressing techniques, etc.	70	10	20	20	120
7. Social activities required, e.g. Day Centres, Rehabilitation Centres and Clubs	110	20	20		150
8. Rehousing required.		10	10		20
9. Intensive rehabilitation work needed. This implies frequent and regular visiting, possibly over several months, and includes any or all of the types of work described in 1–7 above.			30	20	50
10. Reassessment for additional aids or adaptations required.	150	20			170

203

There are indications that early closure of cases is becoming increasingly a matter of policy. Early closure may not necessarily be something to be deplored for, as Neill remarked as early as 1973, "it may be that clients who received relevant help over a brief period felt better served than those who were put on to on-going caseloads for unspecified reasons".[5] Cases involving specific requests for aids and adaptations are among those most likely to be closed as soon as these have been provided. What is, however, essential is a clearly-defined policy towards the closure and review of cases in every area office and, if possible, one that is consistent throughout the whole social services department.

(c) *The need for better record-keeping; some relevant research*
Two notable studies, one in Kensington and Chelsea, the other in Southampton, into what happens to cases concerning the elderly and physically handicapped have already been discussed in another context. They co-incided with the period in which interviews were being held with senior staff in the Greater London boroughs about the numerous processes involved in providing aids and adaptations. The Kensington and Chelsea study looked at the processes of referral, the proportion of cases dealt with by intake teams and the proportion that went on to long-term teams, in a twelve-month period beginning, like the Greater London study, in the autumn of 1974 and ending in September 1975.

The second study was centred on one area office in Southampton where the researchers were able to make use of "a social worker oriented Case Review System developed in close collaboration with a group of fieldworkers in an area office".[6] This study was able to give a computerised breakdown of the services provided for all referrals from 1 February 1975 to 30 June 1975, a cut-off point which approximated closely to the cut-off point for the interviews for the Greater London study. Details concerning cases involving the elderly and physically handicapped – unfortunately still classified together – are reproduced below in Table 18.[7]

The above percentages were based on all Open cases and a one-in-twelve sample of Closures.

When the survey was extended beyond the original cut-off point it was found that of the longer term cases which were still open 61 elderly and physically handicapped people had received more wide-spread practical help – 2.6 per cent compared with 1.2 per cent for those that had been closed by the end of the study period. "Practically all – 93 per cent – had received some practical service [and] over half aids and adaptations".

The research officers in Kensington and Chelsea were unable to obtain the same degree of cooperation as those in Southampton and

Table 18 – Summary of Help Given and Reasons for Closure

Social Workers' Activities	Percentage	Practical Services	Percentage
Mobilising Resources	69	Aids and Adaptations	36
Information/advice	46	Meals on Wheels	23
Review visiting	29	Home Helps	22
Problem solving	14	Assistance with Applications	16
Sustaining	10	None	16
Assessment	69		
Outside Agencies Involved		*Reasons for Closure*	
G.P.'s	44	Aims achieved	30
Hospitals	32	Department withdrawn	22
H.V.'s and nurses	30		
Housing Department	12		
DHSS	11		

therefore examined the situation in each of the borough's three areas as it existed. Although the statistical returns from each area were standardised it was found that the methods of evaluation by social workers differed in each area and so did policies about the early closure of cases. The Kensington and Chelsea figures are of particular interest because the administrative staff in each area were required, in their quarterly statistical returns, to separate the "elderly" from the "physically handicapped who were not elderly". Even so 13 out of the 20 cases recorded as physically handicapped in one area were re-classified as elderly by the research officers. Nor do the statistical returns allow for varying interpretations of primary and secondary problems.

All referrals coming into the area offices were analysed according to the category of client for a twelve-month period. A detailed analysis of what happened to the cases referred – whether the intake teams took no further action, which cases were held by the intake team for short term action before closure and which cases went on to long-term teams – was confined to the month of March 1975.

The highest number of referrals coming in during March 1975 was to the Northern Area (216) where the social work team was housed in an Information and Aid Centre.[8] The lowest number of referrals for March 1975 was in the Central Area (99) which had not then moved its office to premises more accessible to personal callers. In the South Area (123) the number of referrals was still less than half of those in the North Area.[9]

A number of explanations for the variations in the referral rate were put forward. These include the existence of a predominantly young and transient population in the Central Area, a higher proportion of elderly in the South Area and the advantage, in the North Area, of clients who were uncertain about the services they required being able, if necessary, to see a social worker, housed in the same building, on the same day and without having to do any further travelling. However when one examines what happened to all the referrals coming into the different area offices significant differences in policy are revealed.

In the South Area 63 per cent of cases concerning the social problems of the elderly and all cases of physical handicap went on to become "longer term cases". In the Central Area the corresponding figures were 62.5 per cent (elderly) and 66 per cent (physically handicapped but not elderly); while in the Northern team the figures were 43 per cent (elderly) and 50 per cent (physically handicapped but not elderly). However when one looks at the figures given for cases still open after nine months the percentage of the elderly still receiving care had dropped in the South Area from 63 per cent to 5 per cent and in the Central area, from 62.5 per cent to 7.5 per cent. The Northern area classified cases still open according to the kind of problem and not according to the category of client but it was remarked that many of the long-term cases received so little further action that they were virtually indistinguishable from cases involving no further action (NFA).

No figures about cases of physically handicapped people who were not elderly and whose cases were still open after nine months were given for any of the areas. The implications of the findings of the research unit were clear but area team managers were initially reluctant to co-operate with the research unit in making changes about the way in which client needs were evaluated and records kept, partly because of other pressures on their fieldwork staff. However by 1978 the need for an efficient case review system was acknowledged.

On the other hand researchers in Southampton set out from the beginning to proselytise, raise questions about current practices and their effects on clients and to "encourage a climate favourable to possible changes".[10] These, it was hoped, would not only include a revised attitude towards evaluating and reviewing cases but might also prepare the way for a much more obvious orientation towards the community.

The TENTH STEP: Review of cases

Some cases which have to be closed prematurely are "put by" with a note for them to be brought up for review at stated intervals. This may be important for clients with degenerative diseases and for those whose clinical symptoms are likely to be exacerbated by family problems.

One category which is all too frequently neglected by the social services is that of the young adults with severe physical handicap who have come to rely on the continuous and intensive care of specialists in schools and centres and are thus left stranded. The gap between school and life in the normal world is very imperfectly bridged at the best of times, partly because of poor liaison between the schools, the DROs and social services departments and partly because of the acute shortage of social workers with the necessary experience.[11] The younger physically handicapped were found in one of the Southampton studies to be the least willing to tolerate visits from untrained social work assistants[12] and the most vocal in their demands for continuity of care.

Aids that were once appropriate may become less so as the condition of clients changes. Some may no longer be needed, whilst others may have become useless or even dangerous. Some still in use may be adding to handicap rather than overcoming it. For these reasons, occupational therapists are concerned that reviewing clients at fixed periods is seldom done. In only three boroughs were head occupational therapists certain that all clients in need of periodic visits received them at the intervals believed to be essential. These intervals varied from three months through six months to one year, and it must be stressed that it is the condition of the client as well as the condition and suitability of the aid that dictates the need for such visits.

Two boroughs used students to review the less distressing cases. Three boroughs used social work assistants but only one borough was using volunteers to review clients by the end of 1976.

The use of voluntary workers
Many physically handicapped people feel that they need some continuity of social work support and some disabled people are beginning to feel that they themselves might be able to help the social services by advising them on the kind of support needed. This feeling, which was referred to in the report by the Central Council of Education and Training for Social Work[13] is well summed up by the husband of a disabled client who was interviewed in one of the Southampton studies in 1975.

"I think they [the Social Services department] need more direction. After getting all the aids and things it stops. There is a need for continuation, not just giving things to you but ways of adding to the Social Services. Well, one doesn't want to be a busybody but if they asked we could have helped. We could do more for each other, make some continuous contact."[14]

This couple also felt that they should be more involved with the community and that the community should certainly be more involved with physically handicapped people in general.[15]

207

In spite of the recommendations of the Seebohm Report[16] and the Gulbenkian Report,[17] the development of community work has been patchy and in some areas negligible.

The Gulbenkian Report saw community work as the necessary background to all voluntary enterprise but failed to distinguish between the involved citizen who visits and "befriends" on his own initiative and the volunteer who is pointed in a particular direction by a paid community worker and then briefed – and even supervised – by trained social workers or occupational therapists. There is still a noticeable reluctance on the part of many professional workers and volunteers to supervision, although very tactful "guidance" may be an acceptable alternative provided it is made quite clear both to the volunteers and the clients concerned that the volunteer is in no way deputising for a member of the social services department but offering services which the department could not otherwise provide – in fact the role of the volunteer must be continually stressed as extending and not superseding the work of the statutory services. The emphasis, in the Seventies, also falls much more heavily on actual tasks performed rather than on the vague concept of "befriending" although friendship, provided this arises spontaneously and is likely to endure, is not positively discouraged.

A Report published in 1969, *The Voluntary Worker in the Social Services*,[18] recognised the need to direct volunteers towards the work for which they appeared to be most suited and had suggested the formation of "Volunteer Bureaux" which were to be financed in part by voluntary organisations including local trusts, by local councils of social services and by grants from local authorities. These were seen as rallying points for volunteers who wished to be of use to the community but were not always certain how to go about it but "their primary function was to help the services rather than to assist individual volunteers".[19] They were to direct volunteers to a number of different agencies of which the local authority social services department was only one.

In 1976 there were volunteer bureaux in sixteen of the Greater London boroughs. The main work for the disabled that volunteers were asked to undertake was to provide transport. They drove disabled people to clubs, took them shopping and out for jaunts in the car and on occasions drove them to and from their work, while they were waiting for their own specialised transport to be delivered or repaired.[20]

Volunteers are also likely to be directed to work in clubs, luncheon clubs and day centres run by local authorities as well as in local branches of voluntary associations in need of help of various kinds. Many voluntary associations train and supervise the volunteers whom they enlist in much the same way as local authorities are doing.

208

Voluntary associations which put their members in uniform have long had clearly specified aims.

Other forms of "practical assistance particularly welcomed by disabled people include bringing in coal, laying fires, chopping wood, cleaning windows, doing the shopping and gardening, writing letters and doing manicures. The performance of such tasks, many of which can not be covered by the home help service, are much valued although most volunteers are likely to see them as a short-term commitment. Jobs of this kind were frequently undertaken by sixth-formers working to a school teacher with special responsibility for community involvement under the scheme known as Task Force.[21]

By the end of the study, in late 1976, nine of the Greater London boroughs were employing community workers at a senior level, most of whom served two functions. The first was to involve volunteers with community affairs in general and the second to select some of these volunteers to do specific tasks for which they had the time and capability. In two boroughs new divisions of their social services departments, one called Community and Day Care and one called Health and Family Services, had recently been established. These new divisions, under newly appointed assistant directors, superseded the outdated concept that residential and day care were inextricably involved. In two other boroughs community workers had succeeded in getting "Road Teams" of volunteers established in the areas they served. These teams helped the disabled, particularly in emergencies and were felt to be an improvement on paid "Good Neighbour" schemes which had not always been successful.

In four boroughs carefully selected volunteers had been attached to occupational therapists in much the same way as in other boroughs paid social workers assistants had been seconded to work exclusively with physically handicapped people. The volunteers were taught how to check that aids were safe and how to instruct clients in the safe use of newly issued aids. In one of the boroughs the head occupational therapist was using a team of volunteers to review, in alphabetical order, every client who had received an aid. No confidential details about the medical condition of the clients were revealed, but each volunteer was briefed about things to look out for before making the first home visit, and was expected to report back on the condition of the client as well as on the condition of an aid. In another borough volunteers attached to a community worker were allocated individual case-loads of twenty disabled clients.

In the five boroughs referred to above it becomes difficult to see the volunteer as anything but a substitute for the paid social work assistant yet it is of considerable importance to clients that voluntary workers are seen to retain their independence and that it is obvious that they are not at the beck and call of statutory policy-makers. It

209

would be sad indeed if volunteers, whether as individuals or as members of voluntary associations, should forfeit the power to initiate experiments in exchange for a quasi-professional expertise.

The tradition of voluntary service in the United Kingdom has long been associated with the middle classes, but during the Seventies volunteers have been drawn from a much wider section of society. Only a fine line divides some of the work done by volunteers recruited by bureaux and community workers based on social services departments from that done spontaneously by a vast variety of friends, relatives and neighbours.[22] These come from all classes of society and provide a vast potential of recruitment for specialised tasks and there is no doubt that the social services departments will make increased use of volunteers from many sources. One Outer London borough had already, in 1975, enlisted the services of the local Polytechnic to provide courses and weekend seminars for volunteers interested in working with the disabled. These courses included a talk on the use of aids. In five boroughs head occupational therapists were making a point of lecturing to groups such as Rotary Clubs and the Round Table as a way of encouraging feedback about cases of physical handicap. Much more feedback could also be provided by both volunteers and professional staff working in luncheon clubs and centres run by voluntary organisations.

Research done by a member of the research department of Islington social services[23] in 1976 and 1977 defines three distinct types of volunteers. One is the Volunteer Group Model found in three out of the borough's ten areas, where the volunteers organise themselves into groups. In two other areas there is a Volunteer Organiser Model, with a voluntary organiser co-ordinating and supervising volunteers. The third model is the Social Work/Area Team Project Model which exists in six of the ten areas. In this model a senior social worker, basic grade social worker or a community social worker assumes responsibility for coordination and supervision. Volunteer projects are treated by the social services departments as Area Team Projects and awarded lump sums out of the social services budget.[24]

The Islington study suggests that community service volunteers, who may put in as much as forty hours a week, "are quite subtly accorded higher status", given case-loads and seen as potential or trainee social workers.

Volunteers in Islington undertake a much wider range of tasks than the paid workers employed by the borough under the "Good Neighbour" scheme. Good Neighbours work almost exclusively with the elderly housebound and the physically handicapped. Many of them were unmarried mothers who found the pay – up to a maximum of £5 a week – a useful supplement to social security benefits. The scheme was also thought, in a phrase with an oddly Victorian ring, "to improve the image of the poor".

The need for Good Neighbours to live locally raised special problems about confidentiality. The question of how much social workers should tell one local resident about the problems of another local resident is also common to all forms of unpaid voluntary work. The growing habit of paying expenses to volunteers is also beginning to blur the distinction between paid Good Neighbours and volunteers.

Twenty-five per cent of Islington's volunteers had formerly been clients for whom voluntary work was recognised as a form of therapy. This in itself might suggest a need for some form of guidance and supervision.

Perhaps the greatest gift that voluntary workers bring with them is their time – more often than not time in the evenings and at weekends when professional social workers are no longer willing to make themselves available. It is however probable that the proportion of volunteers who express a preference for work with the disabled will remain small. As the Aves Report says :

"The disabled people who were interviewed had on the whole received less help [than other categories] from voluntary visitors and some of them would have liked more".[25]

This is perhaps a cogent reason for encouraging more disabled persons to take part in comunity activities as distinct from organised "self-help" groups and pressure groups.

Re-calling Aids

In the days when the Red Cross Society acted as agent for the supply of aids to health and welfare departments, members of their local branches frequently collected aids to daily living that were no longer needed and continued to do so until the Society disengaged itself from the issuing of anything but aids to home nursing. Officers in two social services departments in the Greater London area recalled having used Boy Scouts at one time for the collection of aids and a third mentioned that police cadets were still being used. Otherwise collection was only being undertaken by local authority vanmen asked to go to specific homes.

At the time of the study a number of Greater London boroughs were still spending a good deal of time and money on writing letters to clients asking them to return unwanted aids, in tracking down aids by means of Change Reports[26] and Death Lists[27] and in various haphazard ways. Frequently storemen who also delivered aids took it upon themselves to check up on aids they suspected to be unused or defunct. One said he "wandered about a bit looking under stairs" and another, who did not deliver aids "shoved a fistful of cards into the vanman's hands".

211

In most boroughs where policy about the recall of aids was as haphazard as this, it was usually attributed to lack of sufficient clerical staff to keep tabs on the aids supplied. Only four boroughs had decided to write off all aids that were not returned spontaneously on the grounds that the process of retrieval cost more than the value of the aids thus retrieved. For the rest, such declared policy as there was varied from one social services department to another. One borough, following the by-gone practice of the old LCC welfare departments, wrote off all aids costing less than £1. This took care of all the non-slip bathmats which, in 1975, still cost only 98p; two boroughs wrote off all aids costing less than £5; and one borough had decided that no aid whose initial cost was less than £10 was worth the expenses involved in retrieval. Two social services departments had limited such activities to recalling only the larger aids such as hoists, special beds and wheelchairs but one clerk explained ruefully that comfortable geriatric chairs[28] also had a habit of "escaping" over borough boundaries when clients moved. In view of the time clients are kept waiting for aids in the first place their reluctance to go through it all again in a different borough is hardly surprising. The process of tracking down such aids is undertaken with a view to extracting a contribution towards their initial cost from the borough to which the client has moved.

One third line manager said that if social services departments provided a truly "client-orientated" service then the clients themselves, or their relatives, would return unwanted aids; the head occupational therapists in three other boroughs also depended on the initiative of clients for the return of aids; but one principal officer, less sanguine, instructed his clerk not only to keep an eye on the Death List but to send out letters at six monthly intervals as well.

Six boroughs sent out letters at periodic intervals, one every three months, three every six months and two annually – all by First Class Mail "in case clients thought they were bills and did not open them". All enclosed adressed envelopes bearing second class stamps for the clients' replies. If clients replied saying that they had aids they wished to return then a further letter was sent telling them on which day to expect a van. In four boroughs staff interviewers were not sure whether or not letters were still being sent.

Details about the procedures adopted in different social services departments are to be found in Table 19 below.

With sufficient fieldwork staff to review clients at adequate intervals the recall of aids that were no longer appropriate or needed would have automatically fallen within the province of social workers, occupational therapists, auxiliary workers and possibly any voluntary workers attached to fieldwork staff. In such circumstances it would be the fieldworker and not a centrally based clerk who would

212

	Number of boroughs
1. No recall as declared policy	4
2. No recall because of lack of policy	2
3. No recall because of lack of staff	2
4. Policy not known	4
5. Haphazard recall	4
6. Letters sent out – every 3 months	1
every 6 months	3
annually	2
7. Reliance on client initiative	3
8. Use of Change Reports	1
* 9. Use of Death Lists	4
10. Aids written off – under £1	1
under £5	2
under £10	1
stock aids only	1
11. Only large aids tracked down	2
12. Check by – auxiliaries	2
volunteers	1
13. Special exercise conducted	1
14. "Paper" exercise pending	1
15. Recall for cosmetic reasons	1

* Some methods of recall were used in addition to dispatch of letters.

be the first to know if an aid were no longer appropriate, or if a
client had died; and it would have been the fieldworker, not the
officer who completed the Change Report, who would have initiated
the process of recalling aids.

Only one social services department appeared to recall aids for
cosmetic reasons. In this borough a clerk took a positive delight in
up-dating aids. In other boroughs occupational therapists did not
feel justified in recalling aids that, although ugly and cumbersome,
still did an adequate job of reducing handicap. However, should
such aids be in need of repair they would automatically be replaced
by their more modern counterparts.

Recalling, or replacing, an aid to daily living can be a much more
delicate matter than recalling an aid to home nursing. When patients
no longer need aids to home nursing it frequently means that they
have recovered and will not need the aids again, although some
patients will, of course, have been receiving terminal care. The
majority of aids to home nursing, however, do not remain with the
same patient for more than six weeks, they are frequently re-usable
after cleaning and quickly back in use by someone else.

Aids to daily living present a rather different picture as many of
them have been in use for years. Often recall may mean that the
client's condition has degenerated to such an extent that the aid
originally issued is no longer effective[29] or that the client had eventu-

ally died. In such circumstances even the most tactfully worded routine letter is liable to cause distress to the relatives of the client. Such matters need to be handled personally wherever possible, especially when the cases of such clients have long been closed.

Comparatively few of the most frequently issued aids to daily living can be re-cycled. Bath aids with cork seats are usually permanently stained, as are many kinds of raised toilet seats. The cost of removing grab-rails from toilets and bathrooms might not justify their recall, but new tenants might object to rails in kitchens and passageways if not to bannister rails. Dismantling anything fixed to walls or ceilings automatically involves redecoration and many clients, particularly in the private sector, are as likely to lie low and say nothing as to take steps to get them removed.

The need to make cuts in public expenditure from 1976–77 onwards may however reverse attitudes to recalling and reclaiming aids. One borough photographed an attractive occupational therapist amid a welter of commodes, toilet seats, tripod crutches, hoists and walking frames and published the picture in the local press. Response was said to be minimal. A neighbouring borough, impressed by the photograph, was "about to do a paper exercise on wastage". The results of this exercise are not known. The social services department of another borough. Hillingdon, in co-operation with domiciliary occupational therapists and social work assistants, followed up five kinds of aids in common use[30] – bath seats, bath rails, chairs of all kinds, walking frames, and raised toilet seats – and found that the 173 clients interviewed had been issued with a total of 297 aids of which almost one quarter were no longer in use for a variety of reasons including such obviously avoidable ones as a bath seat no longer being needed after a bath had been replaced by a shower. Of these one third had been returned to the department and only one client had reported having to wait more than one month for the "pick-up" service to collect an aid.

Of much greater importance than the number of aids that should have been returned to the department was the number of aids found to be unsafe, e.g. bathrails that had come loose, screws and wheel nuts that had loosened in walking frames, raised toilet seats that slipped. Of the 28 clients who had been issued with walking frames eight were no longer using them; 17 clients claimed they had not received any instruction in their use and nineteen reported that no one had been to see them since they first learned to use them. Five of these eight no longer used their frames and the other three did not use them although they had received a follow-up visit.

The Hillingdon study went into considerable detail about design faults in many of the aids used. Some of those issued by social workers before the appointment of domiciliary occupational therapists in

214

1974 had clearly been inappropriate at the time of issue. On the other hand the design of some aids issued by domiciliary occupational therapists had also proved to be unsatisfactory; this was particularly true of well-known makes of chair that are frequently issued throughout the Greater London boroughs. Of the 45 chairs in the sample eight were found to be too high, four were too low, 2 tipped when the client got up and 3 tipped when the client sat down; two had the wrong length of arm; thirteen clients found sitting on chairs covered with PVC uncomfortable. Thirty-eight of the forty-five clients usually sat in their chairs even though 14 of them were not at all happy with them. Clearly more attention needs to be paid to the kind of chairs issued and to modifying them to suit the needs of individual clients.

The conclusion of the Hillingdon study was that the only satisfactory method of recalling aids was by personal contact :

Communication with the Department
"It emerged very clearly from the survey that personal contact is the only effective way of discovering clients' difficulties with their aids. Although all clients are given a card with their OT's phone number, they mislaid these, or did not have a telephone, could not easily post letters, could not remember who had dealt with their case and couldn't cope with finding the right person to speak to, and did not want to take the initiative in complaining because they were afraid of being thought ungrateful or bothersome. The interviewer's personal call overcame these difficulties with the result that four out of every ten clients asked for some message to be given to the department or other agency; three out of every ten had a message for the OT section. It should be pointed out that it was not part of the questionnaire to ask if the client wanted a message passed on – this was a spontaneous reaction to the appearance of someone who seemed to be the right person to tell."[31]

The fact that messages needed to be passed on underlines the importance of continuing contact with disabled clients irrespective of whether or not any reusable aids might come to light. As a result of the survey, the London borough of Hillingdon decided to mount a deliberate campaign which would also make use both of volunteers, people from the borough "Job Recovery" programme and secondary school pupils with time on their hands between examinations and the end of term. All volunteers would be required to present themselves to clients as "messengers" who would report to appropriate borough departments (e.g. the occupational therapists of the social services department) and every care should be taken by them not to give the appearance of doing an assessment themselves. Altogether, 3,650 closed cases would need to receive a "check call" in 1977.[32]

215

A national survey on wheelchairs and their users, conducted by the Office of Population Censuses and Surveys at the request of the Department of Health and Social Security in 1973, throws additional light on the non-use of certain aids.[33] In addition to questions about wheelchairs questions were included in the interviews about certain aids to mobility – walking frames, ramps, hoists, lifts, hand-rails; and also about toilet aids, back seats, other washing aids and dressing aids. It seems likely that these national findings mirror what was happening in the Greater London boroughs at the time but it must be remembered that, as in the London borough of Hillingdon, between 1973 when the interviews were conducted and the publication of the report in late 1976,[34] all but two of the Greater London boroughs had increased the number of domiciliary occupational therapists and that the proportion of aids which were not being used because they had been wrongly issued in the first place is likely to be considerably less than the findings drawn from the national sample in 1973. The two tables that follow are nevertheless of interest.

Table 20 – Possession and use of walking aids

	Stick	Walking frame	Tripod	Elbow crutches	Shoulder crutches	Calipers
	%	%	%	%	%	%
Does not have this aid	54	73	90	90	96	86
Has this aid						
uses indoors only	11	13	4	2	1	2
uses outdoors only	4	1	1	1	1	1
indoors and outdoors	19	6	3	4	3	9
does not use	12	7	2	3	–	2
Base (100%) – adult wheelchair patients	978	978	978	978	978	978

Of the expensive aids, for example hoists, over a quarter were not in use, i.e. 29 out of 107, at the time the survey was made. A similar proportion of walking sticks and walking frames had also been discarded, the walking sticks in favour of walking frames in one third of the cases :

"... of those who had walking sticks but did not use them, as many as a third said they now used a walking aid which provided more support and about a quarter said that their condition had deteriorated to such an extent that they were now confined to using a wheelchair. Similarly, of those who had walking frames but did not use them, over a half said they were now confined to using a wheelchair. Among other reasons given by patients for not using walking aids in their possession were a few where patients no longer felt safe using a particular aid and others where patients found a particular aid uncomfortable or difficult to use. In a small number of cases patients had stopped using an aid because they had experienced a fall when trying to use it."

216

Table 21 – Possession and use of other mobility aids

Whether patient has this aid	Ramps	Hoists	Lifts	Hand-rails	Toilet aids	Bath seats	Other washing aids	Dressing aids
	%	%	%	%	%	%	%	%
Has aid	25	11	6	39	38	25	8	4
Cost								
Paid full cost	8	1	1	11	8	7	3	1
Paid part cost	1	1	–	2	4	–	–	–
Did not contribute towards cost	16	9	5	26	26	18	5	3
Whether uses this aid								
Uses aid	23	8	6	34	34	19	8	3
Does not use aid	2	3	–	5	4	6	–	1
Base adult wheelchair patients	978	978	978	978	978	978	978	978

217

No details are given in the report of the number of clients using walking aids who were receiving periodic visits from social workers, social work assistants or occupational therapists; nor of whether those who were not using them, for example because of a fall, had been in touch with their social services departments. That some of these cases were clearly in need of review is evident. But the argument for not necessarily recalling the majority of the aids not in use is clearly stated in the report from Hillingdon :

"Some clients' condition has deteriorated so that they would no longer use their aids but it would be psychologically unwise to make it explicit to them that this was likely to be permanent, even when it was."

The decision not to recall aids is one that voluntary workers might find more difficult to make than domiciliary occupational therapists and, on balance, it would seem to suggest that it is better to rely on the initiative of clients, or their relatives, for the return of many of the aids.

An area health authority in the north-east of England[35] has found that an annual appeal from the regional radio station has resulted in the return of far more aids than any methods previously used. This is something that might be initiated by the London Boroughs Association so that the results of such an appeal could be synchronised and the boroughs readied to allocate staff to receive aids for a short intensive period. Television might also be used to advantage.

6. *Repairing Aids*

Facilities for repairing aids are few – they are sometimes done by storemen and very occasionally by instructors at day centres – and it is often probably more economic to issue a new aid than to send an old one back to a factory which in any case may no longer be making the old model.

Certain expensive aids, especially aids operated by means of electricity and hydraulic aids are usually repaired in situ by engineers attached to the manufacturers or by repairers approved by them. Disabled clients and their relatives are often seriously inconvenienced by delays over sending people to repair such aids. Another problem about electrically operated aids is that disabled people living alone can be put at risk by failures of electricity. One client reported having been suspended helplessly in mid-air in a patient-operated hoist for several hours and it is suggested that no aids dependent on supplies of electricity should be installed without a battery-operated alarm. If social workers and occupational therapists were to insist on this manufacturers would be obliged to comply. The danger inherent in

218

all alarm systems – that they can lead to helpless people being robbed and property vandalised – has to be balanced against the danger to the disabled person if his equipment fails to operate.

7. Cleaning of Aids

The cleaning of aids that have been recalled for re-cycling presents difficulties. In some boroughs they are cleaned by people at day centres for the mentally handicapped – a fact about which the directors interviewed were apt to be somewhat ashamed. In a few boroughs they were cleaned by storemen or their assistants. One borough had them cleaned at great cost by staff of the sanitation department who were paid overtime rates plus "dirty" money. Office cleaners in another borough were occasionally persuaded to clean them for extra money and in one borough the lady clerk in charge of ordering aids was required to "Dettol" toilet seats that had been sent back. The clerk resigned. Volunteers have been known to be more willing to clean aids to toileting than paid staff.

In these days of scarce resources the deployment of staff to write letters enquiring about aids, collect aids and clean aids that have been recalled would appear to be uneconomic except for very large and expensive aids which the relatives of clients are likely to return of their own initiative should they no longer be required. Two officers suggested that in a time of economic crisis it was important for the public image to be seen to be cutting down on the wastage of aids whether or not this was cost effective. The use of volunteers to write and deliver letters of enquiry and also to collect unwanted aids would help to keep down the expenses of retrieval. No officer in a social services department in the Greater London area was able to give any indication of how much money, if any, was being saved by existing methods of retrieval.

With waiting lists as long as they are in most boroughs it is essential to speed up the processes by which to get much-needed aids to clients in the first place rather than to attempt to return to circulation aids that have fallen into disuse, but the need for a periodic review of aids by professional staff remains the only guarantee of safety and is therefore the main argument against the growing trend towards the premature closing of cases in which aids are known to have been issued.

This chapter concludes the study of the processes by which aids to daily living provided by social services departments reach disabled and frail elderly clients who live in the Greater London area. The processes have been divided into ten distinct steps with gaps between each of them which represent varying periods of delay. In some boroughs these delays have been reduced by re-deploying staff resources, by increasing the number of staff employed for specific tasks and even by reorganising the structure of the social services department. Volunteers have been used to help with follow-up and the recent growth of community services, such as road groups, is providing and extending continuity of care to include the integration of the disabled with the rest of the neighbourhood. The need to be accepted as a person and not merely as someone whose only interest lies in his or her disability is one that many disabled people have come to regard as one of their most important needs and also as their indispensable right.

Subsequent chapters will deal with the part played by minor and major adaptations in keeping clients in their own homes and in the financial and administrative processes involved in their provision.

NOTES

1. A manual breakdown made at the request of the social services directorate of a Northern borough showed that in 1974 the average time in one area, between ordering an aid from the central divisional store and its delivery was 27.5 days; the longest time was 91 days, the average 56 days. The area health authority did only slightly better averaging 30 days between request and delivery. Much of the area was however rural. See Melotte, C. J., "The Supply of Aids and Adaptations", *Cleaning House for Local Authority Social Services Research*, (1976), No. 5.
As a result of this research a joint working group of staff from the Social Services Department and the Local Area Health Authority was formed to discuss the possibility not only of joint storage of aids "but also of joint or coordinated assessment and supply services."
2. A study by a Cheltenham intake team gives "a 'rough' estimate of the length of time between referral and assessment" before and after the establishment of the team in 1974. " . . . 73 per cent of the September '74 allocated referrals received an assessment within three weeks of the original referral being made compared with 29 per cent in '73 . . . 87 per cent of the '74 referrals had been dealt with within 5 weeks compared with 59 per cent for '73". See Wetton, Kate, "The Cheltenham Intake Team: An Evaluation", a study by the Gloucester Social Services Department, *Clearing House* (1976), No. 2.
3. "Occupational Therapy Services in Hillingdon", the London Borough of Hillingdon, Social Services Research Department. In *Clearing House for Local Authority Social Services Research* (University of Birmingham), 1975, No. 7.
4. The Greater London boroughs used to provide all their field-workers with a standard visiting card on which they filled in the telephone number of the office from which they worked, their names and the number of their extension. This practice has been discontinued in many boroughs because of the rising costs of printing.
5. *Op. cit.*, p. 20.
6. See p. 173, note 7 and p. 174, note 19.
7. Goldberg *et al.*, *op. cit.*, 1977, Table 3, p. 257.
8. This is the Westway Centre which also houses the Citizens Advice bureau, the Housing Action centre, the Community Aid Centre and the Voluntary Workers bureau. The average number of referrals in the Southampton study was between 170 and 240 a month.
9. The actual numbers of clients who were physically handicapped but not elderly referred in March were, in all areas, very low – 4 out of 123 in the South; 6 out of 99 in the Central area and in the North area just 3 out of 216. Explicit reasons for their referral are given for the North area. One concerned a younger physically handicapped person in need of sheltered accommodation; a second an epileptic with multiple sclerosis whose wife was about to divorce him; and the third concerned a physically handicapped person who needed extra clothing and help in sorting out bills.
10. Goldberg, E. Matilda *et al.*, "Towards Accountability in Social Work: a Case Review System for Social Workers". *British Journal of Social Work* (1976), Vol. 6, No. 1, p. 18. This study preceded the analysis of referrals published in *BJSW* in 1977. (See Chapter Eight, p. 159).
11. Towards the end of this study, senior social workers with special responsibility for the younger handicapped had been appointed in two Greater London boroughs.
12. Glampson, Ann, *et al.*, *op. cit.*, p. 9.
13. CCETSW, Paper 9.
14. Glampson *et al.*, *op. cit.*
15. A Wandsworth Day Centre makes available a telephone line, manned by disabled volunteers, every weekday from 2–4 p.m. to help with emergencies and to advise on welfare rights. A housebound disabled person in Newcastle-on-Tyne operates a similar service from her own home and puts

disabled people who need emergency transport in touch with volunteer drivers. It is hoped to promote a national network of help of this kind, to be known as the Disabled Advice Service (DAS).

16. *Op. cit.*, para. 489.
17. *Community Work and Social Change: a Report on Training.* Report of a Working Party set up by the Calouste Gulbenkian Foundation, published 1968.
18. *The Voluntary Worker in the Social Services.* Report of a Committee jointly set up by the NSCC and NISWT under the chairmanship of Geraldine M. Aves. (The Bedford Square Press of the NSCC and George Allen & Unwin Ltd, 1969), pp. 126 and 189.
19. *Op. cit.*, p. 126.
20. The DHSS is also prepared to pay for transport to work in such circumstances, but few disabled people were aware of this.
21. Task Force employed over 12,000 volunteers in the Greater London area and was used in all but two of the boroughs. These boroughs discouraged any form of individual voluntary activity including volunteer help with meals on wheels, although there was considerable pressure by social workers for more involvement with the community as a whole.
22. See the Aves Report, *op. cit.*, p. 118 and Mitchell, Ann, *An Enquiry into the Use of Volunteers Directly Responsible to Social Work Departments and into the Relationships between Social Services Departments and Voluntary Organisations* (Scottish Council of Social Services, 1977).
23. See Allen, D., *The Use of Volunteers in the Social Services Departments* (unpublished research). Quoted extensively in the NCSS Briefing for February 1978.
24. Grants to Voluntary Associations by local borough councils showed wide variations in the Greater London area with Islington leading with a grant of £805,000 for 1976–77. This worked out at £7.02 per head of the population. Camden provided £6.46 per head, Wandsworth £1.74 and Hammersmith £1.24 per head. Among the Outer London boroughs the figure for Brent was just £1.00 a head and for Croydon £0.49p. The Wolfenden Report, *op. cit.*, Appendix 6.
25. *Op. cit.*, p. 63.
26. All field workers are expected to fill in Change Reports if a client of theirs is known to have moved out of the area, to have gone into residential care or to have died.
27. Lists of residents of the borough who have died are compiled every month. Copies are sent to the secretariat of the social services department and to area officers. Clerks are expected to track down any names known to the social services and to inform the social workers concerned. By the time this happens relatives have often moved away and houses have been sold or let to new tenants.
28. Most aids have labels stuck on them saying they are the property of the social services department and that they are issued on loan. In one borough the local hospital sent out aids charged to the social services vote with labels saying they were the property of the hospital. Auxiliary social workers had to be sent to scrape them off.
29. Progressive stooping from arthritis can reduce the height of a client from 5′ 6″ to 5′ 2″. This means that the walking frame originally issued will be too high. Similarly people using wheelchairs frequently become obese and are often ashamed to report that they have overgrown the model issued.
30. Social Services Research, *Domiciliary Services Evaluation. Part II. Five types of Aid in Common Use* (November 1976).
31. *Five Types of Aid in Common Use. Part II*, p. v.
32. *Ibid.*, A.g.
33. Fenwick, D., *op. cit.* (HMSO, 1977).
34. See above, p. 124.
35. Durham Regional Area Health Authority – participant at a seminar arranged by the King's Fund on 15 May 1977.

221

CHAPTER ELEVEN

MINOR AND MAJOR ADAPTATIONS :
SOME DEFINITIONS WITH COMMENT;
GETTING MAJOR ADAPTATIONS DONE IN
THE PUBLIC SECTOR (1)

Many of the problems over getting adaptations done, particularly major adaptations, were closely bound up with how adaptations were defined. There were as many definitions as there were Greater London boroughs.

1. *Variations in defining adaptations*

One of the most useful ways of classifying adaptations is by purpose : that is, by the way in which they help clients to overcome specific handicaps such as the inability to move about freely inside the house, to get into a sitting position in bed, to get out of bed, to go to the toilet unaided, to cook in the kitchen, to use a wheelchair inside the home and out of doors, to get outside the front door or to open the garage door. Because disabled people frequently have poor circulation and feel the cold badly, adaptations may be needed to provide warmth and to retain heat. Other kinds of adaptations may be designed to help the relatives of clients who would otherwise have to go into residential care to continue looking after them at home.

The list that follows shows the type of adaptations undertaken by an Outer London borough in 1973–75.[1]

TYPES OF ADAPTATIONS

1. MOBILITY – OUTDOOR :
    Ramp – front.
    Ramp – back.
    Ramped path.
    Handrails (on footpath, garden steps, etc.).
    Landing level to garden.
    Steps altered.

2. MOBILITY – INDOOR :
    Handrails.
    Grabrails.

Lift.
Platform (raise floor level).
Sliding doors.
Door restrainers.
Door alterations (widened, handle moved, etc.).
Wall knocked down.
Steps altered.
Raising /lowering – electric points
                – gas fire controls
                – gas meters
                – shelves, coathooks, etc.
Hoists – Wessex
        – Commodore.

3. HEATING, LIGHTING & VENTILATION :
Power points installed.
Gas fire installed.
Central heating installed.
Pipes lagged.
Pipes and radiators boxed in.
Immersion heater installed.
Ceiling airer installed.
Louvre windows installed.
Double glazing installed.

4. KITCHEN :
Kitchen equipment/units installed.
Kitchen equipment/units raised or rearranged.

5. TOILET AND BATHROOM :
Shower units installed.
Toilet installed.
Bathroom alterations (raise bath, etc.).
Toilet extension.
Clos-o-mat, Perdisans, etc. installed.
Grab/handrails in bathroom/toilet.
Lever position changed on toilet.

6. COMMUNICATION :
Bell transformer.
Intercom system.
Possum selector unit.

7. CARS :
Automatic garage doors.
Carports, crossover and hard-standing.

8. MAJOR EXTENSIONS TO HOUSE:
  Bathroom built on.
  Bedroom built on.
  Toilet built on.

9. MISCELLANEOUS:
  e.g.
  Gate installed at top of stairs.
  Garden fence fixed.
  Drainage corrected.

An example of the types of adaptations supplied shows that some of the items listed as adaptations are clearly connected with the installation of aids, e.g. shower units, special doorbells, chemical closets, hoists, inter-com systems and "Possums" (patient operated selector units). Others, such as grab-rails, handrails and hoists would be considered as aids in some London boroughs and as minor adaptations in others. Items such as altering steps, putting in concrete ramps, making a gate at the top of a staircase or raising and re-arranging kitchen units are likely to be universally regarded as minor adaptations, while building on a whole bathroom or bedroom is obviously a major adaptation. Nevertheless, at the time of the study there was no single agreed definition distinguishing between a minor adaptation and an installation, or between a major adaptation and a minor one. It was therefore not possible to draw any valid conclusions about true levels of provision from the comparative statistics available.[2]

We must consequently examine some of the differing interpretations offered by London boroughs and by the City of London, their relevance in terms of statistical returns, and the implications of these statistics for forward planning.

The two main sources of statistical information, as indicated in Chapter Four, are the figures provided annually by the Department of Health and Social Security and by the Chartered Institute of Public Finance and Accounting (formerly the Institute of Municipal Treasurers and Accountants). This latter body makes no attempt to define adaptations, nor to separate them from aids. The Department of Health and Social Security, on the other hand, classifies the number of households receiving personal aids separately from those receiving adaptations, and makes a definite distinction between minor and major adaptations, albeit in the private sector only. In the public sector they are classified together.

Since the first annual returns were made for the year 1972–73 any adaptation in the private sector costing less than £150 has been treated as a minor adaptation. Any adaptation costing more than £150 is automatically classified as major. That the distinction is regarded as arbitrary is shown by the fact that in only one of the

Greater London boroughs and the City of London was it thought worthwhile to use the sum of £150 at any point in their internal administration. This was done purely to simplify the preparation of the statistical returns.[3]

Typical returns for the year 1973–74 are given in Table 22 (DHSS R1) which follows, Form RI for the Department of Health and Social Security returns for 1972–73.[4] Because of restrictions of space figures are given below for only four boroughs, two Inner and two Outer, and these are for the highest and lowest number of adaptations provided.

Table 22 – Estimated number of households receiving certain kinds of assistance during the period 1 April 1972 to 31 March 1973

Households where assistance was provided for the following items

Column 1	Columns 2–9 give details about	Adaptations/ private property		Adaptations to LA dwellings
Inner and Outer boroughs named	radio and television supplies, rental and attachment and personal aids	Minor (Less than £150)	Major (£150 or more)	
(1)	(2–9)	(10)	(11)	(12)
Inner (highest figure)		183	1	97
Inner (lowest figure)		6	1	1
Outer (highest figure)		405	61	167
Outer (lowest figure)		13	6	29

The number of households given assistance was further broken down into single person households, multi-person households, households with handicapped children under sixteen, and households whose composition was not known. With the exception of households with a handicapped child, the adaptations do not necessarily refer only to households with a physically handicapped member and will usually include households with a member who is elderly frail. The breakdown of households appears on a separate table, DHSS R4, in the annual returns to the Department of Health and Social Security.

There is criticism by local authority social services staff about being required to return statistics of aids and adaptations by "households" as a unit approach to statistics is being increasingly adopted by local authorities for their own purposes. This means that separate statistics have to be compiled for the Department of Health and Social Security by staff who feel they are already overworked. But statistics of this kind enable the Department of Health and Social Security to see what degree of priority is awarded to handicapped people who

225

are also elderly and living alone;[5] and also what number of households there are with handicapped children under sixteen who might be eligible for additional help with adaptations from the Family Fund.[6] It would appear that the Department of Health and Social Security was apparently more interested in monitoring activity, in both the private and public sectors, than cost.

No change in the format of the statistics has been made since they were first called for in the year 1972–73. This is surprising as the Housing Act 1974 made grants available to a disabled person living in the private sector to cover "work required for his welfare, accommodation or employment where the existing dwelling is inadequate or unsuitable for those purposes." An anticipated result of this legislation was that not only would more adaptations to privately owned and privately rented property be carried out, but that these would also be more extensive and more costly; and that in some instances social services would be paying the client's share of the total cost.[7]

At no time has the Department of Health and Social Security asked for returns based on a financial dividing line between minor and major adaptations in the public sector. This may be because there is no standard procedure for deciding what proportion of the cost, if any, would be borne by local authority housing departments. The joint consultative paper issued for internal circulation to the departments concerned in November 1976 spoke of a 50/50 split between local housing departments and local authority social services departments as probably the most likely division of costs. It also went on to say that probably only in the larger County and Metropolitan boroughs would social services departments be able to shoulder the whole burden of this expense. In the Greater London area it was the social services departments which were largely responsible for the financing of both minor and major adaptations to property in the public sector. The disparities between the ways in which these were financed in various London boroughs has already been discussed in Chapter Four.[8]

Another reason why the Department of Health and Social Security may not have asked for statistical returns based on cost may have been because local housing authorities were accountable to the Department of the Environment for any expenses they incurred – and subsidies received – other than those for work chargeable against the social services vote. These figures would not be available to the clerks in the social services departments dealing with the returns of statistics.

If statistics in the form laid down by the Department of Health and Social Security were to be used for forward planning, details of the cost of minor and major adaptations would need to be covered not only for the private but for the public sector as well. The need or otherwise for more purpose-adapted property, more purpose-built property, or even for a policy of more extensive housing of disabled people, ought in part to depend on the availability of reliable information about the number of major and minor adaptations undertaken in any given financial year. This in turn will depend on rationalising the distinction made between minor and major adaptations.

Typical of this kind of confusion is a written instruction sent to a team of fieldworkers dealing exclusively with work for the disabled in an Outer London borough :

"An adaptation is anything that involves the structure of a dwelling or its surround. However if a member of the [borough's own] Industrial Centre is employed or any member of the staff of the [borough's] Housing Maintenance then even the installation of the smallest grab-rail must be entered in the Adaptations ledger and the money for it must come out of the Adaptations budget".

This definition is nevertheless valuable because it takes notice not only of adaptations to the structure of a building but also to its surround. This permits the installation of garages with "magic eyes", car-ports, levelling of gradients, building on balconies and laying down patios. It is illuminating because it highlights the common practice of regarding any work supervised or undertaken by staff from other borough departments under the system of "local orders"[9] as some form of adaptation both for budgetary and statistical purposes.

A number of boroughs used references to altering the structure of a dwelling as an indication that an adaptation was a major one, and six offered definitions that attempted to distinguish between minor and major adaptations by implying some difference between the fabric of a dwelling and its structure. Under definitions of this kind, cutting out a panel from the wood surrounding an old-fashioned bath in order to accommodate the leg of a hoist would not in theory count as any kind of adaptation; sinking a socket into the bathroom floor to take the leg of a heavy-duty patient lifter would be classified as a minor adaptation; reinforcing a wooden floor with concrete to support the weight of a heavy bath unit would be a major adaptation.

To find a definition which was meaningful, it was necessary to go outside the Greater London area into an adjacent County borough. As in the majority of the Greater London boroughs, an aid was defined as "anything removable" (i.e. a wooden but not a concrete ramp), but this borough *budgeted for aids and minor adaptations together*. Minor adaptations clearly included all work of *installation* for they were defined as "including anything screwed to the fabric of the dwelling". On the other hand "anything that altered the structure of the property", no matter what it cost, was automatically classified as a major adaptation. Responsibility for aids and minor adaptations was vested in a principal officer who had previously been a head occupational therapist who worked direct to the assistant director of the fieldwork division. Responsibility for keeping progress checks on major adaptations, all of which were done by the borough architects' department, was vested in an administrative officer (AP 3) in the social services department. An indication of the relative volume, if not the relative importance, of the work being done in the two different divisions can be construed from the fact that the budget for "Aids and Minor Adaptations" (including installation) in 1974–75 was £53,000, whereas only £28,000 was allocated for "Major Adaptations".

The researcher seeking a common denominator between what each of the 32 Greater London boroughs and the City of London considers to be a major adaptation is left in the last analysis with nothing more than the availability of finance at the time an adaptation is requested. The Brunel study foresaw this in 1974 :

"For example, in the case where a social worker was applying for a costly adaptation to the home of a physically handicapped person he, the administrator, might in a certain situation say in effect 'you need the approval of a more senior officer for this work', or, 'we are over-spent on the budget and I cannot therefore agree to proceed without further authority'. In both these situations some clear policy-bar is apparent. In other cases his response might be, in effect, 'I note your application for certain adaptations but are you aware that many of your colleagues are specifying such-and-such things which are cheaper'."

The Brunel study goes on to say that it would clearly be inappropriate for an administrator to suggest that a fieldworker had made a bad judgement, that other clients' needs were greater or that the client would surely be better off in residential care. Should such comments appear to be justifiable then they could only rest appropriately with the superior of the case-worker concerned.[10]

Unfortunately it is often much simpler to abandon projects about which an administrator feels uncertain than to invite an interchange of views at case conferences between senior officers of the social services secretariat, who are accountable for finance, and senior case-workers, who are accountable to clients. Without such safeguards built in to the process by which scarce resources have to be rationed, the apparent large differences in expenditure between one local authority and another reflect the policy of the social services departments rather than the needs of clients and their relatives on whose behalf fieldworkers make applications for costly aids or adaptations.[11]

Any form of delay compounds the rationing of scarce financial resources, and what the Brunel study pin-points as the inability of one officer to proceed further without authorisation from a superior has already been discussed in detail in Chapter Nine, where Table 14 on pages 180–81 shows the varying sums of money which could be authorised at different levels of the hierarchy in different Greater London boroughs during 1974–75. In essence the figure chosen by each of them to indicate that an adaptation is considered to be major was directly related to the hierarchical structure and to the financial ceiling above which applications for adaptations had to go before the social services committee. These, it was found, varied from a figure as low as £25 up to £2,000, with four directors having complete discretionary powers.

In one Outer London borough the limit of financial authority in approving adaptations permitted the director of social services was £500 in 1973–74. Representations were made, based on the figures that follow, to have this sum raised to £1,000.

Cost of Adaptation	Number of Adaptations
£500–£1,000	18
More than £1,000	20
Total (more than £500)	38

In this borough a breakdown of expenditure showed that the average cost of all adaptations, including installation of aids and minor adaptations, was £133, but that the average range of cost was from £50 for adaptations to help with indoor mobility (mainly handrails) to an average of £2,000 for major adaptations including extensions.[12]

These findings also suggest that the figure of £150 set by the Department of Health and Social Security[13] is unrealistically high for the majority of minor adaptations and unrealistically low for the majority of major adaptations. If the figure of £1,000 were used as a cut-off point instead of £150 a much more valuable index of the provision of major adaptations could be provided through routine monitoring by social services staff of all adaptations costing more than £1,000 of which the whole or part of the expenditure comes out of the social services vote.

The consultative paper of November 1976[14] suggested that throughout England and Wales responsibility for all major adaptations should, in the long term, be transferred to local housing authorities with the social services departments assuming an advisory role.

229

In the short term it suggests, under the heading "Proposals for the Immediate Future", that

(a) Housing authorities should finance any work which would become a part of the structure of the dwelling and would be a normal feature of any new housing for disabled people.

(b) Expenditure on any other features (which would be expected to be non-structural, i.e. in the nature of portable equipment) should be met by the Social Services authorities who would consult as necessary with the health authorities.

The paper goes on to say that the Department of the Environment "recognises that certain practical difficulties arise from these proposals", particularly between over what should be considered "structural alterations" and what might be defined as "non-structural alterations".

Attention is also drawn to the fact that the statutory provisions relating to the functions of social services and housing authorities overlap and that the effect of existing legislation on schemes of adaptations and improvement for disabled people is different in the private sector and the public sector. Before local authority housing departments would assume responsibility for adaptations in the private sector there would have to be new legislation.

Meanwhile the need to secure some consistency, not only in the boroughs represented by the London Boroughs' Association but throughout the United Kingdom as a whole, would seem imperative. The circular of guidance issued in August 1978 substitutes "structural" for "major" but admits to difficulty in separating "structural" from "non-structural" work. It makes no attempt to isolate the "aids" component in e.g. portable hoists and lifts from the "structural" work of installing them, and so to some extent leaves confusion that much more confounded.[15]

2. Getting major adaptations done in the public sector

(a) The involvement with other borough departments

The Greater London borough which, at the time of this study, provided both the greatest number of purpose-built dwellings and the greatest number of adaptations for disabled clients, also had the simplest definition of what constituted a major adaptation.

"A major adaptation is work that involves any outside agency including other borough departments."

This definition recognises that much of the work of installing aids and also that of many minor adaptations may fall well within the competence of handymen and technicians based on social services departments. Unlike the definition used in the majority of the

Greater London boroughs it does not seek to distinguish between minor and major adaptations by using relative costs as a criterion.

This definition also recognises the reality that many outside agencies have to be involved in any major work of adaptation. This, in turn, means problems of administration, liaison and overall control that are common to every borough in the Greater London area no matter how the staff of their social services departments attempt to deal with them. Of these the factor common to all of them which involves the greatest period of delay is the need to get planning permission – this was invariably sought after, and not before, the social services committee had approved the project. In none of the Greater London boroughs did staff feel able to seek planning permission, even in the public sector, concurrently with the many other processes that lead up to the point at which committee sanction is requested, even although these preliminaries may well take as long as six months. Having to get planning permission, according to one third line manager in a social services department, was also the main reason why no really major adaptation, no matter how urgent it might be, could ever be completed in less than nine months from the date of referral.

This statement was endorsed by all the appropriate staff interviewed throughout the Greater London boroughs although the majority of them extended the nine months to "at least a year" with the exception of the two adaptations most frequently provided – showers and stairlifts. All the officers of the secretariat interviewed who dealt with adaptations were asked what was the shortest possible time in which (i) an extension with a shower and (ii) a stairlift involving some alterations to the existing layout of the stairs had been achieved. In the 25 boroughs which had put in shower extensions the shortest time was six months in two of them and nine months in the rest. No borough which had installed a stairlift had managed to do so in less than nine months. Both these adaptations were held up by the need to get planning permission from health and sanitation authorities and, in the case of stairlifts, fire risks had also to be assessed.

Next to obtaining planning permission the next most frequent source of delay occurred before a request for an adaptation went to committee. Unless a property were owner-occupied, no work could be initiated until permission had been obtained from the landlord. In the public sector this is the local authority housing manager, in his capacity as landlord, or the appropriate official of the Greater London Council, usually the housing manager of the district concerned. As landlords they have the power to withhold permission or, having satisfied themselves that an adaptation is necessary, practicable and feasible, grant permission subject to the approval of the social services committee. This applies equally to an adaptation in a council dwelling on a vast council estate or to an isolated house that has been bought up by the council as an "in-fill" in an area scheduled for development or rehabilitation. Occasionally a director of housing would buy an unoccupied house because it would lend itself to inexpensive adaptations for specific elderly or disabled people on the council's waiting list, but this was exceptional.

Directors of housing, borough housing managers and district housing managers require, in the same way as private landlords do, that any damage to the fabric arising from structural alterations shall be made good and that all necessary works of redecoration will be carried out. Some of them also insist that adapted property is restored to its original condition if the disabled client ceases to live in it for any reason. The study revealed occasional cases of semi-permanent ramps and handrails and ceiling track hoists being removed – the expense of their removal was invariably charged against the social services vote – without any attempt having been made to match the vacant property, as adapted, to a disabled client on the council or GLC waiting list. The more enlightened housing officials attempted to look upon adapted property as something to be pooled on behalf of those disabled in need of re-housing. It is realised that there are human and practical difficulties in asking tenants to move out should a disabled member of the family die, be taken into a residential home or enter a hospital for terminal care, but provided the need to move out in such circumstances had been explained to the family at the time any major adaptations were made, a decent period allowed for mourning and an attractive alternative home offered at a comparable rent it was claimed by housing officers and social workers that no difficulties had arisen over what had amounted to forcible re-housing.

On the whole both re-housing disabled people – provided there is adequate housing stock – and making major adaptations to the property in which they live is comparatively less complicated in the public sector than in the private sector, though all major adaptations involve a multiplicity of processes. Not for nothing have the adventures encountered by domiciliary occupational therapists after initiating a major adaptation been named "The Thirty-Nine Steps", and as will be seen in Section 5 of this chapter it would seem that twenty-nine steps appears to be the minimum possible.

3. *The Processing of Major Adaptations in the Public Sector*

In the Greater London boroughs much of the work of processing major adaptations is taken out of the hands of the staff of the social services departments both before and after the project is put to the social services committee for approval. Even so those fieldworkers who attempt to keep in touch with the progress made on behalf of their clients will find themselves dealing, both by telephone and on paper, with officers from a minimum of three other borough departments and in personal contact with the mix of direct labour and private contractors which one or more of these departments will be employing.[16] Frequently two surveyors, each from a different borough department, will be involved in the initial site visit, one, a quantitative surveyor coming perhaps from a borough architects' department and a second, in cases such as the installation of a lift, an electrical engineer coming perhaps from a borough engineers' department. Or both of these advisers might be based on a large housing department or a department of technical services.

The existence of a number of departments doing similar work under different names throughout the whole of the Greater London area was at first bewildering to the researcher. Those boroughs which had become sufficiently interested in theories of corporate management to re-organise their internal structure had cannibalised some of these departments into single larger departments bearing names like Planning and Development whilst retaining, in new divisions, some of the staff of the departments that had been assimilated. Many senior architects, job architects, draftsmen, surveyors, engineers and technicians were for the most part still doing recognisably the same jobs and still handing out work to the same builders and contractors on the same approved lists. The exceptions were the officers who came from those departments which had formerly been headed by borough treasurers and who, whether or not they had been obliged to merge with the department of the chief executive (still frequently referred to as the town clerk), preserved a measure of autonomy. Some of these officers, at a high level, might hold watching briefs during crucial stages in the financing of adaptations and others, at a lower level, were involved with assessing clients for financial contributions but none were to be found amongst any of the amalgams referred to above. Housing directors, in addition to granting approval for adaptations in the public sector, might release housing maintenance staff and builders to do all or part of the physical labour of demolition and construction. Or they might request officers of the housing department to undertake the processing of all work of all kinds connected with major adaptations in council property.[17]

Whichever borough department assumes responsibility for overseeing the work involved in major adaptations the fact remains that officers and fieldworkers employed by the majority of the social services departments are required to stand aside from the time of the first site visit to the final completion of the adaptation, except for two brief interludes. The first of these is when "sketch plans", always beautifully drawn, and "rough estimates" are put forward by directors or assistant directors of social services to the social services com-

233

mittee. The second is when the final tender or negotiated price goes to committee for approval. There may even be one other session with the social services committee if, as is often the case, an insufficient number of tenders has been submitted or the final cost looks like exceeding the rough estimate.

Having the processing done in this way by employees of the departments most concerned with the actual work of adaptation has the advantage of taking a great deal of work off the staff of the social services department. The majority of them do not have in their employ officers who can, for example, decide on the merits of one tender as against another or what material for a new wall combines the best value for money with the maximum safety for bearing special equipment or the amount of reinforcing needed for a floor or ceiling.[18] But it also means that almost all the work involved in a major adaptation, whether manual, clerical, administrative or supervisory, can become totally divorced for long periods of time from the client on whose behalf the adaptation is being undertaken and also from the social services department against whose vote the cost of these many and various services is being entered.

Attempts by both fieldworkers and officers of the secretariat to exercise some form of control over the progress made are not always well received. In three boroughs surveyors and technicians who were interviewed, although they were not based on social services departments, complained vociferously that social workers and domiciliary occupational therapists "changed their minds about plans", "got in the way of builders" and "encouraged clients to ring up and make complaints". On the other hand the advice of domiciliary occupational therapists and especially that of head occupational therapists was usually welcomed at the time of the first visit to the site and joint visits at this stage were the exception rather than the rule. In one borough the head occupational therapist had also been asked to draw up a written brief on the main rules that need to be observed when doing major adaptations.

Officially all supervision of works of major adaptations was undertaken by a Clerk of the Works. But as these borough employees had so many calls on their time inspection of major adaptations (always classified under "Minor Works") were frequently random and intermittent.

Attempts to keep fieldworkers, their clients and officers of the social services secretariat informed about the progress being made assumed many guises. The most frequent was to ask a clerk or administrative assistant to act as a "chaser" and, in addition to her various other duties, to ring round the other borough departments involved at discreet intervals to "have a chat" about how things were getting along. Questions frequently asked included whether builders had actually begun work, had overcome delays in getting certain necessary materials,[19] had returned to the site after absences for unexplained reasons and whether they expected to complete the work by the date specified in some, but by no means all, contracts. There appeared to be an unwritten code which ensured that clerks were never so impolite as to telephone surveyors until at least six weeks after every detail of the major adaptations had been approved, while surveyors clearly considered it impolite to make any kind of contact with the approved builders for at least two weeks after work on the site was presumed to have begun.

In five boroughs "progress sheets" were optimistically attached to the front of a client's confidential file and monitoring by area based clerks then proceeded on much the same lines. In every borough a system of sending duplicate forms to a clerical or administrative officer in the social services departments secretariat prevailed but not – as was equally desirable – to fieldworkers involved with the case. None of these forms did anything to speed up progress between the different points at which such forms could be signed and copies forwarded.

The most satisfactory method of keeping checks on progress involved the use of "aids and adaptations officers" who had themselves come into administration "with knowledge of the building trade", but only three boroughs employed these on the staff of their social services departments. These officers, graded as AP 3 or AP 4 and SO 1, were based strategically on teams led by head occupational therapists. All knew the builders who were working on the adaptations personally, and, although not entirely acceptable to senior officers brought up to administer "by the book" managed to keep things moving with the minimum of inter-departmental wrangling.[20] In two boroughs fieldworkers followed the old "welfare" practice of attaching a volunteer to keep an eye on how things were going and, incidentally, how the disabled clients and their families were standing up to the inconvenience that is inseparable from having structural alterations made to homes in which people are living at the time. In this respect one should remember that whereas people who are not handicapped can get up and go out for a walk or leave the key with a neighbour and go out to work, many people so severely disabled that they need major adaptations will not only be housebound but may even have to sit in the same room where walls are being banged down and new doorways made.

4. *Typical procedure for major adaptations in an Inner London borough – Public Sector – 1974–75*

The need to keep revelant staff in the social services department

235

constantly informed about the progress of major adaptations is fully recognised in the written instructions issued by a third line manager in the social services secretariat in 1974. The document assumes that the most appropriate fieldworker in cases involving a major adaptation will be the occupational therapist based on the social services office for the area in which the client lives. The appropriate officer in the social services secretariat to monitor a major adaptation from start to finish is the Consultant for the Physically Handicapped, a principal officer placed just one grade below the assistant director (finance) who took the final decision about which of the requests for major adaptations he was prepared to submit to the social services committee. The instructions which follow in Section 5 below were drafted by the head occupational therapist,[21] based on a day centre, who saw no need to be kept informed officially as she held weekly meetings with the area-based occupational therapists who also called in daily. Four copies of the many forms needed were made. The top copy was kept by the officer in the borough architects' department responsible for overseeing the progress of the work. The second copy was sent to the Consultant for the Physically Handicapped in the social services secretariat and the third to the area-based occupational therapist, who put it on the client's file, the fourth went to an appropriate officer in the borough treasurer's department.

At different stages of the adaptation, different staff of the borough architects' department were involved. If the occupational therapist asked for an adaptation that was obviously going to be extensive and costly, the senior borough architect might go along on the initial site visit together with one of his quantity surveyors and perhaps an engineer. He would then draw up the first plans before handing over to a "job" architect or to the surveyor. None of the borough's three senior architects held any special qualifications in designing for the disabled, but one of them was known to be particularly interested in the problems of the disabled. The Consultant for the Physically Handicapped who had worked closely with him for three years said that he had read Selwyn Golsmith's book[22] and attended seminars at which Selwyn Goldsmith had been speaking. It was therefore considered unnecessary to call in a consultant architect even for the more elaborate major adaptations. When this architect was not available – he was becoming heavily involved with plans for a large housing estate – then the Consultant for the Physically Handicapped had to rely on the expertise and tact of the occupational therapist to ensure that the plans drawn up were appropriate to the needs of the handicapped.

The procedures fall into eight stages with the departments assuming responsibility for each stage clearly defined. Stage One – referral, initial site visit, sketch plans, costing, second site visit – involve both the borough architects' department and the social services department. (Steps 1–8 inclusive). Stage Two involves only the borough treasurer's department. Stage Three takes matters back to the borough architects' department. (Steps 12 and 13). Stage Four is a purely internal matter for the social services department and its committee, and so on. Officers of all these departments can be seen to be actively involved at different stages but none are actively involved all the time. This is why four copies of each major decision are made so that if necessary there can be verbal consultation between the officers of the different departments at crucial points of the procedure; e.g. Stage Five is the responsibility of the borough treasurer, Stage Six of the borough architect and Stage Seven unites all departments concerned on the completion of the adaptation.

No attempt has been made, in Section 5 that follows, to show the twenty-nine steps in the form of a diagram because this would give to the reader a false impression of speed and ease in what is a massively cumbersome operation. It is essential that he should climb the steps laboriously, pausing in particular at those marked with an asterisk to gaze at vistas of almost boundless delay. He should also remind himself constantly that the average time taken in this borough on any major adaptation was said by its director of social services to be two years with one year the minimum time needed to put in a stairlift that was urgently needed because of a risk to health involved.

5. *The Twenty-Nine Steps: the progress of a major adaptation in the public sector* (Major areas of delay are shown by *)

Stage One: The Preliminary Stages
  1. The disabled client is referred to an occupational therapist.
  2. The area occupational therapist visits the client at home and assesses need. If she decides that a major adaptation is considered necessary for the client's greater safety, comfort and convenience – and possibly also to allow the client to continue to work at home – she will then
  3. telephone an officer in the borough architects' department to ask for a joint visit to the site at a mutually convenient time that will also be convenient to the client.
  4. The area occupational therapist confirms the time of the appointment in writing.
  5. The site visit takes place. The feasibility of the adaptation proposed by the occupational therapist is discussed and modifications or an alternative plan agreed on.
  6. Sketch plans are made and costing done by staff of the borough architects' department.*

7. One copy of the estimate and one copy of the sketch plan go to the Consultant for the Physically Handicapped (CPH) in the secretariat. One copy of the estimate and one copy of the plan go to the borough treasurer's department. One copy of the estimate and one copy of the plan go to the area occupational therapist for placing on the client's file. The top copies of both estimate and plan are retained in the borough architects' department.

8. If the plan is sanctioned by both the CPH and by the borough treasurer the area occupational therapist then visits the client for the second time, either with a surveyer or if the adaptation is a costly or difficult one, with a senior borough architect. The details of the plan are explained to the client and the client is told that he may be required to contribute towards the cost.

Stage Two – Involvement of the borough treasurer's department
9. The area occupational therapist writes to the borough treasurer's department asking him to arrange for the client's income to be assessed and the cost of the proposed adaptation to the client determined.*

10. The client signs a letter of consent (four copies).*

11. The borough treasurer's department informs the CPH that Step 10 has been completed (copy to borough architect and to the occupational therapist).

Stage Three – Back to the borough architects' department
12. The borough architect invites two, three or five tenders according to the estimated cost of the adaptation but is prepared if need be, to accept two realistic tenders if no more than two are forthcoming.*

13. The borough architect advises the CPH of the lowest tender. (Copy to borough treasurer and area occupational therapist).

Stage Four – The social services department takes over
14. (a) The CPH discusses the case with the assistant director (finance). If he approves, then
    (b) a full report on the needs of the client is prepared for the next session of the social services committee. This will include recommendations arising out of the client's financial situation, a detailed plan from the borough architects' department and the price of the lowest tender.

15. If the social services committee approves the adaptation the director then informs the borough treasurer.

Stage Five – Re-involvement of the borough treasurer's department
16. The borough treasurer writes to the client offering him a firm

238

price. (Copies to CPH, the borough architect and the area occupational therapist).

17. The client then either (i) accepts the offer, (ii) asks for a less expensive version or (iii) decides to give up the idea of an adaptation altogether.*

18. The borough treasurer writes to the CPH to say whether or not the client has accepted the offer on the terms put forward. If so steps 18–25 inclusive will be necessary. If a modified version is required a new site visit, new sketch plans and new estimates will be needed. In effect the whole process will then revert to Step 2.

19. The CPH sends a written order for the adaptation to the borough architect.

Stage six – The borough architect's department takes over

20. Planning permission is now sought by the borough architect.*

21. The borough architect places an order with a contractor and agrees a starting date and an estimated date by which the work ought to be completed.

22. The borough architect advises the area occupational therapist of the starting date and the possible date of completion.

23. A Clerk of the Works is asked to supervise the contractor's work while it is in progress.

24. On completion of the work the borough architect advises the borough treasurer and the director of social services of the final cost. (Copies to the CPH and the area occupational therapist).

Stage Seven – Back to the social services department

25. The area occupational therapist visits the client to check that the work as completed fulfils the purposes for which it was planned and that it has been done to a satisfactory standard. Also that all interior decorating has been made good before the period of guarantee, usually six months, expires.
    Notes on this visit are placed on the client's file.

26. The administrative assistant to the CPH notes the final cost of the adaptation on the original order form and in a ledger that records the running total that is kept for budget purposes.

27. The director of social services asks the borough treasurer to release payment to the builder.

Stage Eight – The borough treasurer's department presides over the completion of the adaptation

28. The borough treasurer's department releases payment to the builder pointing out that he has warranted the work for six months or one year as the case may be.

29. Assuming no structural faults appear the adaptation is considered to be complete.

Delays varied slightly with pressure of work on the other borough departments involved and also with the speed in which clients returned forms. When faced, after many months of waiting, with a final price (step 6) often in excess of what had originally been expected, clients who were expected in this borough to contribute towards the cost of adaptations in the public sector, often liked to consult relatives before making a final decision and might delay doing so for some weeks.

The cost of major adaptations in this borough was higher than average. This was partly because all delays affect prices in an inflationary situation and partly because a number of factors had combined, in the words of its assistant director (finance) "to give the borough a bad name with builders". This meant that the system of tendering, although theoretically operating, had broken down in practice and that the borough architect was left with no alternative but to accept a very high price as the lowest of two bids or even fall back on a price negotiated with the only builder willing to undertake the work.

The borough architects' department employed three qualified architects none of whom had had any previous experience of or training in designing for the disabled but all of whom were said to have "enjoyed learning on the job". Enthusiasm, coupled with delays in processing, had however led to as many as twenty estimates being submitted to the social services committee on the same day, a practice which was avoided in all other boroughs. Those directors and assistant directors who took adaptations to committee in blocks usually limited the number to not more than four; others preferred to put up only one costly adaptation at a time.

Nevertheless, very few boroughs had found ways of eliminating any of the "twenty-nine steps" listed in Section 5 above, or of reducing the time scale to less than twelve months.[23]

NOTES

1. See "Occupational Therapy Services in Hillingdon", *op. cit.*
2. In addition statistical entries may vary not only with local definitions but also according to the practice of the clerk making the returns. It is arguable that all hoists, which are removable and portable, should be regarded as aids issued on loan and that the cost of installing them should be a separate entry. Frequently, however, the cost of the aid is not separated from the total expenditure involved, which in 1976 often exceeded £150. In 1973 a popular hoist costing £87 could be bought and installed for little more than £100. In 1976 this type of hoist cost £120, which together with the rising cost of labour, meant that over £150 had to be spent before the aid could be used by the client. Clerks interviewed in five boroughs now list this aid as a major adaptation when it is installed in the private sector as well as including it on DHSS Form R1 under "other Personal Aids". Stairlift, stair climbers and lifts, which are also removable, though not portable, may appear as aids or as major adaptations according to local practice with consequent anomalies. For example, one make of stair climber that takes a wheelchair costs over £2,000 but as it requires no modification

to the stair-well could appear as an aid, while a much cheaper stairlift costing several hundred pounds to install, might be shown as a major adaptation.

3. The sum for which an area team manager could authorise aids and adaptations was raised from £100 to £150 in one borough at the request of the assistant administrative officer responsible for the statistical returns.

4. *Local Authority Social Services Departments – Aids to Households. Details of certain assistance provided to households by social services departments during the 12 months ending 31 March 1973.* Department of Health and Social Security Statistics and Research Division 6 (September 1973).

5. Many of the elderly in these returns would have been "impaired" (according to the definition of impairment used in the OPCS report) rather than handicapped.

6. See Chapter Three, p. 64.

7. See The Housing Act 1974, para. 56 as amended by the House of Lords, and Circular 160 (Department of the Environment) to accompany the Housing Act (December 1974).

8. See p. 88 above.

9. See Chapter Nine, p. 194.

10. Brand Institute of Organisation and Social Studies, *Social Services Department* (London, 1974).

11. See the monograph, *The Implementation of the Chronically Sick and Disabled Persons Act* (Action Research for the Crippled Child, 1973).

12. An analysis of the figure for the first quarter of the following financial year, 1974–75, showed that 12 major extensions were still waiting the committee's decision.

13. Of the total of 633 adaptations notified to the Department of Health and Social Security 61 were listed as costing over £150 in the private sector, 405 cost less than £150 and the cost of 167 in the public sector was not specified.

14. *Op. cit.*

15. See Joint Circular DOE 59/78.

16. Two of the Greater London boroughs used only direct labour for major adaptations.

17. *Ibid.* The smooth transition hoped for in this circular is more likely to be achieved in those few boroughs already using housing department staff.

18. This is particularly true when new materials are being used. Nevertheless it was a senior administrator in a social services department who volunteered the information that none of the walls in a new council estate could stand the strain of as much as a grab-rail and that the installation of even a small aid could mean a major structural alteration. Such mistakes can prove very costly indeed. Examples were found in the course of this study of surveyors who did not know the local by-laws, e.g. a drawing was made which put in a toilet without a handbasin. This led to having to make a larger extension before planning permission was granted, to re-costing and then back to committee – a delay of four additional months.

19. In many boroughs the builders ordered toilet suites and shower cabinets from their regular contacts and although a spot check in two boroughs showed that equally good models were available the builders preferred to wait several months to have their original order filled.

20. As Administrative and Professional Staff or Senior Officers of the Secretariat, these Adaptations Officers carried more weight than others, similarly titled, who were appointed as clerical or even "miscellaneous" grades.

21. The head occupational therapist, after discussion with both the Consultant for the Physically Handicapped and representatives from the borough architects' department, also drafted the many forms used.

22. *Op. cit.*

23. The role of the occupational therapist will, it is hoped, remain essentially unchanged throughout Stage One, Stage Four, step 14(b) and Stage Seven, step 25. *Ibid.* para. 16.

CHAPTER TWELVE

GETTING MAJOR ADAPTATIONS DONE IN
THE PUBLIC SECTOR (2): TENDERS; THE POLICY OF
THE GLC; CHANGING POLICIES TOWARDS
MAJOR ADAPTATIONS

1. *Introduction*

In the previous chapter the main areas of delay over getting adaptations done in the public sector were identified as

(a) getting the financial and legal work done,
(b) "client vacillation"
(c) getting builders to submit reasonably priced tenders and
(d) delays after the builder chosen had started work on the adaptation.

The marked reluctance of builders to work for the borough analysed stemmed from problems about payment. In boroughs which made interim payments builders appeared to be marginally more willing to tender. In most boroughs officers of the chief executive's department were unacceptably slow in releasing payment after a major adaptation had been completed. This was reported as one of the main reasons why builders were dissuaded from submitting realistic tenders. As the system of tendering affects both the public and private sectors alike, it needs to be considered in some detail.

2. *Tenders and Negotiated Prices*

Of the social services departments in the Greater London area only one required no estimates at all in both the private and public sectors; all the others except those using direct labour required varying numbers of estimates in the public sector only, and one, which used direct labour in the public sector, sought three estimates in the private sector. The number of estimates required varied from two to five, the social services department which required five having a sliding scale with only one estimate required for anything likely to cost less than £50 and five for anything costing over £2,000. Other social services departments operated sliding scales according to price with three estimates being required in most of them for estimates over £500.

The requirement to give a number of estimates bore little relation to the number of estimates that would actually be received. The local authority requiring five estimates had not once received as many as five and it was current practice to "make do" with three. Another authority requiring five estimates had not once received as many as "two honest estimates", the operative word here, and in the matter of all estimates, being the word "honest". In many local authority areas builders were unwilling to take on the smaller jobs of adaptations but, as they were anxious to remain on the list of approved builders because of the large projects that departments such as housing have to offer, tendered but submitted a price so unrealistically high that the tender would automatically be dropped. In one borough the Chief Architect could get minor adaptations done only by "adopting a stick and carrot approach" – no minor adaptations tendered for, no large contracts.

The advisability or otherwise of a system of tenders is a matter both of individual opinion and of the corporate policy adopted by social services committees. By 1975 only one social services department had substituted a negotiated price for all adaptations. On the other hand a social services department which had monitored negotiated prices over the previous year and had mounted a paper exercise with prices that had gone out to tender found that the negotiated price was never less than twice as much as the lowest of three tenders. This social services department reverted, in the financial year of 1976–77, to a system of tenders.

Waiting for estimates to come in is a major source of delay and one that could only be justified in terms of saving public money. There is no evidence, beyond that given by one borough, that money is in fact saved or that the lowest estimate is as low, or lower, than a negotiated price. Nor is it always advisable to make a point of accepting the lowest estimate. Only one borough reported having called in a private consultant architect to decide which of three tenders gave the council the best value for money, something quite different from the cheapest.

Another factor that needs to be considered is that approved contractors differ widely in their general capabilities and also in their ability to do certain specific kinds of work. Some may be good at ramps but not good with steps; some can handle any electrical work involved and others have to subcontract. Some builders take on more work than they can cope with reliably and employ unskilled "cowboy" labour for jobs requiring skill. There is no reason to assume either that the highest estimate will produce the most satisfactory work or that the lowest estimate will produce less satisfactory work. The quality of materials to be used, which are usually specified in the estimates, also needs to be evaluated against final cost as does the figure included for "making good" any damage done during the process of adaptation, e.g. if a wall has to be re-papered and the original paper cannot be matched the builder may estimate for one wall in a different paper of the client's choice or estimate for re-decorating the whole room.

The practice of going out to tender, unless the tenders are deliberately rigged, makes it purely a matter of chance if the most suitable choice for a certain job happens to submit the lowest, or most sensible, estimate. Everyone who has "had the builders in" knows the difficulties that have to be encountered when work is in progress and the need to escape from them by going out whenever possible. For some of the disabled any such escape from the work of adaptation is impossible, and the housebound will have to endure without respite the inevitable mess and inconvenience. The more quickly the work is done the better but frequently there are delays between starting a job and finishing. These may leave a disabled person at risk when in similar circumstances a normal person would be able to step over a pile of material or negotiate a hole in the floor without difficulty. One of the reasons given by builders for such hold-ups is that they are waiting for materials, but other hold-ups are known to occur because they had already started on a non-borough job whilst waiting to hear if their tender had been accepted. This means that they may be juggling with more work than they can manage in a reasonable length of time and, unless their contract with the borough includes a specific date by which the adaptation must be finished, the work for the disabled may well be subject to intermittent periods of delay. This is another reason why interim payments for work in progress are to be encouraged. Such payments also help small builders who may run out of money – and credit – with which to buy some of the materials needed for a major adaptation.

Towards the end of the study in late 1976 when the Housing Act 1974 was beginning to make itself felt, further complications over tenders arose in those cases when property in the private sector had to be brought up to standard before application for an improvement grant could be made. Builders were refusing, in some boroughs, to submit estimates for the repairs unless the borough department concerned would guarantee that they would also get the contract for the adaptation. This it was not possible for the department to do if any share of the cost of the adaptation were likely to fall on the client. The client might change his mind for a variety of reasons, including rising costs, during the nine months or so when negotiations about repair grants and the actual completion of repairs and improvements to sub-standard property were in progress.[1]

The research department of the London borough of Hillingdon published an analysis in 1975 of the time taken from referral to completion of thirty-nine adaptations begun in 1973–74[2]. The time taken waiting for estimates to come in was 45 per cent of the whole of the time taken from start to finish.

3. Time taken in the provision of adaptations: an intensive study by an Outer London borough

This study by Hillingdon had a number of purposes, one of which was "to examine the service being given to clients of the occupational therapists living in their own homes; and in particular the time taken to undertake adaptations." It was discovered that the simple sequence of request, assessment, order and completion was frequently compounded by delay. The speed with which assessments were made depended on the availability of occupational therapists' time and borough architects' time. Ordering was often delayed many weeks whilst clients made up their minds whether or not to have a hole knocked in the wall or not. As time went on the condition of clients sometimes deteriorated so that adaptations had to be altered after they had begun. In certain cases the process of adaptations was a continuing one with further adaptations being undertaken. Not surprisingly wide variations were found in the time required for each stage. Some urgent cases were dealt with quickly but for the most part the time taken between the request for an adaptation and the request for an estimate reflected not only the nature of the adaptation – how simple or complicated it was in terms of design and construction – but also the backlog of work which existed during the period studied.

An attempt was made to make a manual analysis of 39 major adaptations – in this borough adaptations costing £500 or over – but "because very few had been finished when the research work was done, it was not possible to carry the analysis further, to the completion of the work". However valid conclusions could be drawn about the process of authorisation.

"Referral to the Assistant Director (Day Services) usually amounted to a few days only; this period, securing authorisation, and going through the necessary financial and legal procedures took in total about 5 weeks for adaptations of £500 to £1,000 and six weeks for those costing £1,000 upwards".

The six weeks reflects the committee cycle. All adaptations costing more than £500 had, at the time of the study, to go up to committee. (This sum was raised to £1,000 as one of the results of the study).

A more ambitious study followed in which all adaptations both major and minor, ordered in 1973–74 were analysed. The results which came off the computer gave the time between request and order placed, order placed and completion (where available) and request and completion (where available) and were presented in the form of the three graphs reproduced opposite in Table 23.

The graphs have considerable value because they show not only the time scale for adaptations but also the volume and pressure of work caused by the large number of minor adaptations, 522 of which were being dealt with concurrently with the major adaptations by the same occupational therapists. In this borough however minor adaptations – that is those costing, at the time of the study, less than £500 – were done by staff in a different division of the borough architects' department, although still theoretically under his supervision. This left staff immediately responsible to the borough architect free to deal with major adaptations which, although relatively few in number, need a good deal more in the way of processing and almost inevitably require planning permission. Both divsions of the borough architect's department worked to the same brief, which had been drawn up by a senior – later head – occupational therapist and which insisted on "traditional materials in traditional designs".[3] It therefore ensured that new walls would be able to bear, among other things, the weight of grab-rails together with that of the disabled clients using them.

All the minor and major adaptations ordered in this borough in 1973–74 were broken down into kind and unit cost as in Table 24 below. Those done in the public and those done in the private sectors are not distinguished.

The borough was exceptional in that it was the only one in 1973–74 where the housing department assumed financial responsibility for the total cost of all adaptations to council property. This accounts for the exceptionally high cost of £65,834 in relation to expenditure in the other Greater London boroughs.

After this borough had completed its first study of minor and major adaptations, it was decided to make another study of adaptations requested between 1 April 1975 and 1 August 1975 in order to see whether these four months revealed any change in workloads or in trends. The figures showed a massive increase in both volume of work and in the real value of the cost of the work undertaken. The findings are reproduced in the following table, Table 25.

Table 25 shows that the 220 adaptations ordered in the first four months of the financial year 1974–75 showed an increase of 24.8 per cent above the annual rate of 1973–74. Expenditure was growing even more rapidly with the value of work ordered (£59,000) already approaching the total for 1973–74 and running at two and a half times the level of the previous year. The share of adaptations to help mobility, both outdoors and indoors, had risen but that of major extensions had fallen – possibly because of more deliberate attempts

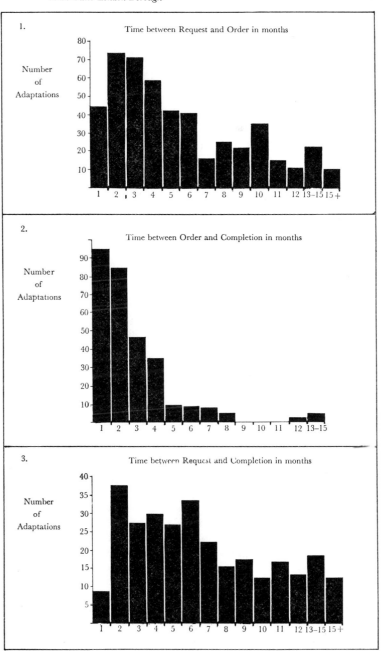

Table 24 – Numbers of and expenditure on adaptations by type (Private and public sectors) in an Outer London Borough – 1973–74.

Type of Adaptation	Number	Expenditure £	Percentage of total spent on adaptations	Unit Cost £
Mobility, Outdoor	77	6,893	10.5	90
Mobility, Indoor	268	13,272	20.2	50
Heating, Lighting and ventilation	24	1,191	1.8	50
Kitchen	9	764	1.2	85
Toilet and Bathroom	187	22,740	34.5	122
Communication	6	306	0.5	51
Access to Car	8	1,765	2.7	221
Major Extensions	9	18,870	28.7	2,096
Miscellaneous	3	33	0	11
TOTAL	591	65,834	100.1	Av. 133

Table 25 – Percentage of different types of minor and major adaptations ordered in 1973–74 and from 1 April – 31 July 1975.

	1973–74 (whole financial year) %	1974–75 (4 months) %
Mobility, Outdoor	10.5	17.3
Mobility, Indoor	20.2	32.0
Heating, Lighting and ventilation	1.8	1.5
Kitchen	1.2	0.3
Toilet and Bathroom	34.5	30.0
Communication	0.5	0.0
Access to Car	2.7	0.0
Major Extension	28.7	18.6
TOTAL	100.1	99.7
Total Number of adaptations undertaken	591	220
Cost of adaptations	£65,834	£59,000

to re-house people. However twelve major extensions were awaiting final authorisation on 1 August 1975.

Expenditure on all extensions to increase mobility had tripled in the first months of 1974–75 and the unit cost of toilet and bathroom extensions had doubled. A much more detailed analysis of invoices would have been necessary to decide how much of this increased expenditure was due to inflation, but it was reasonably clear that inflation played a lesser part than the fact that the nature of the work undertaken was more extensive in 1974–75 than in 1973–74. The share of adaptations in the privately-rented sector also increased in 1974–75 but remained low re absolute numbers. No separate figures were given for these or for adaptations done to owner-occupied property.

The main recommendations of this study concerning the provision of adaptations were (1) that the delegated powers of the assistant director (day services) should be raised from £500 to £1,000; (2) that there should be an increase of two in the establishment of occupational therapists; (3) that a post of occupational therapy technician be created; (4) that there should be an increase of one "aide" [social work assistant] for each area occupational therapist, [bringing the number of "aides" per head up to two], and (5) that a post for a head occupational therapist should be created.

As this borough already employed the highest number of occupational therapists in the Greater London area, with one senior and one basic occupational therapist in each area, now to be backed up by two social work assistants, the implication is that other boroughs may be seriously understaffed. As all adaptations in the private sector were also done free of charge to the client, the finance department did not have to be brought in to assess clients' incomes for contributions, thus eliminating a major area of delay. Nor were clients who were not being asked to pay as likely to vacillate about whether or not they wanted an adaptation done.

Work on bathrooms and toilets heads the list of work undertaken – indeed this was found to be the case throughout the Greater London boroughs. Table 25 shows that in Hillingdon they accounted for over one third of the total cost. A further breakdown of expenditure shows that the average cost of all adaptations (including installation, minor and major adaptations) was £133 in 1973–74 but that costs ranged from £50 for minor adaptations to assist indoor mobility (such as handrails) to £2,000 for major adaptations (such as full bathroom extensions). Increases in the cost of individual adaptations was considerable but the increase in the numbers of adaptations required was even more marked.

The work done by the research teams in this borough confirms the verbal reports of vastly increased demand given in interviews by senior officers in other Greater London boroughs.[4] Two of the major areas of delay – client vacillation and waiting for builders to tender – were also common to all the Greater London boroughs. Obtaining planning permission, generally considered to be a major area of delay was however a speedier process in Hillingdon than in the majority of boroughs and the time spent over legal work – a mere five weeks – considerably less than average.

4. *The use of direct labour for major adaptations*

The borough of Hillingdon used private builders for 74 per cent of adaptations and direct labour for installing aids in council property.

Senior administrators in the majority of the Greater London boroughs were convinced that private contractors were cheaper for small jobs and this has already been commented on in Chapter Nine. For major adaptations however the reverse was true in three out of the four boroughs which had direct labour. In these a sliding scale operated with the housing department bearing a higher percentage of the cost of large jobs. The bigger the job the smaller the percentage charged against the social services vote so that, for adaptations costing more than £1,000 in the public sector, the housing department might well shoulder 90 per cent of the cost leaving only 10 per cent to come out of the social services budget.[5]

Some boroughs were obliged to use direct labour for major adaptations irrespective of comparative costs. In one borough a council with a conservative majority insisted that all work liable to cost more than £150 had to be given to private contractors but in two other boroughs anything costing more than £50 was allocated to the direct labour force. In two of the boroughs where social services departments employed special adaptations officers the services of the borough architect were called in for any work costing more than £500 in one of them and more than £1,000 in the other. More boroughs made use of direct labour for surveying and designing major adaptations than for minor adaptations in the public sector. In one borough the borough architect took over all work costing more than £400 in both the public and private sectors and in only two boroughs was a consultant architect called in by the social services department concerned, which also paid his fees, to decide which of the designs submitted for two major adaptations in the private sector were the best value for money. Some boroughs encouraged clients living in the private sector told to find builders for themselves. In each case this meant that they had to persuade three builders to tender. Many boroughs used a mix of direct labour and approved private contractors for major adaptations in the same way as they did for installations and minor adaptations.

None of the directors and assistant directors interviewed were very clear about how the cost of direct labour was calculated but four believed that private contractors would have been both cheaper and quicker. All the senior administrative staff interviewed were convinced that the use of direct labour did nothing to speed up the time taken to complete a major adaptation although no tenders had to be submitted, money for building materials was theoretically always available and the processes of accounting simplified. The less senior administrative staff and the clerks involved in "chasing up" direct labour resented the time taken up by trying to overcome delays that they considered to be largely unnecessary.

5. The Policy of the Greater London Council towards Major and Minor Adaptations: delays over giving permission for adaptations

At the time of the study the official policy of the Greater London Council was that it stood in relation to social services departments as any other landlord. Where the installation of aids or the provision of minor and major adaptations in any GLC property situated within the Greater London Council was concerned, the policy which was confirmed in writing in August 1976 was :

"Adaptations are made to GLC property by the local social services departments to their own standards much the same way as would apply to property in other ownership. The procedures do not differentiate but, of course, GLC personnel are usually better informed on these matters than the typical private landlord and there is scope for exchange of ideas."

In practice the GLC, in its capacity as landlord, refused permission in every single borough in the Greater London area for borough employees to make any structural adaptation to their property without their own surveyors first seeing at least a careful sketch plan. Also the time taken in arranging for GLC surveyors and borough surveyors to meet in order to "exchange ideas" was one of the largest single delaying factors in getting work done in GLC property. Officers in the social services departments of all but two Greater London boroughs spoke with varying degrees of bitterness about the administrative costs of urging surveyors of both departments to make appointments for initial site visits and of the time taken in chasing up GLC housing officers to give written permission for work by borough surveyors to go ahead.

In two boroughs, staff of social services departments reported that the GLC had occasionally allowed its own direct labour force, if times were slack, to install things like grab-rails but it was not known if the cost of labour had been later charged to the social services departments. This was, however, exceptional and likely to be seasonal, as the normal practice was for the GLC, if its direct labour force undertook any work of adaptations, to do so as agents of the local authority with all the delays that the submission of sketch plans and estimates involved. Conversely, if a Greater London borough preferred to call in private contractors for work done in GLC property, then the GLC insisted on its officials examining the plans drawn up by the borough surveyors and draftsmen, evaluating the estimates in relation to the quality of the work that needed to be done and inspecting the work when it was finished. In most cases all of the cost was borne by local authority social services departments.

251

By 1976 the social services departments of three boroughs had come to a gentleman's agreement with the managers of GLC districts over grab-rails and bannister rails. This allowed local authority borough surveyors to decide if these could be fitted safely. No agreement over ramps had been successfully negotiated in any Greater London borough because it was felt there might be possible dangers to the neighbours of the disabled person who would also be tenants of the GLC and to whom the GLC would be answerable if accidents occurred. All installations of ramps, whether portable or permanent, had to receive prior agreement and subsequent inspection.

Complaints about the slowness with which GLC staff came to decisions were so rife that the researcher felt it important to invite three senior officials of the GLC to comment on delays in general. One explanation offered was that the GLC was re-deploying staff and some districts were completely without district surveyors between late 1974 and early 1976. This also explains why officers in two of the "satisfied" social services departments spoke of an excellent liaison with district surveyors who had been recently appointed. In the third borough the director of social services reported a "staggering improvement in relations" with the district surveyor's office but attributed this entirely to the perseverance of his head occupational therapist in bringing this about. The directors of the three boroughs who expressed complete satisfaction about liaison with GLC staff at all levels were all interviewed in 1976 after the newly deployed GLC district surveyors had taken up their posts. By this time there were 17 district surveyors to cover the 32 boroughs and the new surveyors may have established better liaison with social services departments than had hitherto been apparent in boroughs visited in 1974 and early in 1975.

Dissatisfaction was by no means confined to one side. Housing staff from the GLC also felt a sense of grievance over what they felt to be a lack of co-operation by directors of social services departments when senior housing officers of the GLC made recommendations. The letter already quoted above refers to the reluctance of some social services departments to :

"undertake certain types of adaptations, for example, where a disabled person is re-housed into a property needing adaptation, or where some permanent improvement to the property is involved."

Distrust and lack of confidence was frequently mutual but early in 1976 a working party was set up to consider ways of ironing out the problems and grievances of both sides by means of joint consultation. The working party consisted of representatives from the London Boroughs Association together with representatives of GLC housing and architects' departments. This working party held several meetings at which ways of simplifying and standardising certain procedures were discussed. The possibility of the GLC housing department paying a fixed proportion of the costs of adaptations in the properties they administered was also on the agenda.

The working party reported privately in September 1976, but their report had still not been printed for public circulation by 1 March 1978. This, it was said, was mainly because of the impossibility of sparing staff from the London Boroughs Association to prepare it for the printers. Another acknowledged reason for the delay was that, together with officials from every other housing department in the country, senior housing officers of the GLC were waiting to learn what proposals would be put forward in the long promised circular of guidance from central government departments on the future responsibilities of housing departments.

6. *Sharing the cost of adaptations in the public sector*

There was a general feeling among the senior officers of social services departments who were interviewed in the course of this study that, in spite of the provisions of Section 2 of the Chronically Sick and Disabled Persons Act, both the GLC and the local authority housing departments ought to contribute financially to the cost of adaptations to the homes of their disabled tenants. Exactly how much local housing authorities could have contributed, had they been so minded, lurked in the administrative shadows in a "grey area" which, unlike the "grey areas" between different kinds of aid, had still not been acknowledged overtly by the majority of local housing authorities. Adaptations had not been listed as "admissible expenditure" in 1971, but on the other hand nor had they been listed as "inadmissible expenditure". Only three housing authorities in the Greater London area had, however, been content to help in any way with expenditure (through sliding scales) and only one had been willing to assume financial responsibility for the total cost of all adaptations needed by its disabled council tenants. This borough, in 1973–74, had secured permission from the Department of the Environment to include a sum for adaptations to existing property in anticipation of requests from its social services department which went in as a separate item under Housing Assessments and actual expenditure on adaptations was then monitored during the succeeding financial year. This is still current practice in this one borough in 1977–78.

Until the Department of the Environment issued Circular 74/74 no guidance about housing for the physically disabled was forthcoming either to social services departments, under section 2 of the

253

Act, or to local housing authorities under section 3. The circular avoided all reference to finance but, a year later, the Rents and Subsidies Act 1975 introduced special exchequer subsidies for two of the kinds of housing referred to in Circular 74/74 – wheelchair housing and mobility housing. A subsequent circular[6] left local housing authorities in no doubt about the value of applying for these extended yardstick allowances and of their obligation to provide an unspecified proportion of new housing of this kind. No specific reference was made to adaptations in the private sector.

At the same time the Housing Rents and Subsidies Act 1975 made more exchequer money available to local housing authorities who, instead of having to dip into their Housing Revenue Accounts for any additional money needed, could now apply for a 66⅔ per cent subsidy under a "new capital costs element of housing subsidy". Details of this general subsidy can be found in Part II of the Department's Manual for 1975[7] which attempted to make matters more explicit in the following paragraph :

"4.14. The effects of paragraph 8(4)(a) of Schedule 5 with Part II of Schedule 6 to the 1975 Act is that the cost of improvements to local authority dwellings is moved from paragraph 3(1)(c) of Schedule 1 to the 1972 Act into a new sub-paragraph 3(1)(a)(iv) of that Schedule, i.e. such costs are now accounted for in the same way as the costs of new building schemes".

But the manual also included, at long last, a clear directive about the application of the general subsidy for adaptations to existing property or at least for those adaptations which involve additions. This is printed in two columns as follows :

2.5.17 Additions to existing dwellings to make them suitable for old or handicapped people.	The amount approved by the Department as a limit for subsidy purposes.

In Appendix D4 the manual also includes a reminder that claims for yardstick allowances for disabled persons can be made, and, again by implication, that when these are applicable to existing property they may be made in addition to a claim for the general subsidy.

The procedure for applying for the yardstick allowance was also simplified in 1975. Instead of asking local housing authorities to submit schemes, control by the Secretary of State was in future to take the form of a fixed expenditure allocation to each authority. This sum could not be exceeded without the approval of the Secretary of State.

Why then did the majority of local authority social services departments fail to get together with local authority housing departments and agree on schemes involving a division of expenditure in the ratio of 66⅔ per cent by local housing departments and 33⅓ per cent by social services departments? In view of the fact that local authority housing departments could reclaim the whole of their share up to the fixed financial allocation this would have seemed a logical procedure.

There are three reasons. The first, that the staff of social services departments had not, apparently, seen the Housing Manual or heard of the new subsidy. The second – and at first sight a truly formidable obstacle – that every request for an adaptation to existing property, no matter how small, still had to be applied for separately and in advance. (Presumably those administrators who were aware of the subsidy were daunted by the conditions of application). And third that, had the Department of the Environment positively encouraged retrospective claims by social services or housing departments, the system would have become unmanageable.

The assistant director of the Research and Development department of an Inner London borough did however become aware, in 1975, of the existence of this subsidy. He also succeeded in convincing officials of the Department of the Environment that it was unreasonable to expect administrators to submit one-off applications for any but the largest adaptations. In the public sector the bulk of adaptations done were relatively minor, and filling page after page of the ledger with grab-rails, bannisters and handrails being the most frequent.[8] As an experiment permission was given for the social services department to submit applications in blocks and at the end of the financial year 1976–77 the Department of the Environment took the unusual step of giving retrospective approval for all the adaptations done in the public sector, backed up by a refund of 66⅔ per cent of the money the social services department had spent on them. This procedure is now established practice in this borough. A second borough succeeded in 1977–78 in getting the expenditure on the part of the social services department reduced to 33⅓ per cent of the total cost of all sorts of adaptation for disabled clients but in this borough it was the housing department which claimed the retrospective 66⅔ per cent and billed the social services for only a third of their current cost.

The success of both these experiments depended initially on securing the goodwill of the housing manager – particularly as in the first experiment it cut out the need to involve any administrators in the housing department either in the business of making applications for the subsidy or in billing expenditure against the social services vote. The first experiment concentrated all administrative procedures in a single department – in this case the social services department – and treated direct with the Department of the Environment. The second experiment followed a more orthodox line with similar success financially but without streamlining the administrative processes involved.

Whether or not a 2:1 ratio of expenditure should become common to all of the Greater London boroughs is a question which has been overtaken by the appearance on 29 August 1978 of the promised Circular of Guidance from the Department of the Environment and the Department of Health and Social Security. Policy about how adaptations were to be financed had tended to remain suspended like a fly in amber. This was already beginning to prove bad for the morale of the staff of some boroughs in the spring and summer of 1976 when the last interviews for this study took place. This feeling was exacerbated by the need to make cuts in local authority expenditure. A clear-cut financial policy – and shared financial responsibility – would have cut down delays in decision-making and also the cost of administration.

If the recommendations of the joint circular are followed local authority housing departments will be required to take full responsibility for all "structural" adaptations, both major and minor, to council property, backed by subsidies from central government of $66\frac{2}{3}$ per cent. What the circular does not say is who pays the remaining $33\frac{1}{3}$ per cent, the social services department or – subject to local practices about means-testing – the client? Whatever local practices may be, the majority of social services departments will, in theory, be better off by the sum of $66\frac{2}{3}$ per cent of the total cost and this, in turn, could mean that they can take on a much larger share of the cost to the disabled clients living in the private sector. It is interesting that the borough which was the first to experiment with a retrospective grant of $66\frac{2}{3}$ per cent for adaptations in the public sector has, in 1977–78, changed its policy to ensuring that all major adaptations in the private sector are provided free of charge to the client.

7. The policy of social services committees towards adaptations in the public sector

Personal interviews with senior officers in social services departments revealed considerable differences in the policy of social services committees – especially towards the end of the study when cuts in local government expenditure were beginning to make themselves felt. Should the social services committees provide a few spectacularly expensive adaptations? Or should it use the bulk of the money allocated for a large number of less costly adaptations, for example a telephone shower instead of a shower cabinet or a shower cabinet instead of a whole bathroom extension?[9]

It is regretted that the opportunity was missed to press for more exact details. A breakdown of actual expenditure on adaptations into those costing under £500, over £500, over £1,000 and over £2,000 would have provided valuable data about the way in which policy decisions by social services committees had been influenced by cost and also on their declared policy on re-housing. Directors with adaptations costing more than £6,000 already in the pipeline were quick to volunteer this kind of information but others kept silent. With hindsight it would have been useful to learn what was the biggest figure their department had ever spent on any one single adaptation in any one year and also how frequently such large sums were likely to receive committee approval in the future.

Such information as did emerge from interviews with senior officers suggested that for the majority of the Greater London boroughs a sum of around £500 was the most that social services committees were prepared to approve in either the public or the private sector. One senior officer spoke of 24 adaptations completed, but not begun, in May 1975, but only one of these had cost over £500 out of a total budget for adaptations of £8,000.[10] Another borough with a reputation for a high provision of services for the disabled had contributed towards only eleven adaptations costing more than £500 during a period of five years. In three boroughs the average number of adaptations costing more than £500 done in any one financial year was twelve. One borough had never done any adaptation costing as much as £500 and one, in 1976, had done only two adaptations since the Act was passed, neither of them costing more than £200.

Between 1974–75 and 1975–76 only four social services committees had made re-housing, rather than adaptation, a deliberate policy, much to the advantage of their social services budgets. In one of these boroughs no help was provided with any adaptation costing over £1,500 either in the public or the private sector. Four other boroughs said that it was their policy to re-house whenever possible for anything costing more than £200 in the private sector and £500 in the public.

Already by the middle of 1976 it was becoming the established policy of many local authorities to re-house council tenants rather than provide them with costly major adaptations. As over 40 per cent of disabled people in one London borough were not only council tenants but "council tenants with housing needs"[11] this suggests that a considerable number of disabled people throughout the Greater London Area as a whole will either have to accept re-housing or go without the adaptations needed to keep them where they are.

Quaife reported, in 1975, that over 50 per cent of disabled people

257

living in London were willing not only to be re-housed but to move out of their borough.[12] It is probable that, as the Government survey pointed out in 1971, it is the younger physically handicapped who are the most willing to move and that elderly people, even if they have no inside toilet and cannot climb stairs, are more anxious to stay where they are.[13]

Difficulties about matching disabled clients to new purpose-built bungalows and new mobility units are reported by the Central Council for the Disabled to be less widespread than is generally believed.[14] However, senior officers in some social services departments gave examples of purpose-built housing standing empty until public pressure forced local housing authorities to allocate it to families without a disabled member.

A point raised by the same report, and one that is all too frequently overlooked, is that

"the question of waiting time can be very crucial where disability is concerned since it can strike very suddenly and any real adjustment to the new condition can be made impossible in the limbo land between one housing situation and another."

Indeed "in the meantime [a disabled person] may quite possibly enter institutional accommodation and disappear from view altogether".

One way of preventing this – and there are very real difficulties about providing one-off housing quickly – would be to establish half-way houses while disabled people wait for accommodation. The working party also suggests "short-term lets" for families with a disabled member who are inadequately housed and draws attention to the yawning gap "between current housing and social services provisions, i.e. between sheltered housing schemes and residential homes".

In spite of the difficulties about finding suitable wardens for sheltered housing – and the known over-provision of sheltered accommodation for the younger physically handicapped by some voluntary organisations – social services committees cannot draw up an effective policy towards adaptations unless they also take into account both the availability of short and long term residential accommodation, which they provide, and of sheltered accommodation which is provided either by local housing authorities or by housing associations.

In the long term all decisions about whether or not to re-house disabled people living in the council sector or to provide major adaptations is directly related to available housing stock. There may be a number of high-rise buildings which, even if the lifts are wide enough to take wheelchairs, may still not be suitable for adaptation.

Terraced houses on steep hills may well be impossible to adapt for severely handicapped people. If there are relatively few dwellings suitable for adaptation for disabled people the chances are that there will also be relatively few dwellings suitable for re-housing them. Such boroughs will therefore have a poor record on both fronts. Even in boroughs which are less badly off as regards housing stock disabled clients can seldom be provided with a truly effective choice by social services departments.

During the interviews with senior officers in social services departments the researcher was surprised to find how little was known about the number of council tenancies that had been adapted at some time or other to meet the needs of a disabled tenant. Four housing managers were said to keep tabs on such properties but only two allocation officers were known to take a special interest in such properties. The GLC had begun to feed details of the kind of disability from which clients suffered into its computer by 1976, in addition to whether or not the tenant used a wheelchair. In five boroughs, head occupational therapists were collating data in 1975 and 1976 about adapted property known to them; and in two boroughs consultant aids and adaptations officers were doing the same. They had been greatly assisted by the old "welfare" habit of keeping wall maps on which the homes of all disabled people were marked with coloured flags, a practice which is also useful if clients are in need of review.

Re-housing council tenants because adaptations, although feasible, would be costly raises moral issues that are not easily resolved. Once it has been clearly established on clinical, social and compassionate grounds that a major adaptation will enable a disabled person to go on living in the same dwelling, the social services committee has a statutory duty under the Chronically Sick and Disabled Persons Act to assist in the provision of the adaptation. The Department of the Environment Circular 74/74 also emphasised the value of "established links with relatives and friends nearby". There is therefore no excuse for re-housing disabled clients and their families against their will unless the proposed adaptation is structurally impossible. On the other hand central government in Circular 12/70, has made it equally clear that local authority social services departments can only meet acknowledged need within the limits of their budget. The fact that, in real terms, local authority resources have suffered several cutbacks since 1974–75 means that inevitably social services committees will have had less money to spend although faced with increased demands for services.

One of the categories of client most likely to suffer from a hardening of policy is the middle-aged person suffering from a degenerative disease. Few medical practitioners would be willing to commit themselves on how long, in terms of years, such a patient would continue to benefit from any costly adaptations proposed; nor to hazard a guess as to how long specific relatives could be expected to stand up to the increasing physical and emotional strain inseparable from caring for advanced cases at home. The decisions that have to be made by fieldworkers on whether or not to press for major adaptations in such cases are painful, all the more so because the only alternative is usually to put a middle-aged man in need of long-term care in a geriatric hospital ward.[15] One head occupational therapist admitted frankly to leaving such applications to sink to the bottom of the pile. In two boroughs any such cases, accompanied by very detailed reports, went up to the social services committee on an "ad hoc" basis and, if successful, the cost of the adaptation to the social services budget was then paid for out of a special supplementary grant. Supplementary grants were however discontinued in 1976–77 as yet another way of decreasing public expenditure. Only two Inner London boroughs insisted that the need of the disabled person and not the availability of public money must remain the only criterion and that clients with an uncertain prognosis should be subject to the same careful balancing of needs as all other clients, irrespective of whether they lived in the public or private sectors. In one of these boroughs it was the deliberate policy of the social services committee to pay 50 per cent of the cost of major adaptations in the private sector irrespective of family income, "a lesson", said the director of social services, "in equity". An Outer London borough agreed to pay the whole cost of a £4,500 adaptation for a middle-aged client living in his own heavily mortgaged property who had been obliged as a result of multiple sclerosis to accept supplementary benefit on behalf of his wife and schoolboy sons.

By the end of 1975–76, the need to formulate an overt policy about major adaptations for clients with a poor prognosis was lost sight of when the majority of the Greater London boroughs decided to stop providing costly major adaptations for all categories of client. Diminishing resources were to be concentrated on providing as many minor adaptations as possible and the chances of any application for major adaptations reaching the social services committee were extremely unlikely unless a strong local pressure group or a "difficult" Member of Parliament had taken up a particular case.

Children suffering from severe degenerative diseases fared little better than adults though, by 1976, the expectation of life of a child with severe spinal bifida and hydrocephalus might well exceed thirty years. Evidence was accumulating by the end of this study that the parents of such children who lived in council property were under increasing pressure to accept re-housing instead of a major adaptation, often on new estates at some distance from the neighbourhood support on which they and their handicapped child had come to rely.

A much publicised case of a social services committee which refused to pay £6,500 for a major adaptation to the home of a severely handicapped thirteen year old child highlights one of the recurrent problems that bedevil fieldworkers. This case was eventually taken by the local Member of Parliament to the Ombudsman who – obliged to leave aside any clinical, compassionate or social definitions of need – gave judgement in favour of the council. The grounds for this decision were that DHSS Circular 12/70 made it quite clear that "criteria of need are matters for the authorities to determine in the light of resources". Details of the case as such therefore fell outside his jurisdiction.[16]

Attempts by pressure groups to have Circular 12/70 withdrawn have been unsuccessful.

Families of children living in the private sector have marginally better chances of securing financial help for a major adaptation since the establishment of the Family Fund in 1974 – but as help from this Fund is closely tied in with a matching contribution from the social services committee – or at least a willingness to meet an agreed share of cost – they may well find themselves up against the same insurmountable barrier of the local authority budget.

In both the public and the private sectors evidence was accumulating throughout this study of families who were running heavily into debt either because they were not fully aware of the statutory help available or because the condition of the disabled member was so severe that they could no longer tolerate the delays associated with help from local authority departments and other agencies.

Until the dilemma posed by undefined "need", on the one hand, and unspecified "resources" on the other is resolved, inequitable treatment and unnecessary hardship will persist and the resulting anxiety and stress will involve not only the disabled clients but also the social services staff who are anxious to help them to live as normal a life as possible within the context of their families and neighbourhood.

NOTES

1. In early 1978 one assistant director of social services reported that an adaptation involving both renovation and improvement grants for a disabled client in the private sector meant that the minimum time from start to finish would be two years. This was true even when the accepted minimum of renovation was done under Section 65 of the Housing Act, 1974.
2. "Occupational Therapy Services in Hillingdon". See above, pp. 245–9.
3. See above, p. 241, n.16.
4. See Chapter Eight, section on the Waiting lists, pp. 161–66.
5. The Chief Architect of the LCC had made a flat-rate charge of 5 per cent for direct labour used at the request of other departments.
6. Circular DOE 92/75.
7. Manual on Local Authority Housing Studies and Accounting, (Joint Publication with the Welsh Office), HMSO 1975.

8. These did not count as aids in this borough.

9. Showers were the most frequent of the adaptations mentioned in interviews. Their installation, although cheaper than building on a bathroom extension, is still expensive, especially if a bath has to be removed. On some disabled people who can only bath with help from a hoist – and from other people – a shower may confer independence but a Hillingdon research study found that just under a third of clients for whom showers were installed were unable to use them alone. Hillingdon installed 45 showers between 1973 and 1976. An equal proportion of families still had baths but where the shower had replaced the bath nearly half the clients reported that their families missed bathing.

The interviews, with 37 out of the original 45 clients, also revealed a number of faults in planning and lay-out (e.g. flooding) and in the design of the showers themselves especially for people with bad hands who could not control the temperature of the water or the angle of the nozzle.

In the English climate if the bathroom is unheated showering can be anything but a pleasurable experience especially for people with circulatory problems.

Only one of the 37 clients interviewed in Hillingdon complained of delays by the contractor over installation, for which the average time was nine months.

10. This borough was moving steadily towards a policy of re-housing instead of adaptation.

11. See report of the working party for the Central Council for the Disabled, *op. cit.*, p. 56.

12. Quaife, Patricia, "One Year On: the CCD's Housing Advisory Service" in *Contact* (London November/December 1975).

13. *Op. cit.*, Vol. II, p. 53, and p. 83, Table 8. The proportion of "potential movers" among all disabled people was given in the report of the National Survey as 1:4. Young disabled people in both the public and private sectors were more willing to move than disabled people over 65 irrespective of whether or not they lacked the basic amenities. The main reason for wanting to move was the desire to get around the house more easily.

14. *Op. cit.*, pp. 52–3.

15. According to Dr Dunwoody, speaking in the Standing Committee debate on the Chronically Sick and Disabled Persons Bill in January 1970, many disabled people aged 38–49 were in geriatric wards. Of those aged between 50 and 59 the majority were in geriatric wards, *loc. cit.*, col. 131.

16. See *The Sunday Times*, 3.5.75.

CHAPTER THIRTEEN

GETTING ADAPTATIONS DONE (3):
THE PRIVATE SECTOR

(a) *Disabled People living in the private sector of housing*

The 1968 National Survey found that approximately one in twenty of all adult disabled people (5 per cent) rented property from private landlords; 29 per cent were owner-occupiers, an estimated nine per cent of whom were buying their homes with the help of a mortgage; and a further 29 per cent – the same figure as for owner-occupiers – rented council property. The remaining disabled adults either lived with relatives or were in some form of residential care. Somewhat more than 34 per cent of the adult disabled population were therefore to be found, in 1968, in the private sector against only 29 per cent in local authority housing.[1]

The National Survey also pointed out that disabled people living in the private sector were the most likely to need adaptations – especially to dwellings with stairs which they could not climb and toilets which were inaccessible – or to be rehoused[2] This was because

"of all tenancies, privately rented unfurnished and furnished accommodation are the worst equipped for the basic amenities."

In spite of a certain amount of re-housing since the Chronically Sick and Disabled Persons Act 1970 and the identification of considerably higher numbers of disabled people in both the private and public sectors than had been anticipated by the national survey, there is no evidence to suggest that the balance of disabled people living in the private sector and those living in the public sector has been altered. A working party of the Central Council for the Disabled reporting in 1975 continued to accept the assumptions of the national survey as basic to their findings and suggestions.

Nevertheless an examination of the annual returns of statistics submitted by the social services departments of the Greater London area for the financial year 1973–74 shows that although more adaptations were carried out in the private sector if the total of all the adaptations done in 32[3] boroughs is considered, the figure is only tenuously related to the exceptional needs of the private sector. In all 8,059 adaptations of all kinds were carried out in the private sector against 7,511 in the public sector. The difference, which is just 548 or approximately 6.8 per cent, is slightly more than the extra 5 per cent of disabled persons in the national sample who were not living in council tenancies. Again, of 8,059 adaptations done in the private sector only 352 or 4.4 per cent cost more than £150 – a very low figure indeed if one takes into consideration the frequent lack of basic amenities.

Apart from the fact that the Department's statistics do not give figures for the total expenditure on adaptations in either sector, the separate borough statistics are not susceptible to easy or valid interpretation. To some extent they must be presumed to reflect the composition of the housing stock in a particular borough, as well as the political attitudes to housing that have prevailed in the past. A borough with a history of buying up private houses under compulsory purchase orders is likely to have far fewer disabled clients needing adaptations to privately rented accommodation than a borough which has hardly any municipal housing projects whatsoever. On the other hand there are boroughs with a considerable mix of housing stock which also have a history of imposing a high level of rates and an equally high level of expenditure on the social services. In these boroughs entrenched habits of expenditure may lead to a higher than average provision of adaptations, especially major adaptations, in both the public and private sectors.[4] The only safe deduction that can be made from the statistics collected by the Department of Health and Social Security is that policy appeared to vary from one borough to another. The study was to reveal that the cause of the variations in the provision of adaptations in the private sector was at least as much attributable to widespread uncertainties about what policy to pursue as to differences in the way policy was defined.

(b) *The policy of social services committees towards adaptations in the private sector from 1971–74*

Until the Housing Act 1974 all responsibility for the provision of adaptations had been vested in local authorities since Section 29 of the National Assistance Act 1948. These responsibilities were re-affirmed by the Chronically Sick and Disabled Persons Act 1970 which made no distinction between disabled people living in the public and in the private sectors. The underlying assumption was that the new social services committees would help all disabled people according to their needs. Once need had been established the 1970 Act also placed them under a statutory obligation to provide assistance towards meeting it although a subsequent circular preserved the right of local authorities to decide whether or not clients should contribute towards the cost of any services provided.[5]

Few social services committees were entirely happy about the idea of spending public money for major adaptations in the private sector as these might prove of considerable financial advantage to private property owners. In the majority of boroughs they either withheld financial help, imposed severe means testing or sought various ways of ensuring that any increase in the market value of an adapted property accrued to the council in proportion to the amount of public money spent. Steps were also taken to ensure that the relatives of the disabled people on whose behalf the adaptations were carried out did not benefit as the result of the expenditure of public money. One London borough which gave evidence to the working party of the Central Council for the Disabled already referred to said in evidence that

> "despite its statutory obligations the uncertainty of the future use of adaptations provided discouraged them from providing major adaptations in the private sector."

Other senior social services staff were found by the researcher to share this view. Indeed only two of the directors of social services interviewed said that their committees insisted on equity in the treatment of clients irrespective of tenure. In one of these the whole cost of the adaptations was paid out of the social services vote and in another, which operated means testing in both sectors, clients were never required to pay for more than half of the cost of an adaptation in either sector. Senior staff in all the Greater London boroughs were however convinced that there would inevitably be fewer major adaptations done in the privately rented sector partly because of the difficulty in getting permission from private landlords. Problems over gaining permission also arose in the owner occupied sector if the property was being bought with the help of a mortgage. These and other difficulties peculiar to getting adaptations done in the private sector are discussed below.

(c) *Problems associated with adapting Privately Rented Property; getting the landlords' permission*

Getting the landlords' permission
No adaptation of any kind, however minor, can be carried out in privately rented property until the social services department has received written permission from the landlord. This applies as much to fixing a grab-rail on to a toilet wall as to building on a whole toilet and bathroom extension. Waiting for landlords to give written per-

265

mission was described by clerical administrative staff interviewed in every Greater London borough as one of the major delaying factors.

Procedure in all the boroughs was for a clerk or administrative assistant to begin by sending a brief letter to the landlord explaining why a disabled person needed a certain adaptation and what the adaptation would consist of; that it was feasible to carry it out; and that the council undertook not only to make good any damage done but also to restore the property to its original condition should the landlord require them to do so if the disabled person were to die or move elsewhere. In spite of the reasonableness of these initial letters clerks throughout the Greater London area reported that many of them were not even acknowledged. Further letters, frequently written by staff of increasingly higher rank, would then follow. Telephone calls were also made to enquire if one or more of these letters might possibly have gone astray. However the net result of all this time-consuming activity was just as likely to be a refusal to grant permission as a willingness to co-operate with the social services department.

The worst offenders, from the point of view of delay, were some large property companies whose shareholders were represented at several removes by agents. If the property owned was dilapidated, or the controlled rents provided an uneconomic return on capital, the first response from the agents was reported to be, as likely as not, an offer to sell the property to the council. If the council refused to buy it the company frequently showed no further interest beyond continuing to withhold permission for the adaptation. Even in those boroughs where clerks had succeeded in establishing a reasonably good working contact with the agents – some of them for instance knew the ex-directory numbers of the agents' secretaries or were able to talk without impediment to the agents themselves – little could be done to break the deadlock. The agents were bound by the policies of the companies employing them which often took no note of the needs of individual tenants. The policy of what were invariably referred to as "the giant property companies" was referred to again and again as being "diabolical" – a popular adjective at the time of the study.

Less evidence was forthcoming about the attitudes of small private landlords – the sort of landlord who lived in the same house as the tenant or who owned probably not more than three houses altogether, let off as flats and rooms – but it was generally conceded that, as long as the landlord would not be out of pocket, a more humane attitude could usually be expected. Cases existed in which permission for an adaptation was withheld in an attempt to force the disabled person to move before his or her condition deteriorated to a point when it became a burden to the landlords or other tenants. There

266

were also landlords anxious to re-possess rooms who hoped that a refusal to allow an adaptation to be made would result in the disabled person being taken into care. These were thought to be the minority. In the small sample taken of clients receiving aids and minor adaptations over a three month period,[6] out of six landlords who were asked to give permission for bannister rails to be installed, four were found to have refused permission for reasons unknown, one had not replied and one had replied saying that he would prefer to arrange and pay for their installation privately. This was the only instance available to the researcher of a landlord offering to pay for an adaptation and it is not known whether or not the bannisters were in fact provided.[7]

On the whole landlords in the private sector were content to leave any necessary surveying of the property to council employees. A few however insisted on sending in their own private surveyors whose services would then be paid for – as in the case of boroughs employees – out of the social services vote.

If landlords, either large or small, withheld permission for an adaptation then there was nothing the social services department could do about providing it. No machinery existed by which compulsory powers to adapt property could be assumed in the way that compulsory purchases of property could be made under certain conditions, e.g. in slum clearance areas, or compulsory improvements forced on landlords under section 92 of the Housing Act 1974. Short of persuading a housing manager or housing director to buy a particular property – and then only if it were on offer – the whole question of adapting the property would have to be dropped. This meant that a large number of disabled clients were condemned to live in unsatisfactory conditions, often for many years.

(d) *Problems associated with adapting owner-occupied property*

(i) *Mortgaged properties*
The National Survey reported that 9 per cent of the 29 per cent of disabled people who were owner-occupiers were buying their homes with the help of a mortgage. In fact senior finance officers reported during the course of this study, in 1974–76, that second mortgages are also frequently taken out and even, on occasion, there will be a third mortgage as well. Houses were also found to have been pledged against bank loans and overdrafts and against loans from finance houses. Consequently no adaptations to any property that was apparently owner-occupied could go ahead until true ownership had been identified. This was said by one senior administrator to involve a certain amount of delicate detective work and probably a scrutiny of documents deposited with the land registry office. In the case of an unencumbered owner-occupancy, provided planning permission

could be obtained, arrangements for an adaptation could then go ahead. Otherwise permission would first have to be obtained from the building society, bank or loan company involved in the same way as permission was sought from private landlords. The decision as to whether or not to give permission for an adaptation was usually forthcoming more speedily from building societies than from private landlords although building societies were more likely to insist on surveys being made by their own surveyors. Should the surveys show that an adaptation was practicable, permission was usually granted provided the social services department accepted full responsibility for the cost of the adaptation. Problems about the legal title to the enhanced value of the property after it had been adapted were dealt with, in all but two boroughs, by borough legal staff.

(ii) *Problems arising out of the need to determine enhancement values*
Major adaptations to privately-owned property were assumed automatically to raise the market value of the property.[8] The addition, for example, of a downstairs toilet and shower unit or of an extra downstairs room and a patio for a child in a wheelchair could, it was felt by social services committees, add several thousands of pounds to a re-sale price and their members needed to be assured that the borough would benefit from the increased value of the property in proportion to the money it had contributed towards the adaptations.

Decisions on the exact amount of enhancement value conferred by individual adaptations were taken by borough surveyors and valuers. The cost of their services, like those of any legal staff involved, were entered against the social services vote. The policy of using borough staff to deal with the necessary preliminaries to any decisions about major adaptations were calculated by one assistant director of social services to amount, at times, to as much as 16 per cent of the total cost. If, for one reason or another, a client then found that he could not face going ahead with an adaptation, in all but two of the Greater London boroughs he would not be one penny out of pocket. This in itself is a valuable and usually unrecognised contribution by social services departments to clients living in the private sector.

Clients living in the private sector in the Greater London area were more likely to be asked to contribute[9] towards the total cost of the building work involved in a major adaptation than if they lived in the public sector and the ceilings below which adaptations might be provided free were usually lower. But as the scale for assessing contributions which had been drawn up by the London Boroughs' Association was considered to be heavily weighted in favour of the clients,[10] the amount paid by clients, as reported by senior administrators, had been considerably less, between 1971 and 1974, than subsequent legislation was to impose on them.

(e) *The effects of the Housing Act 1974 on the provision of major adaptations for disabled people living in the private sector*

(i) *The amended clause 56 (2) a*

This highly controversial clause, which extended improvement grants to disabled people needing major adaptations to private property, was not in the Housing Bill as originally presented. The Bill was concerned with rehabilitating property, not people, and had made no provisions for help from central government in a matter which had been firmly defined as the responsibility of local authority social services departments by the Chronically Sick and Disabled Persons Act, 1970. But for pressure groups, increasingly concerned about under-provision by local authorities, exchequer help appeared to be essential if the number of such adaptations were to be significantly increased. The recent circular, *Housing for People who are Physically Handicapped*, issued by the Department of the Environment only a few weeks previously,[11] had put the official stamp of approval on adaptations – which it considered to be of even more value, in certain circumstances, than new purpose-built properties – but it had entirely ignored the financial problems facing the social services departments. The Housing Bill was therefore seized on as an opportunity to air grievances and to focus the attention of central government on the special problems of disabled people needing major adaptations in the private sector.

Strong lobbying resulted in a concerted move by politicians of all parties to negotiate some form of "Disability Grant" and it was decided that the simplest way to do this would be to force through an amendment to an existing clause relating to improvement grants.

(ii) *The Amendment to Clause 56(2)a of the Housing Act 1974*

Government spokesmen in both the House of Commons and the House of Lords were firmly against the idea. They insisted that all the legislation needed to help disabled people with adaptations was already contained in the Chronically Sick and Disabled Persons Act 1970. The attention of Members of Parliament would, it was considered, be better directed towards making sure that local authority social services departments implemented that Act rather than towards grafting an entirely new concept on to a clause in the Housing Bill which had been drawn up with a totally different purpose in mind. The matter was dropped in the Commons but the parliamentary pressure group was not to be deflected and it was re-opened at the Report Stage in the House of Lords. Whilst there was a general agreement that the provision of adaptations by local authority social services departments was desirable, opinion in the House of Lords continued to view the introduction into the improvement grant system of specific provisions for meeting the needs of disabled people as a much needed "belt-and-braces" operation.[12] Eventually, albeit with unconcealed reluctance, Lord Hughes, who was responsible for seeing the Bill through the Lords, went against his brief and accepted a hastily constructed amendment:

> "with the Opposition, the Cross-Benches, my own supporters and the Church now all lined up against me, although I remain of the opinion that it will not necessarily be helpful, it is correct that I should accept the feeling of the House on the matter. On reflection I accept the amendment."[13]

In this way Clause 56(2)a of the Housing Act 1974, as amended, came into being.

(iii) *DOE Circular 160/74*

Subsequent events were to prove Lord Hughes right in his assumption that the amendment would be likely to prove unhelpful. For one reason it was completely unrelated to the reasons why improvement grants had originally been introduced in 1969. The intention of the government at that time had been "to preserve equity between residents in general improvement areas (GIAs) whether the dwellings were privately or publicly owned."[14] The Department of the Environment saw improvement grants as part of a continuous on-going system for re-habilitating property in run-down areas. For this reason, the grants, which were discretionary, were firmly related to the condition of the property and any rehabilitation of the people living in it was a consequence of the grants and not a reason for awarding them. Officials of the Department were now being asked to tie improvement grants to the condition of a disabled owner, a disabled tenant or a disabled member of a family, a concept which cut right across the existing administrative framework. That they did not like the idea, any more than Lord Hughes had done, is clear from the first circular issued after the Act:

> "As a result of an amendment during the House of Lords Report stage the description in Section 56(2)a of works for which an improvement grant may be given was extended to refer to registered disabled persons. *Although the precise effect of the amendment is not altogether clear* it would seem that where the dwelling concerned is to be occupied by a registered disabled person, (normally either the applicant or a member of his household), the grant can cover 'works required for his welfare, accommodation or employment where the existing dwelling is inadequate or unsuitable for his purpose.' " [author's italics]

The Circular also takes note of the fact that intermediate grants

270

will be available to "any registered disabled person" living in a property in which standard amenities already exist but which "are inaccessible by virtue of his disability", but it was not until January 1976, over a year later, that a subsequent circular[15] exempted disabled people from having to wait a statutory twelve months without an accessible amenity before they could apply for an intermediate grant. This later circular also lifted the restriction, for disabled people only, that had confined improvement grants to properties built before 2 October 1961. In all other respects, however, disabled applicants came up against the same restrictive conditions as other applicants for improvement grants. This meant that they could not apply if the property they lived in had – in the Greater London area – a rateable value of over £300. Any application for an improvement grant would be conditional upon bringing the property up to standards laid down by central government. Disabled people were also bound by the same ceilings (i.e. the upper limits of the cost of works eligible for grants from central government) and these had been set unrealistically low.[16]

The rateable value limit was raised to £400 in 1977, but it is doubtful whether rateable value is a reliable index of ability to pay. A Green Paper (1977, Cmnd. 6851) indicates the willingness of the government to introduce legislation to enable local authorities to waive the rateable value limit in the case of disabled persons. This however is still for the future.

The percentage of the cost that disabled clients could receive by way of improvement grants was left to the discretion of local housing authorities but there was a remarkable degree of uniformity throughout the country. In the Greater London boroughs this was 50 per cent for properties in areas that had not been specially designated as in need of general improvement. If the property were in a General Improvment area, the owner would only have to pay 25 per cent of the permitted cost and in cases of undue hardship the owner's share might be further reduced to 10 per cent.

"Undue hardship" has proved consistently difficult to define but Circular 160, which was not unsympathetic to the problems of disabled people – as distinct from the problems created by the amendment – suggested that

"very sympathetic consideration should be given to any applicant whose principal source of income consists of a state retirement or a disability pension."

It does not, however, suggest that contributions by all disabled people should be limited to a flat rate of ten per cent irrespective of their incomes; nor does it insist that persons on supplementary benefit should automatically be exempt from contributions. As all social services departments in the Greater London area had hitherto assumed full responsibility for adaptations for families on supplementary benefit the amendment, in this respect, conferred no benefits whatsoever on the category of disabled people who were most likely to be in need of financial assistance for its adaptations.

In fact as a result of the amendments it seemed at times that social services departments were likely to benefit more than clients. Assuming the amount of improvement grant to be 50 per cent, then the local authority housing department could claim back three quarters of the remaining 50 per cent from central government and the remainder, which was then debited to the social services department, would be just one-eighth of the total cost of the adaptation. This was frequently much less than social services departments would have paid before the extension of improvement grants to disabled people, and some of them are now paying the client's share as well.

The severity, and the rigidity, of the conditions attached to improvement grants were to prove so discouraging that rather than be tied to unfavourable conditions (for example it might be necessary to have a damp course installed before some financial help for an indoor toilet was forthcoming) many owner-occupiers preferred to by-pass the system and to proceed piecemeal, in their own time and at their own expense. Private landlords were even more unlikely to avail themselves of grants which were tied to bringing dilapidated property up to standard and disabled tenants would be even more dependent than before on financial help from social services departments.

The amendment to the Housing Bill which was to result in Section 56(2)a of the Housing Act 1974 served only to increase dilemmas over the provision of major adaptations in the private sector. It had been hastily introduced and as hastily drafted and it had given no indication of whether or not disabled people should receive what came to be known as "disability grants" as of right, although this is presumably what the parliamentarians intended. Circular DOE 160 did little to clarify the amendment which had not been sufficiently thought through.

(f) *The legal implications of the improvement grant for property in which a disabled person is living: maturity mortgages, loans and liens*

The need for disabled clients to raise money to cover the difference between the amounts they receive in grants from central government and the total cost of completed adaptation has resulted in additional legal work for local authority staff.

Circular 160 pointed out that local authorities are empowered to grant maturity mortgages and that "capital advanced in this way need not be repayable until the end of a fixed period or ... on the happening of a specified event before the end of that period."[17]

The specified event was taken, in the Greater London boroughs, to mean either the death or the removal of the disabled person on whose behalf the mortgage was issued. The London boroughs varied in their attitude to these mortgages and in some officials had still not made up their minds what to do about them by the time they were visited in late 1975. Two social services departments had decided not to give any form of financial help whatsoever to the client, but in others decisions were still pending in 1975 about the period before "security mortgages" became payable. One borough had decided to tie the loan to a period of five years, three chose a period of ten years and two of fifteen years. In one borough the period before which a maturity mortgage would have to be repaid varied with the prognosis of the client's condition and could be as short a time as three years or – in the case of a disabled child – as long as 20 years.

Boroughs also varied on whether the money lent took the form of an interest free loan (3 boroughs); a restricted interest loan (4); or a depreciating rate of interest over a period of ten years after which no further interest was charged (2). Some boroughs, on the other hand, expected clients to begin paying off loans, together with the agreed rate of interest, from the moment a major adaptation was completed.

There was also considerable variation over the way the loan was tied up – the lien. Two senior officers were quite harsh about tying it to the death or removal of the disabled person who was the occasion for the maturity mortgage or loan. All the boroughs visited tied the loan to the sale of the property but three boroughs did not insist on the property being sold once the disabled person was no longer living in it. In these three boroughs the lien was attached to the spouse of the disabled person or, if need be, to whichever relative was living in the property and looking after the disabled person.

No evidence was forthcoming at the time of this study of borough legal departments entering into agreements about improvement grants on behalf of disabled tenants with private landlords.

Instead of a straightforward system of means testing, with the local authority social services department making up the difference, the social services departments now found themselves in the position of money-lenders, albeit the terms on which the money was lent were more favourable than those of the open market. In some cases, where interest-free loans were provided, if the cost of legal and adminstrative expenses were offset, then the social services departments operated at a loss.

273

(g) *Problems arising out of the need to bring property up to the required standard*

In order for a property to qualify for an improvement grant its condition had to satisfy the local housing authority on ten points.[18] All the points insisted on are desirable but in terms of cash outlay they can be very formidable. A dwelling must, at least in theory :

  (i) be substantially free from damp
 (ii) have adequate natural lighting and ventilation in each habitable room
(iii) have adequate and safe provision throughout for artificial lighting and have sufficient electric socket outlets for the safe and proper functioning of domestic appliances
 (iv) be provided with adequate drainage facilities
  (v) be in a stable structural condition
 (vi) have satisfactory internal arrangements
(vii) have satisfactory facilities for preparing and cooking food
(viii) be provided with adequate facilities for heating
 (ix) have proper provision for the storage of fuel (where necessary) and for the storage of refuse, and
  (x) conform with specifications applicable to the thermal insulation of roof spaces laid down in Part F of the Building Regulations in force on the date of the grant.

For a disabled person desperately in need of an indoor toilet, or perhaps a stairlift to get to a bathroom or bedroom, the Ten Points are discouraging even although *repair grants* – part of a package deal by central government for improving dilapidated properties – may also be applied for. In 1975 and 1976 these had an upper limit of only £800, of which the exchequer was unlikely to contribute more than half.

Of more importance for disabled applicants was the fact that, because improvement grants were discretionary, local housing authorities could, if they so wished, waive some of the Ten Points.[19] This was not generally realised by social services departments at the time of this study, although in late 1977 the research division of one of them was to take a test case to the Department of the Environment in an attempt to determine what was the policy of central government towards disabled people in urgent need of a major adaptation and what was a purely local variation. For the most part, however, disabled people are, yet again, still liable to be penalised because they happen to live in a borough which is not disposed to interpret liberally policies which central government has deliberately left inexplicit.

(h) *The role of the improvement grant officer*

Not all the Greater London boroughs were employing improvement grant officers at the time of the study but the numbers of such officers was increasing in 1976 and more social services departments were making use of their knowledge and experience. While most improvement grant officers were based on housing departments or on housing aid centres, some were to be found in what were still called borough treasurer's departments and one was based on the department of public protection.

All the improvement grant officers were said to have been helpful to the staff of social services departments and their clients in setting up arrangements for what the officers themselves referred to as "disability grants". One experienced improvement grant officer interviewed in the course of this study said that the only points he insisted on – out of the possible ten – were that the dwelling should be structurally sound, reasonably free from damp and have roofing insulation. This last point could be insisted on, as extra money from central government is available to pay for it. Otherwise he saw his job in terms of putting as few obstacles as possible in the way of disabled people applying for grants towards the cost of adaptations.

Not all members of local authority housing departments were prepared to use their discretionary powers in as generous a manner, although there is a growing tendency to take decisions on individual cases.

Another improvement grant officer said that the attitude of the director of social services had been less than constructive. As a courtesy he had been consulted before applications were approved and all but one of them had been turned down on the advice of fieldworkers who had considered either that the disabled persons were not in need of a major adaptation or not able to raise the money for their share of the total cost.

(i) *The attitude of social services departments to improvement grants for disabled persons*

Circular 160 was issued on 26 November 1974 and took effect from 2 December 1974. This was three months after visits to the Greater London boroughs in connection with this study had begun and it was thought at first that the impact of the new legislation might involve return visits to those boroughs in which interviews had already taken place.[20] In fact the effect of the amendment to the Housing Act 1974 remained negligible for almost the whole of the next two years, both in the Greater London boroughs and throughout the country as a whole. Senior officers of social services departments interviewed in the summer of 1975, six months after Circular 160 had been issued, had not only not read it, they had not even heard of it.[21]

From the outset directors of social services interviewed in the Greater London area were unanimous in expressing their doubts about the practicability of improvement grants for the disabled. They all saw the grants as yet another delaying factor in a chain of delays that was already far too long. One director described the help given by central government as merely "robbing Peter to pay Paul", and that as 60 per cent of all local authority expenditure already came out of the Rate Support Grant it would have been far simpler to increase this than to embark on subsidies which in the end, and after a great deal of time-consuming administrative processes, merely produced additional aid to the tune of one eighth of the total cost of a major adaptation. Two directors of social services thought that some form of specific grants to social services departments for major adaptations would have proved more effective. All the social services staff who were interviewed in 1975–76 felt that the cost of administering what came to be known as "disability grants" was out of all proportion to any apparent financial gain and if their social services committees was prepared to pay the client's share of a major adaptation, or that of a recalcitrant landlord, they might well be landed with the cost of necessary repairs as well. One social services committee decided, as a matter of declared policy, to ignore the amendment to clause 56a of the Housing Act and to continue to pay the whole cost of any adaptation done in the private sector. Two other boroughs decided to have nothing whatsoever to do with improvement grants and continued to provide means-tested adaptations on the basis of Section 2 of the Chronically Sick and Disabled Persons Act 1970. The majority remained extremely wary of the whole situation.

Towards the autumn of 1976, when estimates for the subsequent financial year were being considered, there was however a noticeable shift in the attitudes of senior social services staff in those boroughs which saw assistance towards adaptations in the private sector as a moral obligation as well as a statutory duty.

If cuts in public expenditure meant that they would have to scrape the bottom of the barrel if they were to come up with any money at all for major adaptations in the private sector, then senior administrators felt that they ought to take a fresh look at what central government was offering. One social services department, which had hitherto put very little pressure on disabled people to take up improvement grants, expected to recoup about £13,000 in the eighteen months beginning on 1 October 1976. This meant that major adaptations costing around £104,000 had already been commissioned in the private sector, to which clients would be contributing approximately £52,000, central government £39,000 and the social services department only £13,000 or one eighth of the total cost. The £39,000 re-claimed from central government was considerably in excess of any sum that might have been raised from applying a means test, but there were still doubts about the cost-effectiveness of the exercise. A great deal of extra work would be required by staff in the borough's finance and legal department – this would be billed against the social services vote – and the additional delay and inconvenience caused to disabled clients in need of major adaptations had also to be offset against the financial gain.

Further impetus may have been given to the take-up of grants in 1977 when the rateable value for eligible property was raised from £300 to £400 along with the upper limits of work that could be grant-aided. These increases had been steadily pressed for by local authority housing departments throughout 1975 and 1976, but any benefits that they may confer on disabled people will be purely accidental. They were presented to the House of Commons as part of a vast infusion of capital to help the crippled and ailing construction industry and no mention of disabled persons was made.[22] In this the policy of central government has not changed since its resistance to the amendment of the Housing Bill in 1974.

No figures were available to the researcher in 1976 for the number of "disability grants" that had been approved since Circular 160 became effective on 2 December 1974, either for the country as a whole or for the Greater London boroughs. But they are known to have been disappointingly small, with probably, not more than one or two a year being taken up in most boroughs and none at all in some.[23] At the time the study was completed, in the Summer of 1976, no major adaptation in the private sector which involved both an improvement grant and a repair grant had been completed but it was estimated that applications for repair grants, waiting for approval, getting a builder to undertake the repairs and then waiting for the repairs to be inspected added a minimum of nine months to the time taken for completing the actual building work needed to keep the disabled person in his own home. The processes involved in applying for an improvement grant would then demand at least another three months so that a major adaptation would take a full year longer to complete, and perhaps up to three years, instead of two from start to finish.

The basic problem of whether discretionary grants are the best way – or even an appropriate way – of providing assistance by central government for major adaptations in the private sector remains unresolved. The proposal in the consultative paper that they should become the responsibility of local housing authorities[24] can be con-

277

strued as an awareness of widespread concern about the present in-
adequacies of provision and the amount of additional delay that the
need to comply with their conditions imposes both on local authority
social services departments and on disabled individuals. The joint
circular (para. 7) hopes that the improvement grant scheme will be
employed as flexibly as possible and recognises that for some disabled
people convenience is more important than bringing a property up
to standard[24]

(j) *The Role of the Family Fund*

For families with a severely handicapped child under the age of
sixteen a certain amount of help with major adaptations in the
private sector may be obtained from the Family Fund. In 1975 the
administrators felt that the difficulties of administering the new kind
of improvement grants, together with the need to cut local authority
expenditure, would result in still fewer major adaptations being
undertaken in the private sector. They therefore revised their policy,
for a second time, and are now once again prepared to offer a
considerable amount of help towards major adaptations in the private
sector, provided local authorities are also willing to make some contribution. If a local authority social services committee does not, however, consider that it has sufficient resources to do this then the
Family Fund will not be able to help in this way. Recent statistics
provided by the Department of Health and Social Security are not
encouraging.

(k) *Re-housing in the private sector as an alternative to major*
    adaptations

(i) *Difficulties over re-housing owner-occupiers*
By the end of 1976 a number of boroughs appeared to favour a policy
of re-housing rather than adaptation even if this meant offering
council property to people living in the private sector, and there were
suggestions by senior officers interviewed that local authority social
services departments were beginning to reach breaking point over the
strain that major adaptations in both sectors were putting on their
resources.

Three Outer London boroughs, each with above average stocks of
housing that had been purpose-built for the disabled made conscien-
tious attempts at re-housing clients in the private sector in council
property. Two other Outer London boroughs tried to re-house clients
in council property that might not be immediately suitable but which
would nevertheless be cheaper to adapt. The Inner London boroughs
tended to have less housing stock available although the housing
managers of two of them had initiated a policy of buying up available

private houses that were suitable for adaptation and then adapting the ground floors with specific elderly or disabled people in mind. One Outer London borough had a similar policy. These "infills" as they were called, helped the elderly and disabled to remain integrated with the community but there was a strong feeling on the part of the occupational therapists interviewed in these three boroughs that the elderly continued to be given precedence over the disabled. The same was said of property adapted by housing associations which, at the time of the study, were said to be actively concerned with the problems of the disabled in only four of the Greater London boroughs. The help that housing associations can offer the disabled clients of social services departments, especially since the Housing Act 1974, is one to which senior staff in local authority social services departments might well give more attention. At the time of this study there was a tendency to look on borough policy towards housing associations as a matter that was purely the concern of the housing department.[25] It has, in fact, wider implications that could affect the policy of social services departments towards adaptations in the private sector. Much more might be done, in co-operation with housing associations, to re-house those disabled clients who live in privately rented accommodation. The comparative freedom offered by housing association tenancies might encourage disabled people accustomed to living in the independence of the private sector to accept "fair rent" accommodation when council tenancies, should any be offered, would be unacceptable.

Suggesting to disabled owner-occupiers – or owner-occupiers with a disabled member of the family – that they should give up the independence conferred by ownership is a task that needs handling with delicacy. A senior administrator in an Outer London borough which refused to provide any adaptations costing more than £1,500 to privately owned property admitted to "doing a bit of arm-twisting" to get owners to sell their property to the council.[26] This borough claimed to buy these properties at the "going market price" but it proved to be the market price for property with a sitting tenant. Until the owner was safely re-housed he had no chance to sell the property more favourably and no chance of being re-housed by the council unless he accepted their offer to him as a sitting tenant. Such a state of affairs is far from satisfactory. Nor had a number of the administrators interviewed taken into account the effect that losing their own home might have on the physical and emotional condition of disabled clients who, after years of independence, might feel a loss of status on becoming council tenants. On occasion disabled people were said to have been glad to have been relieved of the burdens of home-ownership but this was exceptional. The majority felt that owning their own property, no matter how dilapidated or unsuitable

279

it might be, offered them a greater feeling of security than the money they received from the sale of the property. Borough legal advisers frequently offered free legal advice on how to invest this money so that it would "give them a nice little income" – they were, for example helped to invest it in equities or unit trusts – but the effect of owning capital was vitiated by the need to pay rent and by the effect of inflation generally. At a time when the value of property is increasing, encouraging people to sell their houses to the council, rather than helping them to remain in their homes by providing major adaptations, appears a questionable way of adding to local authority housing stock, particularly as legal agreements can be entered into to ensure that the borough does not lose from the eventual sale of the property.

No other social services committees had declared their policy about major adaptations by fixing a financial limit – in the borough referred to it was £1,500 – but senior administrators in some boroughs suggested that bars above certain sums existed. In three boroughs assistant directors were said by less senior staff to refuse to take anything in the way of an adaptation to private property costing over £500 to committee. These boroughs also had no declared policy about buying properties in need of adaptation.

Owner-occupiers who sold their homes to the council were the only category of disabled people throughout the Greater London area who were able to jump the long housing queues for council tenancies. In such cases disability might thus be seen as conferring a dubious privilege.

(ii) *Difficulties over re-housing disabled clients living in the privately rented sector*

Re-housing as an alternative solution in the privately rented sector was beset by many of the same difficulties as for owner-occupiers : Clients did not want to leave the area in which they were living. Many did not relish becoming council tenants, which they saw as a sacrifice of the greater independence offered by the private sector. In some cases moving into council property would also mean giving up a much-loved pet – disabled people frequently rely heavily on dogs for company and for protection. But the possibility of finding more suitable accommodation in the privately rented sector at a controlled rent they could afford to pay was so remote that re-housing by the local authority housing department was, more often than not, the only solution. This might well take some years as they were unlikely to have accumulated sufficient "points" to ensure speedy re-housing. All the local housing authorities in the Greater London area were using a system of points which, with a few local modifications, had been in operation since the Second World War. Although a disease such as tuberculosis might result in the re-housing of families that were living in overcrowded conditions, physical disability – even when backed up by letters from doctors – did not attract enough additional points to move people significantly higher up the waiting list. Moreover, few disabled people living in the privately rented sector had thought of putting their names down on local authority waiting lists or, if they had, had not done so a sufficient number of years ago – a degree of foresight which they could scarcely be expected to have shown.

Even in those boroughs which had embarked on a good deal of purpose-building for the disabled, tenants living in privately rented property were less likely to get first choice of any specially designed bungalows and flats available than disabled people living in council property. Indeed cases were cited of properties that had been purpose-built for the disabled going to families urgently in need of housing for reasons totally unassociated with disability. This was said to be because none of the disabled on the waiting list suffered from the specific disabilities for which the properties had been designed; or because no disabled council tenants were near the top of the waiting list at the time. Domiciliary occupational therapists in three boroughs expressed indignation that properties of this kind had not been allocated to disabled people irrespective of their place on the waiting list. According to the National Survey disabled people living in the privately rented sector had to wait at least twice as long as council tenants before being re-housed. The number of purpose-built bungalows and flats was in any case only a very small proportion of housing stock.

In cases of exceptional need such as, for example, when the clinical condition of a client is so bad that the only alternative to re-housing would be a geriatric ward or other type of residential care, directors of social services have the power to put forward the name of a disabled person as a priority nomination. This happened very seldom as directors were unwilling to appear to abuse this privilege. Also disabled people are only one of many categories in urgent need of suitable housing.

(iii) *Possible solutions to the problems of re-housing persons in the private sector*
A possible solution would be for local housing authorities to keep two waiting lists, one of them a separate list for families with a disabled member who live in unsuitable accommodation. Another solution – and one that would probably be easier to operate – is to encourage housing associations to design more of their newly built properties as "mobility housing" and to ensure that an agreed percentage of these is set aside for disabled persons. This was beginning to

receive the attention of the special projects unit of the Housing Corporation for the year 1977–78 and is one of the more encouraging of recent developments, particularly as the Department of the Environment has estimated that only 27 per cent of all new housing projects is likely to be suitable for disabled people. This represents only a small fraction of their total housing stock and as priority in the allocation of new mobility dwellings is still likely to be given to persons who already live in council property, a great many disabled people now living in the private sector are likely to remain in unsuitable housing for many years, in spite of the fact that the Chronically Sick and Disabled Persons Act provided a legislative framework within which local authorities were expected to take steps to ensure the "greater safety, comfort and convenience" of all disabled clients in need.

NOTES

1. Buckle, J., *op. cit.*, Vol. II, para. 12.8, p. 68 (HMSO, 1971).
2. *Ibid.*, Table 87.
3. One borough did not submit statistics that year.
4. See Davies, B., *Variations in Services for the Aged: a causal analysis,* Occasional Papers in Social Administration, 40 (London, 1974).
5. See the Joint Circular (DHSS 12/70).
6. See Chapter Nine, p. 183.
7. A further eight requests for minor adaptations had been considered impracticable by technical staff. In one instance a wall was found to be too damp to support bannisters but no machinery existed for reporting this either to the landlord or to the public health authority. This again emphasises how limited the powers of social services departments are in the private sector.
8. Cases were cited by domiciliary occupational therapists of adaptations which might be considered to be the reverse of enhancement, e.g. when a small garden had to be turned into a garage. Nor would the addition of a downstairs bathroom necessarily increase the value of a property. Social service committees however persisted in regarding all adaptations as enhancements.
9. The amount clients were expected to contribute varied throughout the country. One client, referred to in a speech in the House of Lords in 1974, who had an assessable income of £5 a week had been required to meet the whole cost of a major adaptation. See Report Stage of the Housing Bill, *Parliamentary Report (Lords), Vol. 352, col. 1706.*
10. The scale is discussed in detail in Chapter Four, p. 93.
11. DOE, Circular 74/74, May 1974, para. 10.
12. Parliamentary Report (Lords), Vol. 352. Report stage of the Housing Bill, 1974. Cols. 1708–9.
13. *Ibid.* Col. 1712.
14. The Housing Act 1969, Section 38.
15. Circular DOE. 13/76.
16. In 1975 and 1976 the upper limit for intermediate grants – the grants concerned with the provision of essential basic amenities such as an accessible indoor toilet and a supply of hot water – was £700. For improvements (i.e. major adaptations in the case of disabled persons) the ceiling was £3,200 or, for a 3-storey dwelling, £3,700. If repairs were necessary before these grants could be applied for then the ceiling for grant-aided work was £800.
17. Para. 55.
18. These points, which had been reduced from 12, are laid down in the DOE Housing Manual for 1975.
19. The Housing Act 1974, Section 61(4) which allows the local housing authority to "reduce the required standard by dispensing with the condition in question to such extent as will enable them, if they think fit, to approve the application".
20. In 1977, after interviews for the study had officially been completed, return visits were made by the researcher to five boroughs and to three independent Housing Advice Centres and "Shelter".
21. This suggests that circulars issued by the DOE which touch on matters which are also the provinces of social services departments should be issued jointly. And also that much more publicity should be given to joint circulars, many of which seem to remain for unduly long periods in the in-trays of senior officials without their contents being communicated to staff lower in the hierarchy or to fieldwork staff.

22. The new proposals raised the figure for intermediate grants from £700 to £2,000 and for repair grants from £800 to £1,500 – massive increases of 285 and 88 per cent respectively. Discretionary improvement grants were increased by 56 per cent, from £3,200 to £5,000.

23. Figures published by the Department of the Environment reveal a notable fall in the number of improvement grants taken up between 1974 and 1976 by owners of private property. In 1974 improvement grants to 91,184 owner occupiers and 36,513 other owners were approved, making a total of 127,697. By 1976 these figures had fallen to 47,507 and 13,872 respectively, a total of 61,379 (a decrease of 52 per cent). Figures for the number of intermediate and repair grants approved also show a steady decline from a total of 21,593 in 1974 to 11,383 in 1976 – a drop of 47 per cent. See Department of the Environment: *Housing and Construction Statistics* (April 1977).

24. See the DOE Consultative paper of November 1976; Joint Circular DOE 59/78, para. 15.

25. Senior staff in local authority housing departments were not interviewed as this fell outside the brief for this study.

26. One owner in this borough took his case to the local MP. The social services committee, after a good deal of pressure, agreed to adapt the property instead of buying it.

CHAPTER FOURTEEN

CONCLUSIONS

1. *Unmet Need*

All the directors of social services, senior administrative staff and domiciliary occupational therapists interviewed freely acknowledged that there was substantial unmet need. None felt able to estimate the extent of it. The identification of it remains a challenge for the local authority social services departments.

Nevertheless since the Chronically Sick and Disabled Persons Act 1970 a revolution has been taking place both in attitudes towards the disabled and in activities to help them. The disabled are now able to point to legislation and say "we are entitled to help, why are we not receiving what is due to us?" And as a result of technological advance, many more aids are available to help overcome handicap. They also come in more attractive forms. The availability of public money has created a demand which the commercial market has not been slow to meet. The pressure of demand also extends into wider fields including purpose-built council housing and help from public funds for adaptations to homes in the private as well as the public sector.

Why then, when so much is being done is there still so much unmet need? First the surveys of need required by Section One of the Chronically Sick and Disabled Persons Act 1970 were conducted in the Greater London area, as in the country as a whole, with varying degrees of success. Secondly the volume of demand was far greater than anticipated. This put a great strain on the newly created local authority social services departments. They had scarcely begun to get into their stride when demand threatened to overwhelm them. Waiting lists of clients needing aids and adaptations grew steadily longer. In spite of increases in the number and kind of staff employed in administering and providing aids and adaptations, the number of new cases requiring attention remains far in excess of the number of cases dealt with and closed.

A third reason stemmed from the fact that many social services departments in the Greater London area continued to interpret the Chronically Sick and Disabled Act 1970 in the light of Section 29 of the National Assistance Act 1948. This defined eligibility for a service in terms of "substantial" and "permanent handicap". It implied that only clients with static and severe disabilities should be provided with help from local authority welfare departments. Although local authority welfare departments had been urged by the then Minister of Health to give as liberal as possible an interpretation of the word "permanent", this unrepealed Act continues to provide grounds in some local authorities for excluding whole categories of disabled people from services which would benefit them. People with physical impairments which are fluctuating or degenerating in character, such as arthritis, may not qualify for the aids and adaptations they need or may not get them soon enough. Rationing services in this way goes against the spirit as well as the title of the Act.

In some boroughs on the other hand the majority of the aids unqualified social workers and assistant social workers before disabled and chronically sick people really need them, may have an adverse effect on their condition. It can lead to rapid degeneration. The study revealed that a great many aids, especially bathing aids, were being issued indiscriminately. Over-provision of this kind meant less money to meet essential need.

During the financial year 1975–76, the second year of the study, there was evidence that even more rigid criteria were being employed in some of the Greater London boroughs. Only those who were not only substantially and permanently handicapped but also at risk qualified for help with aids and adaptations. It appeared probable that some other boroughs intended to follow suit.

In some boroughs on the other hand the majority of the aids issued, especially bathing aids, were going to elderly persons who were handicapped by the disabilities normal to their age. This raised the question of whether there ought to be a separate budgetary allocation for the frail elderly as distinct from the disabled. In three boroughs with a higher than average number of elderly in the population, special sums of money had been voted for the needs of the over-eighties. The provision of aids to daily living for the frail elderly was found to be putting a disproportionate strain in some boroughs on the limited resources available for the disabled of all ages. This has implications for the planning of policy in the future. In the case of the frail elderly many of the functions of social services departments overlap with those of health authorities. One of the Greater London boroughs had appointed a senior social worker jointly with the area health authority to deal specifically with the needs of the over-eighties, including the provision of aids and adaptations for them.

2. Shortage of finance

The Chronically Sick and Disabled Persons Act 1970 contained no special financial provision for money from the exchequer. Although the majority of the Greater London boroughs actually tripled their expenditure on aids and adaptations between the financial years 1972–73 and 1975–76, there was still not enough money allocated to keep up with both increased demand and rising prices. Senior staff in three of the Greater London boroughs reported that all cases of identified need were continuing to be met. But in nineteen of the boroughs it has been calculated that the amount of expenditure on aids and adaptations decreased in real terms between 1974–75 and 1975–76 by figures varying from 3.6 per cent to 52.9 per cent. These figures do not however take into account the fact that many of the boroughs showing a decrease in expenditure over the previous year had spent exceptionally high amounts in 1974–75 and that some of them were undoubtedly living to a certain extent off well stocked cupboards.

The number of directors of social services given complete discretionary powers, or delegated powers to spend considerable sums of money on aids and adaptations, increased during the course of this study. They in turn were able to delegate decision-taking. The lower down the line authority was given to spend the faster decisions could be made. But as more needs are identified a point is inevitably reached where discretionary powers come up against the barriers of the budget. The efficient deployment of available resources is therefore all the more essential.

Two boroughs were experimenting, in 1976, with area budgeting for aids, but not adaptations, as a way of establishing the right priorities in a situation where money was limited. As the provision of telephones also came out of the same allocation, there was a risk that the number of other aids issued might be drastically reduced. In a third borough, which had operated area budgeting for some time, adaptations also came out of the area budget and no adaptation in this borough was allowed to exceed £300 for any one client in any one financial year. It was found that the three boroughs with area budgeting spent less on aids and adaptations than the majority of boroughs where control of the budget was centralised. It was however thought that increased autonomy for the area offices had resulted in quicker decision-making and therefore less delay in the provision of aids and adaptations for those clients who had satisfied area criteria.

3. Shortage of staff

All the Greater London boroughs were short of trained and experienced social workers and many were also short of essential specialist staff such as domiciliary occupational therapists. The speedy provision of aids and adaptations depends in the first instance on a quick and accurate assessment of physical handicap. In all but two of the Greater London boroughs[1] the appointment of an adequate number of domiciliary occupational therapists to make these assessments, to recommend correct and appropriate aids and to advise on necessary adaptations was seen as crucial. To back them up, handymen and technicians had to be readily available to install aids and make minor adaptations. More administrative and clerical staff were needed and at up-graded levels, to keep pace with the volume of work.

Improved and larger stores were also found to be necessary. These required storemen who were capable of dealing with the rapid turnover and at the same time ensure that basic stocks of those aids most constantly in demand were maintained. Transport emerged as a key service and extra vans and vanmen were still needed in some boroughs.

The cost of salaries accounts for a major part of expenditure on the social services as a whole and staff appointed to provide and administer aids and adaptations have increased proportionately more than those providing other services. Vacancies for domiciliary occupational therapists, technicians, handymen and supporting clerical staff had been frozen in some boroughs. Some boroughs, in particular those with a less good record for providing aids and adaptations, had failed to fill all the posts advertised for domiciliary occupational therapists and senior social workers with the result that undue reliance was being placed on auxiliary staff, many of whom were carrying out assessments for which they were neither briefed nor qualified. The dilemma posed by long waiting lists on the one hand and a shortage of professional staff on the other was common to all the Greater London boroughs. Those boroughs which had acquired a reputation for an inadequate provision of aids and adaptations could not attract the staff needed to improve their services for the disabled, although they were making conscious efforts to do so.

4. Delay in providing aids and adaptations

The combination of a shortage of staff, a shortage of available money and the unanticipated high level of demand resulted in delays in providing aids to daily living to all but the most urgent cases. Even urgent cases, such as people recently discharged from hospital, frequently had to wait as long as three weeks. Delays occurred between the request for an aid by or on behalf of the client and allocation to a fieldworker; between allocation and assessment, and between the request for an aid by a fieldworker and its authorisation by a superior officer. Manufacturers of aids often took six weeks or more to meet an order. In two boroughs clients had been on an unselective waiting list for over three years and it was thought unlikely that they would ever be visited unless they became "contingencies". In most boroughs there were two waiting lists, one that had been inherited which might go back as far as 1972, and a more current one drawn up by recently appointed staff. In two boroughs, fieldworkers reported delays of between six and nine months before clients on the current waiting list were visited. On the other hand a senior administrator in a borough that had failed to fill an advertised post for an occupational therapist said that the criteria for aids and adaptations were so rigid that such applications as there were could be dealt with "more or less as they came in."

Delays over providing adaptations were considered inevitable in all the Greater London boroughs. The chief reason given was the need to get planning permission. The average length of time quoted for getting a stairlift installed or a shower to replace a bath was nine months. Only two boroughs had succeeded in cutting this down to six months. For major adaptations to the home such as building on a bathroom extension or a downstairs bedroom, a period of nearly two years was not uncommon and it was exceptional for any major adaptation to take less than twelve months.

A further major source of delay was said to be the vacillation of clients, especially if they are asked to contribute towards the cost. There were also delays in obtaining estimates from contractors, delays on the part of contractors attributed by them to a shortage of building materials and – the largest area of delay – the need, in most boroughs, to take all cases of major adaptations up to the social services committee. Until the social services committee had authorised an adaptation and accepted an estimate none of many other processes involved could proceed. Delay over going to committee frequently engendered secondary delay because prices had risen in the meantime. This involved taking a revised estimate, either for the same adaptation or for a modified version of it, back to the committee for it to be approved all over again.

Against the long waiting list must be set the figures for the number of households provided with personal aids collected annually by the Department of Health and Social Security. These show a steady rise in all the Greater London boroughs between 1972–73 and 1975–76. But the level of provision although high is clearly insufficient and likely to remain so in the present economic climate. Attempts to shorten the length of waiting lists by the application of more rigid criteria can only be viewed as a retrograde step. Powers that remained permissive under the National Assistance Act 1948 for twelve years have been mandatory since Section 2 of the Chronically Sick and

Disabled Persons Act came into operation in November 1971. Local authorities have a duty once they are satisfied of the existence of a need to help the client with aids and adaptations. Waiting lists run the risk of being used by some local authorities as a means of rationing rather than of provision.

5. *The role of the domiciliary occupational therapist*

The speedy and efficient provision of appropriate aids and adaptations depends in the first place on a rapid and skilled assessment of the disabled client, preferably in his or her own home. One of the main findings of the study was the crucial role played by domiciliary occupational therapists based, as the Seebohm committee recommended, on local authority social services departments.

The number of experienced domiciliary occupational therapists varied from borough to borough. Two boroughs felt that they needed only one senior occupational therapist (a senior occupational therapist is one who has had more than three years experience since qualifying) if used strictly as a consultant by social workers in need of expert advice on aids and adaptations. At the other end of the spectrum, the director of the borough which provided the largest number of adaptations in the Greater London area had succeeded in getting an establishment for one senior domiciliary occupational therapist and one "basic" (less experienced) domiciliary occupational therapist in each of seven areas. In addition there were two "floating" occupational therapists to look after clients in day centres and problems of access for disabled persons in public conveniences, public buildings, educational institutions and places of entertainment. By the end of 1976 a head occupational therapist had also been appointed. The majority of directors felt that one domiciliary occupational therapist to each area, if properly used, was probably sufficient with one floating occupational therapist and perhaps a head occupational therapist.

The attitudes of other senior staff towards the appointment of a head occupational therapist varied, but all the area domiciliary occupational therapists interviewed felt that a head occupational therapist was essential if they were to be adequately represented at managerial meetings. They felt that they were uniquely placed to identify need and to comment on unmet need but all too often they had no means of feeding this knowledge up the hierarchy. A head occupational therapist, it was also frequently suggested, was the best person to disseminate knowledge about the latest kinds of aid, issue warnings about aids and materials that were unsafe or uneconomic and to control stock. Head occupational therapists saw themselves as not only supervising the work of area-based occupational thera-

289

K

pists but also as organising the work loads. All the occupational therapists interviewed reported that they felt worried, frustrated – at times even guilty – about the cases that they did not have time to get round to. They wanted someone to take off their shoulders the burden of deciding between cases that seemed equally in need of a visit. Head occupational therapists were also felt to be ideally placed to establish priorities for the work connected with adaptations that was undertaken by staff in other borough departments and for making useful contact with the staff of local hospitals and area health authorities.

During the course of the study the number of boroughs employing head occupational therapists rose from six to ten; at its conclusion two directors were still trying to persuade their social services committees to establish a post in spite of cuts in the social services budget; and a further two had succeeded in persuading their committees to create an establishment for posts although the newly created vacancies had to be frozen immediately. Only three directors felt able to resist pressure from the area occupational therapists already employed to create a post for a head occupational therapist, fearing that such an appointment would result in the formation of an élitist clique in the middle of what they referred to as otherwise "open" departments. There was some evidence that this had happened, or was likely to happen, in those boroughs already employing a head occupational therapist. There was also some resistance to the appointment of a head occupational therapist among senior administrators who were unwilling to see their own responsibilities curtailed, particularly those concerned with the future planning of services for the disabled. In all the boroughs employing them it was the head occupational therapist who assumed responsibility for forecasting the amount of money that would be needed for aids and adaptations in the next financial year and who fought hard to see that the sums did not suffer unduly in the revised estimates.

The increase in the demand for aids and adaptations throughout the country as a whole revealed a serious shortage in the number of domiciliary occupational therapists available for work with local authorities. None of the Greater London boroughs succeeded for long in keeping established posts filled. In those boroughs where social services committees had been slow to recognise their value, some of the vacancies for domiciliary occupational therapists had to be frozen, as the result of the cuts in public expenditure, before they were filled. Encouragement by central government to make joint appointments with health authorities, backed up in 1976 by the availability of joint finance, went some way to fill such gaps but even so only three social services departments in the Greater London area considered that their establishment for domiciliary occupational therapists was adequate. The remainder had to rely on untrained social workers and social work assistants to make assessments.

A compromise over the use of unskilled social workers had been achieved in three of the Greater London boroughs by detaching selected auxiliaries to work exclusively responsible to area-based domiciliary occupational therapists. This has placed a further burden on the occupational therapists to provide what may in effect be a form of in-service training. When "aides" of this kind were provided preliminary visits were made noticeably sooner after referral, the simpler cases closed more quickly and the length of the waiting lists reduced. Auxiliaries used in this way were able to screen cases so that occupational therapists could concentrate their professional skills where they were most needed.

Domiciliary occupational therapists were often being deployed as consultants rather than as general practitioners. They made a skilled assessment and diagnosed the appropriate aid or adaptation and then passed on to the next client. The only way found to reduce the length of waiting lists was to hand over cases, once a clinical assessment had been made, to social workers. Because of a shortage both of social workers in general and of social workers willing to work with physically handicapped people in particular, this did not happen very frequently. As a result, occupational therapists were often obliged to assume the role of the general purpose social worker and provide a comprehensive service for a few disabled clients at the expense of the majority. The greater part of the time of the occupational therapists was taken up with the provision of aids and adaptations at the expense of other elements of their job descriptions, especially work with the mentally handicapped.

Review, both of aids and the conditions of clients using them, was one area of their work about which all but a few occupational therapists felt uneasy and to which they knew they were unable to give enough attention. One borough used specially attached auxiliaries to visit clients at fixed intervals to check on aids – whether they were being used properly, were not being used or were no longer appropriate – and to report back to occupational therapists on any obvious signs of deterioration in clients who could then receive a follow-up visit from an occupational therapist. Rehabilitation work also had to take second place to the provision of aids and adaptations. Few occupational therapists were able to find time to give personal instruction to clients in the use of their aids which can often be a vital part of the process of rehabilitation.

Occupational therapists found the work of monitoring the progress of adaptations time-consuming because the staff of at least two borough departments, other than the social services departments, were involved in decisions about them for lengthy periods of time.

Routine phone calls were made by clerks at fixed intervals, and the use of clerks as "chasers" was common to all the Greater London boroughs. Circular 59/78 assumes that domiciliary occupational therapists will continue to represent the needs of clients and give technical advice to housing departments.

A considerable amount of the time of domiciliary occupational therapists was devoted to the purely technical aspects of adaptations – the design, the appropriate materials to use, etc. Many of the occupational therapists interviewed were doubtful about the advisability of their tackling problems for which their training had not been planned. But it was thought that until the Greater London boroughs employ architects, surveyors and engineers with special knowledge of work for the handicapped, it is not a responsibility which they can evade. One department of development and planning had gone part of the way towards solving this problem by detaching four officers – a surveyor, an electrical engineer, a draftsman and a job architect – to work exclusively on adaptations required by the social services department. Two boroughs were beginning to make use of private consultant architects with special knowledge of designing for the disabled.

The responsibility of establishing priorities between one adaptation and another was often undertaken by senior or head occupational therapists. This might include decisions on whether one part of an adaptation ought to go ahead before others. Cases were found in which clients had to remain indoors for several months because no orders could be given for a ramp to be installed until the social services committee had decided whether or not to authorise a major bathroom extension. While it is obviously wise to try and avoid splitting contracts between different contractors – there is already upheaval enough in the client's home without work being done by different builders – there are times when one part of an adaptation clearly needs to be done more rapidly than the other work set out in a contract. A head occupational therapist can decide the order of priorities, in terms of the needs of clients, whilst leaving the choice of contractors in the hands of appropriate staff in other borough departments. But here again the choice of builders is very relevant to client need. Not all builders are good at working round people and handicapped people may be unable to get out of their way.

6. The Adaptations officer

One solution to the problem of monitoring adaptations which was said to work well was to appoint an adaptations officer.[2] Four boroughs had adaptations officers, based on the social services department, whose qualifications for the job included a knowledge of the building trade. These officers made the initial site visit after an adaptation had been requested and were able to say at once, without the request leaving the social services department, whether it was feasible and practicable and also give a preliminary estimate of the cost. They were also able to advise on the kind of materials that should be used. There is for example a danger in using new materials unless they have been tested to ensure that they can take the strain of the kinds of aid which will probably need to be installed. The adaptations officers were also able to advise on the competence of those private builders who were willing to work on adaptations. If on occasion an adaptation involved sub-contracting work such as electric wiring or plumbing, they were able to see that the work was synchronised and that unnecessary and lengthy hold-ups were avoided. They were also able to tell builders who were waiting for supplies of materials from one merchant where supplies were available from another.

These activities were not always welcomed by staff in other borough departments to whom such duties had traditionally fallen. In two of the four social services departments employing them, the adaptations officers not only advised on which builders would be most suitable for certain kinds of jobs, but also handled the submission of estimates and awarded contracts for all but the most costly major adaptations. For staff in other borough departments, the provision of adaptations on behalf of the social services department was only one of many other duties. Not surprisingly, it was found that estimates came in more quickly, committee decisions were communicated more promptly and work begun and completed sooner in those boroughs which employed adaptations officers as intermediaries and supervisors. This post should be re-created in the housing departments.

7. The shortage of builders and contractors

In spite of a recession in the building trade between 1974 and 1976 officials interviewed reported a continuing shortage of builders and contractors willing to undertake works of adaptation. Getting minor adaptations done was often a major problem. One borough architect used a "stick-and-carrot" approach, by awarding major contracts only to builders who had done several smaller pieces of work for him. Many of the builders on the lists approved by councils were slow and reluctant to tender even for the larger contracts. One reason for this was that some boroughs had got a bad name because their finance departments were slow to release payment – a number of clerks believed that small builders had been bankrupted as a result of the council's slowness in releasing payment – and it was found that in

the five boroughs which released interim payments there was less difficulty over getting in tenders although the need to do so still remained
a major source of delay. Officials repeatedly spoke of the impossibility
of getting in the number of tenders officially required and of the
need to persuade social services committees to accept "two honest
estimates instead of three estimates". Some boroughs had dropped
the system of tenders for minor adaptations in favour of a price
negotiated directly between the builders and a member of staff from
whichever department was looking after the work. Only one borough
had felt able, at the time of the study, to substitute a negotiated
price for all works of adaptation irrespective of their estimated cost.

8. *The use of direct labour*

Direct labour was one way of eliminating tenders but opinions
differed about the success of this solution. One social services department in a borough with a long history of employing direct labour
sought and obtained permission to use private contractors. In another
borough the director of social services, disillusioned by the attitudes
and low standards of workmanship shown by private contractors,
reverted to using direct labour only. In a third, which had never
employed direct labour, the director was satisfied with the services of
a small private builder who, although expensive, made up for it in
speed. The majority of boroughs relied on a mix of direct labour and
approved private builders with the bulk of the work of installation
and minor adaptations being done, far too slowly, by direct labour
and the bulk of major adaptations, in the public as well as the
private sectors, being given to private enterprise. Generous interim
payments in some other boroughs had reduced the reluctance of
some contractors to tender.

9. *Installation: The uses of handymen and technical assistants*

A considerable proportion of aids – 60 per cent was calculated in our
small sample – need installation or involve minor adaptations to the
fabric of the building. In all but one of the Greater London boroughs,
delays in installing handrails and grab-rails of up to six months were
not exceptional. Social services departments which did not employ
their own handymen, or who had only limited access to handymen
from other departments, could not begin to keep up with the
demand for the installation of aids. Backlogs persisted even when
social services departments had increased the number of handymen
on their establishment. But at least the most urgent cases stood more
chance of being dealt with when priorities about the order in which
work was done could be sorted out daily by a head occupational
therapist or an adaptations officer.

In addition to installing grab-rails, bannister rails and wall-mounted hoists, handymen did small jobs like adjusting the legs of chairs and beds and fitting portable wooden ramps. But they did no electrical work. Two boroughs were fortunate enough to have one handyman for each area office, each with exclusive use of a social services van. In two other boroughs two peripatetic handymen managed to cover all the areas once a week.

For work needing rather more skill but not necessarily professional qualifications, four boroughs employed technical assistants. These were based on social services departments and employed as "miscellaneous" staff. They delivered aids to clients in both the public and private sectors in vans which were for their exclusive use. In the private sector they also installed all but the most complicated aids. They had access to work benches with electric vices at day centres or in the aids store. In two of the boroughs they also had facilities for work with metal and plastic and could therefore repair aids and make some aids of their own design. From time to time there were complaints from employees in other borough departments that the safety of clients should not be entrusted to men whose qualifications were insufficient to allow them to join an appropriate union. It was important to ensure that they limited themselves to work within their capabilities.

For really difficult and complicated work, and for any work in which the safety of clients would be dependent on professional skill, the social services departments needed to use qualified technical officers lent to them by other borough departments or outside contractors supervised, where possible, by borough technical officers.

10. *Problems about the safety of aids*

Social services departments have a moral obligation to ensure that the question of safety is not overlooked. This goes beyond getting indemnities or taking out comprehensive insurance policies. It is all the more necessary because commercial manufacturers will not guarantee clients against accidents.[3] Nor are they legally obliged to do so. There is no government inspectorate checking on the manufacture of commercial aids as there is in the case of appliances. Nor have uniform standards, (comparable to British Standards in, for example, the building trade), been laid down. An efficient and reliable system of checking the installation of aids is therefore needed and of instructing the clients in their correct use. Such a system was not in use in any of the Greater London boroughs at the time of this study. But a series of accidents had, by 1977, led the Department of Health and Social Security to issue instructions about the need to check certain kinds of vertical wheelchair lifts and stairlifts. This might well be extended to other aids requiring installation, including some types of so-called thermostatically controlled showers which have resulted in disabled clients becoming badly scalded. The research division of the Department of Health and Social Security had already evaluated certain other kinds of electrical equipment, including alarm devices. Direct intervention to prevent unsatisfactory aids being put on the open market has not, as yet, proved possible.

11. *Transport: problems of organisation and employment*

Transport, not only of aids from the stores to the clients but also of employees involved in providing and installing them, and in carrying out and supervising work of adaptation, was shown by the study to be a key factor.

Social services departments which had to rely for transport on a general pool serving the whole borough provided a far less speedy service than those where the social services department had its own fleet of vans. Those social services departments which had detached vans for the exclusive use of personnel did better still. Storemen/drivers with their own van or one special vanman to make a daily delivery of aids produced the speediest results. Assistant technicians delivering the aids they were to install cut out at least two steps in the process between the requests for an aid and its safe use in the client's home. Handymen with their own vans could fix as many as eighty grab-rails a week. An intelligent policy of assisted purchase and a generous use of essential car user's allowances for staff, such as occupational therapists and technicians, also resulted in more flexible and rapid services.

12. *Storing Aids: shortage of space*

Another problem which continually exercised the minds of senior staff in social services departments was that of storing aids. The stock carried was constantly growing in relation to storage space. The capacity of purpose-built stores, such as those designed for inclusion in day centres, was proving inadequate by the time the buildings were completed. Moreover the cost of storage is one of the major items of social services departments' expenditure on aids. The bulk buying of a wide range of aids may be less of an economy than might appear at first sight, particularly when the design of the aids, and the materials in which they are made, carry with them a built-in obsolescence. Clients are becoming more sophisticated in their demands as they become aware of the pleasing and practical designs available on the commercial market. Aids made in metal and synthetic materials may have a higher initial cost than older aids made in materials such as wood and cork but this cost may be offset by greater durability and the possibility of re-issuing them. Careful appraisal of stock could lead in the long run to significant economies.

Though experienced clerks based on the secretariat also showed a considerable knowledge of the aids market, central ordering under the supervision of a head occupational therapist seemed to have considerable advantages. For maintaining stocks of certain aids at essential level, a "Kalamazoo" system of filing was recommended in four boroughs to help clerks re-order in time. Those areas which operated their own budgets were still well advised to use central facilities both for storing and ordering aids. Control of this at the area level could be wasteful and result in discrepancies in price and quality. Equity for clients living in different areas is as important as it is for clients living in different boroughs.

Areas do need however to store certain small aids which are in constant demand, including such items as Zimmer frames which need to be carefully matched to the needs of clients. When some of the social services departments' supply of Zimmer frames was stored in hospitals, patients could be discharged with one which had been correctly fitted. The question of what other aids might be stored by hospitals on behalf of social services departments merits considera-tion, as does the extension of permission to head occupational thera-pists in hospitals to order aids direct from manufacturers but against the social services vote. A possible money limit might be £400 in 1977 prices for any one aid.

13. *Siting stores for aids*

Where to site stores for aids was a problem of general concern. Combining them in a general purpose store serving the whole borough or even the whole of the social services department did not produce satisfactory results. It led to delay in the issue of aids and it was difficult to keep stocks turning over and up to date. Ideally the main aid store needs to be accessible to all areas, even equidistant, but a good system of transport can help to overcome bad siting if a particular site has the advantage of space to park cars and load and unload vans. Residential homes and day centres generally have space for ambulances and vans : outbuildings were often used to provide satisfactory stores for aids.

Anything which relieves pressure on local authority storage space saves money. As a result, efforts were being made in most boroughs to off-load aids belonging to area health authorities which the social services departments had been storing on an agency basis. This may, however, prove to be a short-sighted policy. Larger joint stores

297

K *

may well come to be seen as the most effective solution, particularly as the same aid can be both an aid for nursing patients at home, and therefore chargeable to the area health authorities, or an aid to daily living, and therefore the responsibility of the social services departments, at different phases of its re-cycling.

14. *The Grey Areas*

There were considerable difficulties about the definition of certain aids and therefore about who should pay for what. Which were aids to daily living chargeable to social services departments and which were nursing aids chargeable to the health authorities? No generally accepted definition exists for such aids as hoists, hospital-type beds, ripple beds and electric beds. At the time of the study, senior staff in only two Greater London boroughs felt any need for central guidance on definition – the same staff who said they would welcome an inspectorate. Most of the rest felt that the answer lay in better liaison with the staff of the new district health authorities. But he development of good relations between the different levels of social services staff and health staff appeared to be depressingly slow. A good deal of time had been taken up in hammering out definitions which were purely local in application. In one borough which was co-existent with two district health authorities, beds were provided by the health authority in one half of it and by the social services department in the other and there were many examples of inequity in distribution as between one borough and another. Health authorities were frequently said by senior staff of social services departments to have less money to spend on aids and that many of the aids they provided were poorer in quality.

15. *Joint storage of aids with area health authorities: payment by proportion*

An alternative solution to the problem of payment by definition had been found by a local authority outside London. A joint store housing aids to daily living and aids for nursing patients had been established which served both the social services department of a large city and the coterminous area health authority. This store was due to expand to serve the whole county as well. All expenditure was financed jointly with six-tenths of the total cost being paid by the social services department and four-tenths by the area health authority. This proportion had been agreed after the aids ordered in the two previous years had been examined. It was found that fewer aids had been ordered by the staff from the health authority and that the aids they ordered also had a more rapid turnover. They were also less likely to be in need of repair when returned to stock. This may have been because they tended to be issued only when a district nurse was attending the patient and were therefore less likely to be mis-used. District nurses and health visitors also tended to see that aids were returned promptly although there were sometimes breakdowns in administration over their collection. On the other hand aids for nursing patients at home needed cleaning more often. Aids for daily living tended to be out for much longer periods of time and they also included a higher number of expensive individual items.

The money allocated for this successful joint store covered not only the cost of the aids themselves but also the cost of maintaining the store and the salaries of the staff ordering, issuing, administering and transporting the aids – all in the proportion of six-tenths from the social services department to four-tenths from the area health authority. Agreements on some such proportional basis might be achieved with advantage in the Greater London area.

16. *The duties and responsibilities of storemen*

The pressure of demand for aids and the shortage of space had placed noticeable strains on some of the storemen. In a number of boroughs it was thought that the post needed to be up-graded from that of a warehouse-keeper pure and simple – or a storeman/driver – to that of someone capable of ordering aids, doing simple book-keeping, maintaining stocks at prescribed levels and supervising transport rather than having to lock up the stores and deliver aids. The duties of warehouseman would be combined with all the other functions usually performed by aids clerks based on the secretariat. Although almost all the aids clerks interviewed showed a high degree of competence, there are clear advantages for the person who orders and issues aids to be in the same place as the aids are stored.

At the time of the study only two boroughs had up-graded the post of storeman and the up-grading of the post was being discussed in three others. Two others provided their storemen with part-time clerical assistance.

There was an urgent need for asistant storemen who were physically capable of helping to load and unload heavy equipment, which many vanmen refused to do or were forbidden to do by their union. Only three of the Greater London boroughs had appointed assistant storemen for this purpose and one of these doubled as a craft instructor. If boroughs appoint assistant storemen the "flexibility" of job description provided by the "miscellaneous" grade allows other gaps in staffing to be partially filled.

If costs were to be shared with area health authorities the duties and responsibilities of storemen would increase but so would the money to pay up-graded salaries and to provide posts for assistant storemen of various kinds.

17. *Cleaning Aids*

Cleaning aids presented a considerable problem and in only four of the Greater London boroughs were storemen or assistant storemen prepared to do this. Various solutions were offered ranging from using clients attending centres for the mentally handicapped, to using assistant storekeepers and lady clerks (one of these promptly resigned) or to paying overtime and "dirty" money to employees of the sanitation department. None of the boroughs were asking volunteers to do this, although it is something that they might be more willing to do because they would be more concerned about performing a service than about maintaining their status.

18. *The use of voluntary workers*

The use of voluntary workers is likely to play an increasingly important part in the extension of statutory services for the disabled, especially since money from central government was specifically allocated to voluntary organisations in the financial year 1976–77. At the time of the study, volunteers were however still not welcome in two of the Greater London boroughs, as it was thought they might pose a threat to the existing labour force. Only one borough was using volunteers to keep an eye on the progress of adaptations and only one borough was using them to review clients who had received aids more than six months previously. Three boroughs employed specialist community workers and in one of these "street teams" had been formed to look after the needs of disabled residents. In one borough volunteers attended a special weekend course at the local Polytechnic on the problems of the disabled which included a talk on aids and adaptations. On the whole there appeared to be far less emphasis on using volunteers than there had been after the National Assistance Act 1948.

19. *Wastage of aids*

Senior officials frequently commented, in the course of the interviews, on the wastage of aids and in particular, of the wastage of aids for bathing. A national study of wheelchairs and their users found that many walking aids fell into disuse, mainly because the condition of the clients had degenerated – a finding confirmed by an intensive study of unused aids in an Outer London borough. The majority of the Greater London boroughs did not however attach much importance to reclaiming unused aids. But the need to make cuts in expenditure led some boroughs to take a greater interest in the cost-effectiveness of recall. It is by no means certain that the administrative cost of reclaiming aids when compared with the value of the aids returned justifies the amount of staff time. Most boroughs write off aids such as non-slip bathmats and other aids costing less than £2, though £5 might by now be a more realistic figure. Some only actively pursue expensive aids such as hoists, wheelchairs on temporary loan, beds and special chairs. Those boroughs which rely on the initiative of clients and their relatives to return unwanted aids found that the majority of the larger aids came back on the death of a client, or on removal to residential care, but not necessarily when a family moves across borough boundaries. In all circumstances the solution to wastage is more likely to lie in not issuing unwanted and unnecessary aids in the first place and in teaching clients to use those that are needed, so that they are not left lying around neglected. A regional health authority in the North of England found that two radio appeals a year put out from the local radio station produced more returned aids than any other method, including stamped and addressed letters and house to house collection by volunteers.

20. *The distinction between aids and adaptations and the effect on contributions by clients*

Aids, whether defined as aids for nursing clients at home or as aids for daily living are provided free, though on loan, throughout the Greater London boroughs. In the case of adaptations clients may be asked to contribute towards the cost of adaptations in all but one of the boroughs under certain locally defined circumstances. But different boroughs class the same item differently. Handrails and bannister rails, for example, were treated as aids to daily living in some boroughs and as adaptations in others. More expensive items such as stair lifts and vertical ceiling lifts which may cost more than £1,000 if the cost of installing them is also included, were sometimes treated as aids, on the grounds that if they are removable they can be lent, and sometimes as adaptations. Hoists, if they need installation, were also classed as aids in some boroughs and adaptations in others. Thus in some boroughs bannisters, lifts and hoists were being installed free of charge to the client; in others the lifts, hoists and bannisters were lent free of charge but the clients had to pay for the whole or part of the cost of installation; and in still other boroughs clients were assessed on their ability to pay both for the aid itself and the cost of installing it. Some generally agreed definition of what is an aid and what is an installation is needed and these should be independent of

301

cost which, in an inflationary situation, quickly ceases to be a useful yardstick. This would not only simplify the work of social services departments engaged in the day by day implementation of policy, but it would also enable more valid comparison of provision to be made between one borough and another from the annual statistical returns made by the Department of Health and Social Security.

Installations should be listed as a separate category of expenditure and clients assessed, where it is council policy to do so, for contributions only towards the cost of the installation and not of the aids themselves.

21. *The changing role of the housing department in the provision of adaptations*

Radical changes involving the relative responsibilities of social services departments and local authority housing departments were foreshadowed in a consultative paper issued by the Department of the Environment in November 1976. Some of these became recommendations in a joint circular issued in August 1978. This wisely substituted the words "structural" and "non-structural" for "major" and "minor" but still admitted difficulty in drawing a distinction between them. An attempt to clarify matters by listing examples of both has met with only limited approval from senior administrators partly because some of the items listed cut across local definitions that have been working well but mainly because the circular fails to isolate the "aids" component in listed items such as electric hoists and stair-lifts from the work of installing them. As definition determines who pays, as well as whether the whole or part of the items listed is eligible for subsidy by central government, the need for a single, nationally acceptable, definition remains.

Agreement on such a definition should not be impossible and perhaps the London Boroughs' Association, or the research department of the GLC, might give a lead. Precedent exists in the former's aids, all of which, they suggested in 1973, should be issued free and on loan to the client. All bathing aids were classified as aids to daily living and therefore chargeable to the social services vote. This took the largest proportion of all aids issued out of the "grey areas". The scale drawn up and recommended by the London Boroughs' Association for assessing the ability of clients to pay for adaptations was used, with slight local variations, in all of the Greater London boroughs save one. The same criteria were applied by all social services departments when deciding whether or not to provide telephones. Machinery clearly exists for producing workable and agreed definitions of aids and adaptations which might also prove acceptable on a national basis.

The subsidies available to local housing authorities, as the result of the circular, should result in a considerable increase in the number of 'structural adaptations' made to council property in the future. All such adaptations will now qualify for a general subsidy of $66\frac{2}{3}$ per cent of their total cost and – a gratifying break with precedent – these subsidies will no longer have to be applied for individually. This is the direct result of research undertaken in two London boroughs between 1976 and 1978. Provided the total cost does not exceed "the delegated costs limits set" applications may now be submittted in blocks and retrospectively. This is a tremendous breakthrough.

On the problem of who is to pay for the remaining third of the total cost of "structural" adaptations to council property the circular remains silent. The role of local housing authorities in the private sector is discussed in section 25 below.

22. *Re-housing as an alternative to major adaptation*

One of the results of passing full responsibility for adaptations over to housing departments might be a noticeable increase in the number of disabled people for whom re-housing instead of adaptation is seen as the alternative. It is not a matter which can be solved by establishing a general policy. Where adaptations to the home of a disabled client are feasible, the choice between adaptations and re-housing should rest with the client. There are a great many factors to be taken into consideration. It is important that social services departments ensure that the client is aware of these rights from the start. Cost is not the only consideration. Also relevant is the period of time likely to elapse between the request for an adaptation and its completion, during which considerable disruption of the house will have to be endured. The prognosis of the disability is a further consideration but it will need the most delicate handling. Some clients will prefer at all costs to spend the last few years of their life in their own homes while others may prefer to sacrifice familiarity if suitable re-housing can be offered at once. What is of prime importance is that disabled persons should not be rushed into a decision. Wherever possible, a choice of alternative housing should be offered – for example, the choice between a converted ground floor flat in an old house with an established garden purchased by the council as an in-fill, a ground floor flat in a brand new block possibly constructed as "mobility" housing, or a purpose-built flat or bungalow. The ability to offer such alternatives varied from borough to borough. But there were signs during the study that suitable housing stock was increasing. For example, a number of local authority housing departments had already begun to offer agreed percentages of new ground floor accommodation for allocation to disabled people.

23. *Under-use of housing associations for re-housing the disabled*

At the time of the study there appeared to be little or no awareness on the part of senior officers in social services departments of how much more might be done by housing associations to re-house disabled people living in unsuitable accommodation in the private sector. The part they could play is of particular importance as these disabled clients are the least likely to be on waiting lists for council property. Housing associations in the Greater London area tend to think first in terms of re-housing elderly people who may or may not be disabled. In their evidence to a working party of the Central Council for the Disabled in 1975–76 they criticised the inadequacy of grants for converting property for use by disabled people. It was argued that unless grants from central government were increased, the housing associations could not bring the accommodation they provided for the disabled up to Parker-Morris standards of acceptability.

More consultation between representatives of housing associations and local government departments would clearly be desirable. This is recommended by the joint circular of 1978.

24. *The revised policy of the Family Fund*

Another source of finance for major adaptations for disabled clients living in the private sector is the Family Fund. It is now willing to match contributions by local authority social services departments – and in some cases pay a larger proportion of the cost – both for adaptations in owner-occupied and in privately rented property. This revision of policy needs to be more widely known as many senior staff of the Greater London boroughs were still over-reacting to suggestions, in 1975, that the Family Fund was being unduly exploited. The return to a more generous policy by the trustees of the Family Fund arose out of an awareness of the way in which cuts in public expenditure would almost certainly curtail expenditure by social services departments on major adaptations and particularly on major adaptations in the private sector.

25. *Major adaptations in the private sector; amenity and*
   improvement grants; improvement grants; loans and liens

The process of adapting houses in the private sector involved disabled clients in many additional complications which tenants living in council and GLC property were spared. Not the least of these was the need, if they were not owner occupiers, to get permission of landlords or, if the house was mortgaged, of the company holding the mortgage.

In the case of major adaptations for owner-occupiers councils usually took "liens" on the enhanced value of the adapted property. If disabled people lived in a private dwelling which qualified for an improvement grant or an amenity grant then the need to bring the property up to standard added still further to the delays in getting the adaptation started. In spite of the willingness of many councils to lend money (in the form of "maturity mortgages") to help clients pay their share of the total cost, many disabled people, discouraged by mounting delays, preferred to opt out of the improvement grant system in favour of doing the adaptations they wanted bit by bit, in their own time and at their own expense.

Until the new legislation, proposed in the consultative paper, is passed the role played by local housing authorities in the provision of "structural adaptations" will continue to be limited to approving applications for Improvement Grants. The circular recommends a more flexible approach and points out that, to a disabled person, "convenience" may well be more important than bringing the property up to standards. This should dispel any remaining confusion about what is the policy of central government towards disabled people living in the private sector and purely local interpretations of previous directives.

Disabled people who were not eligible for improvement grants might also get financial help from social services departments on very favourable terms but, as in all but two boroughs this meant submitting to a means test, many of these also opted for independence.

The rateable value limit of property in the Greater London area was raised from £300 to £400 in 1977 and a green paper of the same year indicates the government's willingness to pass legislation that will do away with the limit altogether. But meanwhile many disabled people in the private sector may either do without a necessary adaptation or incur worrying burdens of debt.

26. *Means-testing for adaptations*

There was no uniform policy about means testing in the Greater London boroughs beyond the fact that no disabled person receiving supplementary benefit would be asked to pay for anything. Otherwise, with the exception of two boroughs, the social services departments provided adaptations free up to whatever ceiling had been determined locally – £200 was the most frequent sum in both the private and public sectors – and then proceeded to assess the ability of the clients to contribute towards the whole or part of anything

305

above that ceiling. No attempt had been made to increase the ceilings in order to keep pace with inflation, with the result that what had started off as a generous policy appeared to be unduly stringent by the end of 1976.

Ceilings need to be revised and updated annually and perhaps, as subsidies from central government increase, it may be possible in the not too distant future to see an end to means testing altogether, at least for clients living in council property. Between 1976 and 1978 two more social services departments decided not to operate a means test even in the private sector and there is evidence to suggest that more will follow suit, particularly as the contributions made by clients provide only a fraction of the total cost of the budget.

27. *The effects of inadequate provision on staff morale*

During the financial year 1974–75 the study revealed a noticeable buoyancy amongst the staff of those social services departments which had greatly increased the provision of aids and adaptations and whose records, as revealed in the annual statistics of the Department of Health and Social Security, showed them to be near "the top of the league". Much less satisfaction – there had never been any complacency – was encountered in those social services departments when visited a year later, even before the effects of cuts on public expenditure began to make themselves felt. Problems of provision which it had been thought were in sight of being mastered were now seen as well-nigh intractable even in those boroughs which had increased both the money available for aids and adaptations and the staff to prescribe, order, issue, transport and generally administer them. Frustration, guilt and even despair were frequently referred to in interviews with senior staff.

28. *Rehabilitation Teams and Multi-disciplinary Teams*

The study revealed a number of changes in staffing patterns which had arisen out of the unprecedented demand for aids and adaptations. One of the most successful was the creation of special rehabilitation teams led by a head occupational therapist. These consisted in each area of at least one domiciliary occupational therapist, backed up by an adaptations officer, one or more assistant technicians and a handyman all based on the social services department and with their own transport readily available at all times.

It was advisable for domiciliary occupational therapists to have desks in the areas they served, as well as at the place where the head occupational therapist was based. Attending allocation meetings in the areas and possibly working shifts on intake teams would go some way to involving them with other staff in social services departments. More important, it would allow some of their professional knowledge and expertise to stimulate enthusiasm for working with the disabled among area-based social workers and assistant social workers, particularly in areas where the senior social workers had little experience of the problems of disability.

Two boroughs preferred to use a Multi-disciplinary Team which included former nurses as well as occupational therapists. Because of the shortage of occupational therapists more boroughs may adopt this pattern of staffing.

29. Lack of adequate clerical support

In all but one borough complaints were made that the establishment for clerks and typists was inadequate to cope with the increased provision of aids and adaptations. This was particularly true in the case of the team of specialist officers which also looked after the registration of the disabled. It applied equally to all the rehabilitation teams whose single clerk was required to take over duties that had formerly been done by area-based clerks and administrative assistants. In those boroughs which had not extracted specialist teams a shortage of clerical staff in the domiciliary section was constantly mentioned by senior administrative officers. Only one assistant director believed the solution to lie in rationalising the work done by the clerks rather than in increasing their numbers.

30. The need for well-designed forms

The study revealed a proliferation of ill-designed forms with, in some boroughs, different forms for similar purposes in different areas. Many of the forms appeared to have been primarily designed to ease the task of submitting statistics to the Department of Health and Social Security and for handling by computer, rather than to help with the provision of aids and adaptations. But certain of the details asked for by the Department of Health and Social Security (e.g. those about age and whether the client lives alone) provide an essential context to the provision of services. Some boroughs found that the use of tear-off slips cut down on paper-work and also permitted all those members of staff who were involved with providing aids and adaptations to know how far the processes of provision had gone at any given time. Staff based on the secretariat were found for the most part to be insufficiently aware of the importance of letting field-workers know that an aid had been delivered – and by inference that a home visit was needed to instruct the client in its use. A prompter feedback on whether works of adaptation had been satisfactorily completed might have resulted in a prompter release of payment to builders and thence to better relations between builders and councils.

Well designed forms would also speed up the process of provision of information whilst eliminating the collection of unnecessary data. This question might well be considered by a working party of the London Boroughs' Association or a group such as the Social Services Research Group which has already turned its attention to the format for the statistics required annually by the Department of Health and Social Security. This group recommended that the Department should discontinue asking for data about households and that the forms should be re-designed on the unit basis preferred by the majority of local authorities. Serious attention to the design of local authority forms would necessarily involve some re-designing of the Department's forms as well. This would again depend on the general acceptance of clear definitions of aids and adaptations and of a continued belief in the value of the data collected.

31. *The need for advanced training courses for social workers in work with the physically handicapped*

The long waiting lists had led nearly every borough to compromise over who made the first visit to assess the client. This was done by untrained social workers or social work assistants in every borough visited except where cases were clearly in need of skilled and urgent clinical assessment. Temporary measures, such as more rigorous screening before a client's name is entered on a waiting list or calling a halt to further deliberate efforts to identify new needs, have had to be accepted in some boroughs. But needs which are not identified do not cease to exist. Whether they are on an official waiting list or not clients are still waiting for help.

In the long term more domiciliary occupational therapists will need to be trained and this has been accepted by the Department of Health and Social Security. Advanced courses for experienced social workers who have already had a "generic" training in work with families are also needed. Courses of this kind which have been recommended by the Central Council for Education and Training in Social Work have yet to materialise. The staffing position is likely to remain intractable for some time to come.

32. *The wider perspective*

This study has described the situation found in London in the period 1974–1976. But there is also a need to step back and consider wider questions. Are the local authority social services departments, as they have evolved over the past six years, able to provide the services envisaged by the Seebohm Report or have they already grown too big? How does the way in which they are organised affect the implementation of the Chronically Sick and Disabled Persons Act, itself a massive and cumbersome piece of legislation? Should the trend to more autonomy in the areas be encouraged and if so what effect would a "geographical" rather than a "hierarchical" pattern of administration have on services for the disabled? The London Boroughs' Association has already helped to standardise some of the better practices of administration. The next step might be to test out solutions for common problems which depart from established norms.

Study is needed on how best to ensure that aids and adaptations are provided promptly for clients on discharge from hospital and that there is more follow-up for young people with multiple handicaps when they leave their special schools. The whole question of whether the elderly frail should be classed with the physically handicapped – and financed from the same allocation – needs to be thoroughly examined especially as they receive more aids and minor adaptations than any other section of the population. Research undertaken for the Merrison Commission on the needs of clients suffering from rheumatoid arthritis has already been completed and the report is likely to reinforce the need to consider additional ways of financing aids and adaptations for this identified group of clients. The Family Fund Research Project, based on the University of York,[4] has already issued a number of papers all of which have a direct bearing on the provision of aids and adaptations for children under sixteen with very severe handicaps. The possibility that similar agents of central government might be established to meet the needs of other categories of client, for example the elderly, should perhaps be considered. The increasing interest shown by Colleges of Engineering, Technical Colleges and Colleges of Further Education, as well as by Universities, in the problems of the disabled is continually widening the field of research. On a smaller scale local authority social services departments in the Greater London area might perhaps look more often for help with one-off aids to retired mechanical engineers who are willing to give their services free under the wings of the organisation known as "Remap".

Although local authority policy about the provision of aids is clearly defined throughout the Greater London boroughs, policy about adaptations is clearly in a state of flux. All too often lack of a clearly defined policy means that a series of ad hoc decisions, each subject to long delays, takes the place of smooth and swift administration. Social services committees and housing need to state their policy on adaptations, as on aids, in no uncertain terms so that it can be understood at every level of the chain of command and by other local authority departments as well. A deliberate policy makes delegation of responsibility possible and delegation in turn can result in swift decisions. All delay costs money. It is an illusion to suppose, especially in terms of economic stringency, that the less said about finance the more likely money is to be forthcoming. Resources are scarce, both of manpower and money, and rationing essential. Solutions will only be found by facing squarely up to these issues and taking carefully considered, planned measures to deploy existing resources in the best possible ways.

No matter how good these planned measures may be, their usefulness will depend on co-operation between the staff of social services departments with the staff working in other borough departments, the GLC health authorities and outside agencies such as voluntary associations. Unless they have the confidence of general practitioners, hospital ward sisters, borough surveyors, engineers and technicians, health visitors, geriatric visitors and district nurses, the interests of the disabled will continue to be served less than well. Nor is it merely a matter of establishing a good liaison with the staff of outside bodies at all levels. People on the outside must know whom they need to contact about a service. General practitioners frequently complain that the rapid turnover of social workers makes it impossible for them to know whom to ring up about a patient. Whatever the structure of the area office, and of the secretariat, the person with overall responsibility for a particular aid or adaptation ought to be clearly designated and readily accessible to enquiries. The growing use of intake teams in area offices has gone some way to improving communications as has the appointment of area domiciliary occupational therapists and, at a higher level, head occupational therapists.

The possibility of not only extracting teams of specialists led by a head occupational therapist but also of creating special Centres for the Disabled to which all enquiries must be addressed could be one possible solution. In such centres aids could be stored on adjacent premises – both aids for home nursing and aids for daily living – and there could be a permanent exhibition of aids, on the lines of that provided by the Disabled Living Foundation in Kensington, to which clients might be brought and where they could be instructed in their safe use, whether or not the aids were provided by the local authority. Other services for the disabled such as the provision of outings, holidays, telephones and radios which are already administered by a special division of the secretariat in the majority of boroughs could just as readily be administered from a centre. The siting of such a centre in a large borough would certainly present difficulties, but many of these could be overcome by an improved system of local authority transport. Such a centre would take a good deal of the work of reception and referral off the staff to area offices. A head occupational therapist or a specialist senior social worker skilled in working with disabled people and their families could be based on such a centre instead of in the offices of the secretariat, thus ensuring the availability of expert professional advice, something which, because so few social workers have received specialist training in working with disabled people and their families, very few area offices can be sure of providing. The need to provide constantly updated information about available services could be provided by a Citizen's Advice Bureau worker attached to the centre.

Another possibility would be to link such centres to the catchment areas of teaching hospitals, in which case they might serve more than one borough and still not be too large to meet their original purpose. District nurses and health visitors might, with advantage, be based on the same building. Such a centre might be a suitable subject for joint finance with money made available by the local area health authorities involved.

Some opposition to specialist centres can be anticipated from the disabled themselves on the grounds that they would segregate services for the disabled at a time when they, and their families, are beginning to win acceptance from the community. But properly conceived, such centres could provide more broadly based services than area social services offices without losing touch with localised activities. Indeed a community worker might also be based on the centre.

The importance of providing a total assessment of the needs of disabled people in as wide a context as possible implies a need to see all available services for the disabled as a whole. These should also include the services provided not only by the Health Authorities but also by the Department of Education and Science, Employment and – most important of all – the Department of the Environment. The need for joint planning, if not joint care, is becoming steadily more apparent in an economic situation where available resources cannot possibly meet all the needs identified.

Since the National Assistance Act of 1948 local authorities have been asked to interpret "needs" and "handicap" as liberally as possible. But the only way to ensure that the maximum number of services will reach the maximum number of people is to see that the public money available for spending on them is used to the best possible advantage. Instead of seeking the easy way out by rationing scarce resources through the application of rigid criteria, it would be far better to look for more economic ways of deploying them, and this will inevitably involve re-thinking existing patterns of local authority administration.

1. In these two boroughs it was a matter of policy to use what they called "Seebohm" (i.e. "general purpose") social workers in all circumstances. Advice on aids and adaptations was forthcoming at consultant level by experienced officers who had worked in welfare departments and who believed the proper context for occupational therapists to be a hospital or health authority, in spite of the recommendation by the Seebohm committee that they should be transferred to local authority social services departments.

2. This kind of adaptations officer should not be confused with ex-welfare officers with the same title who have been appointed as special consultants on the needs of the physically handicapped. These may hold a rank as high as principal officer although the officers of this kind interviewed also had a practical knowledge of building work and were prepared, if necessary, to visit sites with social workers.

3. Accidents can, and do, occur for other reasons. One example is of aids left by vanmen on doorsteps or in narrow passageways which stay in the path of disabled people who may find it difficult to avoid them until someone eventually comes to instal them.

4. See above, p. 63.

APPENDIX

Table 1 – Extracts from *Social Services Statistics: Estimates 1974–75*
(Chartered Institute of Public Finance and Accountancy and Society of County Treasurers). in £'s.

Column No.	1	6	14	67	68	69	75	82	89	90	91	92
Borough	Total population	Total per 1000 population £	Nos. of handicapped at 31.3.75 (General)	Multi-purpose 18 and over	Elderly 65 and over	Younger P.H. population 18–64	No. of Home helps per 1000 pop.	Meals % of total directly supplied by the authority	Telephones	Aids and Adaptations	Holidays	Travel Concessions (over 18)
				Net expenditure per 1000 population £ Day Centres and Clubs					*Net expenditure per 1000 population £*			
Camden ..	193,000	36,918.0	3,460	–	6,922.1	760.4	1.97	50	233.2	483.0	411.6	24.0
Greenwich ..	214,000	40,485.9	3,548	778.6	1,544.7	188.1	1.83	52	220.2	84.0	587.8	66.1
Hackney ..	211,000	28,791.3	4,500	657.6	5,269.6	–	2.01	46	68.7	42.7	576.7	97.4
Hammersmith..	173,500	26,929.4	2,117	–	2,644.1	918.9	1.38	62	61.9	112.9	170.5	41.0
Islington ..	182,830	31,116.6	3,500	114.4	5,130.2	15.1	1.18	83	219.6	77.0	397.1	181.5
Kensington ..	172,500	19,448.9	2,240	135.5	691.8	–	0.70	60	64.1	42.1	91.2	68.0
Lambeth ..	289,924	28,150.2	4,750	646.8	9,090.3	–	1.34	46	←—— 203.4 ——→		241.2	22.0
Lewisham ..	254,100	24,847.6	4,863	–	8,837.2	1,066.7	0.81	40	124.0	125.0 ——→	456.3	31.5
Southwark ..	242,150	30,354.7	7,025	–	8,105.0	–	1.73	46	63.5	79.0	184.4	33.5
Tower Hamlets	148,000	35,410.9	2,202	–	3,616.4	1,329.3	1.17	41	←—— 200.8 ——→		824.1	46.0
Wandsworth ..	292,000	21,968.1	4,400	190.7	4,386.7	363.0	1.05	54	170.2	179.7	435.6	38.4
Westminster ..	219,000	25,707.7	2,450	8.2	4,813.1	1,027.7	1.05	93	124.8	88.9	336.4	9.2
City of London	7,500	23,422.7	800	–	3,745.2	4.2	1.60	67	133.3	76.0	146.0	16.2
Barking ..	157,000	14,587.9	2,660	445.3	5,485.7	1,380.7	1.19	35	72.5	89.8	221.6	90.9
Barnet ..	302,100	9,708.9	4,000	25.4	1,969.1	179.9	0.50	67	40.5	128.2	46.9	23.6
Bexley ..	217,076	9,997.6	1,950	679.5	1,650.3	387.7	1.23	66	66.7	110.6	37.4	38.0
Brent ..	275,000	17,147.1	3,750	–	2,214.2	497.5	0.56	63	149.1	98.0	221.1	108.2
Bromley ..	306,000	8,463.9	2,756	47.3	1,762.0	79.6	0.50	10	23.6	99.3	19.1	36.9
Croydon ..	333,000	11,378.3	6,659	–	55.8	29.0	0.48	70	25.4	82.7	32.7	73.9
Ealing ..	292,500	15,047.8	4,390	–	436.5	549.8	0.75	92	55.2	121.8	59.7	11.5
Enfield ..	264,700	9,240.8	4,000	–	1,021.9	762.8	0.79	82	32.6	75.0	43.0	57.1
Haringey ..	233,800	18,900.9	2,200	–	5,750.7	57.6	1.34	55	45.8	209.8	183.8	57.3
Harrow ..	204,700	11,092.0	1,764	74.6	3,307.1	216.3	0.65	27	27.1	258.4	170.1	38.8
Havering ..	246,600	10,601.9	2600	–	2,506.8	475.4	0.81	12	85.2	280.8	138.8	30.7
Hillingdon ..	232,957	12,479.4	3,000	–	2,908.5	240.5	1.20	15	139.7	402.4	353.8	53.0
Hounslow ..	207,500	13,051.4	3,400	57.8	2,007.4	231.1	0.73	44	53.5	119.3	18.6	57.2
Kingston ..	136,400	12,710.2	1,200	–	1,819.3	555.9	0.51	66	36.3	89.2	49.5	5.5
Merton ..	176,400	14,372.6	3,900	111.4	5,130.2	15.1	1.21	56	121.9	354.1	95.3	115.8
Newham ..	226,000	13,384.7	4,000	–	3,223.6	776.7	1.27	35	16.8	115.5	42.9	75.6
Redbridge ..	236,000	10,053.1	2,770	–	1,941.0	5.3.6	0.68	71	46.6	108.2	160.6	78.6
Richmond ..	169,423	9,937.9	3,150	–	2,089.7	23.7	0.59	40	129.9	36.6	54.9	22.5
Sutton	169,860	9,616.5	2,295	–	788.2	266.2	0.57	48	46.5	108.3	22.7	22.7
Waltham Forest	235,100	32,178.4	4,000	–	1,349.2	385.9	1.02	48	78.7	52.6	88.9	48.7

Table 2 – Attitude of Metropolitan Borough Councils towards the use of private contractors.

	1 Allow without reservation	2 Allow subject to rigorous control	3 Allow except for elaborate work	4 Direct labour	5 Committee's decision in each case
Battersea	X				
Bermondsey			X		
Bethnal Green	X				
Camberwell			X		
Chelsea		X			
City of London	X				
Deptford					X
Finsbury					X
Fulham				X	
Greenwich					X
Hackney				X	
Hampstead	X				
Hammersmith				X	
Holborn	X				
Islington		X			
Kensington	X				
Lambeth			X		
Lewisham			X		
Paddington	X				
Poplar				X	
St. Marylebone	X				
St. Pancras	X				
Shoreditch				X	
Southwark					X
Stepney				X	
Stoke Newington		X			
Wandsworth	X				
Westminster					X
Woolwich					X

BIBLIOGRAPHY

1. *Books*

Action Research for the Crippled Child, *The Implementation of the Chronically Sick and Disabled Persons Act* (ARCC, 1973).

Blaxter, Mildred, *The Meaning of Disability* (London, 1976).

Blau, P. M., *The Dynamics of Bureaucracy. A Study of Interpersonal Relations in Two Agencies*, revised edn. (Chicago, 1963).

Brunel Institute of Organisation and Social Studies, *Social Services Departments* (London, 1974).

Consumer's Association, *Coping with Disablement* (Which, 1974).

Davies, B., *Variations in services for the aged: a causal analysis.* Occasional Papers in Social Administration, 40 (London, 1971).

Goffman, E., *Asylum* (Pelican Books, 1971).

Goldsmith, Selwyn, *Designing for the Disabled; a manual of technical information* (R.I.B.A., 1963).

Hall, Anthony S., *Point of Entry: A study of Client Reception in the Social Services* (London, 1975).

Hall, Penelope, *Social Services in England and Wales*, 9th edn. (London, 1975).

Jerman, Betty, *Do Something! A Guide to Self Help Organisations* (London, 1971).

Jones, Kathleen (ed.), *The Year Book of Social Policy in Great Britain 1973* (London, 1974).

Levy, Hermann, *National Health Insurance: A Critical Study* (Cambridge, 1944).

Mayer, J. E. and Timms, N., *The Client Speaks* (London, 1970).

Moore, S., *Working for Free* : The Essential Handbook of Voluntary Work (London, 1977).

Ripley, B. J., *Administration in Local Authorities* (London, 1970).

Sainsbury, S., *Registered as Disabled*, Occasional Papers in Social Administration, 35 (London, 1970).

Shenfield, D., *Social Policies of Old Age* (Birmingham, 1957).

Smith, Marjorie, *Professional Education in Social Work in Britain* (London, 1953).

Symons, J., *Care with Dignity* (London, 1972).

Thomson, D., in *New Cambridge Modern History*, XII, Chapter 2.

Townsend, Peter, *The Last Refuge: A Survey of Residential Homes and Institutions for the Aged in England and Wales* (London, 1962).

2. *Reports, Surveys and Studies*

Beveridge, Lord, *Social Insurance and Allied Services* Cmd. 6404, (H.M.S.O., 1940).

Birmingham, University of, *Report to the D.H.S.S.* (1976).

Buckle, Judith, *The Handicapped and Impaired in Great Britain*, Vol. II, "Work and Housing of Impaired Persons in Great Britain" (H.M.S.O., 1971) for the O.P.C.S.

Central Council for the Disabled, Report of the Working Party on Housing, *Towards a Housing Policy for the Disabled, January 1974 – November 1975* (C.C.D., 1976).

Central Council for Education and Training in Social Work, *Paper 5 and Paper 9* (London, 1974).

D.H.S.S., *Report of the Committee on Local Authority and Allied Social Services*, Cmnd. 3703 (H.M.S.O., 1968).

Fenwick, D., *Wheelchairs and their users: a survey among users of National Health Wheelchairs in England and Wales, to establish their characteristics and attitudes to the operation of the wheelchair service* (H.M.S.O., 1977). By O.P.C.S. Social Survey Division on behalf of the D.H.S.S.

Gulbenkian (Calouste) Foundation, Working Party Report, *Community Work and Social Change: A Report on Training* (1968).

Harris, Amelia, *The Handicapped and Impaired in Great Britain*, Vol. 1 (H.M.S.O., 1971) for the O.P.C.S.

Miners, D., and Plank, M., *Housing for the Disabled in Greater London* (G.L.C., 1975).

Ministry of Housing and Local Government, The Ninth Report of the Housing Management Sub-Committee of the Central Housing Committee, *Council Housing, Purposes, Procedures and Priorities* (H.M.S.O., 1969, "The Cullingworth Report".

Mitchell, Ann, *An Enquiry into the use of Volunteers Directly Responsible to Social Work Departments and into the Relationships between Social Services Departments and Voluntary Organisations* (Scottish Council of Social Services, 1977).

Mitchell, Peter, *Report for the Fund for Research into Crippling Diseases* (February 1973).

N.S.S.C. and N.I.S.W.T., *The Voluntary Worker in the Social Services* (London, 1969). Report of a Committee under the Chairmanship of Geraldine M. Aves.

Report of the Committee of Inquiry into the Care and Supervision provided in relation to Maria Colwell (H.M.S.O., 1974).
316

Report of the Royal Commission on Local Government in England 1966–69, Vol. I, Cmnd. 4040 (H.M.S.O. 1966), "The Redcliffe-Maud Report".

Royal Surgical Aid Society, *77th Annual Report* (1940).

Seebohm, Sir Frederick, *Report of the Commission on Local Authority and Allied Personal Social Services*, Cmnd. 3703 (H.M.S.O. 1968). "The Seebohm Report".

Skinner, F. ed., Tower Hamlets Council of Community Services, *Physical Disability and Community Care* (1969).

Social Services Research Group, Working Party Report, *D.H.S.S. Statistics of the Personal Social Services* (London, 1974).

Tester, Sue, *Housing for Disabled People in Greater London, Interim Report of a Pilot study prepared for the Greater London Association for the Disabled* (University of London, 1969).

Wolfenden Committee, Report of, *The Future of Voluntary Organisations* (London, 1977).

Wright, Fay, *Public Expenditure Cuts Affecting Services for Disabled People* (London, 1977).

York, University of, Department of Social Administration and Social Work, Family Fund Research Project. Papers – *Some Practical Consequences of Caring for Handicapped Children at Home* (1976); *Variations in provision by local authority social services departments for families with handicapped children* (1976); *Housing Handicapped Children and their Families* (1977).

Younghusband, Eileen, *Report of the Working Party on Social Workers in the Local Authority and Health and Welfare Services* (H.M.S.O., 1959).

Younghusband, Eileen, *Report on the Employment and Training of Social Workers* (Carnegie U.K. Trust, 1974).

3. Articles

Bowl, R., "Survey of Surveys", *New Society*, 28 October 1971.

Glampson, Ann, and others, "Post-Seebohm Social Services : (2) The Consumer Viewpoint", *Social Work Today*, Vol. VIII, No. 6 (November 1976).

Goldberg, E. Matilda, and Others, "Towards Accountability in Social Work : A Case Review System for Social Workers", *British Journal of Social Work* (1976) Vol. VI, No. 1.

Goldberg, E. Matilda, and others, "Towards Accountability in Work : One Year's Intake in an Area office", *British Journal of Social Work* (Autumn 1977) Vol. VII, No. 3.

Hall, A. S., "Client Reception in a Social Services Agency", *Public Administration* (1949), Vol. XLIX.

Hillingdon, London Borough of, "Occupational Therapy Services in

Hillingdon", *Clearing House for Local Authority Social Services Research* (University of Birmingham, 1975), No. 7.

Loewenstein, Carole, "An Intake Team in Action in a Social Services Department in an Inner London Borough", *British Journal for Social Work* (1975), Vol. IV, No. 2.

McKay, Ann and others, "Consumers and a social services department", *Social Work Today*, Vol. IV, No. 16 (November 1973).

Melotte, C. J., "The Supply of Aids and Adaptations". Occasional Paper No. 3, Research, Planning and Training Sector of the Kirklees Metropolitan Council Social Services Directorate. *Clearing House for Local Authority Social Services Research* (1976), No. 5.

Neill, June E., and others, "Reactions to integration", *Social Work Today*, Vol. IV, No. 15 (November 1973).

Quaife, Patricia, "One Year On : the C.C.D.'s Advisory Service". *Contact* (London, Nov/Dec. 1975).

Royal Borough of Kingston-upon-Thames, "A look at Duty Day Work – Overview" in *Clearing House for Local Authority Social Services Research* (1975) No. 4.

Smith, G. and Ames, Janet, "Area Teams in Social Work Practice : A Programme of Research", *British Journal of Social Work*, Vol. VI, No. 1 (1976).

Wetton, Kate, Gloucester Social Services Department, "The Cheltenham Intake Team", *Clearing House for Local Authority Social Services Research*, No. 4.

4. *Unpublished Research*

Allen, D., *The Use of Volunteers in Social Services Departments* (quoted extensively in N.C.S.S. Briefing, February 1978).

5. *Acts of Parliament*

National Insurance Act, 1911.
Blind Persons Acts, 1920 and 1938
Disabled Persons (Employment) Act 1944.
Education Act, 1944.
National Insurance (Industrial Injuries) Acts, 1946, 1965, 1967.
National Health Service Act 1946.
National Assistance Act 1948.
Mental Health Act 1959.
Health Services and Public Health Act 1968.
Housing Acts, 1969, 1974.
Local Authority Social Services Act 1970.
Chronically Sick and Disabled Persons Act 1970.
National Health Services (Charges) Regulations Act 1971.

Housing Finance Act 1972.
Housing Rents and Subsidies Act 1975.

6. *Parliamentary Debates*

HC Debates, Chronically Sick and Disabled Persons Bill, Standing
Committee "C", Report, Session 1969–70, Vol. II.
HC Debates, Chronically Sick and Disabled Persons Bill, Second
Reading, Session 1969–70, Vol. 792.
HC Debates, Session 1976–77, Vol. 935.
Lords Debates, Vol. 352, Report stage of the Housing Bill, 1974.

7. *Government Departments: Circulars, Leaflets, Papers, etc.*
Circulars

Ministry of Health 48/47.
Ministry of Health 118/47.
Ministry of Health 70/48.
Ministry of Labour 87/48.
Ministry of Health 15/60.
D.H.S.S. 12/70 (joint with D.E.S., M.H.L.G., M.O.T.).
D.H.S.S. 27/71 (joint with D.O.E., D.E.P.).
D.H.S.S. 45/71.
L.A. 18/71.
D.H.S.S. 35/72.
D.O.E. 59/75.
D.O.E. 74/74 (joint with Welsh Office).
D.H.S.S. 282/74 (joint with 7 other departments).
D.O.E. 59/74 (joint with Welsh Office).
D.O.E. 160/74 (joint with Welsh Office).
D.O.E. 92/75 (joint with Welsh Office).
HC(76) and LAC (76)6.
D.O.E. 13/76 (joint with Welsh Office).
HC(76) 18, LAC(76) 6.
D.O.E. 59/78 (joint with D.H.S.S. and Welsh office).

Leaflets
D.H.S.S. Aids for the Disabled (1976).

Booklets
D.H.S.S. *Equipment for the Disabled*. Booklet series (by the Oxford
Regional Health Authority for D.H.S.S.).
D.H.S.S. *Surgical Appliances Contract 1976*. The "Yellow Book".
Welsh Office (NHS) *Provision of Medical and Surgical Appliances*
(1974). The "Orange Book".

Consultative Documents
D.H.S.S., the Future Structure of the National Health Service (H.M.S.O., 1970).
D.O.E., D.H.S.S., W.O., Adaptations to Housing for People who are Physically Handicapped (H.M.S.O., 1976).
D.H.S.S., The Way Forward, Priorities for Health and Personal Social Services in England (H.M.S.O., 1976).

White Papers
Public Expenditure to 1978–79, Cmnd. 3879 (H.M.S.O., 1975).
Public Expenditure to 1979–80, Cmnd. 6393 (H.M.S.O., 1976).
The Government's Expenditure Plans, 2 Vols., Cmnd. 6721–I and II (H.M.S.O., 1977).
The Government's Expenditure Plans 1978–79 to 1981–82, 2 Vols. Cmnd. 7049–I and II (H.M.S.O., 1978).

8. *Statistics*

D.H.S.S., Statistics and Research Division 6., *Local Authority Social Services Departments, Aids to Households* (Annual).
Annual Abstract of Statistics for Greater London.
Chartered Institute of Public Finance and Accountancy and the Society of County Treasurers, *Social Services Statistics: Estimates 1974–75* (Annual).

9. *Reports for internal distribution*

London Borough of Hillingdon Social Services Research *Domiciliary Services Evaluation, Part II, Five Types of Aid in Common Use* (internal publication, 1976).
Neill, June E., *A study of referrals.* Research Unit internal publication (National Institute for Social Work, 1974).
Royal Borough of Kensington and Chelsea, Research Section. *Report on New Referrals to the Social Work Division Northen Area office* (internal publication, 1975).
D.H.S.S., *The Remedial Professions, a report of a Working Party set up by the Secretary of State for Social Services* (H.M.S.O., 1973). "The McMillan Report".
D.H.S.S., *Report of the Committee of Inquiry into the Pay and Related Conditions of Service of the Profession Supplementary to Medicine and Speech Therapists.* (H.M.S.O., 1975). "The Halsbury Report".